MW01121716

Failure to Prevent Gross Human Rights Violations in Darfur

International Criminal Law Series

Editorial Board

Series Editor

M. Cherif Bassiouni (*USA/EGYPT*)

VOLUME 6

Failure to Prevent Gross Human Rights Violations in Darfur

Warnings to and Responses by International Decision Makers (2003–2005)

By

Fred Grünfeld
Wessel N. Vermeulen

in cooperation with

Jasper Krommendijk

BRILL
NIJHOFF

LEIDEN | BOSTON

Library of Congress Cataloging-in-Publication Data

Grünfeld, Fred, 1949- author.
  Failure to prevent gross human rights violations in Darfur : warnings to and responses by international decision makers (2003-2005) / by Fred Grünfeld, Wessel N. Vermeulen in cooperation with Jasper Krommendijk.
    pages cm. -- (International criminal law series ; volume 6)
  Includes bibliographical references and index.
  ISBN 978-90-04-26031-3 (hardcover : alk. paper) -- ISBN 978-90-04-26040-5 (e-book)
  1. Sudan--History--Darfur Conflict, 2003--Law and legislation. 2. Genocide intervention--Sudan--Darfur.
  I. Vermeulen, Wessel N., author. II. Krommendijk, Jasper, author. III. Title.

  KZ6795.S73G78 2014
  962.404'3--dc23

                                                2014011149

This publication has been typeset in the multilingual "Brill" typeface. With over 5,100 characters covering Latin, IPA, Greek, and Cyrillic, this typeface is especially suitable for use in the humanities. For more information, please see www.brill.com/brill-typeface.

ISSN 2213-2724
ISBN 978-90-04-26031-3 (hardback)
ISBN 978-90-04-26040-5 (e-book)

This book is printed on acid-free paper.

Printed by Printforce, the Netherlands

Contents

Preface

This book is the capstone of a research project on the prevention of genocide, with a focus on the study of early warning and early action of genocide since the end of the Cold War. In particular it examines the idea that fifty years after the Holocaust, genocides again took place and that any prevention or rescue operation failed. The obvious first question to investigate is whether warnings were sent to decision-makers and whether they were acted upon in a timely fashion. If these warnings were not reacted upon, they could have been unclear or unreliable and therefore failed to persuade decision-makers in other states and international organisations to react. Else, if warnings were available, believed and combined with policy recommendations, dynamics within the decision-making process need to explain failure to prevent Gross Human Rights Violations.

Gross Human Rights Violations are of great societal concern. The academic field to research them in an interdisciplinary way is still undeveloped, as was also noted by Amnesty International in a small booklet called "the forgotten science."[1] This was exactly the reason why the PIOOM[2] foundation was established; to start interdisciplinary research on the causes of Gross Human Rights Violations, first at Leiden University and later with a chair on the "Causes of Human Rights Violations" at Utrecht University. Fred Grünfeld was appointed as the second chair holder in 2003 for ten years at Utrecht University in different departments. Maastricht University welcomed this Utrecht professorship in continuing his full time employment as associate professor at the Department of International and European Law in Maastricht. The extraordinary professorship took place at the Netherlands Institute of Human Rights (SIM[3]) in the Faculty of Law (2003–2007) and at the Centre for Conflict Studies (CCS) at the Faculty of Humanities (2008–2012). The research was initially on the relationship between three different levels of conflict (violent, low intensity and high intensity) and five different

---

1 Amnesty International Nederland (1991), *Een vergeten wetenschap; van onderzoek naar actie: over schendingen van mensenrechten en hoe die voorkomen kunnen worden*, Mets, Amsterdam, [A forgotten science; from research to action: on human rights violations and how they can be prevented].

2 Abbreviation from Dutch "Programma voor Interdisciplinair Onderzoek naar Oorzaken van Mensenrechtenschendingen" [Programme for interdisciplinary research to the causes of human rights violations].

3 Abbreviation from Dutch "Studie- en Informatiecentrum Mensenrechten" [Study and information centre human rights].

scales of human rights violations. Civil and Political Human Rights and
Social, Economic and Cultural rights were both included but no very clear
cause–effect relationship could be discovered neither between the two categories of human rights violations nor between human rights violations and
conflict escalation.[4] It became increasingly clear that improving early warning systems – in order to make the warnings more accurate and hence more
convincing for actors – is a fruitless attempt. This is because warnings have
always been transmitted and received but they have mostly not been reacted
upon by the bystanders for other reasons than the reliability of the warning.
The research therefore changed its focus from modifying and making the
warnings more sophisticated to the decision-making level to explain the acting or non-acting of the bystanders. The early warnings however, remained
the starting point for this research on genocide prevention; any stage in an
emerging genocide consists of a specific warning and enables actors to use
appropriate instruments to prevent.[5]

It was in the thirties of the last century when Albert Horstman on his bicycle
in Germany became aware of the aims and intentions of the Nazis. When
returning home, he tried to warn the authorities in the Netherlands but he was
not believed. During the war he became a resistance fighter rescuing Jews in
hiding and saving British and American pilots as well. After the war he decided
to start a fund to invest in research in early warning and action.[6] It was the
financial support of this fund that made the research assistance for this project
possible. The appointments of Wessel Vermeulen (2007–2008 and 2013), David
Taylor (2008–2010) and Jasper Krommendijk (2013) were fully subsidised by
the Horstman Foundation. Without their contributions this study would not
have been published.

This study into Darfur started with interviews in 2005, which were conducted during the stay of Fred Grünfeld in the US for a book on the Rwanda
genocide. These interviews reflect the very fresh impressions on Darfur in May
and June 2005 at the UN Headquarters in New York of officials from the different UN units. Contrary to the previous studies in this project on Rwanda and
Srebrenica, no inquiry reports and hardly any secondary literature on Darfur

---

4   Frederik Grünfeld, inaugural speech, Utrecht University, 10 December 2003, "Vroegtijdig
    optreden van omstanders ter voorkoming van oorlogen en schendingen van de rechten van
    de mens" [Early action of bystanders for the prevention of war and human rigths
    violations].

5   G.H. Stanton (1996), *The 8 Stages of Genocide,* Genocide Watch, available at www.genocidewatch
    .org/aboutgenocide/8stagesofgenocide.html [accessed 23 December 2013].

6   Stichting Albert Horstman Fonds.

was written at that time. That is why in 2008–2009 Wessel Vermeulen set up a timeline of primary sources of all the events in Darfur, in order to enable researching the transmitted messages with this information to the decision-makers. David Taylor continued this work and he also started to describe and analyse this information. It is his historical descriptions that are reflected in the introductions of the Chapters five to nine.

It was possible to work with Wessel Vermeulen again in 2013, who had in the mean time obtained his PhD from the University of Luxembourg and had started at the University of Oxford, to finalise and publish this study. Drawing conclusions based on hypotheses and all the material he knows so well was a nice common research activity for the two authors. We could add new sources of information such as the WikiLeaks cables (containing, for instance, relevant information on the referral of the Darfur issue to the ICC). In addition, we had more interviews with policy-makers to supplement the public information available to us. The perceptions and evaluations of such decision-makers were very useful additions to further the understanding of the policy process. In order to avoid relying too much on subjective interpretations, we at last undertook a short research into the archives on Darfur at the Ministry of Foreign Affairs of the Netherlands. We furthermore complemented these primary sources with the academic literature of the last decade on this topic. It is in this finalisation stage of the book that Jasper Krommendijk – a PhD student in international law and international relations at Maastricht University – became involved since August 2013 as a research assistant. This published book is the result of this strong cooperation between Fred Grünfeld, Wessel Vermeulen and Jasper Krommendijk.

We thank in particular those who were interviewed for this book, the Ministry of Foreign Affairs in the Netherlands to allow access to their archives, Simon Dennett for his proof reading of the manuscript in Oxford and the editors Lindy Melman and Bea Timmer of the publisher Brill, Martinus Nijhoff, in Leiden.

Fred Grünfeld was able to do this research because the institutions and departments at both Maastricht University and Utrecht University allowed and encouraged him in this research. In particular with respect to the study on Darfur these are the Faculty of Humanities and the Centre for Conflict Studies at Utrecht University and the University College Maastricht, the faculty of Law, the Department of International and European Law and the Maastricht Centre for Human Rights at Maastricht University. Fred Grünfeld is in particular grateful to Fons Coomans who made it possible, as the chairman of the Department in Maastricht, for him to concentrate fully on this research in the finalisation of this publication in 2013.

At last, this book brings not only this project to a close but also the three institutions and boards that empowered and stimulated this research together. These are the Albert Horstman Foundation (boarded by Isaac Heertje, Roel Klaassens and Jaap Roodenburg), the PIOOM foundation (boarded by Johan Bom, Adriaan Dorresteijn, Gerard van Lennep and Johan Scholten) and the PIOOM Chair with the board of governors: Georg Frerks, Duco Hellema, Ellie Lissenberg, Johan Scholten and Harmen van der Wilt. We thank you all very much.

Fred Grünfeld and Wessel Vermeulen

List of Abbreviations

AU	African Union
AMIS	African Union Mission in Sudan
CHD	Centre for Humanitarian Dialogue
CHR	Commission on Human Rights (UN)
CPA	Comprehensive Peace Agreement
DFID	Department for International Development (UK)
DPA	Department of Political Affairs (UN)
DPA 2006	Darfur Peace Agreement
DPKO	Department of Peacekeeping Operations (UN)
EU	European Union
EU Council	EU Council of Ministers
ICC	International Criminal Court
IDP	Internally Displaced Person
IGAD	Intergovernmental Authority on Development
JEM	Justice and Equality Movement
NATO	North Atlantic Treaty Organization
PSC	Peace and Security Council (AU)
OCHA	Office for the Coordination of Humanitarian affairs (UN)
OIC	Organisation of the Islamic Conference
SLM/A	Sudanese Liberation Movement/Army
SPLM/A	Sudanese People's Liberation Movement/Army
UN	United Nations
UN SG	United Nations Secretary-General
UN SGSR	United Nations Secretary-General Special Representative
UNAMIS	United Nations Advanced Mission in Sudan
UNHCR	United Nations High Commissioner for Refugees
UNMIS	United Nations Mission in Sudan
UNSC	United Nations Security Council
UK	United Kingdom of Great Britain and Northern Ireland
US	United States of America
USAID	United States Agency for International Development

Biographic Note

Fred Grünfeld

(1949) is associate professor of International Relations and of the Law of International Organizations at the Department of International and European Law of the Faculty of Law at Maastricht University and at the Maastricht Centre for Human Rights. He teaches also at the University College Maastricht. Fred Grünfeld was professor in the Causes of Gross Human Rights Violations at the Centre for Conflict Studies in the Department of History of the Faculty of Humanities at Utrecht University. Fred has studied Political Science at the VU University in Amsterdam. His current research is on comparative genocide studies (Rwanda, Srebrenica and Darfur) and in particular the failures of Third Parties to prevent the genocide.

Wessel N. Vermeulen

(1985) is a post-doctoral research fellow at the Oxford Centre for the Analysis of Resource Rich Economies (OXCARRE) at the Department of Economics, University of Oxford. Wessel graduated in Economics at Maastricht University and obtained his PhD (2013) in Economics from the University of Luxembourg with a dissertation on the macroeconomic consequences of the exploitation of natural resources. His main research topics include migration of labour, international finance and the economics of natural resources.

Jasper Krommendijk

(1985) is a PhD in International and European Human Rights law at the Maastricht Centre for Human Rights, Faculty of Law, Maastricht. As of July 2014, he will be assistant professor of European Law at the Radboud University Nijmegen. Jasper studied International and European Law as well as International Relations at Groningen University. Jasper has published on matters of EU law, international investment law and the law and politics of human rights. His PhD (2014) deals with the domestic impact and effectiveness of the recommendations of UN human rights treaty bodies in the Netherlands, New Zealand and Finland.

CHAPTER 1

Introducing the Research
Questions and Methodology

1.1 Introduction to the Research

This book is part of a larger research project on the failure to prevent genocide, ethnic cleansing and gross human rights violations in Rwanda (1994), Srebrenica (1995) and Darfur (2003/04). In addition to providing in-depth analysis on the international response to the crisis in Darfur, this book has a limited comparative scope. It will compare the qualitative evidence collected for these three conflicts and make some broader generalisations in the final chapter.

The central proposition in these three projects is that the third party or external bystander matters for the outcome of (intra-state) conflicts.[1] When we study international relations from the perspective of the bystander-actor at the international level, we think that other states and international organisations have the ability to shape the course of a conflict. The latter also assumes that there is a certain degree of international order and a degree of international responsibility or even duty for a state beyond its own borders.[2] This assumption has consequences for the academic theoretical approach we may use in the study of our topic, since it implies that we can use other theoretical approaches that deal with international norms and roles for international organisations. At the international political level, that responsibility was expressed in the doctrine of "Responsibility to Protect," which was affirmed by all UN member states in the Outcome Document of the World Summit in 2005 and reaffirmed in a Security Council resolution in 2006.[3]

One underlying objective of this study is to critically reflect on certain justifications or excuses used to deny any responsibility.[4] Bystanders of the Shoah

---

1   Staub, E. (2000) "Genocide and Mass Killing: Origins, Prevention, Healing and Reconciliation," *Political Psychology*, Vol.: 21(2), pp. 367–382; Smeulers, A. and Grünfeld, F. (eds.), (2011) *International Crimes and other Gross Human Rights Violations. A Multi- and Interdisciplinary Textbook.* Leiden, Boston: Martinus Nijhoff Publishers, Brill.

2   Barnett, M. (2012) "Duties beyond borders," in Foreign policy. Theories, actors, cases, by Smith, S., Hadfield, A. and Dunne, T. (eds.), Oxford: Oxford University Press.

3   UN Docs.: A/Res/60/1 (2005) and S/Res/1674 (2006).

4   See also Power, S. (2007 [2003]) *Problem from Hell: America and the Age of Genocide.* New York: Perennial, London: Flamingo, p. xvi; Cohen, S. (2001) *States of denial: knowing about atrocities and suffering.* Cambridge: Blackwell Publishers.

© KONINKLIJKE BRILL NV, LEIDEN, 2014 | DOI 10.1163/9789004260405_002

during WOII, and later of the genocides in Rwanda and Srebrenica during 1990s can be characterised as idle and passive onlookers.[5] Four arguments are always used to explain why these bystanders did not act to rescue the victims:

(1)   The notion that "we did not know" about what was going on exactly (in German this sounds even more alarming[6]);
(2)   Had we known it, we could not have responded to it, because we did not have the appropriate means or instruments to react;
(3)   A response would likely have counterproductive effects;
(4)   In case we have the knowledge and the warnings and the instruments are available to act with no serious counterproductive effects, the political will to act was lacking.

In this book we will address all four notions and counter these arguments in order to determine that international bystanders did know what was happening, they did have the instruments available to act to stop the Gross Human Rights Violations (GHRV) and acting was less harmful than not acting. Moreover, in our view the very general and rather vague concept of "political will" needs to be unravelled in order to truly understand the behaviour of third parties on gross human rights violations and that is why, among other reasons, we will pay attention to domestic (internal) influences and cognitive and psychological mechanisms in analysing the foreign policy-making of the bystander states.

1.2   Research Questions

The research questions in this study are linked to the four defensive arguments put forward in hindsight by the bystanders when they express their remorse or apologies for not acting. We would like to falsify these four excuses for the case of Darfur in answering the following questions for the policy-makers in other states and international organisations:

---

5   Grünfeld, F. (2014), "Do bystanders exist?," in *Facing the Past*, by Malcontent, P.A.M. (ed.), forthcoming.

6   The infamous excuse for not acting or rescuing the victims of all bystanders at all levels during the Holocaust/Shoah was "Wir haben es nicht gewusst," Bart van der Boom explained that these words did not mean the literal "not to know" or "to ignore" but signified an insincere attitude of burying your head in the sand (in Dutch "een onoprechte houding van alsof je neus bloedt," see Boom, B.E., van der, 2012, *Wij weten niets van hun lot.* Amsterdam: Boom, p. 8).

(1)   Whether and when were the policy-makers aware of the severity of the impending crisis in Darfur (the knowledge question)?
(2)   Were the policy-makers advised on feasible instruments to prevent conflict escalation and a deteriorating human rights situation (the early warning question)?
(3)   Were instruments available for the policy-makers to deploy in order to effectively prevent or de-escalate the situation (question on availability of means)?
(4)   Did the policy-makers deploy these available instruments in time and effectively, taking into account the need to alleviate or stop the suffering (question on decision-making)?
(5)   What other circumstances, such as international and domestic support to act, or situations in other parts of the world, affected the decision-making (a question on the environment and political will)?

The last question refers in particular to public opinion, sovereignty of states, position of the five permanent members of the Security Council, support or opposition from the Arab world, Islamic states and the African continent, solving the North-South conflict in Sudan and other conflicts such as the global "War on Terror" and the backlash due to the intervention in Afghanistan and Iraq.

1.3   Methodology

This research is not (purely) deductive in the sense of testing hypotheses or theories. Neither is it exclusively inductive or focused on the establishment of mere facts and observations related to the prevention of Gross Human Rights Violations in Darfur. We can position the methodology of this research using the four dimensions in social science research as summarised by Todd Landman.[7] The dimensions are: (1) from a specific context towards universal knowledge; (2) from inductive towards deductive reasoning; (3) from qualitative and quantitative evidence based inference towards inference without evidence; (4) from sub-national to single country studies and comparative studies towards global coverage and general theoretical constructs.

   Our study is in the middle of all four dimensions. More specifically, the four dimensions are addressed in this study in the following way. Firstly, it goes

---

7   Landman (2009) "Social science methods and human rights," in *Methods of Human Rights Research*, by Coomans, H., Grünfeld, F. and Kammingo, M. (eds.), Antwerp: Intersentia.

beyond the particular specific context situation by making comparisons of the Darfur situation with the Rwanda and Srebrenica situations. Secondly, it is based on theories in international relations, genocide and human rights literature. The theories have been used to inform and structure the empirical analysis, and make sense of and interpret the data. Thus, this research is not exactly testing the theory but it is more than merely gathering data without theoretical considerations. In short, it is inductive and analytical. Thirdly, inferences are made in this study on quantitative data in searching and counting all early warnings on the situation in Darfur to the national and international decisionmakers. These messages were discerned from all available primary sources such as newspapers, diplomatic messages from WikiLeaks – see below for its limitations – and the archives of the Ministry of Foreign Affairs in the Netherlands, NGO reports and in particular the messages from and within the UN such as the IRIN press. Finally, the empirical scope is at three levels of analysis: the sub-national for the domestic influences on the foreign policy-making process, the national for the foreign policy of the United States, Netherlands, United Kingdom in particular, and the international for analysing the decisionmaking in the European Union, African Union and the United Nations. As said before, it includes a comparative part making use of similar dimensions and theoretical frameworks among the three cases of Darfur, Rwanda and Srebrenica.

In short, positioned in the middle of the elaborated methodological continuum of Landman, this study is a "theory-driven empirical analysis that is inductive, comparative and seeks to make broad generalizations."[8]

1.4   The Theoretical Context

Methods and substance of research are closely related. We will set out here the relevancy of International Relations theories for our research, while in the next chapter we offer a more detailed overview of the different theories with respect to the study of genocide prevention and conflict. This book adopts a pluralistic theoretical approach, because we believe that by comparing and contrasting different frameworks we can see what each magnifies, highlights and reveals as well as what each blurs or neglects.[9] We believe that using different "lenses" to approach the subject matter will lead to different and richer explanations.

---

8   Ibid., p. 29.

9   Allison, G.T. and Zelikov, P. (1999) *Essence of Decision: Explaining the Cuban Missile Crisis*. 2nd edition. Pearson Publishers, p. x.

Another reason for embedding our analysis in a broader theoretical context is that much has already been written about the international response to the conflict in Darfur in the past decade. The aim of this book is not so much to document and provide an exhaustive account of the international response to the conflict, but rather to move beyond "unique explanations" towards "characterization of these phenomena at a more general level."[10] The major categories of perspectives in international relations are the state-centric approach of realism, the multi-centric approach of pluralism and the global-centric approach of globalism.[11] Each approach has different actors and different assumptions. In particular, realism and pluralism/liberalism have been used in this book to inform and structure the empirical analysis and make sense of and interpret the data. For a more detailed discussion of these and other theories, see Chapter 2.

The literature on human rights violations and the causes of conflict makes a distinction between root-causes, proximate causes and triggers.[12] The proximate causes are the subject of this research whereas the root-causes are taken as a given environment, and triggers are too short-term to be reasonably taken into account as informative signals to decision-makers who have the power of preventing escalation. The proximate causes are all such events that ought to result in (preventive) action, and are closely related to the literature on early warnings. Following this literature, the analysis tries to filter out crucial moments of decision-making, the processes that lead up to such moments as well as the key players involved. Proximate causes are translated to early warnings of a possible (that is, preventable) future conflict and atrocities (or the continuation or escalation of a on-going conflict). Subsequently, decision-makers need to choose to act or not act based on these warnings and their actions or in-action is related to the further development of the situation. In order to establish what bystanders and third parties could have done to prevent escalation of the conflict in Darfur it is imperative to account precisely when credible warnings on the crisis were voiced to the policy-makers, which policy options were available and proposed, and subsequently which actions were taken (see Section 1.5).

---

10   Allison and Zelikow (1999), p. 389.

11   Viotti, P.R. and Kauppi, M.V. (1999) *International Relations Theory.* Longman Publishing Group, p. 2 and 10. The fifth and most recent edition of this handbook includes more IR theories (Viotti, P.R. and Kauppi, M.V., 2012, *International Relations Theory.* Longman Publishing Group, p. 12).

12   Grünfeld, F. and Verlinden, S. (2012) "Mensenrechtenschendingen als vroegtijdige waarschuwingen voor conflictpreventie," *Vrede en veiligheid: tijdschrift voor internationale vraagstukken,* Vol.: 40(2/3), pp. 167–185.

The literature on early warning shows us the immense gap between warnings and actions in previous comparable situations. The largest part of this literature has concentrated on how to predict genocides and conflicts arising and how an accurate early warning system can be set up. The focus has been on the way early warning systems have operated in practice with a view of developing better and more valid qualitative and quantitative indicators and improving the collection of data.[13] Other scholars have focused on the need for formulating explicit and politically feasible strategic policy options and recommendations for action for policy-makers as a way to ensure action.[14] The rationale behind much of this work is the belief that early action is more likely once the quality of information is better and convincing policy recommendations are formulated. Harff and Gurr, for example, state: "if researchers can forecast more accurately the sites and sequences of crisis escalation, policy-makers will be more likely to act early than late."[15]

Nonetheless, such views actually neglect the reality that reliable warnings have frequently been ignored or dismissed and atrocities have been allowed to happen. Often, the problem is not one of limited intelligence as the previous views imply, but a problem of failing to use and act upon the information that is available.[16] Scholars focusing on this 'warning-response gap' have analysed why warnings have often failed and only sometimes succeeded. The focus is on the way and conditions under which warnings have been received, paid attention to, accepted and prioritised by decision-making actors. Prominent examples in this field include Adelman and Suhrke's and Piiparinen's works on the international community's failure to prevent the genocide Rwanda and George

---

13   See for example, Schmeidl, S. and Jenkins, J.C. (1998) "The early warning of humanitarian disasters: Problems in building an early warning system," *International Migration Review*, Vol.: 32(2), pp. 471–486; Harff, B. (2003) "No lessons learned from the Holocaust? Assessing risks of genocide and political mass murder since 1955," *The American Political Science Review*, Vol.: 97(1), pp. 57–73.

14   See, for example, Adelman, H. (1998) "Defining humanitarian early warning," In *Early Warning and Early Response*, by Schmeidl, S. and Adelman, H. (eds.), Columbia International Affairs Online, p. 57. Clarke, J.N. (2005) "Early warning analysis for humanitarian preparedness and conflict prevention," *Civil Wars*, Vol.: 7(1), p. 81.

15   Harff, B. and Gurr, T.R. (1998) "Systematic early warning of humanitarian emergencies," *Journal of peace research*, Vol.: 35(5), p. 552.

16   Jentleson, B. (ed.), (2000) *Opportunities missed, opportunities seized: Preventive diplomacy in the post-Cold War world*. Lanham: Rowan & Littlefield Publishers, p. 12; Suhrke, A. and Jones, B. (2000) "Preventive diplomacy in Rwanda: Failure to act or failure of actions?" in *Opportunities missed, opportunities seized: Preventive diplomacy in the post-Cold War world*, by Jentleson, B.W. (ed.), Lanham: Rowan & Littlefield Publishers, p. 252.

and Holl's study into the warning-response problem in relation to several conflicts.[17]

The warning-response literature has initially not been explicitly connected to or framed in theoretical terms, but is more empirical or practical in nature with its focus on identifying factors or explanations as to why early warnings have not resulted in (early) action.[18] These studies highlighted the unwillingness of states to act and the lack of political will as a crucial factor. Many analyses about the international response to the conflict in Darfur have also focused on the 'lack of political will' as the primary explanation for the late or insufficient response to the unfolding tragedy.[19] This was mentioned as the final argument of all the excuses above. Other studies have pointed to realist explanations, such as the absence of strategic national (security) interests or the presence of other more important conflicting interests that prevented states from taking action. For example, guaranteeing the flow of oil (China), the maintenance of arms trade (Russia) or the safeguarding of the Sudanese cooperation in the field of anti-terrorism (United States). Such explanations are valid and should not be discarded.

We think that the concept of 'limited political will' should be analysed more thoroughly. The factor of political will is characterised under the broader umbrella of pluralism/liberalism, taking into account that political will is not a fixed concept and may change under the influence of internal and external influences. We agree with Evans when he argues that: "the difficulty with most discussions of political will is that we spend more time lamenting its absence than analysing what it means."[20] Cushman also found the notion rather

---

17   Adelman, H. and Suhkre, A. (1997) "Early warning and response: why the international community failed to prevent the genocide," *Disasters,* Vol.: 20(4), pp. 295–304; George, A.L. and Holl, J.E. (1997) *The warning-response problem and missed opportunities in preventive diplomacy.* Carnegy Commission on Preventing Deadly Conflict, Carnegie Corporation of New York; Suhrke and Jones (2000); Piiparinen, T. (2010) *The transformation of un conflict management. Producing images of genocide from Rwanda to Darfur and beyond.* London, New York: Routledge. For more references, see Meyer, C.O., Otto, F., Brante, J., and De Franco, C. (2010) "Re-casting the warning-response-problem: Persuasion and preventive policy," *International Studies Review,* Vol.: 12(4), p. 561.

18   Meyer et al. (2010, p. 562–563) noted that the literature on the warning-response gap has remained under-theorized.

19   Bartrop, P.R. and Totten, S. (eds.), (2013) *The genocide studies reader.* London, New York: Routledge, p. 5.

20   Evans as quoted in Woocher, L. (2001) "Deconstructing 'political will': explaining the failure to prevent deadly conflict and mass atrocities," *Journal of Public and International Affairs,* Vol.: 12, p. 181.

simplistic and highlighted the insufficiency of simply reducing the failure to prevent genocide to such an "amorphous variable."[21] Likewise, Piiparinen noted that: "Lack of political will should be construed less as an explanatory factor per se than as a factor to be explained by reference to the 'trouble-making' mechanisms that produced and compounded it."[22] This book hence aims to conduct a more thorough and structural analysis of the concept of political will in order to unearth such structural or institutional causes and underlying mechanisms. The latter is another reason for a (pluri)theoretical approach.

Several studies on recent genocides also went beyond this explanation based on the lack of political will to include broader cognitive, psychological and organisational and institutional dimensions. For example, they focused on structural shortcomings in the UN early warning system, including the poor organisation of the collection and analysis of early warnings and the disconnection between the analysis and the development of policy options. Other explanations were sought in the presence of confusing and ambiguous signals prone to different interpretations, the distortion of objective analysis as well as the information overload and "vast quantity of noise from other crises that preoccupied world leaders."[23] These studies also pointed to some psychological 'strategies' or cognitive factors, including the tendency to deny the possibility of genocide out of disbelief, the refusal to take the warning seriously because of a fear of over prediction ('cry wolf phenomenon') and the inclination for decision-makers to wait as a result of the prospect of a 'slippery slope'.

One illustration of an attempt to go beyond the lack of political will as the predominant explanation is the formulation of five reasons for inaction by the former Dutch Minister for Development Cooperation and the Special Representative for the Secretary General in Darfur from 2004–2008 Jan Pronk. Besides opportunism ("It is not in our interest"), Pronk listed four others: fatalism ("They have always been killing each other down there"), shrugging off the responsibility ("It is all their own fault"), pragmatism ("What is one to do? We did not act on other occasions either"), and outright indifference ("The victims are far away and anonymous").[24] These reasons show a remarkable

---

21   Cushman, T. (2003) "Is Genocide Preventable? Some Theoretical Considerations," *Journal of Genocide Research*, Vol.: 5(4), p. 526.

22   Piiparinen, T. (2008) "The Rise and fall of bureaucratic rationalization: Exploring the possibilities and limitations of the UN Secretariat in conflict prevention," *European Journal of International Relations*, Vol.: 14(4), p. 719.

23   Adelman and Suhrke (1997), p. 301.

24   Pronk as quoted in NCDO (1997) *From early warning to early action. A report on the European conference on conflict prevention*, Amsterdam: NCDO, p. 16.

resemblance with the many reasons for denial of past atrocities as has been explained in *States of Denial* by Stanley Cohen.[25]

Chapter 2 will discuss the several theoretical approaches that are used in this research more in-depth.

1.5 Defining Early Warning and Early Action

Our research is first aimed at discovering what information was known to the decision-makers at what moment.[26] Before any third party can act in response to an emerging crisis or conflict situation, it must have information on that situation in the target country. This information must then be processed in order to develop policy options on how best to act. The concept of 'early warnings' thus encompasses the signals of a deteriorating situation in the target country in combination with the advised policy options on how to act. Relevant decision-makers in the intervening country or organisation should receive and believe these early warnings, and then decide whether to intervene in the target country to prevent further escalation of the conflict or atrocities.

'Early warning' refers to the collection and analysis of information about potential and/or actual conflict situations, as well as the provision of policy suggestions to important decision-makers at the national, regional and international levels with a view of avoiding a conflict (escalation).[27] Austin underlines the importance of formulating concrete policy options to the relevant decision-makers in addition to the gathering information.[28] Thus, 'early warning' is not merely distributing information about a deteriorating situation, but it also requires that experts analyse the information, and subsequently send

---

25 Cohen (2001).

26 This section is largely based on Grünfeld, F. (2012) "Early Warning, Non-Intervention and Failed Responsibility to Protect in Rwanda and Darfur," in *Human Rights and Conflict, Essays in Honour of Bas de Gaay Fortman*, by Boerefijn, I., Henderson, L., Janse, R. and Weaver, R. (eds.), Antwerp: Intersentia, pp. 131–132; Smeulers and Grünfeld (2011), pp. 369–375.

27 West African Network for Peacebuilding (2000) *Preventive Peace Building In West Africa: West Africa Early Warning And Response*. Network training module, Accra, Ghana.

28 "The term early warning systems will be used generically to mean any initiative that focuses on systematic data collection, analysis and/or formulation of recommendations, including risk assessment and information sharing, regardless of topic, whether they are quantitative, qualitative or a blend of both" (Austin, A., 2004, "Early warning and the field: a cargo cult science?," in *Transforming ethnopolitical conflict: the Berghof handbook*, by Austin, A., Fischer, M. and Ropers, N. [eds.], Berlin: vs Verlag für Sozialwissenschaften, p. 1).

the appropriate warnings to decision-makers. In addition, to have any impact the message must be received and accepted by the people who actually are in a position to act.

We define 'early actions' as decisions taken by key players that are intended to prevent (further) escalation. These can be relatively minor actions, such as public statements, calling a meeting with others or forwarding the information, but the actions are characterised by the intent to bring a deteriorating situation on the ground to a halt. We acknowledge that it is often extremely difficult to choose the right moment for preventative action. This is further aggravated by the fact that the risks are often not that obvious and imminent in the early stages of a conflict. It can therefore be difficult to obtain the requisite (parliamentary, regional or international) support for action. At the same time, the costs of mounting preventative action at an early stage are much lower than at a later stage. In addition, peaceful settlement is frequently still possible and easier in the early phase of a conflict. Conflict resolution is more complex at a later stage, because often military means are required. The latter is more difficult to realise, since this makes it necessary to encroach upon the territorial integrity and sovereignty of the state concerned. In short, acting at an early stage is to be preferred because it is usually more effective and less costly.

1.5.1   *Operationalising Early Warning and Early Action*
Practically, we see reports or statements on an adverse change, deterioration in the situation, or an expectation thereof, as early warnings. This includes reports on refugee flows, human rights violations, the blocking of access by the perpetrator(s) of humanitarian goods or neutral forces, announced policies (expected to be) adverse to peaceful resolution. In this research we have tried to include all the warnings and reports from credible sources (see Section 1.6 for a further description of data gathering).

It becomes clear that informing key decision-makers on escalating conflicts needs to be combined with appropriate policy options in order to facilitate decision-making. Therefore, if there is a clear recommendation on policy we can rate it as such, but very often warnings and recommendations go together. We believe that policy recommendations are an essential part of early warnings. Therefore, for the quantitative analysis (see Section 1.7.2 and the appendix), the difference should not be taken too heavily.

Another difficulty is differentiating between early warnings and early actions. Some events might be both an early warning and an early action. For instance, when access is denied to humanitarian organisations then this constitutes an early warning. However, when prominent people involved with such an organisation seek the media to speak out against this denied access then it constitutes an early action by said person as he/she tries to pressure the perpetrator into behaving differently. At the same time, this is an early warning as well since he also tries to make third parties aware about the (deteriorating) situation and mobilise them to act against it.

The determination of whether a message can be considered a warning, a recommended action or a decision is based on a qualitative assessment which takes into account the source and the addressee. This assessment is, among other information, based on in-depth interviews with actors involved in the decision-making (see Section 1.6.1 for a further description). These interviews were valuable to obtain insights in the different views of the political processes that cannot easily be derived from the messages only, although we realise that most interviewees will give the researcher a flattering outlook of their own acts and organisations. If decision-making can be seen as a process that takes the messages as input, and of which decisions are the output, then these qualitative data are important.

One advantage of this operationalisation is that it can easily be applied to a wide range of conflict cases. This in turn will make comparative analysis of conflict cases feasible and tractable. The method is therefore able to uncover and highlight similarities and differences in conflict prevention.

1.5.2 Selected Period for Warnings and Actions

We have put forward that this study is focused on the proximate causes in the preventive period. Therefore, we will not address the long history and the possible root causes in-depth as others have done.[29] Chapter 4 will briefly outline the historical background to the conflict in Darfur. Our research starts with the first clear violent act in February 2003. This choice is not without criticism because this first violent act can already be seen as the trigger of the conflict, which we earlier defined as too short-term to be reasonably taken into account as informative signals to decision-makers (Section 1.4). Based on the latter, one would expect this research to focus also on the situation before February 2003, since this is the preventive period *par excellence*. However, the reasons we start in February 2003 is that there are limited warnings from before and hardly any decision-making at the international level, if at all before this moment.[30]

---

29 Daly, M.W. (2010) *Darfur's Sorrow. The forgotten history of a humanitarian crisis.* 2nd Edition. Cambridge: Cambridge University Press; de Waal, A. (ed.) (2007) *War in Darfur and the search for peace.* Global Equity Initiative, Harvard University; Flint, J. and de Waal, A. (2008) *Darfur: a new history of a long war.* London, New York: Zed Books.

30 One exception is, for example, the internal briefing of Alex de Waal of the Dutch Ministry of Foreign Affairs in mid-2000 in which he already warned for future tensions between

The other reason is that prevention does not stop with the first violent act. In Reychler's definition, the prevention stage includes measures to ensure a conflict or atrocities in their early phase do not escalate.[31] In Darfur the violence increased with perhaps a peak in direct related casualties in the winter of 2003–2004. Whereas in the spring of 2004 the warnings were taken into account and in late spring and summer 2004 some decisions at international level to address the gross human rights violations were taken (see also Figure 2 below). We cover this period until March 2005 when the Darfur situation was referred to the International Criminal Court, which eventually led to the arrest warrant for genocide of Sudanese President al-Bashir in March 2009. The conflict has still not ended. As with most conflicts in the world, it has continued in a way, 'muddling through' with occasional flare-ups of further violence and atrocities and a diminishing attention in world politics by both political leaders and the wider public.

1.6   Data Gathering and Sources Used

Before we start the in-depth analysis of decision-making in the Chapters 5 to 9, we will provide a justification for and overview of the sources that we used and how we used them to answer the research questions.

1.6.1   *Information* ex tempore *and* ex post

This study will primarily rely on primary sources such as NGO reports, state reports and declarations and official documents of international organisations such as the UN, AU and EU. There are two reasons to rely on these primary sources. Firstly, to date there has not been a comprehensive study on the Darfur conflict that recounts all relevant warnings. Early studies exist that have recounted many of the relevant warnings and actions.[32] However, new facts, sources and studies have since emerged which put these warnings in context and shed further light on the knowledge question. Secondly, no study has focused exclusively and structurally on the mechanism of early warning and action on the crisis in Darfur.

Khartoum and Darfur (Bieckmann, F., 2012, *Soedan. Het sinistere spel om macht, rijkdom en olie*. Amsterdam: Balans, p. 55).

31   Reychler, L. (1999) Democratic peace-building and conflict prevention: The devil is in the transition. Leuven, Belgium: Leuven University Press.

32   For example, Prunier, G. (2007) *Darfur: An ambiguous genocide. Revised and updated edition 2007*. London: C.Hurst & Co. (publishers) ltd; Daly (2010); Flint and de Waal (2008).

We created a timeline of all these reported events, like the publication of NGO reports, the appearance of a UN representative on international media, as well as the date of adopted resolutions or declarations. Many of those events are public and as such it is not hard to receive a good first overview of who knew what and when and the information was acted on. As will become clear in the following chapters, the Darfur crisis is not known to be characterised by secrecy or the lack of information by policy makers, and this can already be established by public sources alone.

There is always the possibility that decision-makers actually have more information available or receive reports and warnings earlier than the general public (the researcher). During the research we started with public information (the reports and warnings that were public at the time, not in hindsight). This public information was complemented in the analysis with new sources that have become available since. This includes information available to policy-makers but not to the public, such as internal memos and diplomatic cables. The archives of Foreign Affairs in the Netherlands contained messages from other embassies, NGO reports, information from their own diplomats in Khartoum and this made it possible to ascertain what information reached the policy-makers. For the US we could make use of their embassy reports to Washington via WikiLeaks.

This also includes interviews with policy-makers, which were held in the period 2005–2013, to determine their knowledge and to qualify and analyse the warnings and actions (see the Bibliography for an overview of the persons interviewed). We asked in all our interviews with the decision-makers what information they had on the situation in Darfur. The interviews – together with the other sources of *ex post* information – were used together to examine whether decision-making actors had received or were aware of the warnings, whether they actually had more information at their disposal and therefore whether they knew about the scale and severity of the situation.

It is important to note what is not considered thoroughly in the chronological account: events that occur in Darfur. Although this reality is what ultimately matters for the people in Darfur and the effectiveness of the mechanism of early warning and action, the inaccessibility and general remoteness of the region means that there is very little direct – in the sense of time – connection to particular attacks and fighting in Darfur and what policy-makers know. As the situation deteriorated, much information came from refugee camps in Chad with a considerable delay of a couple of days after the attack had already occurred. In this research we chose to record the day the news reports on the attacks were published rather than the moment of the attacks themselves.

1.6.2   *Leaked US Diplomatic Cables*

One new source of information that has become available recently is the collection of US diplomatic cables that were leaked on the Internet during the course of 2010–2011. These cables provided some valuable information on the discussions between the US, EU countries and some African countries with respect to the crisis in Darfur. They allow for insight on the process towards events such as negotiation rounds, UN resolutions and African Union support. Although such diplomatic cables have been used in research for a long time, these were normally only released sparsely by the US government themselves, or with a very long delay. The way that the 'WikiLeaks cables' came into the public domain and the size of this collection of cables is unprecedented, and therefore requires some comments on how one can use this appropriately.

These cables are mostly written by American embassy personnel and are generally of low security level, and as such do not give a comprehensive view of all contacts between US diplomats, international diplomats and other government officials. Secondly, there is no guarantee that the leaked cables constitute the entire set of liaisons with all relevant countries, most likely they do not. Therefore, the cables provide only a snapshot of diplomatic actions, which are nevertheless a valuable additional source next to the public accounts. The cables often report on conversations American diplomats had with foreigners. Such conversations may be very frank, on a personal note and outside publicly stated lines. Therefore not all such reported statements should be taken at face value or be extrapolated to government policy.

We obtained the cables from a WikiLeaks website.[33] There are a total of 251,287 cables available, with relatively more cables available from 2006 onwards compared to the years before. Cables in which "Darfur" is mentioned follow a similar pattern. There are 6285 cables available ranging mostly between December 2003 until February 2010. For the period analysed in this book, February 2003 to March 2005, there are 272 cables available. Many cables come from European capitals as well as from N'Djamena, Chad. However, Berlin and London are notably absent. Also for Paris there is little interesting information in the published cables. However, the American embassies in Brussels, Belgium, and The Hague, the Netherlands, report on many interesting conversations they have with officials. Other important capitals, such as Moscow and Beijing, are completely absent for the case of Darfur. This indicates that there is a clear selection in the cables due to possibly the security clearance of the original leaker, his own interests, as well as other unknown reasons. The implication is that absence of communication in the repository

---

33   http://www.cablegatesearch.net.

has no meaning. That there are no cables of US diplomats discussing Darfur with British officials does not mean it did not happen and we will never make such claims. Instead, we use the available information to gain insights and as such the cables function as additional evidence for analysis based on other sources.

Although the person responsible for leaking the cables was tried and convicted for this act in the US, and some cables may contain sensitive information regarding personalities, we believe it is prudent to use these cables in this research for the purpose of understanding the actions of all relevant parties.

1.7 Visualising the Conflict

We would like to give an overview of the Darfur conflict using two graphs. Firstly, we will give some indication of the severity of the conflict, and how this compared to the perception of policy-makers at the time. Secondly, we will give an overview of the number of early warnings and actions over the course of our research period.

1.7.1 *Visualising the Casualties*
During the conflict, policy-makers made regular statements on the severity of the situation in Darfur. We can use these statements as indicators of policy-makers' attitudes towards the crisis and their information.

In Figure 1 (see next page) we plot the three lines on the number of casualties in the Darfur conflict. The solid line is based on statements made by several policy-makers at the dates indicated on the horizontal axes. For instance, the US State Department estimated in September 2003 that the conflicted had cost 30,000 lives. We take such statements seriously and believe these are truthful depictions of the knowledge of those actors at the time.[34] There have been many statements on casualties over time and our selection of statements is based on highlighting those actors close to the UN Secretariat or Security

---

34   February 2003: Start of conflict; 31 March 2004: 10,000 deaths (EU Parliamentary Doc.:
      Resolution P5-TA(2004)0225); 13 July 2004: 20,000 deaths (UN estimate); 9 September
      2004: 30,000 (US Department of State, Documenting Atrocities in Darfur, State Publication
      No. 11182, 21 September 2004); 11 January 2005: 100,000 deaths (UN envoy Pronk to the
      Security Council, UN Doc.: S/PV.5109); 31 March 2005: 130,000 deaths (statement by the
      United States to the UN Security Council, UN Doc.: S/PV.5158); 18 September 2006: 200,000
      deaths (statement by the United Kingdom to the Security Council, UN Doc.: S/PV.5528); 23
      April 2008: 300,000 deaths (John Holmes, UN head of humanitarian affairs, BBC News).

Council, including representatives of member states. The numbers purposely exclude counts from NGOs or other activists. By focusing on the statement of policy-makers only, we obtain a view on what these actors were willing to acknowledge and their judgment of the situation.

The other two lines are based on *ex post* survey data and can be used to reflect the distance of policy-makers' statements from the truth. These lines are based on data collected in the region and offer estimations of the true number of casualties, but this information was not known at the time.[35] The plotted series are based on data from a study that takes 70 surveys together in order to provide some final estimations on the total cost of human life in the conflict. The dotted and dashed lines can be interpreted as a consensus (average) view, the former for direct violent deaths, the latter taking the broader costs in human lives due to the humanitarian situation. The shaded areas

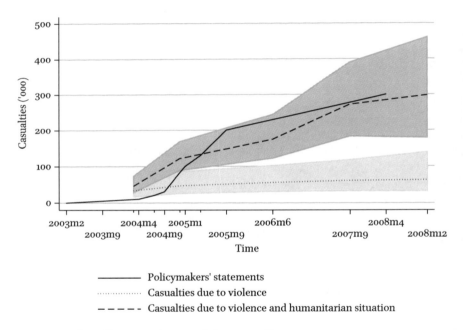

FIGURE 1   *Casualties comparison reported versus reality.*

---

35   Degomme, O. and Guha-Sapir, D. (2010) "Patterns of mortality rates in Darfur conflict," *The Lancet*, Vol.: 375(9711), pp. 294–300. We use the data of their Table 5. Note, there is no survey data available on mortality before September 2003, so casualties from the first 6 months or so are not taken into account. The dashed line and corresponding confidence interval relate to the second baseline estimated of the study.

around the lines represent a 95% confidence interval. The widening of the bands with time, due to variation in the results among the different surveys, attests to the considerable uncertainty around the true number of casualties. Since there is no census that looked at the period before September 2003 the lines start in early 2004 with a count that covers the period since September 2003.

Figure 1 indicates that the policy-makers severely under-reported the number of casualties relative to the true number until mid-2004. The solid line is below the estimated violent deaths, and only barely lies in the lower part of the confidence interval, presenting the most conservative estimates. Moreover, at the time there was some confusion on which numbers included violent deaths only, and which numbers took into account casualties due to the deteriorating humanitarian situation, such as malnutrition and diseases. The statements of policy-makers do not always make explicit to what their numbers relate. The graph suggests that policy-makers switched somewhere in 2004 from violent casualties to a broader measure. Henceforth, they offered numbers that lie well in the area representing survey data, albeit on the high side. Over time, as the surveys are conducted and more information becomes known, the number of casualties reported by policy makers converges to the consensus view of the surveys.

A second observation is that casualties due to direct violence become a less important factor from approximately 2005 onwards. The humanitarian situation improves, evidenced by a flattening of the dashed lines from the start of 2005, but still is growing more quickly that can be explained by the dotted line of violent deaths. Over time the dotted line flattens and the consensus view is that around 62,000 people have died directly due to violence; the total count lies around 300,000 people by 2008. This number, or one that would fall in the confidence band around it, is mostly maintained until today.

1.7.2 *Visualising Early Warning and Early Action*

As stated before, we worked with a timeline-based database in which we recorded all date-based information that we collected during the research period. This qualitative data includes news articles, Security Council resolutions, reports by human rights rapporteurs, reports by NGOs but also facts as stated in accounts of authoritative books. In essence, this database is nothing but a sizeable spread sheet with all kinds of facts and sources. We collected all this information firstly for the aid of research. Now having the data we aim to visualise it, which in turn can give insights on the process of early warning – early action. Naturally, any visualisation is just a stylisation of facts. The aim is to give some broad pattern. There is not much information to be gained in the details due to its level of abstraction. Visualising means quantifying. We simply count and categorise events over time.

The difficulty lies in which items to count, and how to classify them. The criteria we use to include an event are an affirmative answer to the question: Can we be reasonably sure that we included all events of certain actors and are not otherwise biased due to limited information? For instance, it is easy to ensure the inclusion of all relevant NGO reports (of a limited number of NGOs) and all Security Council resolutions. However, we cannot include diplomatic cables or internal memos, because these are not completely available and those that are available are probably not a representative sample of all cables and memos that are still not public. We also did not include articles from news-papers or news websites. The next step is categorising each item as an early warning or early action. Here we follow the definition as set out in Section 1.5 above. The full list of events and further details on the selection procedure are given in the appendix. Although one may dispute the inclusion, exclusion or classifications of individual events, we believe that the resulting pattern as indicated in the figure can be taken as a reasonably objective measure of devel-opment of international activity around the conflict.

Figure 2 presents the result of this exercise. Each month from January 2003 to March 2005 has its own bar that indicates the number of events we have

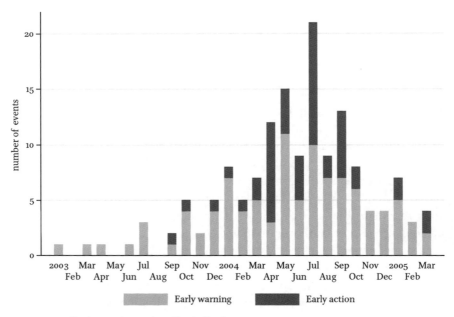

FIGURE 2   *Early warning early action in Darfur.*

recorded for the total of early warnings and early action events. The minimum is zero, notably for some months in 2003, and the maximum is 21, for July 2004. The pattern is similar to what others have presented in terms of media attention of the Darfur conflict.[36] During 2003, the actual conflict had been the most intense, as found by many surveys, but warnings were relatively sparse with none or only single reports issued for the first six months of 2003. The situation changes during the last months of 2003 when the first actions are taken and the number of warnings increases. During 2004 the momentum builds up to the summer months, which relates to intense diplomatic and international activity in the UN, AU and EU. After the establishment of the Commission of Inquiry in September 2004, activity and reports decreases notably. The last spike of March 2005 relates to the three Security Council resolutions. This further supports our selected period of analysis.

1.8   Structure of the Book

The rest of the book is structured as follows. Chapter 2 sets out the theoretical framework which is based on theories of International Relations and foreign policy making. Chapter 3 applies and illustrates concisely the theoretical framework for the genocides in Rwanda (1994) and Srebrenica (1995) with a particular focus on explaining the reasons for the failure to prevent the genocide.

Chapter 4 introduces Darfur, the land and its people, and gives a brief historical context to the conflict. Chapters 5 to 9 discuss thoroughly how and why international decision makers responded to the situation in Darfur. Each of these chapters concludes with a brief reflection on key decisions or events in that period from a theoretical point of view. The analysis ends with the adoption of Security Council's Resolution 1593 of March 2005, which referred Darfur

---

36   For further analysis of media reporting on the Darfur conflict for instance, Grzyb, A.F. "Media coverage, activism, and crating public will for intervention in Rwanda and Darfur," in *The World and Darfur. International response to crimes against humanity in Western Sudan*, by Gryzb, A.F. (ed.), 2010, Montreal: McGill-Queens University Press; Vos, D. (2006) "Een onderzoek naar internationale nieuwsstromen en de Nederlandse nieuwsberichtgeving over de crisis in Darfur in de periode van Februari 2003–2006" [A research to the international news-streams and the Dutch news reporting on the crisis in Darfur in the period February 2003–2006], PhD Dissertation, Utrecht University; Kothari, A. (2010) "The framing of the Darfur conflict in the New York Times: 2003–2006," *Journalism Studies*, Vol.: 11(2), pp. 209–224.

to the International Criminal Court. However, the conflict did not end at this time. Chapter 10 serves to give an overview of the developments since.

Finally, the Conclusion sets out our findings on the decision-making with respect to Darfur and offers a comparative analysis with respect to the cases of Rwanda and Srebrenica as laid out in Chapter 3.

Theories in International Relations

As was said in the introduction, we have used several theories of International Relations (IR) to inform and structure the empirical analysis of the warnings, memos, state reports and UN documents. What is more, the theories have also been used to explain (the lack of) international response to the gross human rights violations in Darfur during 2003–2005. This chapter will present the theories we have used to explain the behaviour of the bystanders at the state and international levels. This includes the theories of pluralism/liberalism which focus on domestic influences on the foreign policy-making. In addition, the decision-making models developed by Allison in relation to the 1961 Cuba crisis will be relied upon as well as psychological and cognitive mechanisms. While this chapter describes these theories, the next chapter will apply these theoretical models to the genocide in Rwanda and Srebrenica in order to illustrate the theories.

2.1 Realism and Pluralism

The dominant theory of International Relations with respect to peace and security is (neo)realism. It treats states as the primary actors in international relations. States are considered as unitary, rational, self-interested, strategic, utility-maximising entities who are predominantly interested in their own power and national (military) security.[1] The major explanation for state behaviour is the anarchic world system which lacks an "international policy force." Because there is no such higher central authority above states, states themselves have to ensure their own "survival," something which is referred to as "self-help." Because states are pre-occupied with their own survival and the realisation of their own national interests ("*realpolitik*"), military and political security elements (the so-called high politics) dominate the agenda. Whereas the suffering of nationals in other states is easily overlooked when it does not have any cross boundary effects. Realists would not be surprised about the failure of the UN or other International Organisations. They argue that these

---

1 Viotti, P.R. and Kauppi, M.V. (2012) *International Relations Theory*. Longman Publishing Group, p. 39–41.

© KONINKLIJKE BRILL NV, LEIDEN, 2014 | DOI 10.1163/9789004260405_003

organisations are used as mere instruments by states and are only as influential as their most powerful members wish them to be. The sovereign, independent and autonomous states determine what these international organisations will do.

The realist theory with its focus on power and security as the main objective of states is important for analysing the international response to the situation in Darfur. It especially offers explanations with respect to the role of the major powers in the Security Council.[2] However, in our view this (neo)realist approach is not wholly sufficient to analyse the role of the third parties with respect to Darfur. Several – in our view important – aspects are ignored or downplayed.

Firstly, given the unitary assumption and its focus on the international system as the predominant level of analysis, (neo)realist accounts are not interested in opening the "black box" of the state to study the internal decision-making process. The state is unitary because any differences of views in a society are resolved and the state can speak as one voice in world politics. That is to say, (neo)realists view the world in terms of states interacting with each other as if they are hard billiard balls. Neorealists, in the words of Mearsheimer, "ignore cultural differences among states as well as differences in regime type, mainly because the international system creates the same basic incentives for all great powers. Whether a state is democratic or autocratic matters relatively little for how it reacts towards other states. Nor does it matter who is in charge of conducting a state's foreign policy. Structural realists treat states as if they were black boxes: they are assumed to be alike, save for the fact that some states are more or less powerful than others."[3] We adopt a multicentric approach following pluralist IR theories. This means that we examine how different opinions within a state matter and that the state is no longer perceived as a unitary actor. This approach also recognises that there is no such thing as one fixed national interest. In the pluralist approach, bureaucracies, interest groups and public opinion will have its impact on foreign policy

---

2 Another prominent rationalist theory which shares many assumptions of neorealism is neo-liberal institutionalism. This strand is slightly more optimistic about the possibility of cooperation between states. It believes that the effects of the anarchic system *can* (potentially) be positively influenced and mitigated by the creation of regimes and international institutions. Scholars study the design of these institutions with a view of identifying features and factors that make them work. Scholars in this tradition would argue that there is a weak international peace and security regime in the form of the UN Security Council, given the presence of the veto power for the five permanent members.

3 Mearsheimer, J.J. (2008) "Structural Realism," in *International Relations Theories*, by Dunne, T., Kurki, M. and Smith, S. (eds.), Oxford: Oxford University Press, p. 72.

decision-making. Likewise, we also aim to extend the analysis to the sub-national and state level instead of primarily relying on the international system as the only level of analysis. The attention for political processes within a society and its influence on the formulation of the foreign policy of the state allows a broader view on the decision-making. This means that we will study the role and behaviour of groups and bureaucracies (Section 2.3) as well as the impact of domestic sources on foreign policy-making (Section 2.2).

Secondly, the rational actor assumption does not fully capture the more complex reality in which decisions are taken; often uncertain crisis situations about which there is insufficient information. Neither do realist theories adequately acknowledge that decisions are taken by human beings, who seldom make a purely rational decision given psychological and cognitive constraints. We therefore include in our analysis cognitive practices such as cognitive dissonance and wishful thinking, as well as heuristic devices such as analogies and stereotypes (Section 2.4).

Thirdly, the focus on states as the main unit of analysis does not fully capture the reality either. We believe that other non-state actors such as international organisations can play an important and different role from the states as well. International Organisations can become or are already independent actors in their own right. Therefore we extend our analysis also to the decision making process within international organisations, such as the UN and EU.

In short, in realist international politics can be represented as a billiard ball game: the states are the billiard balls colliding with one another and the clash – the interaction of sovereign states – of the balls determine the direction and the content of international politics. In pluralism international politics can be viewed as a latticework or cobweb image. This is much more complex with many national and international actors.[4]

2.2   Domestic Sources of Foreign Policy

"It is in the realm of domestic politics that the battle to stop genocide is lost." This was Samantha Power's major conclusion in her book *Problem From Hell: America and the Age of Genocide*.[5] The absence of domestic pressure in a certain country means that there are no domestic political costs for a particular

---

4   Viotti, P.R. and Kauppi, M.V. (1999) *International Relations Theory*. Longman Publishing Group, p. 211.

5   Power, S. (2007 [2003]) *Problem from Hell: America and the Age of Genocide*. New York: Perennial, London: Flamingo, p. xviii.

government in the form of moral shame for inaction. She however, noted that this political calculus and the government disincentive not to act can change as a result of domestic pressure and advocacy. Power described how senior US officials were not interested and unwilling to respond to (early) warning unless there was media coverage and public shaming.[6] Van der Stoel noted the paradox of preventive diplomacy that by the time a conflict receives most people's attention, it is too complicated to stop. At the same time, no action will be taken unless the crisis has people's attention.[7] The domestic sources of foreign policy behaviour are especially addressed in pluralist/liberalist International Relations theories. They were developed in the sixties by Singer and further built on by Rosenau.[8] Rosenau proposed a model on how societies may react towards influences from within when they are internally oriented, or outside the national political system when they are externally oriented, or none when they tend to be non-receptive, or indeed a combination of both when they are dually (both internally and externally) oriented.[9] These patterns are obviously ideal types.[10] In order to explain this model, the following examples can be given in relation to Darfur. A large dictatorial state such as Sudan will primarily be non-receptive; a large democratic state such as the US will be primarily internally oriented; a small democratic state such as the Netherlands will primarily be dually oriented. The consequences are that Sudan is not very willing to accommodate and internal influences will have no effect whereas maximum external influences, such as sanctions to obtain humanitarian access, can have some effect. As will be explained in the following chapters, the US was very much willing to take the domestic views into account, which partly

---

6   Power (2007), p. 270, 281 and 508.

7   Van der Stoel, M. (1999) "Early warning and early action: preventing inter-ethnic conflict," Speech given at the Royal Institute of International Affairs, 20 August 1999, OCSE Doc.: HCNM.GAL/5/99, p. 3.

8   Singer, J.D. (1961) "The level of analysis problem in international relations," in *International politics and foreign policy; a reader in research and theory*, revised edition, by Rosenau, J.N. (ed.), (1969) New York: The Free Press, London: Collier-Macmillan Limited, London (original in *World Politics*, 1961, pp. 77–92). Rosenau, J.N. (1966) "The adaptation of national societies: a theory of political behavior and transformation," in *The scientific study of foreign policy,* by Rosenau, J.N. (1980), New York, London: Frances Pinter Ltd.

9   Rosenau (1966) in Rosenau (1980).

10   Grünfeld, F. (1999) "The effectiveness of United Nations economic sanctions," in *United Nations sanctions: effectiveness and effects, especially in the field of human rights. A multidisciplinary approach*, by van Genugten, W.J.M. and de Groot, G.A. (eds.), Antwerpen: Intersentia.

explains its genocide determination. The Netherlands is also willing to take parliamentary wishes into account but finds its limitation in the external views from Europe and the UN. The latter is, for example, visible in the watering down of the Dutch wishes for a no-fly zone and sanctions on Darfur.

Recent well-known contributions in the liberal IR field come from Putnam and Moravcsik. The former depicts foreign policy-making as a two level game entailing simultaneous negotiations at the domestic level and the international level with other governments. During the domestic game, societal actors pressure the government to adopt favourable policies reflecting their preferences. Domestic political constraints and calculations mean that the government is eager to build coalitions with these groups. At the international level, national governments try to maximise their ability to satisfy these domestic pressures and minimalise negative consequences of foreign developments.[11] The difficulty of the game is that the government often has to reconcile conflicting pressures from both levels.

Putnam's conceptualisation was taken further by Moravcsik and his "new liberalism." The main rationale is that (democratic) governments translate the preferences and demands of domestic actors into foreign policy: "the foreign policy goals of national governments are viewed as varying in response to shifting pressures from domestic social groups, whose preferences are aggregated through political institutions."[12] This argument is built upon the assumption that governments have an interest in being re-elected and satisfying – or at least avoid infuriating – voters.

With respect to (military) intervention and the contribution to peacekeeping operations, it is generally assumed that governments have to weigh the 'CNN effect' against the 'bodybag effect'. On the one hand, there is an incentive for governments to show that they are able to deal with and influence international events in accordance with domestic values, in order to avoid being seen as weak. On the other hand, there is a tendency to avoid pursuing a risky course with uncertain benefits and high costs in terms of casualties and financial resources, because this could lead to domestic punishment.[13]

---

11   Putnam, R.D. (1988) "Diplomacy and domestic politics: the logic of two-level games," *International Organization* Vol.: 42(3), p. 434. See also Peters, G.B. (2005) *Institutional theory in political science: The 'new institutionalism'*. Gosport: Ashford Colour Press Ltd., p. 136.

12   Moravcsik, A. (1993) "Preferences and power in the European Community: a liberal intergovernmentalist approach," *Journal of Common Market Studies*, Vol.: 31(4), pp. 473–524, p. 481.

13   Pohl, B. (2013) "To what ends? Governmental interests and European Union (non-) intervention in Chad and the Democratic Republic of Congo," *Cooperation and Conflict,* forthcoming, p. 3.

There are three domestic mechanisms that discern affecting foreign policy decision-making. Firstly, there is direct public pressure in the form of mobilisation of domestic actors, media attention and challenges from political parties. For many foreign policy issues, there is little or no domestic interest and the public is sometimes seen as apathetic and uninterested in international affairs. Secondly, there are foreign policy elites in political parties, NGOs, academia and (research) institutes, which can also connect or channel public pressure with the government decision-making process. Thirdly, the anticipation of possible public pressure or *ex post* accountability as perceived or assumed by governments.[14] This means that even though there is no direct pressure (yet), there is an inclination to at least act in accordance with the preferences of domestic actors.

2.3   Decision-Making Theories

This section will present the three decision-making models as developed by Allison with respect to the Cuban missile crisis.[15]

2.3.1   *Rational Policy Model*

One of the most widely applied models in foreign policy decision-making is the Rational Policy Model. This model is widely used in (neo)realist theories and it underlies the core assumptions of rationality. In short, according to this model, decisions are made "by calculating the rational thing to do in a certain situation, given specified objectives."[16] The model implies that actors have a prefixed rank of preferences and that an actor aims to realise its interests and maximise its satisfaction. The actor is expected to be capable of differentiating among alternatives and their consequences or outcomes and choose the alternative with the highest pay-off.[17] In other words, state behaviour is "driven by a logic of anticipated consequences and prior preferences"; decisions are the result of a reasoned weighing and

---

14   Pohl (2013), p. 15.

15   Original terms of the model from the article Allison, G.T. (1969) "Conceptual models and the Cuban missile crisis," *The American political science review*, Vol.: 63(3), pp. 689–718; and the books Allison, G.T. (1971) *Essence of Decision: Explaining the Cuban Missile Crisis.* Boston: Little Brown; Allison, G.T. and Zelikow, P. (1999) *Essence of Decision: Explaining the Cuban Missile Crisis.* 2nd edition. Pearson Publishers.

16   Allison and Zelikow (1999), p. 5.

17   Allison and Zelikow (1999), p. 18; Mintz and DeRouen (2010), p. 57–58.

calculation of the consequences, and costs and benefits of alternative modes of action.[18]

2.3.2 Organisational Process Model

The second decision-making model focuses on intra-organisational factors, especially the effects of standard operating procedures, routines (often with little flexibility) and cultures of bureaucracies on decision-making. One of the central tenets of this model is that bureaucracies tend to be conservative, hesitant to adopt new approaches and consider the full range of policy options. Instead they are satisfied with incremental and minor changes on the basis of past decisions and behaviour. This may lead to temporary and imperfect solutions.[19] Only a few authors have looked at organisational and bureaucratic behaviour in relation to the international community's responses to genocide.[20] George and Holl, for example, referred to the inflexibility of organisations and a reluctance to revise the course of action once a policy decision is made. Bureaucracies consequently ignore or dismiss subsequent intelligence (see also the discussion of cognitive dissonance in Section 2.7).[21] Meyer et al. noted the importance of reflecting on organisational dimensions with respect to conflict prevention because formal and informal rules in bureaucratic organisations often determine which warnings are filtered out and prioritised over others.[22]

---

18   March and Olsen (1998), p. 949–950.

19   Mintz, A. and DeRouen Jr., K., (2010) *Understanding foreign policy decision making.* Cambridge: Cambridge University Press, p. 74.

20   Brazeal, G. (2011) "Bureaucracy and the U.S. Response to Mass Atrocity" *National Security & Armed Conflict Law Review*, p. 60. Meyer, C.O., Otto, F., Brante, J., and De Franco, C. (2010) "Re-casting the warning-response-problem: Persuasion and preventive policy," *International Studies Review*, Vol.: 12(4), pp. 562–563.

21   George, A.L. and Holl, J.E. (1997) *The warning-response problem and missed opportunities in preventive diplomacy.* Carnegy Commission on Preventing Deadly Conflict, Carnegie Corporation of New York.

22   Meyer, C. O., Otto, F., Brante, J., and De France, C. (2010) "Re-casting the warning-response-problem: Persuasion and preventive policy", *International Studies Review*, vol.: 12(4), pp. 556–578. Jentleson and Suhkre and Jones also noted bureaucratic factors and dynamics in relation to early action (Jentleson, B. [ed.], 2000, *Opportunities missed, opportunities seized: Preventive diplomacy in the post-Cold War world.* Lanham: Rowan & Littlefield Publishers, p. 11–12; Suhrke, A. and Jones, B., 2000, "Preventive diplomacy in Rwanda: Failure to act or failure of actions?," in *Opportunities missed, opportunities seized: Preventive diplomacy in the post-Cold War world*, by Jentleson, B.W. [ed.], Lanham: Rowan & Littlefield Publishers, p. 256–259).

2.3.3   *Bureaucratic Politics Model*

The third model – sometimes called the governmental politics model – acknowledges that a state is not a unitary actor, but rather "a conglomerate of large organizations and political actors" and "large acts result from innumerable and often conflicting smaller actions by individuals at various levels of organisations in the service of a variety of only partially compatible conceptions of national goals, organisational goal, and political objectives."[23] The model construes foreign policy decision-making as a competitive political bargaining game of (counter-)coalition formation between government actors with competing interests. The main rationale is the political competition ("pulling and hauling") between various bureaucracies and individuals in top positions who not only act to fulfil (their conception of) the national interest. To characterise the bureaucrat in this model Allison stated: "where you stand depends on where you sit," indicating that the view is coloured by the perspective of the organisation to which the actor belongs.[24] Bureaucracies and individual decision-makers also protect their own 'turf', try to maximise their interests and try to control and increase their expertise monopoly and financial resources.[25] Both Power and Barnett noted how bureaucrats are protecting their own careers.[26] Power held that they are therefore not eager to speak up and "rock the boat."[27]

Given its focus on divisions within states between several government departments, the model is particularly adept at explaining (seeming) "contradictions" in the foreign policy of one particular state. This model is also suitable to analyse the decision-making in international organisations and differences between different bureaucratic divisions. Barnett, for instance, pointed to the different subcultures within the UN and the conflicts of interests between different departments with respect to Rwanda, such as the Secretariat, the Security Council and field operations. In this study we will reflect on the struggle and different views of the Department of Political Analysis (DPA), the Department of Peace Keeping Operations (DPKO), the Office of Humanitarian Affairs (OCHA) and the diplomatic representative of the Secretary-General.

---

23   Allison and Zelikow (1999), pp. 3, 5.
24   Allison (1971), p. 176.
25   Allison and Zelikow (1999), p. 255–256.
26   Barnett, M. (1997) "The UN Security Council, indifference and genocide in Rwanda," *Cultural Anthropology*, Vol.: 12(4), pp. 556–557, 562; Barnett, M. (2003) *Eyewitness to a genocide: The United Nations and Rwanda*. Ithaca, N.Y.: Cornell University Press, p. 12.
27   Power (2007), p. 267.

2.4   Cognitive Dissonance and other Psychological Mechanisms

Another theoretical approach related to decision-making processes is a bit different because it primarily focuses on the filters and prisms of all incoming information. The information is often disregarded when this does not fit in the existing mindset. This factor is based on a recognition that decision-makers operate under constraints, like time pressure or domestic and international political pressure, and have limited information-processing capabilities. This means that rational explanations do not suffice, especially in complex and uncertain situations where information is inadequate or flawed. There are psychological and cognitive limitations to the capacity of human beings to grapple with such complex issues. Within the limitations of such 'bounded rationality' actors use mental strategies and psychological mechanisms to cope with their limitations. Actors frequently use mental shortcuts or biases that enable them to make sense of complex information and make decisions more easily without thoroughly collecting and analysing all the information available.[28] This might also (partly) explain why individuals, groups, media, states, international organisations sometimes filter out or misinterpret early warnings. We will underline this factor because in almost all genocide situations this misinterpretation takes place when the very gruesome narrative that is brought to the attention of decision-makers is not taken seriously. Sometimes the message is unbelievable, beyond any imagination and sometimes the message does not fit in the pre-existing strategy with regards to the issue.

In short, cognitive dissonance reduction is the situation whereby actors avoid and discount information that is inconsistent with their prior views and which would require them to adjust their view. One consequence is that disproportionate attention is paid to information that is consistent with their views. George and Holl noted how early warnings are often treated as dissonant information that is often discounted or at least required to "meet higher standards of evidence and to pass stricter tests of admissibility than new information that supports existing expectations and policies."[29] Cognitive dissonance will be further illustrated in the next chapter on Rwanda and Srebrenica.

---

28   For a good overview of these so-called "heuristic devices," see Mintz and DeRouen (2010), pp. 97–104; Stein, J. (2012), "Foreign policy decision making: rational, psychological, and neurological models" in *Foreign policy. Theories, actors, cases*, by Smith, S., Hadfield, A. and Dunne, T. (eds.), Oxford: Oxford University Press, pp. 130–137.

29   George and Holl (1997), p. 23; Jentleson (2000), p. 12. This also reflects Power's observation that allegations are not simply accepted and that there is a tendency to demand constant corroboration (Power, 2007, p. 263).

Another cognitive practice is wishful thinking. Actors convince themselves that negative developments are less or unlikely to occur, while they are considerably more optimistic about the likelihood of positive outcomes. Actors think that their choice will be successful in order to self-justify their decisions or beliefs. One example of wishful thinking relates to the almost naïve trust in negotiations and diplomacy among US and EU officials in situations of genocide (see next chapter).

One example of a 'mental shortcut' which actors use to deal with complex situations is analogies. There is an inclination among decision-makers to reflect back to past events with comparable circumstances. Decisions made and lessons learned with respect to a past event might be copied and used for the current situation. Besides the positive consequences of raising the salience of and attention on a certain issue, the use of analogies might have negative consequences as well. This especially happens when analogies are used too easily when the new situation does not truly mirror a past event. Power held that faulty analogies are more likely to be used when policy-makers have limited prior knowledge about the country.[30] She noted that the use of the holocaust analogy for contemporary genocides or situations of gross human rights violations might lead to a battle over the correctness of the analogy instead of action to address the situation: a "definitional warfare...has often distracted us from the events on the ground and elevated an abstract quarrel over an analogy to centre stage."[31] She also argued that (wrong) analogies might alienate certain people, create a backlash or offer an excuse not to act. She noted that: "Once we realise today's crimes are not exactly 'like' those of the Holocaust, we all too quickly soothe ourselves with the further notion that 'the situation is not so bad after all'."[32] Another example of a mental shortcut to deal with complexity are stereotypes and simplifications. Piiparinen, for example, pointed to a normalisation technique used by actors, by relying on stereotypical and racial images and by describing the conflict in Rwanda as "chaotic, mad and tribal" (see next chapter for a further illustration of this practice).

---

30   Power, S. (2001) "Bystanders to genocide: Why the United States let the Rwandan tragedy happen," *Atlantic Monthly* Vol.: 288(2), p. 8.

31   Power, S. (1999) "To suffer by comparison," *Daedalus,* Vol.: 128(2), p. 56–57.

32   Power (1999), p. 58.

CHAPTER 3

Case Studies
Rwanda (1994) and Srebrenica (1995)

For the comparative section of this study we will examine the genocides in Rwanda (1994) and Srebrenica (1995). This chapter is mainly based on the results in previous studies on this project by the authors.[1] Rather than exhaustively covering both cases, they will be applied to the theoretical part of the previous chapter with the aim of comparing the studies on Rwanda, Srebrenica and Darfur in the concluding chapter.

All three situations are about the prevention of Gross Human Rights Violations by the national and international bystanders. Two of these (Rwanda and Srebrenica) have even been classified by judicial authorities in tribunals as genocide. It is not our purpose to determine whether each situation can be defined as genocide, crimes against humanity or war crimes so we will use the more general label of Gross Human Rights Violations (GHRV).[2] Our aim is to

---

1 Grünfeld, F. and Huijboom, A. (2007) *The Failure to Prevent Genocide in Rwanda: The Role of Bystanders*. Leiden, Boston: Martinus Nijhoff Publishers, Brill; Grünfeld, F. (2008) "The Role of Bystanders in Rwanda and Srebrenica: Lessons Learned", in *Supranational Criminology: Towards a Criminology of International Crimes*, by Smeulers, A. and Haveman, R. (eds.), Antwerp: Intersentia; Grünfeld, F. and Vermeulen, W.N. (2009) "Failures to Prevent Genocide in Rwanda (1994), Srebrenica (1995) and Darfur (since 2003)", *Journal of Genocide Studies and Prevention*, Vol.: 4(2), pp. 221–238; Grünfeld, F. (2012) "Early Warning, Non-Intervention and Failed Responsibility to Protect in Rwanda and Darfur", in *Human Rights and Conflict, Essays in Honour of Bas de Gaay Fortman*, by Boerefijn, I., Henderson, L., Janse, R. and Weaver, R. (eds.), Antwerp: Intersentia. See also in particular Barnett, M. (1997) "The UN Security Council, indifference and genocide in Rwanda", *Cultural Anthropology*, Vol.: 12(4), pp. 551–578; Barnett, M. (2003) *Eyewitness to a genocide: The United Nations and Rwanda*. Ithaca, N.Y.: Cornell University Press; Piiparinen, T. (2008) "The Rise and Fall of Bureaucratic Rationalization: Exploring the Possibilities and Limitations of the UN Secretariat in Conflict Prevention", *European Journal of International Relations*, Vol.: 14(4), pp. 697–724; Piiparinen, T. (2010) *The transformation of UN conflict management. Producing images of genocide from Rwanda to Darfur and beyond*. London, New York: Routledge.; Power, S. (2001) "Bystanders to Genocide: Why the United States Let the Rwandan Tragedy Happen", *Atlantic Monthly* Vol.: 288(2), pp. 84–108; Power, S. (2007 [2003]) *Problem from Hell: America and the Age of Genocide*. New York: Perennial, London: Flamingo.

2 For the differences between Gross Human Rights Violations, War Crimes and Crimes against Humanity, see Smeulers, A. and Grünfeld, F. (eds.) (2011) *International Crimes and other Gross Human Rights Violations. A Multi- and Interdisciplinary Textbook*. Leiden, Boston: Martinus Nijhoff Publishers, Brill, pp. 3–118.

study the international response to these GHRVs. In our view, there is no other situation in the world since the Holocaust/Shoah that encompasses all elements of the meaning of 'genocide' in its entirety as the killings of the Tutsi people in Rwanda. All Tutsi, because they were born as Tutsi, had to be murdered irrespective of their views, age, sex or place of residence in Rwanda. In a hundred days 800,000 were deliberately killed during a genocide which was planned, prepared and organised by the state and its institutions, comparable with the Nazi persecutions of all Jews in Europe. The International Criminal Tribunal for Rwanda decided without any doubt that the Prime Minister of Rwanda at the time, Jean Kambanda, was to be sentenced to life imprisonment for genocide and conspiracy in genocide.[3] The massacre in Srebrenica occurred in July 1995, when during five days, 8000 male Muslims of all ages were murdered. The massacre was considered to be genocide by two international courts because the killing of all male men of that ethnic group in that area irrespective of their age precluded any procreation.[4] The perpetrators in Darfur have not yet been sentenced by a court, although in the arrest warrant against Sudanese President al-Bashir the act of genocide is included as one of the charges.[5]

All three situations – Rwanda, Srebrenica and Darfur – took place after the end of the Cold War, which made foreign intervention somehow easier because the world was no longer divided between Eastern and Western spheres of influence. During the Cold War period, the two major antagonists (the US and USSR) also regularly invoked their veto powers and, hence, obstructed decision-making in the Security Council. Moreover, the end of the Cold War diminished the fear of an American-Soviet confrontation with nuclear arms. All this facilitated international interferences in the prevention of gross human rights violations in general, and genocide in particular.

Another hindering factor is still active: the sovereignty of states. This is particularly felt strongly in the Third World as a result of their relations with former colonisers – the so-called threat of imperialism under disguise of a humanitarian intervention. More generally states still emphasise non-interference in another country and the protection of national sovereignty and

---

3   ICTR (International Criminal Tribunal for Rwanda) in case no. ICTR-997-23-S, September 4, 1998.

4   ICTY (International Criminal Tribunal for former Yugoslavia) in case Prosecutor v. Radislav Krstić of August 2, 2001, IT-98-33-T and ICJ (International Court of Justice) in case Bosnia and Herzegovina v. Yugoslavia, 3 February 2003, available at http://www.icj-cij.org/docket/files/122/8248.pdf [accessed 16 November 2013].

5   ICC (International Criminal Court), arrest warrant of July 14, 2008, ICC-OTP-20080714 -PR341.

territorial integrity. The responsibility to protect, including rescuing populations when gross human rights violations by their own governments take place,
was outside the vocabulary of the Organisation of African Unity.[6] With the
establishment of the African Union in 2002, this changed and Darfur consti-
tuted a first test for this new organisation.

Comparative research is in some way risky because the historical circumstances, the regional and international context and the actors will always be
different. In addition, Rwanda (1994) and Srebrenica (1995) could have influenced the response ten years later in Darfur, especially because of the shock
these genocides caused in the nineties and the critical self-reflection of many
states and international organisations on their behaviour. 'Lessons learned' is
the constantly repeated adagio. So the preparation for a mission is important.
The UN Humanitarian Coordinator for Sudan in 2003 Kapila, for instance,
wrote in his book that he put the critical UN report on the role of the UN in
Rwanda and in Srebrenica in his luggage on his way to Sudan in 2003.[7] The only
book of orientation on Rwanda in their luggage for the Belgian and Canadian
Commanders in 1993 to Rwanda was the tourist guide of Baedeker.[8] The Dutch
peacekeepers of Dutchbat III received only limited military training and no
information on the country, its culture and population. Without any background information the capacity to act without stereotypical images was hampered. The information from the previous peacekeepers Dutchbat II was not
reported to their successors. One of the conclusions of a Dutch inquiry was
that only a military training was insufficient to act in Srebrenica.[9]

Emphasising the uniqueness of each case does not allow us to make any
progress in studying atrocities and genocide. Indeed the Shoah was unique,

---

6   Goldhagen, J.D. (2009) *Worse than war*. New York: Perseus Publishers, see in particular
    Chapter 11, "What can we do", pp. 581–676.

7   Kapila, M. (2013) *Against a tide of evil*. Edinburg: Mainstream Publishing, pp. 16–17. United
    Nations, Srebrenica Report of the Secretary-General Pursuant to General assembly Resolution
    53/35 (1998), David Harland a.o., UN Doc.: A/54/549 (hereafter Harland Srebrenica report);
    United Nations Report of the Independent Inquiry into the Actions of the United Nations
    during the 1994 Genocide in Rwanda, 15 December 1999, United Nations, Ingvar Carlsson a.o.,
    UN Doc.: S/1999/1257 (Hereafter Carlsson Rwanda report).

8   Daillaire, R. (2004) *Shake Hands with the Devil. The Failure of Humanity in Rwanda*. London:
    Arrow Books, 2004, and authors' interview with Luc Marchal, 21 January 2005.

9   Nederlands Instituut voor Oorlogsdocumentatie (2002) *Srebrenica: een 'veilig' gebied.
    Reconstructie, achtergronden, gevolgen en analyses van de val van een Safe Area*. [Srebrenica:
    a "safe" area. Reconstruction, backgrounds, effects and analyses of the fall of a Safe Area]
    Amsterdam: Boom, see in particular Chapter 8 in part II, pp. 1479–1597, "Peacekeeping en
    humanitair optreden" [peacekeeping and humanitarian acting], p. 1485.

but genocide has been repeated in the second half of the twentieth century. The similarities in the organisation and preparation of the genocide on Jews and Tutsi has been studied and revealed by Mukimbiri[10] making use of the eight stages of genocide developed by Stanton.[11] These similarities are remarkable taking into account the modern, technological and bureaucratic way the Nazis in Germany prepared and performed the destruction of all Jews, whilst Rwanda is an undeveloped society where a high number of Tutsi killings were performed with primitive means such as machetes but at the same speed.

In our study, based on theoretical aspects in the academic field of international relations, we will research some patterns in these three case studies. These are the behaviours of third actors at the state and international level of analysis. Both the international, i.e. external, influences for a state and the domestic, i.e. internal, influences will be studied in the foreign policy-making of the states. The attention on internal influences makes it possible to study the process of decision-making in both states and international organisations, such as: rational decision-making, organisational decision-making and bureaucratic politics decision-making. This focus on decision-making is required in order to explain the gap between the warnings and the actions. The triplet 'warnings-instruments-actions' is the guideline in these comparisons.

3.1   Warnings and Knowledge

3.1.1   *Rwanda*
In the case of Rwanda the warnings for an emerging genocide were manifold; not only from NGOs, but also from third states and the UN military commanders of the peace-keeping forces. Since the spring of 1992 Belgium, France, the United States (including its CIA), many UN experts and rapporteurs of the Commission of Human Rights plus Human Rights NGOs like Amnesty International and Human Rights Watch had warned of the deteriorating situation and the possibility of genocide. But no one reacted to these outspoken warnings.[12] The most reliable information came from UN generals in

---

10   Mukimbiri, J. (2005) "The seven stages of the Rwandan Genocide", *Journal of International Criminal Justice*, Vol.: 3(4), pp. 823–836.

11   Stanton, G.H. (1996) *The 8 stages of genocide,* Genocide Watch, Washington D.C. available at: http://www.genocidewatch.org/aboutgenocide/8stagesofgenocide.html [accessed 16 November 2013].

12   Grünfeld and Huijboom (2007), pp. 61–126.

Rwanda and was sent directly to their colleagues in New York. The so-called 'genocide fax' of January 1993 – with the information about the preparation of the Hutu extremists to exterminate the Tutsi – was addressed to the military advisor of UN Secretary General Baril. The UN inquiry commission criticised the UN Force Commander Dallaire for not sending this message to the DPKO but to their fellow Canadian military Baril. However, Baril immediately informed Annan and Riza of DPKO. Annan and Riza did not inform the Secretary-General and they did also not inform the members of the Security Council on the threatening situation. They only instructed that the heads of diplomatic missions in Rwanda should be informed. The inquiry commission later concluded that "the seriousness of the threats in the cable justified informing the Council as whole."[13] This behaviour can be explained by our theoretical frameworks of 'cognitive dissonance,' 'Organisational Process Model' and 'Bureaucratic Politics Model' as we will do in the following section.

3.1.2   Srebrenica
The warnings on Srebrenica were less clear and less specific and they were not issued such a long time before the genocide erupted as in Rwanda. International actors were, nonetheless, aware of the risks for the minorities in several areas. Safe havens were therefore created to have the minorities protected by blue helmets against the majorities.[14] That was the case for the Serbs in Croatia (North and South Kraina plus East and West Slavonia) and the Muslims in Bosnia-Herzegovina. Awareness on the precarious position of these ethnic minorities was known long before the genocide in Srebrenica occurred. The weak position of these enclaves was also clear for the Dutch commander Karremans in Srebrenica. When he was asked in 1994 what would happen if Srebrenica would be attacked, he answered that there was no escape possible and in case they had to fight, they would have needed "a Boeing 747 to transport all the body bags to Holland."[15] Already in spring 1995 he warned several times about the shortage of food, munitions and petrol because of the enclosure by the Serbian army.[16]

---

13   Carlsson Rwanda report, p. 33.

14   Grünfeld (2008), pp. 467–470.

15   Karremans, Th. (1998) *Srebrenica, Who cares? Een puzzel van de werkelijkheid.* Nieuwegein: Arko Uitgeverij p. 7. (In Dutch: Wat gebeurt er als het Bosnisch-Servische leger jullie straks aanvalt? Dan zitten we als ratten in de val. En als we moeten vechten, zullen we een Boeing 747 nodig hebben om alle doden naar Nederland te brengen.)

16   Ibid., pp. 94–109. See in particular his warnings on the deteriorating situation of June 4 and 5, 1995, pp. 312–321.

The UN Secretariat and some members of the Security Council, being NATO allies of the Netherlands, were aware in May 1995 of an impending attack on the enclave Srebrenica. They decided not to inform the government of the Netherlands – notwithstanding the Dutch peacekeepers located in Srebrenica – and they also decided not to have any debate in the Security Council. Afterwards the Dutch Minister of Defence Voorhoeve stated that he only heard of the existence of the most serious warning afterwards. Thus, any preventive military enforcement action was precluded in advance. When the Serbian attack on the enclave started, the UN gave the members of the Security Council "false and incomplete information to let them think that the situation in Srebrenica was not that atrocious."[17] The inquiry report stated:

> In fact, rather than attempting to mobilize the international community to support the enclave's defence we [the Secretary General as the head of the UN Secretariat] gave the Security Council the impression that the situation was under control, and many of us believed that to be the case. The day before Srebrenica fell we reported that the Serbs were not attacking when they were. We reported that the Bosniacs had fired on an UNPROFOR blocking position when it was the Serbs. We failed to mention urgent requests for air power.[18]

These are clear examples of important mistakes from the UN Secretariat, who transmitted false information to the members of the Security Council, so that the international community underestimated and minimised the enormous threat at the brink of the genocide in Srebrenica.

The intention of the Bosnian Serbs to commit genocide was afterwards confirmed in the court decision by the ICJ of 27 February 2007.[19] The Yugoslavia Tribunal also condemned Zdravko Tolimir, the Bosnian Serb commander and assistant of General Ratko Mladić, to life imprisonment because of the genocide in Srebrenica and Žepa. The tribunal determined that the Bosnian Serbs had the explicit intention to exterminate the Muslims from Srebrenica.[20] In May 2013 the Serbian president Tomislav Nikolić for the first time acknowledged

---

17   Authors' interview with David Harland, 2 June 2005.
18   Harland Srebrenica report. There were Dutch appeals for Close Air Support on 6, 10 and 11 July 1995 (Karremans, 1998, pp. 158, 183–187, 194).
19   Bosnia and Herzegovina v. Serbia and Montenegro, Judgement, ICJ Reports 2007.
20   NRC Handelsblad, 13 December 2012, "Levenslang wegens Srebrenica" [Life imprisonment because of Srebrenica].

that genocide was committed in Srebrenica and he asked forgiveness for the crimes perpetrated by the Serbs in Bosnia.[21]

3.2 Responses

3.2.1 Rwanda

Before the genocide, diplomacy had led to the Arusha peace agreement of 4 August 1993 between the Rwandese government and the Rwanda Patriotic Front. For the implementation of this accord and the facilitation of the transitional administration in a stable environment for a government of both Hutu and Tutsi, the UN sent peacekeepers to Rwanda in October 1993.

At the moment of the creation of this peacekeeping force the risks were underestimated and the situation on the ground was such that there was no longer a peace to keep. Warnings were ignored. The only reaction from New York was to continue as before, not taking into account that the situation on the ground had changed completely. After the clear warnings, the UN in New York only informed the Rwandese government of possible dangers. They furthermore respected the Rwandese sovereignty and prohibited their own UN peacekeepers to act beyond self defence against the unfolding security threats such as hidden weapons and the training of the extremist militia. A new policy was not developed and essential information was not forwarded to the members of the Security Council for fear of negatively affecting the reputation to the Department of Peacekeeping Operation in New York. A new mandate to the available peacekeepers was not discussed, although the Canadian leaders of the peacekeeping force requested it.

Available instruments were thus not employed to deter, to prevent or stop the genocide. When the genocide started almost all peacekeepers were withdrawn as was decided by the UN in New York. Withdrawing the peacekeepers meant that a buffer was taken away and the genocide could continue without any hinderance of a third party. The decision to withdraw was taken after the *génocidaires*[22] deliberately murdered ten Belgian peacekeepers at the first day of their atrocities against moderate political leaders and the Tutsi population.

---

21 NRC Handelsblad, 26 April 2013, "Servië betuigt spijt over "misdaad" Srebrenica" [Serbia appologises for "crime" Srebrenica] (Bosnian television interview with President Tomislav Nikolić, 7 May 2013).

22 *Génocidaires* is a French term, which originates from the Rwandan genocide and refers to the perpetrators of the genocide.

It was a well planned and effective action, since the UN gave in and withdrew, removing the last hurdle for a total genocide. Contrary to the aim of genocide prevention the UN and France facilitated the *génocidaires*. Other nations did not act although they had powerful instruments available, such as their robust national armies. US soldiers from Burundi invaded with tanks over land and Belgian, French and Italian special forces were flown in to evacuate their own countrymen but they did not rescue the Rwandese embassy personnel or any other Rwandese who were in peril of death.[23] The genocide ended because of the military power of the army of Tutsis, commanded by Paul Kagame, which invaded Rwanda from Uganda and occupied the whole country. The *génocidaires* of the Hutu extremists consequently lost their power. It was the military power that mattered.

The non-interference in Rwanda was also facilitated in the two following ways. Firstly, France deliberately kept silent during the whole period, whereas it supported the French speaking *génocidaires* (who still represented Rwanda in the SC) during the genocide. Being silent with all the knowledge on the atrocities constitutes to allowing the genocide and helping the perpetrators as collaborators. At the moment the *génocidaires* lost power France directly reacted and was authorised by the Security Council on June 22, 1994 in Resolution 929 under Chapter VII to start a military intervention (*Opération Turquoise*) to help the Hutu militias to escape and to protect and rescue the *Interahamwe* perpetrators in Goma. This military action can primarily be explained from the perspective of the approach of realism in International Relations Theories, because France acted first and foremost to defend its own national interests and to safeguard its sphere of influence (*'la Francophonie'*) in Africa (see also Section 3.3.2).[24]

3.2.2   *Srebrenica*

As was mentioned in the previous section, a UN protection force (UNPROFOR) was created for Bosnia in February 1992. Srebrenica was declared a safe area under UN protection in April 1993. The aim of these peacekeepers in Srebrenica was to protect the population in the enclaves from an attack; in the case of Srebrenica protecting the Bosnian Muslims against the Bosnian Serbs. The UN force was not able to counter the attack and did not even try to deter the aggressors or to defend the so-called safe-areas with Muslims. The area was consequently conquered by the Serbs without any resistance from NATO, the

---

23   Grünfeld and Huijboom (2007), pp. 167–178.

24   Lanotte, O. (2007) La France au Rwanda (1990–1993). Entre abstention impossible et engagement ambivalent. Bruxelles: P.I.E. Peter Lang.

UN and the Dutch peacekeeping force on the ground. After conquering the enclave the genocide took place. There is even evidence that the UN peacekeepers did not obstruct the deportation of the population and thus facilitated the *génocidaires*. Diplomacy was no longer one of the available options. The only answer in this case would be a military counter attack with the air force situated in Italy under French and NATO command. Nonetheless, the UN Secretary-General and the Security Council members had already in May excluded – in secrecy behind closed doors – such a military answer in the form of a military enforcement operation under Chapter VII.[25] Some assistance for the ground forces was requested in July, albeit in vain. This assistance was refused since the *génocidaires* deliberately took some UN peacekeepers hostage and threatened with an ultimatum to kill these soldiers in case of an air attack on July 11, the day of the fall of Srebrenica. The Dutch Minister of Defence Voorhoeve, asked to cancel the air support in phone calls to the Secretary General of the UN, NATO and the French Air Force Commander in Vicenza (Italy, the location of the airbase for the bombers to Bosnia). He also phoned the UN Special Representative Akashi at 4.50 PM. Akashi later blamed the Dutch for this cancellation but it was Akashi who decided earlier on at 4.30 PM to cancel the air support for the peacekeepers. Our conclusion was: "The threat of killing peacekeepers was very effective. In Rwanda, as we have seen, most peacekeeping forces were withdrawn after the killing of ten Belgian peacekeepers. In Srebrenica, military action was aborted following a threat to kill Dutch peacekeepers. The result, in both situations, was that the targeted populations became very vulnerable and were no longer protected; the *génocidaires* were not hindered by any third party."[26]

The genocide in Srebrenica was thus not prevented or stopped by third parties. Decisive military action was only taken after the fall of Srebrenica in the form of bombing Serbian forces and Serbian occupied territories. The instrument of sanctions was used with more effect at a later stage with the tightening of sanctions against the Bosnian Serbs and the lightening of sanctions against the Serbian government and the population in Belgrade, with the aim of a achieving a peace agreement. The sanctions and military retaliation eventually contributed to a diplomatically negotiated peace agreement at Dayton in the US in November 1995. The Dayton Accords endorsed the *de facto* situation on the ground, in other words, the Bosnian Serbs were granted the territory of Srebrenica in Republika Srpska. Consequently, the *génocidaires* still rule over the (former) victims in this area.

---

25   Grünfeld (2008), pp. 467–470.
26   Grünfeld and Vermeulen (2009), p. 228.

3.3   Explaining the Warning-Response Gap for Rwanda and Srebrenica

In order to explain the warning-response gap in the cases of Rwanda and Srebrenica, we will use and apply the theoretical concepts outlined in the previous chapter. For each concept illustrations are provided. The concepts are: (1) Domestic sources of foreign policy, (2) Rational Policy Model, (3) Organisational Process Model, (4) Bureaucratic Politics Model and (5) Cognitive dissonance and other psychological mechanisms. In concluding Chapter 11 these results will be compared with those derived from our Darfur study for the comparative element of this book.

3.3.1   *Domestic Sources of Foreign Policy*
The genocide in Rwanda was not prevented or stopped by third parties, as discussed in the previous section. The non-interference of third parties before and during the genocide can be explained with reference to the pluralist-liberal theories and in particular from the different perspectives the decision-making theories offer. Domestic influences on the foreign policy-making of the third parties were absent before and during the genocide in Rwanda. There was no public pressure which activated Western governments. At the height of the genocide the American official who was the head of the African Division of the State Department even tried in vain to mobilise an NGO such as Human Rights Watch.[27] What is more, the public pressure that was present was also increasingly against a greater involvement in Rwanda. This was especially the case in Belgium. The deliberate murder of ten Belgian peacekeepers at the start of the genocide was an important reason for the – almost complete – withdrawal of the peacekeeping force from Rwanda. This is because the public opinion in Belgium no longer supported the continuation of the peacekeeping mission. Public support was not only lost due to the Belgian fatalities, but also due to the still fresh memory and reminder to the Americans of the murder and slaughtering of American (and Pakistani) peacekeepers in Mogadishu, Somalia one year before. With respect to Srebrenica the story starts before the Netherlands considered participating in UNPROFOR. In the Netherlands the public was shocked by the images like the meagre man behind the fence at the Omarska and Trnopolje camps or the atrocities from Vukovar.[28] This public

---

27   Authors' interview with Prudence Bushnell, 27 May 2005.
28   Nederlands Instituut voor Oorlogsdocumentatie (2002), see in particular Part I, Chapter 6, "De emotionalisering van het debat door de kampen ('Omarska'): juni-augustus 1992" [The emotionalism of the debate because of the camps ('Omarska'): June–August 1992], pp. 579–727.

mood stimulated Dutch parliament to propose a contribution with Dutch blue helmets to the peacekeeping force UNPROFOR in Srebrenica without any conditions in advance for the participation as the Nordic countries had put forward. The Canadians warned the Netherlands of the dangerous situation in this safe haven, but the Dutch accepted the weak military mandate because they were eager to do 'something good'. By contrast, the Scandinavians – in particular the Danish parliament – were only willing to contribute to UNPROFOR in Tuzla when they could bring heavy military material such as tanks for self-defence and for the execution of their mandate, i.e. the protection of the population in the safe haven. The Netherlands was so eager to contribute and make use of its new military unit, 'the Air Manoeuvre Brigade' that the warnings were not heard and the examples and experiences of their close allies were not taken into account. This led to the disastrous result of the genocide which occurred in Srebrenica, while nothing of that scale happened in Tuzla because the Danish tanks in that area could withstand an attack of the Bosnian Serbs 15 months before Srebrenica was conquered. Military deterrence proved to be important. However, we are aware that this provision was made possible because of the considerable domestic influences on foreign policy in the Nordic countries. Such influences were missing in the Netherlands because domestic actors, most notably the Dutch parliament, did not request additional military guarantees.

3.3.2   *Rational Policy Model*

The Rational Policy Model, with its focus on cost-benefit analyses, is able to explain the establishment of both peacekeeping forces before the genocide occurred. A peace agreement for Rwanda was made and these forces could help in implementing the peace agreement. For example, the US President Clinton agreed with the peacekeeping force, because he welcomed a positive international act without any risks, especially after the catastrophe in Somalia for American soldiers. The Rational Policy Model applies to a lesser extent to the peacekeeping forces in Srebrenica and other safe havens in Bosnia. The (potential) costs for peacekeeping by third parties in Bosnia/ Srebrenica were considerable. That is to say, many diplomatic efforts had failed, the situation on the ground was risky and minorities in these areas were in danger. The benefits for governments were primarily domestic political in nature. By contributing to a peacekeeping force, governments would be able to show to their population that they were responding to domestic pressure and actively addressing the situation. The Rational Policy Model is even better placed to explain the warning-response gap and the near absence of efforts by the international community to prevent the genocide. Most analyses of the international response to intra-state conflicts and genocides have focused on the lack of political will and the absence of strategic interests. Such explanations fit well with the Rational Policy Model. Samantha Power concluded in her study on the US response to several genocides in the 20th century, including Rwanda and Srebrenica, that the responses reflected a deliberate decision not to respond after weighing the costs and benefits. US policy-makers pursued two goals. On the one hand, avoid becoming involved in conflicts which do not or hardly affect American interests. On the other hand, minimise the political costs and moral shame by giving the impression that the maximum achievable is being done. The costs of avoiding engagement were significantly lower than the costs for increasing the involvement.[29]

The Rational Policy Model can also explain the silence of France in the Security Council during the genocide in Rwanda because a Hutu victory was a French interest in Africa. The French military action to protect the Hutu *génocidaires*, who fled to Goma in Eastern Congo after the genocide, was also a clear rational French decision to protect their interests in the region. The Rational Policy Model also offers an explanation for the non-provision of information on the situation in Rwanda by the UN Secretariat to the Security Council. The Secretariat estimated that forwarding the information to the Security Council would contribute to the derailment of the peace process. By contrast, ignoring the warning would involve considerably less costs and not raise any expectations. A Polish major who served in UNAMIR noted: "this is one of the UN typical tactics: do not reply, then the problem does not exist. If you reply, you admit you [need to] solve it."[30]

The Rational Policy Model also explains why international actors were primarily interested in rescuing only their own nationals and officials. At the start of the genocide in Rwanda a huge fighting force arrived to evacuate mostly Western foreign nationals. A total of over 1700 elite troops from the US, France, Italy and Belgium were either flown in or put on standby in neighbouring countries immediately after the attack on President Habyarimana's plane when the evacuation of their nationals was ordered. If these 1700 well-armed and trained elite troops had been added to the 2500 UNAMIR soldiers, the total number of troops on the ground in Rwanda would have been 4200 – exactly the number of soldiers all Rwandan parties to the Arusha Peace Accords had asked for in 1993 and the number that was considered realistic by the military who prepared the peacekeeping mission.[31] A possible combination of this

---

29   Power (2007), pp. 508–509.
30   Piiparinen (2010), p. 112.
31   Grünfeld and Huijboom (2007), p. 177.

strong military force with the weaker UN peacekeeping force was never tabled in the decision-making processes of any Western capital or at UN Headquarters – a clear signal for the *génocidaires* that no one from the outside world would oppose the genocide.[32] Likewise, the decision in Srebrenica not to strike from the air with a bombardment on the ground in Srebrenica after the genocide had started can be seen as a rational decision to protect French and Dutch soldiers (part of it as hostages) on the ground instead of the Muslim Bosnians.

3.3.3   *Organisational Process Model*

The organisational process model is very apt in explaining the early-warning-response gap, because it focuses on bureaucratic cultures within states and international organisations. The most prominent example of work that is focused on bureaucratic culture is the writing of Barnett on the genocide in Rwanda.[33] Closely linked to the organisational process model is the phenomenon that big organisations can become detached from their aims in underlining the organisational bureaucratic interests. A bureaucratic culture produces "powerful and autonomous bureaucrats who could be spiritless, driven only by impersonal rules and procedures and with little regard for the people they were expected to serve."[34] This contributed to the "production of indifference" by ensuring that the UN avoids operations with little chances of success which would threaten its interests by damaging its reputation and image.[35] Piiparinen likewise pointed to the phenomenon of bureaucratic rationalisation, whereby rules and procedures, such as the principles of neutrality and impartiality, become ends in themselves rather than the means to realise a certain objective – in this context peace and security.[36] The model explains very well why the peacekeeping forces maintained the strict and limited standard operating procedures and routines for keeping the peace even though the situation on the ground was rapidly deteriorating. In the months preceding the genocide in Rwanda, all early warnings were received by the UN but they failed to effect a change in the decisions of the UN Secretariat. The Secretariat remained unyieldingly committed to thinking in terms of peace and security and the post-conflict transformation process of installing a new multi-ethnic government.[37]

---

32   Smeulers and Grünfeld (2011), pp. 398–399.
33   Barnett (2003).
34   Ibid., p. 7.
35   Barnett (1997); Barnett (2003).
36   Piiparinen (2008), p. 714.
37   Smeulers and Grünfeld (2011), p. 396. Barnett (2003), Melvern, L. (2005) "The Security Council in the face of genocide", *Journal of International Criminal Justice*, Vol.: 3(4), pp. 847–860.

On 5 April, the Security Council approved the continuation of the peace-keeping force in Rwanda for another six months without receiving or taking into account the information on the deteriorating situation. This prolongation was simply presented as a routine decision.[38] This was one day before the crash of the plane with President Habyarimana, which was the trigger of the genocide. The following day, 6 April, at the outbreak of the 'politicide' followed by the genocide, the peacekeeper commander general Dallaire phoned five times with the heads of the DPKO in New York Kofi Annan and Iqbal Riza, but they decided to prohibit the use of force to give safety to the members of the moderate Rwandese government. DPKO top officials reacted according to the organisational process model as if it was a routine decision even though the Prime Minister and members of his government were killed.[39] A day later on 7 April, ten Belgium peacekeepers were deliberately murdered by the Rwandese *géno-cidaires*. That day the Belgian ambassador in New York, Noterdaeme, asked for the protection of the Belgian nationals and a more forceful role of the peace-keepers. The answer from Annan was again that all actions had to be in accordance with the existing rules of engagement.[40] Annan's reply was the routine answer in line with the organisational process model which highlights standard patterns of behaviour.

In their bureaucratic vision, the UN had to maintain a traditional neutral peacekeeping role and not take sides against the perpetrators of the impending genocide with forceful action as was requested by, for instance, the Canadian UNAMIR commander, Roméo Dallaire, and many others, such as the Belgian government. The typical answer derived from this organisational process model is of withdrawing almost all peacekeepers when some soldiers were murdered. The soldiers could no longer stay without the consent of the parties as being one of the conditions for peacekeeping operations. Changing one's views when the situation has changed is not within the limited routinised way of thinking that is characteristic for this organisational process model.

The most reliable warnings coupled with a policy recommendation of how to act were without doubt forwarded and received in New York. However, as a result of decisions taken in the UN DPKO by persons such as Kofi Annan this information, including the rapidly deteriorating situation, was not forwarded to the members of the Security Council who were thus precluded from taking any action whatsoever.[41] A bureaucratic calculation as to the costs of

---

38   Grünfeld and Huijboom (2007), pp. 151, 254.

39   Ibid., pp. 166, 255.

40   Ibid., p. 181.

41   Smeulers and Grünfeld (2011), p. 396.

forwarding the warning signal to the Secretariat played a role. One important element that was taken into consideration was the political capital of the Secretary General. It was argued that when he goes (too) regularly with warnings to Security Council, he might not be taken seriously any more, especially if it later turns out to be a false alarm. Besides, he might set himself on collision course with the (permanent members) of the Security Council. This would jeopardise his (future) working relations with the Council. Another consideration which prevented the Secretariat to inform the UNSC was the estimation or anticipation that the Security Council would not authorise any (enlarged) intervention anyhow.[42]

Neutrality and impartiality were the tasks belonging to classical peacekeeping forces of the first generation. Neutrality and impartiality became ends in themselves rather than the means to realise a certain objective. It is not unreasonable to argue that genocide requires a total opposition to the United Nations, because genocide can be seen as threatening everything the UN has stood for, as laid down in its Charter. But this did not happen. Instead, the UN and UN officials were primarily concerned with the interests of the UN. A UN official in New York stated: "I was more committed to the survival of the UN than I was to the Rwandans."[43] There was a clear attempt to avoid damaging the reputation and image of the UN as a whole and the Department of Peacekeeping Operations in particular (see below at Bureaucratic Politics Model).

In her analysis of the US response to Bosnia/Srebrenica, Power also highlighted several elements reflecting the organisational behaviour model. First of all, the impossibility of US military intervention was treated as a given and shaped the thinking of many (lower) officials. Officials simply assumed that intervention was unacceptable and would not happen, so they did nothing. They hence internalised the policy constraints and the indifference at the top-level. One US official noted the consequence of this posture: "When it [the Administration] adopts a defeatist mode...it's going to get defeatist results."[44] Another example for this Organisational Process Model is the statement of the Secretary-General of the UN at the brink of the genocide in Srebrenica against a military defence: "peace should be pursued only through non-military methods because he was against what he called a culture of death."[45]

---

42   Barnett (2003), p. 15.
43   Barnett (1997), p. 573.
44   Power (2007), pp. 266–267, 287, 315 and quote from p. 313.
45   Carlson Rwanda report, para. 497.

3.3.4   *Bureaucratic Politics Model*

This is the model *par excellence* to explain the behaviour of the UN in both genocides. The Security Council did not adopt any resolution or take any measure to stop the atrocities in Rwanda and Srebrenica. On the contrary, DPKO did not provide the full information to the members of the Security Council for fear of harming their own administrative unit. They misinformed the Security Council in both cases and they did not provide the perspective that the peace was no longer to be maintained and restored but an emerging genocide with slaughtered peoples had to be feared.

The administrative unit DPKO feared that a failure in the operation after Somalia may endanger the existence of this administrative unit and future peacekeeping operations across the world. All instructions on Rwanda were in accordance to the rules of DPKO as just elaborated and all events and information was coloured to benefit their sub-organisation. They did their utmost to distort all incoming information by rejecting all that might have changed the views that the peace could no longer be kept, the Bosnian Serbs had aggressive aims or that the Rwandese rulers were preparing a genocide. Other UN departments should obviously be involved in such extreme cases of genocide or aggression, which are linked to the major aims of the UN and its activities in maintain peace and security and the protection of fundamental human rights. However, DPKO left no room for other departments to get involved. In order to defend their unit, Annan and Riza deliberately did not inform the Security Council members of the worsening security situation on the ground but instead labelled it as a civil war or tribal struggle, and misinformed on the outspoken Serb aggression and their attack on the hills around Srebrenica.

3.3.5   *Cognitive Dissonance and other Psychological Mechanisms*

In our definition of cognitive dissonance we underlined the way actors in the decision-making avoid and discount information that is inconsistent with their prior views and which would require them to adjust their views. In the previous sections, we elaborated that – in line with the organisational process model – all information that did not fit in the routine pattern of decision-making was ignored and disregarded. This mirrors cognitive dissonance. There is consequently no adjustment of the original plan of action. UN officials continued to perceive the situation as a peacemaking process involving the installation of a transitional government and not as an emerging genocide. The UN Secretariat – and in particular the DPKO – therefore favoured a neutral rather than a confrontational position. A shift in perception from facilitating the implementation of a peace accord toward preventing an emerging genocide was needed, but no such shift took place.[46] We also have explained that in the Bureaucratic Politics Model the interests of several – more dominant – UN (or US) departments prevailed in the decision-making and counter information is neglected or changed in a way that it is made consistent with the interests of the unit.

An example of cognitive dissonance was when a Security Council member did not realise and could not believe that his neighbour in the Security Council is a representative of the *génocidaire* Hutu regime in Rwanda. As mentioned, deteriorations in the security situations were primarily seen as "dangers to the peace process" more than as "dangers to Rwandans."[47]

Actors also tended to filter incoming information through previously held views and expectations. UN officials, for example, analysed the incoming information and warnings with a prior bias or prejudice against the Bosnian Muslims. The latter were seen as the ones who undermined the peace process and incited the Serbs.[48] A further complication for international actors, particularly the UK, was the idea that the Serbs in Bosnia were this time the perpetrators committing atrocities against Croats or Muslims, whereas they were heroic in their struggle against Nazi Germany.

Bystanders find it difficult to believe the unbelievable or imagine the unimaginable. For instance, the National Security Advisor to US President Clinton, Anthony Lake said afterwards "I wasn't imagining 'a Srebrenica' because it hadn't happened before."[49] This behaviour is very close to denial, even though it is not outright denial.[50] As a result of this disbelief or denial, atrocities were not recognised or put in a distorted way to fit existing world views. Another mechanism, which is closely related to disbelief, is wishful thinking. Actors convince themselves that negative developments are less or unlikely to occur, while they are considerably more optimistic about the likelihood of positive outcomes. One example of wishful thinking in the case of Rwanda relates to the almost naïve trust in negotiations and diplomacy. The then US Ambassador in Kigali, for example, stated: "The fact that negotiations can't work is almost not one of the options open (...). We were looking for the

---

46   Grünfeld and Vermeulen (2009), p. 233.

47   Power (2001), p. 10; Power (2007), p. 346.

48   Power (2007), p. 398.

49   Ibid., p. 410. On the other hand it was Lake who told the authors that at the start of the genocide in Rwanda he was aware of the magnitude of these atrocities watching the murdered bodies in the river on his satellite screen in Washington (Authors' interview with Antony Lake, 21 May 2005).

50   Cohen, S. (2001) *States of denial: knowing about atrocities and suffering.* Cambridge: Blackwell Publishers.

hopeful signs, not the dark signs. In fact, we were looking away from the dark signs."[51]

After the fall of the enclave of Srebrenica, US and UN officials acted as if they were conducting business as usual. A cable to the UN Headquarters in New York from 14 July 1995, UN Special Representative Akashi started with an enumeration of the amount of food and the shortages in shelter in Tuzla. The disappeared Muslim men were only euphemistically and shortly mentioned in paragraph eight: "We are beginning to detect a short-fall in [the] number of persons expected to arrive in Tuzla. There is no further information on the status of the approximately 4.000 draft age males."[52]

Another psychological mechanism used by actors was a normalisation technique. Several actors relied on stereotypical and racial images. Killings in Africa were neither seen as especially unusual. US Acting Assistant Secretary of State for African Affairs, Bushnell stated: "People didn't know that it was a genocide. What I was told was, 'Look, Pru, these people do this from time to time'."[53] A report of the inquiry commission of the AU afterwards also pointed to "the implicit racism" and the "sense that African lives are not valued as high as other lives" which was visible in the priority given by New York to the peacekeepers in Rwanda to help the rescue of expatriates, even beyond its original mandate (Section 3.3.2).[54] The conflict in Rwanda was also described as "chaotic, mad and tribal."[55] One consequence of portraying it as an impenetrable Somalia-like chaos with little possibility of resolution is that actors are relieved from any duty to act. Another way of diminishing the urgency to act is by describing the situation in Rwanda as a civil war instead of genocide, which may help bystanders at all levels to disregard the cruel atrocities of the perpetrators.[56] The situation in Bosnia was also described as an inevitable "tragedy" or "civil war" as opposed to deliberate and carefully top-down coordinated atrocities

---

51   US Ambassador in Kigali, David Rawson, as quoted in Power (2001), p. 10.

52   Power (2007), p. 403.

53   Ibid., pp. 351, 365. See also Suhrke, A. and Jones, B. (2000) "Preventive diplomacy in Rwanda: Failure to act or failure of actions?", in *Opportunities missed, opportunities seized: Preventive diplomacy in the post-Cold War world*, by Jentleson, B.W. (ed.), Lanham: Rowan & Littlefield Publishers, p. 256.

54   Organization of African Unity, The International Panel of Eminent Personalities to Investigate the 1994 Genocide in Rwanda and the Surrounding Events, available at: http:// www.peaceau.org/uploads/report-rowanda-genocide.pdf [accessed 18 December 2013], para. 21.15.

55   Piiparinen (2008), p. 719.

56   Idem; Piiparinen (2010), p. 76.

committed by a recognisable group of perpetrators.[57] The conflict was portrayed as a civil war in which all sides committed brutalities and which would be difficult to be solved by outsiders. Any military intervention was believed or presented to lead to a "Vietnam-like quagmire."[58] It is remarkable that this analogy of Vietnam was used and not one from WWII. As put forward the decision was already taken by the SC members not to intervene and that is why all information and messages were put to support that view. This is called cognitive dissonance.

In the following chapters we will bring these analytical tools in to practice for Darfur.

---

57   Power (2007), p. 285.
58   Idem.

CHAPTER 4

A Background of Darfur

In this chapter we briefly sketch the historical, socio-economic and political context of Darfur. On the one hand, some of the aspects discussed here might be seen as the fundamental problems of the region of Darfur, which need to be addressed in any comprehensive peace settlement. On the other hand, these fundamental or root causes are less informative in explaining why the conflict emerges so violently in 2003, or how and when bystanders might act. Nevertheless, the location and history of Darfur does explain in part the actions of certain bystanders during the crisis starting 2003. Unlike in the later chapters we base ourselves here mainly on secondary sources. We limit ourselves to a brief overview of the background of Darfur, whereas more elaborate accounts can be found in other sources.[1]

4.1 Composition of Sudan and the Inhabitants of Darfur

Darfur is located in the west of Sudan bordering Chad, Central African Republic and South Sudan. The region of Darfur obtained its name from one of the main people living in the area, the Fur. Together with the Zaghawa and Masalit, as well as several smaller groups they form a population of Africans who have inhabited the area since before modern times. The Fur, the biggest among them, broadly live in and around the volcanic mountain range of the Jebel Mara, the Zaghawa live mostly to the west of this, towards and in Chad, while the Masalit are to be found in south-west Darfur.

Arab tribes are similarly found all over the region, although they dominate more towards the north and east of Darfur. Arabs are said to have arrived later to these lands than the African people, but were already present by the fourteenth century. From these times onwards, the people have mixed and lived

---

1 If not otherwise noted, the main text is based on Daly, M.W. (2010) *Darfur's Sorrow. The forgotten history of a humanitarian crisis.* 2nd Edition. Cambridge: Cambridge University Press. See also Prunier, G. (2007) *Darfur: An ambiguous genocide. Revised and updated edition 2007* London: C. Hurst & Co. (publishers) ltd., Chapters 1–3; Bassil, N.R. (2013) *The postcolonial state and civil war in Sudan. The origins of conflict in Darfur.* London, New York: I.B. Taurus.

together. Hence, what is currently called Arab and African is in reality not strongly based on 'objective' criteria such as race, ethnicity, language or otherwise. The African and Arab tribes have shared Islamic faith for at least two centuries. Denominations are for a large part based on how the people see themselves and others.

This diversity of the people across the region of Darfur has been attributed to its place on old trade routes between north–south and east–west Africa, as well as to the many nomadic people that travel around with their cattle. Estimates of the total population of Darfur ranged between a few hundred thousand to around one million by the end of the 19th century, while closer to six million 100 years later. Numbers have fluctuated heavily over time due to incoherent data and varying environmental-climatic conditions in the region. The share of the different peoples among the total population is similarly hard to gauge since no official census has been held since the 1950s. Broadly speaking, African people make up around half of the population.

4.2   A Long History

Not much of Darfur's early history is known for certain. Only when foreigners from Europe and the Ottoman Empire started to travel through and stay for extended periods in the late eighteenth and early nineteenth century have more reliable records become available. These travellers recounted a kingdom or sultanate led by a royal Fur family. These Fur gained their sway over the region as trade partners to Egyptians in slaves and exotic products from further south in Africa. The state administration around this sultanate was formally organised with offices and titles, but was nevertheless primitive in comparison to rulers in more northern parts of Africa such as Egypt. Its protection from external harassment of other rulers was for a large part due to its geographically isolated location.

Nevertheless, Darfur came under foreign rule for a limited period of time at the final stage of the Ottoman-Egyptian expansion into Sudan. This expansion was undertaken in 1821 for the search of profitable trade and valuable minerals and agriculture. Only the trade in slaves was successful. The Nile area of what is now Sudan (and South-Sudan) was governed for much of the nineteenth century as an extension to the Egyptian province. Egyptian expansion into Darfur was much more limited and only marginally brought modernisation in life and governance. Once the power of the Ottoman Empire was weakening, Egypt lost control over the Sudan in 1882. The United Kingdom, as the new empire, eventually took over even though Sudan and Egypt formally remained part of the Ottoman Empire.

The people in Darfur again experienced a short period of limited independence under an Islamic ruler, called the Mahdi State, which lasted from 1885 to 1898. This regime never obtained direct control over the area. Rather, through constant military incursions into Darfur, it inflicted hardship, causing death and all but ending trade on which the people had relied. In combination with droughts, causing famine, as well as the outbreak of plagues and diseases, this period was one of severe deprivation. By the end of the nineteenth century British troops re-conquered the Sudan but left a Fur to rule in Darfur, in effect allowing for a vassal sultanate. The interest of the British was not so much in the development of Sudan or Darfur, but primarily to guarantee the security of Egypt from the south. Control over Sudan was aimed at deterring further advancement towards British controlled territory by European powers such as France and Belgium, which were expanding their African colonies from the south and east.

Until this time, no previous authority or ruler of Sudan or Darfur had formally drawn a border with its neighbours to the west. This left a question to what extent the tribes living to the west of Fur lands belonged to the region of Darfur, in particular the Masalit. France aimed by the end of the 19th century, as part of the 'Scramble for Africa,' to expand into Darfur by laying claim to all Masalit land. With this advancement of France, through the establishment of Chad, an agreement was required between the UK and France on the exact borders of Darfur. However, this agreement was not reached before the start of the First World War.

In 1916, the British took more direct control over Sudan and installed a bureaucratic administration, more or less independent of Egypt. However, Darfur was notably excluded from central administration due to its remoteness. The cheaper option of leaving a local in charge was deemed sufficient, at least as long as British interests were not harmed. The issue of the border on the east was finally settled in 1921 when France and the UK agreed on the western Sudanese border, encompassing Dar Masalit.

In general, the British were not interested in spending a lot of resources to build up a modern and direct administration for the Sudan and Darfur. Instead they opted for indirect rule and appointed local strongmen where possible under the tutelage of British agents or officials, not unlike the system that was used in India and Nigeria. These appointed local strongmen did not necessarily always have the support from the people and were sometimes badly qualified to run a local administration. In combination with the actions of self-interested tribal leaders the system failed to deliver much for Darfur.

The lack of investment in the development of an education or a health system left the people in Darfur, more than in the rest of Sudan, extraordinarily susceptible to yearly climatic and natural variations of draught, disease epidemics – for both humans and cattle – and pests and plagues on crops. At the beginning of the 20th century, Darfur still lacked the infrastructure that would allow year-round transport. The old caravan, pilgrim and trade routes were never made passable for the rainy season. During the Second World War, when Sudan was caught between Italian ruled Ethiopia-Eritrea on the south-east and Libya on the north-west, the British air force commanded the improvement of infrastructure for supply to airbases in Darfur and further modernization of runways and control towers. However, Sudan and Darfur played only marginal roles in the war and a front was never established.

Already after the First World War a path towards independence from Britain was set in. A series of five-year plans with finance from Britain was arranged for the development of Sudan, including: building law and order, and establishing education, health, agriculture and transport capacities. However, directed by the Sudanese in Khartoum, most of it was spent in the capital, surrounding regions and agriculture production around the Nile. Darfur, just as southern Sudan, received barely anything. By 1953 Sudan was set to become an independent country over a three-year transition period. The treaty that established this was agreed between Egypt, Britain and a council of Sudanese representatives. Ideas for a self-governing, non-Muslim non-Arab South Sudan were raised but quickly abandoned. Darfur was simply considered part of (north) Sudan.

Some form of party democracy was introduced in 1955 in Sudan, leading up to independence in 1956, but the democratic government was quickly overthrown by a military regime in 1958. At the same time, economic development, with help of foreign aid and concessionary loans from abroad, was largely concentrated on the centre, Khartoum. This pattern remained through the change of regimes, juntas and revolutions. Darfur, as well as the southern Sudan, was simply left behind. Local political representation and organisation in Darfur was still largely arranged along tribal lines. The African and Arab peoples in Darfur were, and have never been able to, overcome internal differences to counter central government neglect and abuse. The South rebelled against the government, which resulted in one of the bloodiest civial wars in Africa (see Section 4.4).

In 1984–1985 a major draught caused a famine disaster across a large part of Africa. In Sudan casualities were exacerbated as a result of misconduct of the central government. The government first denied the problem, and later cooperated only reluctantly with international aid agencies.[2] Darfur's remoteness caused additional delay in the arrival of emergency aid.

From independence onwards there was also the tendency from Khartoum's various governments to 'Islamise' and 'Arabise' the rest of the country. The response was increased resistance from the South against Khartoum's dominance, and fighting broke out. These policies had a lesser effect on Darfur, which was already predominantly Muslim and where the majority of the people spoke Arab, if not as their mother tongue then as a second language.

In the 1970s and 1980s the regional dimensions of Libya and Chad became a more important factor for the situation in Darfur. Chadian fighters and Libyan sponsored militias hid in or fled to Darfur. Libyan arms, such as heavy and automatic weapons, also found their ways to the other tribes. Henceforth, local disputes were settled more violently compared to the times such when arms were not as readably available. Tribes and people also became caught up in regional politics. After repeated attempts, Idris Déby, who was backed by Libya and allowed by Khartoum to do so from Darfur, overthrew Chadian President Habré in N'Djamena in 1990.

A military coup in 1989 brought a general called Omar Hasan al-Bashir to power in Sudan, and he would later become president in 1996. The new regime backed off from talks on a peace settlement with South Sudan and vigorously introduced fundamentalist Islamic custom and law.[3] Fighting spread to other parts of the country including the Nuba Mountains and the Blue Nile area in the east. The new Islamist regime then made a peculiar choice in its international friends. It took Iraq's side after it had invaded Kuwait. Sudan supported the Lord's Resistance Army in Uganda, and other rebel groups in neighbouring countries, as well as Hezbollah and Hamas. It had good relations with Osama Bin Laden who stayed for some time in the country. For these reasons the US declared Sudan a 'state sponsor of terrorism' in 1993. The UN imposed a series of sanctions on Sudan, after an assassination attempt on Egyptian President Mubarak at an Organisation of African States summit in Addis Ababa on 1995.[4] In addition, in 1996 the US further imposed unilateral economic sanctions on the regime. In 1997 the US even bombed a

---

2   See also, de Waal, A. (1989 [2005]) *Famine that kills. Revised and updated edition.* Oxford: Oxford University Press.

3   One scholar notes that the new regime was involved in peace talks for a while, but the failure of progress made the military solution a viable option (Verhoeven, H., 2013, "The rise and fall of Sudan's Al-Ingaz revolution: The transition from militarised Islamism to economic salvation and the Comprehensive Peace Agreement," *Civil Wars*, Vol.: 15[2], p. 130).

4   See UN Docs.: S/Res/1044, 31 January 1996; S/Res/1054, 26 April 1996; S/Res/1070, 16 August 1996.

pharmaceutical factory in Khartoum, thought to be a source of bombs for terrorists.

4.3   Low Level Conflict in Darfur and the Rise of Rebel Groups

Under the al-Bashir regime, and with some Libyan involvement, tribal conflict in Darfur became more ideologically racist in favour of Arab dominance. Local Arab tribes took it as an excuse to grab land and cattle from African people. When faced with it, the government looked away selectively. Disputes would occasionally result in tribal violence. The government re-organised regional governance with more centralised power, and gave government positions to allied Arabs.

In the 1990s the African tribes started to organise protests and resistance against central government abuse, for instance through the organisation of a Masalit self-defence unit in 1996. The government's response was to further empower and support Arab tribal militias, including what was to be known as the *Janjaweed*. It led the African people to join causes, and they organised a common rebellion, first politically, later militarily. An anonymously authored "Black Book" was published and distributed in Khartoum and abroad in 2000. It documented the racial bias in Darfur governance, making it clear that Darfur's remoteness was not the cause of its human disaster, rather it was due to Khartoum's policies.[5] More publications on cattle theft and murder followed. The government responded with increasing violence and support for Arab tribes and militias. Authors behind the Black Book organised later in the armed rebel group Justice and Equality Movement (JEM), which was established in 2001 on Islamic foundation and dominated by Zaghawa Kobe and led by Khalil Ibrahim.[6] Around the same time, a secular mixture of Masalit, Fur and Zaghawa organised themselves and planned a first major counter attack against the government, not the Arab *Janjaweed* militias. This band would later become known as Darfur Liberation Front (DLF). Traditional peace efforts between the government and Darfur rebels were half-hearted. Everyone was preparing for war. In February 2002 the

---

5   *The Black Book: Imbalance of Power and Wealth in Sudan* was a stapled-together book written and disseminated throughout Sudan by student activists, detailing the distribution of political and economic power as lying in the hands of members of only three tribes, to the detriment and marginalization of the south, west and eastern areas and tribes in Sudan.

6   Ibrahim held a masters degree in public health from Maastricht University and had worked in the government administration before leading the JEM (Flint, J. and de Waal, A., 2008, *Darfur: a new history of a long war.* London, New York: Zed Books, p. 103).

Darfur rebels attacked and destroyed a Nyala government post. After training from the southern rebel movement, SPLM, the Darfur Liberation Front changed its name to Sudanese Liberation Movement/Army (SLM/A) in 2003.

4.4   North–South Conflict and Peace Process

The South had risen up against the central government of Khartoum out of the discontent caused by the government's forced Islamisation and Arabisation policies, general neglect and marginalisation in the early 1980s.[7] The southern movement (Sudanese People's Liberation Movement/Army, SPLM/A) led by John Garang managed, with some help of neighbouring countries to the south, to maintain against the Sudanese army's offenses. Ideologically the SPLM fought for a new but united Sudan. In the 1990s fighting came to a stalemate between the South and North, and in 1995 the government accepted the start of new talks. By the early 2000s promising talks brought optimism for the first time since the last attempt that was cut short after al-Bashir's coup. Increased international pressure by the US, the UK, as well as others such as Norway and some African states raised the stakes. For the US the interest in a solution to the conflict was due to domestic pressures of Christian groups and the 'Black Caucus'. Additionally, after the terrorist attacks in 2001, and the subsequent 'War on Terror', Sudan saw an opportunity to polish up its international credentials from its notorious record in the 1990s. The US was represented by President Bush special envoy John Danforth, who would be US ambassador to the UN in 2004. The first agreements and protocols were signed by 2002 in Machakos, Kenya, and from then onwards everyone believed a final peace agreement of one of Africa's longest civil wars was imminent. Negotiations were later moved to Naivasha, Kenya. By this time, over decades of civil war casualties are estimated to number around 1½ million deaths.[8] The negotiations centred on the form of self-determination for South Sudan, its borders and the sharing of oil revenues. The deal was finally signed in 2005, and included self-determination for South Sudan in principle, with a new 'Government of National Unity', which would include

---

7   For recent accounts on the civil war in the south see for instance, Johnson (2011 [2003]) *The root causes of Sudan's civil wars. Peace or truce?* Revised edition. Kampala: Fountain Publishers; Leach, J.D. (2011) *War and Politics in Sudan. Cultural identities and the challenges of the peace process.* London, New York: I.B. Taurus.

8   Johnson (2011), p. 143. It should be noted however that such statistics come with great uncertainty.

the SPLM. A referendum on full independence was to be held a few years later. However, there was little belief that Khartoum would accept anything else than a united Sudan.

4.5   Root Causes

Darfur is poor. It had no viable natural resources to speak of during the twentieth century. Its agriculture is highly vulnerable to the severe climatic variation of the region. The benefits from being located at trade routes slowly disappeared when Darfur ceased to function as an intermediary between northern and southern Africa during the 19th century.

Darfur also suffers from a changing environment. In 1930s the first signs of this change are observed through the drying up of water wells. In 1944 a British report predicted mounting water scarcity as supply decreased while economic development would cause increasing demand. There is evidence of declining rainfall over the 20th century. Perhaps the scarcity of water could have been dealt with, but the situation was made worse by the actions of the central government. New wells were drilled at the wrong places, the government never dealt with managing the allocation of land, which resulted in overgrazing, while migrating people came into Sudan from even dryer places.

The argument that such root causes – e.g. poverty, climate, political institutions, ethnicities – are the key to a political solution in Darfur is still debated.[9] The discovery of a huge underground waterbed was hailed as the Holy Grail to finding a political solution in Darfur.[10] However, from the history documented here, it is clear that the Sudanese government could have dealt with natural scarcities found on its lands if it had wanted to. Instead, the outbreak of violence and the stalling of peace can be explained for a large part by the maliciousness of the central government. Indeed, many scholars agree on "the nature of the Sudanese state and the centre-periphery dynamics it produces as the root-cause of endemic conflict."[11] The foregoing events were all precursors to the situation

---

9   See for instance, de Waal, (2007b) "Sudan: The Turbulent State," in *War in Darfur and the search for peace,* by de Waal, A. (ed.), Global Equity Initiative, Harvard University; Leach (2011); Johnson (2003 [2011]), p. ix; Bassil (2013), pp. xi, 12–13.

10   BBC News, 18 July 2007, "Water find 'may end Darfur war.'"

11   Verhoeven, H. (2011) "The logic of war and peace in Sudan," *Journal of Modern African Studies* Vol.: 49(4), p. 672. This view is echoed in Bassil (2013); Johnson (2011); Leach (2011); de Waal (2007b).

gripping Darfur by early 2003 and were indicative of the notorious human rights record of the Sudanese government as a whole as reported to the UN.[12]

---

12   In a report dated 3 February 1997 presented to the 53rd regular session of the UN Commission on Human Rights, the first Special Rapporteur on the situation of human rights in Sudan, Gáspár Biro reported that government agents had committed "grave and widespread violations of human rights and fundamental freedoms" and that animosities between Arab nomadic tribes and Zaghawan and Masalit tribes had deepened following Khartoum's administrative reorganization of the Sudan (UN Doc.: E/CN.4/1997/58). In 1999, in two separate reports before the Commission and the UN General Assembly respectively, Biro's successor, Leonardo Franco, warned of a "large-scale conflict occurring in West Darfur" (UN Doc.: E/CN.4/1999/38/Add.1, 17 May 1999) and of "extensive violence and human rights abuses against Masalit civilians on the part of Arab militias allegedly supported by the Government" (UN Doc.: A/54/467, 15 October 1999). In the same year, accusations against Khartoum for arming ethnic militias were also made before the Committee on the Elimination of Racial Discrimination. By 2002, Gerhart Baum recounted claims to the General Assembly by the Masalit community in exile that attacks by Arab militias continued in Darfur as part of "a government strategy to alter the demography of the region." Mr. Biro also found evidence to "reinforce claims of the Government's involvement the support of Arab militias" (UN Doc.: A/57/326, 20 August 2002).

Warnings

February 2003–February 2004

5.1 Situation in Darfur: the Start of the Rebellion

The precise date of the start of the conflict in Darfur is debated, with some authors dating it back to 21 July 2001.[1] It is generally accepted that the emergence of the Darfur Liberation Front (DLF) in claiming responsibility for an attack on a military garrison in Golo in the Jebel Marrah region marked the *de facto* beginning of the rebellion. The attack, on 26 February 2003, was mounted against a backdrop of smaller attacks in the years preceding 2003, but with the death of nearly 200 soldiers it was a clear change of pattern and style of resistance against the central government.[2]

Yet, providing an early indication of what was later to become commonplace, the government's response was somewhat contradictory. On the one hand a spokesman dismissed the reports as "exaggerated," but then on the other proceeded to claim that the attackers "are not rebels but bandits," accusing them of having targeted civilians.[3] According to Prunier, by simultaneously sending a mission to negotiate with the rebels, the government "implicitly disowned [this] version," perturbed by the "level of organization" of the attacks.[4] However the attacks were classified, they were a prelude to the March violence in Darfur.

On 25 March 2003 the rebels attacked and took control of Tine on the Chadian border, inflicting severe casualties and loss of life on government troops according to reports.[5] At the same time the Darfur Liberation Army, changed its name to the Sudan Liberation Movement/Army (SLM/A), in a

---

1 Flint, J. and de Waal, A. (2008) *Darfur: a new history of a long war.* London, New York: Zed Books, pp. 116–117.

2 Totten, S. and Markussen, E. (eds.), (2006) *Genocide in Darfur, investigating the Atrocities in the Sudan.* London, New York: Routledge, p. 9; Prunier, G. (2007) *Darfur: An Ambiguous Genocide. Revised and updated edition 2007* London: C.Hurst & Co. (publishers) ltd, p. 92.

3 IRIN, 27 February 2003, "Sudan: government denies existence of new rebel group."

4 Prunier (2007), p. 92.

5 Agence France Presse, 27 March 2003, "Rebels in west Sudan say they captured town on Chad border." AFP claimed to have received a statement by Minni Minawi stating that "government forces fled in disarray leaving 56 bodies behind them" and saying that they captured two armed vehicles.

clear reference to the Southern rebel movement SPLM, which helped them with the provision of arms and creating a bigger political vision. The next major attacks by the rebel forces of the SLM/A and JEM on April 25 2003 proved to be a turning point in the entire Darfur crisis, inflicting severe losses on the government and its proxy forces. SLM/A and JEM rebels simultaneously attacked Nyala in South Darfur and the main Darfur airbase of Al-Fashir from which government forces had launched its own attacks to support *Janjaweed* militias. The operation was devastatingly successful. According to Flint and de Waal (2008), in addition to occupying the base at Al-Fashir, more than 70 government troops, pilots and technicians were killed, all of the military aircraft were destroyed, massive stocks of weapons and ammunition were taken, and the base commander was captured. The rebels had now demonstrated their formidable force.

And yet the rebel attacks continued. An SLM/A assault on a battalion north of Kutum towards the end of May killed 500 government soldiers with a further 300 imprisoned.[6] Retaliation by Khartoum was prompt and calculated; a state of emergency was declared in Darfur, with hundreds of suspected rebel sympathizers arrested and the governors of North and West Darfur dismissed from their posts. A Special Task Force on Darfur was assembled, and the government's plan to initiate further military action to crush the rebels became apparent. Recruitment and arming of Arab militias (non-Arab potential recruits were turned away) began in earnest as the government began to harness the *Janjaweed* as part of its conventional efforts in Darfur under the guise of its Special Task Force. A notorious Arab tribal leader, Musa Hilal, was released from house arrest in Khartoum and appointed overall captain of this *Janjaweed* force. Darfur was on the verge of exploding, with the government ready to increase the intensity of its forces' attacks and transform their very character.

For the remainder of the first semester of 2003 attacks by the rebels continued against designated targets, killing and injuring civilians during their course. The government and its militias retaliated by specifically targeting civilians. In one reported incident on 14 June, civilians including children were killed and women raped in front of their husbands by the *Janjaweed*, who then left with around 400 cattle. Indeed as Daly noted, "[as] JEM and SLA strategy had consisted of surprise attacks on army posts, so the Janjawid would make surprise attacks on civilians in their towns and villages."[7] Daly also described

---

6   Totten and Markussen (2006), p. 11.

7   Daly, M.W. (2010) *Darfur's Sorrow. The forgotten history of a humanitarian crisis*. 2nd Edition. Cambridge: Cambridge University Press, p. 283.

how the "army's role would be largely to provide air support"[8] during these attacks. The legal context within which these operations were taking place had also been manipulated by Khartoum. At the beginning of June 2003 the government disbanded the "special courts" in Darfur, in a move which many see as having been calculated to ensure impunity and "a clear field of action" for the violations in Darfur.[9]

Prunier described how the violence had "assumed a completely new scale" and would involve planes built for transport flying over areas and dropping oil drums filled with explosives and shrapnel, "useless from a military point of view (...) but had a deadly efficiency against civilian targets."[10] The *Janjaweed* would then arrive on horse or camelback, hurling racial epithets at villagers, and would proceed to loot belongings, steal livestock, burn entire villages and brutally kill men, women and children. Rape and sexual humiliation were also common. Eyewitness reports on 7 July recounted an attack of close to 200 *Janjaweed* militias supported by government ground and air forces.

The attacks by both sides to the conflict continued throughout July, killing scores of civilians. Indications that *Janjaweed* militias increased the scale and number of their attacks against Fur, Masalit and Zaghawan villages were rife, with the usual combination of looting, killing and burning. On the other side of the conflict the SLM/A continued to target positions including police stations and army barracks resulting in civilian casualties, as well as suggestions of looting by some rebel ranks. Agence France Presse reported claims by rebel leader Minni Minawi to have killed more than 300 soldiers as revenge for the army's torching of villages,[11] and then later claims that government planes bombed yet more villages causing hundreds of civilian casualties.[12]

The immediate culmination of the July collapse of Darfur came when rebels captured one of the largest towns in northern Darfur, Kutum, on 1 August. In doing so the rebels allegedly killed over 500 government troops, suffering only minimal losses themselves.[13] However, the rebels promptly withdrew, citing

---

8   Idem.

9   Prunier (2007), p. 98. It should be noted that the special courts had been criticized as well for selective prosecution and harsh punishment and treatment of accused (e.g. UN Doc.: E/CN.4/2003/42, 6 January 2003, "UN CHR Special Rapporteur's report on Sudan").

10   Ibid., pp. 99–100.

11   Agence France Presse, 17 July 2003, "Darfur rebels say they killed more than 300 Sudanese soldiers."

12   Agence France Presse, 20 July 2003, "Sudanese planes kill 300 villagers in west Sudan: rebels."

13   Agence France Press, 1 August 2003, "Sudan rebels take town in Darfur, kill 510 government troops: claim."

reasons of protection for the civilian population against government retaliation. Yet, within days SLM/A representatives were accusing government-backed
militias of massacring hundreds of civilians.[14] Similar reports emerged
throughout August of brutal attacks by *Janjaweed* militias with evidence of a
campaign against the civilian population (attacks on villages such as El Malam
near Nyala, Seraf near Kebkabiya, Habila in the west and Kednir in the south
are demonstrative of such a campaign). During many of these attacks wit-
nesses observed government planes in the midst of an apparent bombing campaign responsible for destroying hundreds of villages. Simultaneously however,
rebel attacks were also causing civilian deaths. According to the Associated
Press, the direct consequence of the rebel advance on 1 August had been over
10,000 IDPs from the Kutum area alone.[15]

Estimates emerged of the rapid explosion in the exodus of refugees into
Chad of up to 70,000 people, whilst within Darfur itself over 400,000 had
become Internally Displaced Persons (IDPs) in need of emergency aid.
Although claims that these were the first refugees to cross into Chad were false
(since many civilians had fled across the border as early as April), the numbers
now involved made certain that for the first real time the violence began to
register internationally.

On 17 September, OCHA (UN Organization for the Coordination of
Humanitarian Affairs) announced that an agreement had been reached
between Khartoum and the SLM/A to allow unimpeded humanitarian access to
Darfur, alongside a new plan for humanitarian operations set out by Special
Envoy Tom Vraalsen. This plan, the "Greater Darfur Special Initiative," sought
funds of US$23 million for providing aid, defusing triggers to violence and for
addressing the factors that led to the conflict.[16] Simultaneous to these humanitarian endeavours, rumours of a potential ceasefire between the belligerents
provided at least a glimmer of hope at the beginning of September.

In Abéché, Chad, talks mediated by President Déby between SLM/A commanders and representatives of the Sudanese government also resulted in the
signing of a 45-day ceasefire on 4 September amid reports of refugee flows.[17]
The ceasefire provided for the cessation of hostilities in addition to provisions

---

14   Agence France Presse, 11 August 2003, "Sudan rebels accuse pro-government militia of
      killing 300 in Darfur."
15   Associated Press, 16 August 2003, "Thousands flee fighting in western Sudan."
16   OCHA Press Release, AFR/701 IHA/795, 17 September 2003, "Agreement reached allowing
      humanitarian access to Darfur region of Sudan."
17   See Agence France Presse, 3 September 2003, "Khartoum delegation heads to Chad for
      ceasefire with Darfur rebels."

on the release of prisoners and for the control of irregular armed groups. Accusations of banditry and looting on the part of the rebels, as well as continued air strikes and militia ground attacks by government forces ensured that the newly-signed ceasefire provided little respite for the civilians who continued to be killed or driven across the border into Chad. UNHCR, the UN refugees agency, reported newly arriving refugees in Chad speaking of aerial attacks on their villages.[18] Failure to maintain the ceasefire was thus followed by "swift intensification of the conflict and more attacks on civilian villages."[19]

The humanitarian fallout from the conflict came sharply into focus in October 2003. Médecins Sans Frontières (MSF) was one of the first humanitarian organisations that had a large presence on the ground.[20] It attempted to deliver 33 tons of relief aid to try to alleviate the chronic lack of food, medical supplies and shelter for those caught in the growing catastrophe in eastern Chad.[21] Meanwhile the UNHCR launched an appeal for $16.6 million to avert the refugee crisis on top of the US$23 million already appealed for by the Greater Darfur Special Initiative. At the same time, OCHA warned that the situation continued to deteriorate. The UN humanitarian body declared that "militias continue to destroy livelihoods and cause displacement," looting and burning "over 30 percent of the villages in North Darfur" with the last week of September alone witnessing 23 villages and their crops destroyed.[22] OCHA also detailed the number of IDPs, refugees and displacement camps, as well as the appalling conditions faced by persons having to flee their homes.

This greater awareness notwithstanding, MSF deplored the invisibility of the refugees to the humanitarian community, citing the dire lack of assistance received on the ground. Unlike its previous statements, MSF went further by laying blame firmly at the door of Khartoum, its military response, and the "systematic attacks by Arab militias who seek to crush the rebellion and terrorise villagers" which it claimed the government supported.[23] During the last months of 2003 immediately after the ceasefire, reports from the ground described few, if any, aerial attacks on villages, whilst reports of *Janjaweed*

---

18   IRIN, 15 September 2003, "Sudan: Armed attacks reported in Darfur despite ceasefire."

19   Degomme, O., and Guha-Sapir, D. (2005) "Darfur counting the deaths. Mortality estimates from multiple survey data." Centre for Research on Epidemiology of Disaster, University of Louvain, p. 11.

20   Authors' interview with Olivier Ulich, 1 June 2005.

21   Médecins Sans Frontières, 1 October 2003, "MSF provides healthcare for Sudanese refugees in Chad."

22   OCHA Press Release, AFR/721. IHA/805, 7 October 2003, "Humanitarian situation worsens in Greater Darfur region of Western Sudan."

23   IRIN, 8 October 2003, "Sudan: Darfur refugees 'invisible,' says NGO."

attacks continued to increase. One such report detailed an attack on one day on 15 villages, killing 100 and displacing 15,000.[24]

Government aerial bombardment and brutal *Janjaweed* assaults on villages were interminable throughout November, alongside progressively severe rebel attacks, in the face of an agreed extension to the Abéché ceasefire. UNHCR staff in eastern Chad also reported witnessing first-hand the smoke from burning villages across the border and the aggressive attacks by militias now taking place against refugee and even Chadian communities. Prunier (2007) further asserts that it was at this time that the Sudanese government "took measures which introduced genocidal proportions into the conflict by going deeper than the massacres themselves and targeting [the] very livelihoods of the civilians who had survived the violence."[25] The use of "red tape"[26] to "choke" aid flows and refuse travel permits for US officials are cited by Prunier (2007) as examples that "[d]eath had moved to the administrative level."[27] Khartoum was now using more subtle obstruction tactics in conjunction with the overt use of force.

Due to the worsening security conditions in Darfur, the UN was forced to pull out its staff in late December. The Sudanese military subsequently conducted major offenses in an attempt to crush the rebellion. Demands by the UN to have its staff move back in were initially denied. Access for humanitarian workers was only gradually regained at the end of January 2004.

As the new year dawned, the humanitarian disaster and the ever-intensifying violent conflict became undeniable. The sustained grave restrictions on aid and the continued exodus of civilians from towns and villages around Darfur were catastrophic in and of themselves. Reports from the border between Darfur and Chad put the number of refugees in the latter at upwards of 95,000, with 30,000 said to have fled in December alone, according to the UNHCR.[28] Compounding the misery for thousands of families, it was estimated in mid-January that 85 percent of the (roughly) 900,000 people affected by the violence were inaccessible to humanitarian aid.[29]

Marauding *Janjaweed* militias continued to attack Fur, Masalit and Zaghawan communities, seemingly buoyed by the impunity of their actions and the

24   Agence France Presse, 20 October 2003, "100 killed in western Sudan unrest: report."
25   Prunier (2007), p. 108.
26   Agence France Presse, 10 November 2003, "Khartoum red tape choking aid flows to war-ravaged Darfur: UN."
27   Prunier (2007), p. 108.
28   IRIN, 5 January 2004, "Sudan: Thousands fleeing attacks in western Darfur."
29   IRIN, 16 January 2004, "Sudan: Authorities forcibly close IDP camps in southern Darfur."

support of government planes overhead. Those same Antonov planes had begun to launch daily bombing raids on villages by January, even dropping bombs into Chad where refugees were gathering. One report in the first week of the month claimed that this organised division of labour had killed more than 200 civilians in a single attack on a village in West Darfur, as allegations now emerged with greater frequency that the violence being perpetrated amounted to "ethnic cleansing."[30] Ominously, as the death-toll climbed and the *Janjaweed* continued "burning and looting their way through Darfur,"[31] President al-Bashir issued a chilling warning to the Darfur rebels, implicitly confirming what many civilians fleeing Darfur had already bore witness to. Al-Bashir declared on state television that: "We will use all available means, the army, the police, the *mujahideen*, the horsemen, to get rid of the rebellion."[32] Al-Bashir thus had admitted that he exercised some degree of control over the *Janjaweed.*

At the end of January, JEM rebel official, Abubker Hamid Nour, called upon the "international community" to act to stop Khartoum's "criminal action,"[33] whilst a spokesman for the SPLA rebel movement in South Sudan condemned the "indiscriminate bombardment of innocent civilians in Darfur."[34] At the same time, Sudan was starting to give in to pressure on more access for humanitarian agencies, firstly, through promises, gradually with real actions. On 9 February President al-Bashir claimed victory in his fight against the rebels, declaring that the rebellion had been crushed, and further promised "unimpeded access" to aid agencies. UN humanitarian agencies jumped on this declaration to push their own people in. Among them, Jan Egeland, head of OCHA, immediately welcomed the pledge by al-Bashir, leaving no time to dwell on the rebels' emphatic rebuttal of his claims, no doubt through necessity of trying to organise a rapid humanitarian response.[35] Further, the furore surrounding the

---

30   Agence France Presse, 3 January 2004, "Sudan's Darfur rebels claim government killed 200 civilians."

31   Agence France Presse, 9 January 2004, "Refugees say militia burning, looting their way through Sudan's Darfur: UN."

32   Prunier (2007), p. 109.

33   Agence France Presse, 27 January 2004, "Western Sudan rebels demand condemnation of Khartoum's 'crimes.'"

34   Associated Press, 29 January 2004, "Southern Sudanese rebels criticize government for targeting civilians in western Sudan."

35   JEM and SLM/A rebels contested al-Bashir's claims, saying that they had temporarily fled certain areas of Darfur as a result of heavy aerial bombardment by Government planes, but had not been defeated. The rebels further asserted that "the people who think they are ruling the country always tell lies to the 'international community'" when, "in actuality,

illusive goal of access, which had previously impeded efforts (aid, diplomatic and observer) in Darfur overshadowed an agreement by the rebels to talks in Geneva and provided further cover under which the *Janjaweed* reportedly killed nearly 170 civilians in two days. Perhaps, with hindsight, caution should have prevailed. Indeed, over the course of 11 to 16 February, sharp contradictions were witnessed between the lyrical waxed over the "breakthrough" in Darfur and the actual state of affairs.

Arriving for talks in Khartoum, Tom Vraalsen hailed the positive developments emanating from the capital, as the government declared access corridors open for the flow of aid in Darfur. "We have moral and political responsibility and we are shouldering it" announced Humanitarian Affairs Minister, Mohammed Youssef Moussa.[36] What is more, the government's Foreign Minister Ismail simultaneously announced an ostensible end to the hostilities and the beginnings of the "political phase" of the conflict. And yet the very next day, IRIN reported thousands of people "still fleeing for their lives from militia and aerial bombardments."[37] It was also widely reported on 11 February that the rebels had shot down two army helicopters, with joint attacks by JEM and the SLM/A to take towns and access roads continuing over subsequent days.[38] Details of a major government and *Janjaweed* offensive surfaced on 14 February, purportedly killing civilians, burning villages and destroying water sources in an area said to be inhabited exclusively by (non-Arab) civilians. Once again "ethnic cleansing" was charged.[39] To compound the horrific state of affairs further, aid agencies lamented, "there is absolutely no access to any place, no humanitarian access...[things] are changing for the worse."[40]

At the resumption of the Naivasha peace talks in Kenya at the end of February a spectacular U-turn in optimism had materialised. By now Tom Vraalsen's sanguinity had evaporated, resigned to admitting the impotence of aid workers, persistent fighting, lack of access corridors for aid, and faced with the widespread attention that the massacre of 81 civilians earlier in the month

---

they have been busy killing innocent civilians, looting and burning villages." The rebels called on the "international community" to "come and see for themselves what crimes have been committed" and document those crimes (IRIN, 12 February 2004, "Sudan: Rebels dismiss President's claim of victory in Darfur").

36   Associated Press, 12 February 2004, "Government opens corridors to deliver aid to rebellion-hit Darfur."

37   IRIN, 11 February 2004," Sudan: Thousands still fleeing attacks in Darfur."

38   Totten and Markusen, p. 14.

39   Agence France Presse, 14 February 2003, "Dozens of civilians killed in army offensive in Sudan's Darfur: rebels."

40   IRIN, 16 February 2004, "Sudan: Humanitarian access still difficult, say sources."

now received. Amnesty International, ever at the forefront, condemned the continuing "horrifying attacks," providing details of various acts of violence perpetrated despite al-Bashir's claims of access.[41] Over 10,000 new refugees descended on the camps in Chad, and at roughly the same time a UN Disaster and Assessment Coordination Team (UNDAC). With this team there would be new and detailed reporting that was to be used by Jan Egeland in his briefings to the Security Council later in April (see Section 6.5).[42]

Attacks by rebels reportedly killed over a thousand government troops, *Janjaweed* militias raped women with increased frequency in a wave of new attacks, and government forces continued their bombing campaign, whilst OCHA reported that aid was routinely stolen from its recipients.[43]

5.2   Warnings and Knowledge

5.2.1   *Early Warnings*

The First Warning from NGOs and Humanitarian Agencies

The first warnings were already voiced as early as February 2003. As the previous section already illustrates, the first (public) warnings were primarily issued by NGOs and humanitarian agencies. The NGOs Amnesty International, Médecins Sans Frontières and International Crisis Group are credited with issuing reports at the earliest stages of the conflict.[44] In February 2003, Amnesty International already circulated a press release warning of the deteriorating situation in Darfur and its potential to descend into "another civil war," stressing the subordination of the conflict to the North-South process.[45] Moreover, it called for a Commission of Inquiry by the UN or AU. The release also observed

---

41   AI Doc.: AFR 54/016/2004, 17 February 2004, "Sudan: "international community" must act now to guarantee the protection of civilians."

42   Authors' interview with Jan Egeland, 28 November 2012.

43   OCHA, 27 February 2004, "Sudan: Relief supplies being stolen from recipients in Darfur."

44   Authors' interviews with Jan Egeland, 28 November 2012; Olivier Ulich, 1 June 2005; Isabelle Balot, 2 June 2005; Igiri, C.O. and Lyman, P.N. (2004) "Giving meaning to 'Never again.' Seeking an Effective Response to the Crisis in Darfur and Beyond." Council on Foreign Relations No. 5, 5 September 2004, p. 5–6; Prunier (2007), p. 126; Bieckmann, F. (2012) *Soedan. Het sinistere spel om macht, rijkdom en olie*. Amsterdam: Balans, p. 163–164; UK House of Commons, International Development Committee, "Darfur, Sudan: The responsibility to protect" Fifth Report of Session 2004–2005, Volume I Report, p. 17 (hereafter: UK House of Commons, 2005, Volume I).

45   AI Doc.: AFR 54/004/2003, 21 February 2003, "Sudan: Urgent call for Commission of Inquiry in Darfur as situation deteriorates."

the targeted nature of attacks as almost exclusively against Fur, Masalit and Zaghawa ('African') ethnic groups in Darfur. In March it warned of the restrictions placed on the media in Sudan by government-imposed "red lines [including] the conflict in the Darfur region." and in April it held that "[t]he international community must not watch in silence while the choice of a military solution for human rights problems drags another area of Sudan into disaster."[46]

UN Special Rapporteur Baum

Another timely early warning was the statement of Special Rapporteur on the situation in Sudan, Gerhart Baum, to the UN Commission on Human Rights (CHR) on 28 March 2003. This was also one of the first authoritative warnings of the potential for genocide in Darfur. He presented his report on Sudan following a 2002 resolution of the Commission. His report dated 6 January 2003, does not report on the rebellion, as the organised attacks of February and March had not happened yet, but deals with the flawed justice system in place in Darfur. However, in his statement to the UNCHR he takes the opportunity to update the information. He describes "a serious deterioration of the situation [in Darfur], with a high potential of destabilizing the country." Mr. Baum went further and revealed that sources within Darfur had "reported attacks against civilians and targeting of local tribes, to the point that some accused the government of implementing a clear policy of ethnic cleansing aimed at eliminating African tribes from Darfur." Baum also backed the call of Amnesty International for an independent Commission of Inquiry to further investigate this situation.[47]

Continuing Warnings of NGOs and Humanitarian Agencies

At the end of June the International Crisis Group (ICG) released a Briefing Paper entitled, "Sudan's Other Wars," discussing the need to address all of the conflicts within the country as a prerequisite for the immediate and sustained success of the North-South peace process.[48] The paper devoted a significant section to explaining the crisis in Darfur in relatively clear terms, looking at its antecedents and describing recent events. Although largely detailing the rebel

---

46   AI Docs.: AFR 54/008/2003, 11 March 2003, "Sudan: Restrictions on freedom of expression must be lifted"; AFR 54/026/2003, 28 April 2003, "Sudan: Crisis in Darfur – urgent need for international commission of inquiry and monitoring."

47   Statement by Mr. Gerhart Baum, Special Rapporteur of the Commission on Human Rights on the situation of human rights in the Sudan, Commission on Human Rights 59th session, 28 March 2003.

48   International Crisis Group, Africa Briefing 14, 25 June 2003, "Sudan's Other Wars."

attacks with only some limited explanation of the role of Khartoum, the paper clearly drew attention to the hidden nature of the conflict and its continued escalation, as well as the deliberate military response of the government. Furthermore, it noted that the events in Darfur could pose a threat to the North-South peace, while also having "the potential to trigger intensified ethnic warfare and large-scale forced displacement of the Fur and other African people of Darfur." In July the ICG published a report titled "Sudan Endgame," recommending measures to ensure the success of the latter stages of the North-South peace process.[49] Unlike its previous briefing, the report made only passing reference to the marginalisation of areas including Darfur. It prioritised the North-South peace and reduced concerns over the marginalised areas to the simple solution of being granted some minimal consultation role in the peace talks.

Amnesty International issued another press release in July, reiterating its calls for a Commission of Inquiry.[50] It also criticised the military response of the Sudanese government to the rebellion as ineffective, inflammatory and in violation of human rights, whilst continually restating that the targets of such attacks were members of sedentary groups. Amnesty International also issued a press release at the end of November which included a first eye-witness account of the ethnic dimensions of the conflict by quoting refugees who were told: "As you are black, you are slaves. The government is on our side."[51] An ICG report of 11 December also noted the ethnic character of the conflict: "Government-supported militias deliberately target civilians from the Fur, Zaghawa, and Massalit groups, who are viewed as 'African' in Darfur (...) with no apparent link to the rebels other than their ethnic profile." The report also pointed to the warning against genocide of a Member of Parliament, Mohamed Barka, in a newspaper of 6 November.[52]

There were also more public warnings from NGOs and other civil groups in January and February 2004. The Holocaust Memorial Museum in Washington issued a "genocide warning."[53] Médecins Sans Frontières described the escalation of government bombings and the thousands of civilian casualties.[54]

---

49 International Crisis Group, Africa Report 65, 7 July 2003, "Sudan Endgame."

50 AI Doc.: AFR 54/041/2003, 1 July 2003, "Looming Crisis in Darfur."

51 AI Doc.: AFR 54.101.2003, 27 November 2003, "Sudan: Humanitarian crisis in Darfur caused by Sudan Government's failures"; Hamilton (2011a), p. 21.

52 International Crisis Group, Africa Report 73, 11 December 2003, "Sudan: towards an incomplete peace," p. 19.

53 Totten and Markussen (2006), Ch. Chronology.

54 Médecins Sans Frontières Press Release, 29 January 2004, "Chadian civilians killed and injured by aerial bombings."

Amnesty International said in February 2004: "while news about a forthcoming peace deal to end the 20 year-long civil war in southern Sudan fill the columns of international media, an invisible, vicious conflict is unfolding in Darfur, western Sudan."[55] In no uncertain terms Amnesty International asserted, "the prime responsibility for the grave human rights abuses committed against civilians lies with the Sudanese government and militia aligned to it."[56] The human rights group described in detail these grave abuses, framing the acts in legal terms as violations of international criminal and humanitarian law, perhaps seeking to lay the groundwork for the potential prosecution of acts bearing the greatest responsibility. Using evidence gathered from their own investigations alongside the testimonies of refugees, Amnesty provided concurrent proof of the coordination between government forces and the *Janjaweed*. More significantly, the report also presented suggestions (largely by implication) of the potential genocidal nature of the violence by detailing the "deliberate or indiscriminate" killing of civilians, alongside the telling conclusion that looting the possessions of people who have little to begin with "makes essential acts of life (...) even more difficult."[57]

'Warnings' from the Media

The first international press release was only issued on 17 July 2003 by Agence France Press.[58] According to the annual report of Médecins Sans Frontières highlighting the top ten most underreported humanitarian stories of the previous year, the tens of thousands of people seeking refuge in Chad was the number one issue most overlooked by the us media in 2003.[59] The first major Western news article on Darfur appeared in January 2004. One article in the New York Times of 17 January warned that the "war in Western Sudan overshadows peace in the South."[60] It was only on 25 February 2004 that the genocidal aspects of the conflict were explicitly mentioned in a us newspaper.[61]

---

55   AI Doc.: AFR 54/008/2004, 3 February 2004, "Sudan. Darfur: Too Many People Killed For No
      Reason," p. 1.

56   Ibid., p. 3.

57   Ibid., p. 20.

58   Agence France Presse, 17 July 2003, "Darfur rebels say they killed more than 300 Sudanese
      soldiers."

59   Médecins Sans Frontières Press Release. 6 January 2004, "MSF issues 'Top Ten' list of the
      year's most underreported humanitarian stories."

60   Somini Sengupta, "War in Western Sudan Overshadows Peace in the South," New York
      Times, 17 January 2004. Another article appeared in Le Monde on 7 January 2003.
      Bieckmann (2012), p. 266.

61   Eric Reeves, "Unnoticed Genocide," Washington Post, 25 February 2004.

An internal European Parliament document of February 2004 noted: "The absence of press and film crews on the Sudanese side of the border within the affected areas has made and will continue to make it difficult to generate the amount of international attention that is warranted and commensurate with the size and complexity of this crisis."[62] The first moving images of Darfur of the independent British filmmaker Philip Cox were only shown in early 2004.[63]

5.2.2   Knowledge and Awareness about Darfur

This subsection will examine what various actors knew and at what moment. The subsection will conclude with a reflection as to when actors knew about the (full) scale and gravity of the situation.

UN

One of the first public acknowledgements by the UN Secretariat was the statement of the head of OCHA Egeland on 5 December 2003.[64] Egeland described the situation in Darfur as "one of the world worst humanitarian crisis."[65] Egeland was primarily made aware of the situation in Darfur by UNSG's Special Envoy for Humanitarian Affairs for Sudan, Tom Vraalsen.[66] This assertion was followed by a similar statement of UN Secretary-General Kofi Annan four days later when he expressed his alarm at "the rapidly deteriorating humanitarian situation in the Darfur region of Sudan, and by reports of widespread abuses against civilians, including killings, rape and the burning and looting of entire villages."[67] Annan's statement echoed the confidential note of Vraalsen of 8 December 2003: "militias were launching systematic raids against civilian

---

62   "Darfur Update," undated unpublished background note from Member of the European Parliament Cees Bremmer for the European Parliament Delegation Mission to the Sudan, 19-24 February 2004.

63   Steve Crawshaw "Genocide, What Genocide?", Financial Times, 22 August 2004, referring to a broadcast on British Channel 4 News. Slim (2004), p. 814.

64   Jan Egeland, a Norwegian national, had been active in diplomatic and humanitarian functions. He started as OCHA chief in September 2003 and wanted to make Darfur as a overlooked emergency one of his first priorities (Authors' interview with Jan Egeland, 28 November 2012; Egeland, J. (2010) A Billion Lives: An Eyewitness Report from the Frontlines of Humanity. New York: Simon & Schuster).

65   OCHA Press Release, AFR/784. IHA/837, 5 December 2003, "Humanitarian situation in western Sudan among world's worst as insecurity escalates, says un emergency relief coordinator."

66   Authors' interview with Jan Egeland, 28 November 2012.

67   Statement attributable to the Spokesman for the Secretary-General on the situation in Darfur, Sudan, 9 December 2003, available at http://www.un.org/sg/statements/?nid=689 [accessed 12 June 2013].

populations. These attacks included burning and looting of villages, large scale killings, abductions, and other severe violations of human rights."[68] Bertrand Ramcharan, acting UN High Commissioner for Human Rights, revealed his deep concern at the situation and urged the "international community" to support the parties to resolve the crisis, pointing out Darfur's absence from the Naivasha process.[69]

Besides, these public statements of UN representatives were preceded by internal "warnings" of the UN Resident Coordinator in Khartoum, Dr. Mukesh Kapila, who informed the UN Headquarters in New York about the situation on the ground. Kapila himself received the first "unverified" report on rebel attacks at the end of April 2003.[70] He initially discounted them, as "there were lots of little fights going on all over Sudan."[71] He consequently set up a special team to gather more information on the situation in Darfur. Within days he received other reports on the existence of IDP camps in Darfur, now from his own staff. In the early summer months Darfur civilians fleeing the violence started to arrive in Khartoum and provided him with eyewitness accounts on what is going on in Darfur.[72] In July, Kapila went to Darfur himself together with UN Special Envoy Tom Vraalsen and his assistant Isabelle Balot to review what is necessary in terms of humanitarian aid.[73] Once back in Khartoum, Kapila tried to mobilise some international involvement by sending out alarming reports to the UN Secretariat and to embassies.

One of the first briefing notes from Kapila to New York was from the end of June 2003.[74] A note from 22 June 2003 indicated the potential implications of the unfolding conflict in Darfur: "The present standoff between the government and a well-armed and motivated insurrection movement on Sudan's western border has the potential to further destabilize Sudan,

---

68   Tom Vraalsen, Note to the Emergency Relief Coordinator; "Sudan: Humanitarian Crisis in Darfur," 8 December 2003, available at http://sudanreeves.org/2013/08/05/humanitarian-conditions-in-darfur-a-climate-of-violence-and-extreme-insecurity-2 [accessed 18 November 2013].

69   UNHCR, 29 January 2004, "Acting rights chief concerned over deteriorating situation in Darfur region of Sudan."

70   Kapila, M. (2013) *Against a tide of evil.* Edinburg: Mainstream Publishing, p. 41.

71   Kapila as quoted in Cockett (2010), p. 169.

72   Traub, J. (2006) *The Best Intentions: Kofi Annan and the UN in the Era of American World Power.* New York: Farrar, Straus and Giroux, p. 214; PBS Frontline interview with Dr. Mukesh Kapila, 11 June 2007.

73   Kapila (2013), p. 71–72. Cockett actually stated that Kapila visited Darfur himself for the first time in September 2003 (Cockett, 2010, p. 170).

74   Kapila (2013), p. 70.

whether or not a peace agreement is implemented over Southern Sudan. The similarities between the origins of the conflict in Darfur and that in Southern Sudan cannot be over-looked. (...) The military solution currently being pursued will inevitably increase the level and intensity of armed conflict in Darfur, displace civilians, imperil food security, and create access and security constraints for international assistance organisations."[75] In the last few months of 2003, Kapila became more explicit in his demand for political involvement and precise in his recommendations. He advised the setup of a Commission of Inquiry with the intention of further ICC proceedings in October.[76]

It was on 30 November 2003 that a "political solution" was proposed for the first time in Kapila's memos: "It is, therefore, imperative that the international community exert the strongest political pressure on the Government (...) Any strategy to solve the problem in Darfur should include strong international pressure on the Government of the Sudan to control the militias as a prelude disarmament. International attention should therefore be focused on a political solution."[77] Kapila's note to Egeland one day later asked for his advice on "the UN's political role."[78]

It seems that Kapila's first direct contact with the highest levels within the UN was only at the end of October when, according to him, he met in person with Jan Egeland (OCHA), Mark Malloch Brown (UNDP), Kieran Prendergast (UNDPA).[79] The first memos addressed to these UN representatives specifically are from November/December 2003.[80] On 1 December he proposed in a memo to Egeland that there should be more international pressure on the Sudanese government and that UN SG Annan should come with a high-level

---

75   Office of the RC/HC Sudan, 22 June 2003, "Conflict in Darfur region of Sudan – a briefing note," available at http://www.mukeshkapila.org/book/sudan-archive.html [accessed 22 October 2013].

76   UK House of Commons, International Development Committee. "Darfur, Sudan: The responsibility to protect" Fifth Report of Session 2004–2005, Volume II Oral and Written Statements, p. Ev 53. (hereafter: UK House of Commons, 2005, Volume II.).

77   Office of the RC/HC Sudan, Doc 9, 30 November 2003, "Darfur Update," available at http://www.mukeshkapila.org/book/sudan-archive.html [accessed 22 October 2013], p. 1 and 4.

78   Office of the RC/HC Sudan, Doc 10, 1 December 2003, "Note to Mr. Egeland – Crisis in Darfur Region, Sudan," available at http://www.mukeshkapila.org/book/sudan-archive .html [accessed 22 October 2013].

79   Kapila (2013), p. 112–114.

80   Ibid., p. 164–165. The first memos to the higher level of the UN on Kapila's own website are from 1 and 18 December 2003. Memos available at http://www.mukeshkapila.org/book/ sudan-archive.html [accessed 22 October 2013]. Traub refers to November 2003. Traub (2006), p. 214.

political initiative.[81] On 18 December he sent another memo to Jan Egeland and Kieran Prendergast with a recommendation: "I am informed by diplomatic missions here of their growing view that the international community should press for an all-inclusive, internationally monitored ceasefire."[82] His concerns expressed in person and in writing did not trigger any response from those addressed.[83]

(Western) Embassies in Sudan

The latter quote from Kapila demonstrates that the Western embassies in Sudan were well aware of the crisis unfolding in Darfur in late 2003 as well.[84] US *Chargé d'Affaires* Gerard Galluci stated: "In diplomatic circles in Khartoum by the fall of 2003 Darfur was something we talked about at receptions."[85] The UK embassy especially had a good and broad knowledge analysis of the conflict and the best contacts.[86] UK Ambassador Patey for example, provided the recently arrived Dutch Ambassador Kooijmans information and contacts in order to help him in his attempts in arranging talks and mediation.[87] The French and German ambassadors were reportedly active in visiting Darfur and IDP camps in October and December 2003.[88]

The Dutch and UK missions in Khartoum visited West and North Darfur on 12 and 13 February 2004. They were actually the first to visit Darfur after it had been closed off for international staff and humanitarian workers by the Sudanese government since mid-December. This mission, initiated by the British and Dutch ambassadors, was greenlighted by Sudanese Foreign

---

81 Ibid., p. 165; Office of the RC/HC Sudan, 1 December 2003, "Note to Mr. Egeland – Crisis in Darfur Region, Sudan," available at http://www.mukeshkapila.org/book/sudan-archive .html [accessed 22 October 2013].

82 Kapila (2013), p. 164; Office of the RC/HC Sudan, 18 December 2003, "Note to Mr. Egeland and Mr. Prendergast," available at http://www.mukeshkapila.org/book/sudan-archive.html [accessed 22 October 2013].

83 Traub (2006), p. 217; Authors' interview with Isabelle Balot, 2 June 2005.

84 See also Slim (2004), p. 814; UK House of Commons, 2005, Volume I, p. 19.

85 Gerard Galluci as quoted in Hamilton, R. (2011a) *Fighting for Darfur: public action and the struggle to stop genocide*. New York: Palgrave Macmillan, p. 20. Kapila held that British, French and US diplomats met and discussed the situation in Darfur with Kapila in the summer of 2003 (Kapila, 2013, pp. 48–49).

86 See Bieckmann (2012), p. 257–259, who in this context also relied on Jan Pronk; Kapila (2013), p. 48.

87 Authors' interview with Adriaan Kooijmans, 16 September 2013.

88 Agence France Presse, 20 October 2003, "France contributes to humanitarian operations in Darfur"; Agence France Presse, 10 December 2003, "Sudan's troubled Darfur in dire need of humanitarian aid: diplomats."

minister Ismail and Vice-President Taha. Apart from these ambassadors and a representative of the European Commission delegation in Khartoum, the local EU presidency (i.e. Kooijmans) also included, at their request, the country director of UNICEF and a WFP staff member, as the UN had been barred from visiting Darfur since mid-December. The objective of this visit was also to pressure the Sudanese government by showing the war did not go unnoticed.[89] The mission was free to visit any location it deemed relevant. They had meetings with displaced Sudanese in Darfur and made reports on the situation, including the observations of continued violence. The Sultan of the Massalit tribe in Al-Geneina (capital of West Darfur) informed the mission that the *Janjaweed* were responsible for the massacres and that they were operating under the control of the Sudanese army. When the mission flew out they observed burning villages in the immediate vicinity of Al-Geneina and more burning villages were observed on the flight path to Al-Fashir (North Darfur). The latter also illustrates that the UK-Dutch delegation was completely aware of the connection between the *Janjaweed* and the government. However, the authorities in Al-Geneina denied having any responsibility for the actions of the *Janjaweed*. Denials from Sudanese officials that the government was not responsible for the *Janjaweed* were not believed.[90] It was at this point in time that there was no doubt as for the Dutch Ambassador about the severity of the situation in Darfur.[91]

(Western) Capitals

Apart from the diplomatic missions in Khartoum, their respective capitals were also aware of the events in Darfur. It seems that the governments of the major Western powers were aware of the conflict in Darfur in the late summer of 2003 and sometimes even earlier (see also Section 5.4, Quiet Diplomacy).

In the fall of 2003, Kapila visited some European capitals (Stockholm, Copenhagen, The Hague, Rome and Paris) and the US (Washington) to draw attention to the situation and to call for funding of the humanitarian efforts of

---

89   Dutch Parliamentary Doc.: Tweede Kamer, 2003–2004, 29 237, nr. 13, 13 July 2004, p. 5. Humanitarian workers of the UN had been blocked from entering the region since Kapila had ordered them out for security reasons (Kapila, 2013, p. 194; Authors' interview with Adriaan Kooijmans, 16 September 2013; Office of the RC/HC Sudan, RCHC/SUD/Note 33, 14 February 2004, "Note to Ambassador Vraalsen – Darfur, Eyewitness Accounts of Current Violence," available at http://www.mukeshkapila.org/book/sudan-archive.html [accessed 22 October 2013]).

90   Authors' interview with Adriaan Kooijmans, 16 September 2013; personal communication 29 December 2013.

91   Idem.

the UN.[92] Kapila first met the Norwegian Minister for International Development Hilde Johnson. She was aware of Darfur, but believed that successful finalisation of the North-South talks would allow for a resolution in Darfur as well.[93] In her view, the international community could only manage one conflict at a time.[94]

In London, Kapila was even shown satellite images of burned villages in Darfur. These images gave evidence that the Sudanese government was involved in the atrocities because it was the only force with aircrafts and helicopter gunships to its disposal. Above all, this account also shows that the UK Foreign Office was completely aware of the situation. Kapila actually noted that UK knew more than UN: "They knew already, and in far greater depth than I did."[95]

The US government was aware of the unfolding situation in Darfur at an early stage as well. This was largely the result of the warnings from the head of USAID, Andrew Natsios, and his assistant Roger Winter since the fall of 2003.[96] Roger Winter had visited Darfur already in August 2003 to accompany the first humanitarian delivery, while the first USAID staff even visited Darfur as early as April 2003.[97] Natsios and Winter visited Darfur nine times between October 2003 and May 2004. In briefings with the top of the US State Department, which included Colin Powell himself, Natsios introduced the situation in Darfur, primarily in humanitarian terms. In October 2003, Natsios and Winter expressed their worry for the outbreak of this new conflict right when the North-South conflict was settling. They presented charts estimating death

---

92   The chronological order in Kapila's book is sometimes confusing. In his book, Kapila told about his first visits to capitals right after mentioning the death of Sergio Vieira de Mello on 19 August 2003. At the same time he mentioned that during this tour he tried to reach his US$22.8 million funding target. This target is from the Greater Darfur Special Initiative, which was only launched mid-September (Kapila, 2013, p. 106—107). One source held that Kapila's tours of the capitals was from October 2003 until January 2004 (UK House of Commons, 2005, Volume I, p. 17). Cockett also dated the first round of visits in late October 2003 and the second round in March 2004 (Cockett, 2010, pp. 194, 205).

93   When Kapila told her about the message from Garang, it appeared that this was new information to her, but it did not change her view (Kapila, 2013, p. 106–107).

94   Bieckmann (2012), p. 157.

95   Kapila (2013), p. 108.

96   Kapila (2013), p. 107; Cockett (2010), p. 204–205; Mayroz, E. (2008) "Ever again? The United States, genocide suppression, and the crisis in Darfur," *Journal of Genocide Research*, Vol.: 10(3), p. 362; Authors' interview with Adriaan Kooijmans, 16 September 2013.

97   Testimony of Roger Winter, USAID DCHA Assistant Administrator, on humanitarian crisis in Sudan, Committee on Foreign Relations Committee, Subcommittee on Africa, United States Senate, 15 June 2004.

rates going as far as hundreds of thousands.[98] During those meetings, Natsios tried to make sure – with a "terrierlike" determination – that everyone in the room recognised Darfur as an urgent problem warranting immediate attention.[99] One junior officer who received cables from Sudan remembered their message during those meetings: "We have to respond in a huge way or a million people will die."[100] The first press release by the US State Department about the situation of Darfur was from 16 December 2003. The release, while not mentioning the ethnic dynamics of the conflict, referred to the killings of 3000 civilians, 600,000 IDPs and 75,000 refugees in Chad.[101]

An official of the Dutch Ministry of Foreign Affairs recollected that people at the highest levels were aware of the emerging violence, and that they recognised Darfur as a potential threat to the North-South talks.[102] Especially officials from the Africa Department knew about the conflict in Darfur from early on.[103] The first reports of Amnesty International, Human Rights Watch and International Crisis Group were read.[104]

EU Council and Commission

One of the first public statements on the situation in Darfur was the press release of the EU Council on 22 December 2003 in the context of the EU Sudan Political Dialogue Joint Communiqué in which the EU Council expressed its "deep concern with regard to the developments in Darfur, in particular the humanitarian situation there."[105] This statement was the result of the EU Troika mission, which visited Darfur a couple of days earlier.[106] An EU background document from February 2004 quoted part of the observations of this mission:

> As the EU Troika mission could observe in a very direct, inescapable fashion, normalcy and security have certainly not returned to the Darfur

---

98   Hamilton (2011a), pp. 20, 28.
99   Hamilton (2011a), p. 28.
100   Hamilton (2011a), p. 20.
101   US State Department press release, 16 December 2003, "Sudan: situation in Darfur," as referred to in Hamilton (2011a), p. 29.
102   Authors' interview with Arjan Schuthof, 2 September 2013.
103   Bieckmann (2012), p. 325.
104   Authors' interview with Arjan Schuthof, 2 September 2013; Archive Ministry of Foreign Affairs in the Netherlands, DAF/2010/00185, Period 2003–2004.
105   EU Doc.: 16357/03 (Presse 380), 18 December 2003, "Joint Communiqué EU – Sudan political dialogue," Khartoum.
106   The EU Troika typically includes representatives of the previous, current and next EU president. EU presidencies are rotated every six months.

States. En route by WFP plane towards Al Gineina and in between Al
Gineina and Al Fashir the mission not only observed that tens of villages
had been burnt and were now totally deserted, but, in addition, flew over
villages that were actually burning. Pictures are available on request.
From the air, the pattern of scorched and burning neighbouring villages
indeed seemed to underscore the systemic character of what has been
and is going in the Darfur States.[107]

At the end of January a draft statement was composed by the US, EU, Norway,
Canada and Switzerland expressing their alarm over the recent escalation of
the already dramatic humanitarian crisis in Darfur – 100,000 refugees to Chad,
600,000 internal displaced persons and another three million people affected –
whereas no humanitarian access to the affected population was allowed.
They demanded all appropriate options to provide immediate assistance and
protection.[108]

The European Commission (EC) also showed an adequate understanding of
the conflict in Darfur in its Emergency Humanitarian Aid Decision of the end
of October 2003 by, for example, describing: "The *Janjaweed* militias are currently the main cause of violence, looting, killing, destruction and related displacement."[109] In January the Commission affirmed the dramatic increase of
refugees in a couple of weeks from 40,000 to 100,000 and was aware of the air
attacks on civilians. The Centre for Humanitarian Dialogue asked financial
support from the EC to start mediation attempts in order to prevent both marginalisation and internationalisation of Darfur conflict, which could also be to
the benefit of the Naivasha peace process.[110]

5.3 Reflection: Who Knew What at What Moment?

The account before suggests that many international actors knew about
the developments in Darfur at a relatively early stage. But *what* exactly did

---

107   "Darfur Update", undated unpublished background note from Member of the European
       Parliament Cees Bremmer for the European Parliament Delegation Mission to the Sudan,
       19–24 February 2004.
108   Archive Ministry of Foreign Affairs in the Netherlands, DAF/2015/00646, Period December
       2003–June 2004.
109   EU Doc.: ECHO/SDN/210/2003/02000, 2 December 2003, "Emergency assistance in support
       of population of Greater Darfur Region (Sudan) most directly affected by conflict."
110   Archive Ministry of Foreign Affairs in the Netherlands, DAF/2015/00646, Period December
       2003–June 2004.

they know? Where they able to fully capture the scale of the violence on the ground?

In the first months of the conflict there was a difficulty collecting accurate information and there were insufficient resources to do so, especially at the UN level.[111] The latter is illustrated by the presence of the UN in Sudan. When the new UN Resident coordinator, Dr. Mukesh Kapila arrived in Sudan on 1 April 2003, he was unaware of the escalating conflict in Darfur.[112] He described that vast areas of Sudan were "totally neglected," especially remote regions like Darfur. "Darfur was one of the areas least covered by UN operations. Basically, we had zero presence there."[113] An internal memo of the Office of the UN Residence Coordinator described on 26 July 2003 with the SLM/A claiming "heavy civilian casualties" due to a six-day bombing campaign. However, independent and reliable information on casualty figures, and use of "prohibited weapons" was unavailable because of the inaccessibility to the region.[114] Kapila noted that in October 2003: "a picture was emerging that terrible things were happening, but ours remained a half-formed patchy understanding."[115] One of the first outsiders to really see the atrocities was a representative from the Centre for Humanitarian Dialogue (CHD), who was requested by Kapila in fall 2003 to get first hand reports from Darfur and to know why the rebels are fighting, since that was still "a mystery."[116] It was only on 30 November 2003 that it became clear that the "the crux of the current problem in Darfur is the militias (...) To date, international attention has focused on the SLM/A and the government."[117] When the CHD representative reported back to Kapila in December he still held that "we don't yet know – the full scale of the thing."[118] UN staff were forced out of Darfur in mid-December and only re-established their presence in February 2004. It was only on 5 March 2004 that the UN staff directly witnessed for the first time attacks at the village of Tawila.[119]

---

111   See also Cockett (2010), p. 169.

112   Kapila (2013), p. 19.

113   Ibid., p. 32, 41.

114   Office of the RC/HC Sudan, Doc 3, 26 July 2003, "Darfur Update," available at http://www .mukeshkapila.org/book/sudan-archive.html [accessed 22 October 2013].

115   Kapila (2013), p. 106.

116   Kapila mentioned that he hired Tim Mansfield in late September 2003 (Kapila, 2013, pp. 138–139). Cockett mentioned Andrew Marshall (Cockett, 2010, p. 193).

117   Office of the RC/HC Sudan Doc 9, "Darfur Update," 30 November 2003, available at http:// www.mukeshkapila.org/book/sudan-archive.html [accessed 22 October 2013], p. 3.

118   Kapila (2013), pp. 163.

119   Attacks at the village of Tawilla, private communication, available at http://www .mukeshkapila.org/download/Item%2030.pdf [accessed 22 October 2013]; Kapila (2013), p. 204.

An MSF evaluation report also noted that: "there was little reliable informa-tion on the severity of the humanitarian crisis in its early stages."[120] MacKinnon also held that up to the late summer of 2003, senior UN staff hardly had any first-hand information that would enable an adequate analysis and the well-informed policy recommendations to the UNSC.[121] Likewise, a press release from the Associated Press on 16 August 2003 still referred to the rebels as the Darfur Liberation Front, with no mention of the SLM/A, which might indicate a lack of comprehension of the conflict as well.[122] UN DPA head Prendergast also stated: "I thought it was quite difficult to come to a very clear and full understanding of what you were dealing with. How much of it was a humani-tarian tragedy which was due to the particular climatic conditions, compli-cated, exacerbated by obstructiveness by the government? How much of it was *Janjaweed*?"[123] These limitations to data gathering are also closely related to the restrictions put in place by the Sudanese government on accessing the region of Darfur. These restraints obviously prevented the outside world form-ing a complete picture of the situation on the ground.

It should, however, be acknowledged that the capacity for intelligence col-lection and analysis of the UN is considerably smaller than many of the – more powerful – UNSC members, as the earlier anecdote of the UK satellite images shown to Kapila already showed.[124] The US and the UK especially had a clear picture of the developments in Darfur. Charles Snyder of the Bureau of African Affairs of the US Department of State acknowledged that officials at the US State Department had a "fair idea of what was happening," but he nonetheless questioned the value of such satellite images because they do not reveal every-thing and leave room for interpretation.[125] Other countries however, had more difficulty in collecting information. Former Dutch Ambassador in Khartoum Kooijmans stated, for example:

> There was simply too little information available to fully grasp the nature and scope of the conflict in Darfur. [The Netherlands] had a downgraded

---

120   Médecins Sans Frontières the Netherlands, "Darfur 2004: a review of MSF-Holland's responsiveness and strategic choices," January 2005, available at http://www.alnap.org/pool/files/erd-3291-full.pdf [accessed 18 November 2013], p. 6.

121   Mackinnon, M.G. (2010) "The United Nations Security Council," in *The International poli-tics of mass atrocities. The case of Darfur*, by Black, D.R. and Williams, P.D. (eds.), London, New York: Routledge, p. 86.

122   Associated Press, 16 August 2003, "Thousands flee fighting in western Sudan."

123   PBS Frontline interview with Kieran Prendergast, 29 June 2007.

124   MacKinnon (2010), p. 85.

125   Snyder as paraphrased in Cockett (2010), p. 196.

embassy operating more or less on a shoestring because regular development aid to Sudan had been suspended in light of continuous Sudanese
human rights violations. For that reason I initially started my work in
Sudan in my capacity as Chargé d'Affaires; later on I was upgraded to full
ambassador. I was there with only two diplomatic colleagues mainly
looking after a limited humanitarian aid programme. And then the greatest humanitarian disaster of the last few years breaks out. You barely have
time to delve into the background of the conflict or keep track with daily
developments in Darfur. You are only concerned with the management
of the humanitarian aid bureaucracy. Knowledge about what was happening was, as a result, very limited. Had I been a Minister, I would say: 'I
want a team of the best anthropologists, Arabists and security experts,
who go to Darfur for two months with the task of speaking to everything
and everyone.' But that did not happen of course.[126]

Another matter is when international actors knew about the full scale and gravity of the developments. In the beginning, the crisis was largely represented as
a humanitarian crisis. Médecins Sans Frontières, for example, reported about
the "humanitarian disaster" in eastern Chad on 16 September 2003 but still with
only limited reference to the (political) nature of the on-going violence.[127]
The UK government, and most other Western governments, tended to treat the
situation in Darfur solely as a humanitarian emergency or crisis.[128] Egeland
held that "member states were late in recognising the gravity of the crisis."[129]
Likewise, Prendergast stated that he was under the impression in December
2003 that the access of humanitarian aid was the main issue in Darfur:

> But at that time it appeared to be more a question of obstructing human-
> itarian access than the kind of humanitarian and political disaster that it
> turned into later (...) I would guess that it would be in the very early
> months of 2004, and then we became aware of the death rate – and the
> death rate was mainly from drought and lack of water and from water-
> borne diseases and so on – (...) The early awareness of the crisis was
> among the humanitarians as a primarily humanitarian crisis.[130]

---

126 Authors' interview with Adriaan Kooijmans, 16 September 2003.
127 Médecins Sans Frontières Press Release. "Chad: Thousands of Sudanese refugees caught
     in humanitarian disaster," 16 September 2003.
128 UK House of Commons, 2005, Volume I, p. 32. See also Prunier (2007), p. 126.
129 UK House of Commons, 2005, Volume I, p. 30.
130 PBS Frontline interview with Kieran Prendergast, 29 June 2007.

In addition, the situation in Darfur was initially also viewed as not demanding urgent attention. Kapila wrote on 22 March 2004 that the war in Darfur "started off in a small way last year but it has progressively got worse." According to Dutch ambassador Kooijmans, the conflict in Darfur looked like a "regular conflict" in the fall of 2003 when Chad was mediating between the warring parties.[131] He argued that at that time the conflict was still "a none of my business show."[132] The US also showed little cause for concern in the beginning of 2003. According to the former Presidential Adviser of Peace, Atabani, the US government was initially consciously "looking the other way on Darfur [and were] ready to accept a military solution, if it was a quick, surgical approach," because of their interest in securing a North-South peace deal and obtaining more terrorism intelligence.[133] Mubarak al-Mahdi, a special adviser to the Sudanese government at that time, held that a US diplomat allegedly told him: "We said deal with it quietly and neatly. But they messed it up."[134]

It seems that the ethnic dimensions of the conflict came to the forefront in November/December 2003, with increasing reports from NGOs about the matter.[135] On 11 December diplomats in Khartoum qualified the conflict in Darfur as ethnic cleansing "with Arab militias, possibly backed by the government, destroying entire villages inhabited by dark-skinned people who speak African languages."[136] Likewise, Prendergast said that he became particularly aware of the situation in Darfur towards the end of 2003 and that in the beginning of 2004 he came to realise that the situation had become more serious.[137]

---

131   Letter to State Minister Wahab, Doc. 34, 22 March 2004, available at http://www.mukeshkapila .org/download/Item%2034.pdf [accessed 11 December 2013].

132   Authors' interview with Adriaan Kooijmans, 16 September 2013.

133   Quoted in Cockett (2010), p. 180.

134   Idem.

135   See supra n 25, 51 and 52. The term "ethnic cleansing" was mentioned for the first time in media on 13 November 2003 (Prunier, 2007, p. 90). Igiri and Lyman held that "the ethnic scope of events in Darfur, fuzzy at first, became stunningly clear by spring of 2004." USAID had evidence of ethnic cleansing in the form of satellite images of NASA from April 2004 (Igiri and Lyman, 2004, pp. 6, 11). Eric Reeves claimed that the evidence of ethnic cleansing and genocide were already strong in October/November 2003 (Reeves, E. and Zehnder, M., "Compromising with evil. An archival history of Greater Sudan, 2007–2012. Annex III: Darfur Mortality," available at: http://www.compromisingwithevil.org/pdf/Annex-III.pdf [accessed 20 November 2013]).

136   BBC News, 11 December 2003, "Sudan 'blocks aid to rebel area."

137   PBS Frontline interview with Kieran Prendergast, 29 June 2007.

According to MacKinnon, all SC members were sufficiently aware of the situation from the beginning of 2004: "Members of the Council might have a reasonable 'lack of awareness' defence to explain their collective inaction throughout 2003, but this defence breaks down in 2004."[138]

Leaving aside the exact month, we believe that most government officials at the highest levels were well aware of the severity of the situation and in any case much earlier than when the situation in Darfur was discussed formally at the international level for the first time in mid-2004. Thus, actors knew about the gravity at a time during which much of the violence could still have been prevented. Early warnings were received and read, but they were not sufficiently appreciated and swept under the carpet. As the next section will show, there was a conscious decision to address Darfur silently by using quiet diplomacy and not bring it to the UN Security Council.

5.4   Response

The response of the international community in the first year after the outbreak of the rebellion can be described as follows. Governments, international organisations and NGOs employed a wide variety of activities to address the humanitarian disaster without addressing the underlying (political) causes of the conflict. At the same time, they used quiet diplomacy to put some pressure the Sudanese government behind closed doors, albeit not too much given the on-going North-South negotiations. The latter also contributed to a reluctance or outright denial to put Darfur on the agenda of the Security Council.

Humanitarian Efforts

Governments and the UN already started taking steps to alleviate the dire humanitarian situation in Darfur at an early stage. According to Natsios, USAID had a presence in Darfur since 2003 and had been "spending money to prevent a catastrophe since last May [2003]."[139] Roger Winter allocated US$40 million of emergency aid to IDPs through UNICEF.[140] Likewise, Kapila recounted how he together with the new head of OCHA Jan Egeland, started planning for the humanitarian crisis in Darfur in August 2003. This eventually resulted in

---

138   MacKinnon (2010), pp. 85, 90.
139   Igiri and Lyman (2004), p. 33.
140   Natsios, A. (2012) *Sudan, South Sudan and Darfur: what everyone needs to know*. Oxford: Oxford University Press, p. 156.

the aforementioned humanitarian operation called the Greater Darfur Special Initiative. This Initiative called for US$23 million to bring humanitarian aid into Darfur.[141] This call for funds was also used to bring the situation to the attention of policy-makers. Most European countries as well as the US and Canada funded the Special Greater Darfur initiative and other calls from Red Cross and MSF.[142] At the same time, some UN agencies were unable or unwilling to take any action in the first year of the conflict. UNICEF, for example, held: "we haven't got the staff...we have to get clearance, and is this really our priority?"[143]

The diplomatic missions in Khartoum were also important in ensuring that access for humanitarian aid and staff was not denied by the Sudanese government, especially since the beginning of 2004. UK Ambassador Patey managed in January 2004 to have regular meetings with the government, the UN, humanitarian organisations and diplomatic missions with the view of facilitating the humanitarian efforts and access to Darfur.[144] According to Dutch Ambassador Kooijmans – who also participated in these meeting as acting EU President – these meetings were the starting point of joint donor and UN efforts to gradually increase the pressure on the Sudanese government.[145]

There was a clear preference among (Western) countries to only address the humanitarian dimensions instead of the political and security related aspects of the conflict.[146] These countries were generally eager to fund Kapila's Darfur

---

141 UN Doc.: AFR/701. IHA/795, 17 September 2003, "Agreement reached allowing humanitarian access to Darfur region of Sudan."

142 An internal note from the office of Resident Coordinator indicated that by 22 November US$6.5 million of the US$22.8 million had been committed by European countries only (France, Netherlands, Norway, Sweden and the UK), whereas a US pledge was still "under consideration" (Office of the RC/HC Sudan, 29 November 2003, "Darfur Humanitarian Needs Profile," available at http://www.mukeshkapila.org/book/sudan-archive.html [accessed 22 October 2013]).

143 Kapila (2013), p. 88.

144 The first meeting was on 26 January 2004 (Office of the RC/HC Sudan, RCHC/SUD/Note 25, 28 January 2004, "Humanitarian access in Darfur, Sudan. Note to Mr. Egeland," available at: http://www.mukeshkapila.org/download/Item%2018.pdf [accessed 4 December 2013]). The next meeting was on 9 February (Office of the RC/HC Sudan, RCHC/SUD/Note 28A, 11 February 2004, "Humanitarian access in Darfur, Sudan. Note to Mr. Egeland," available at: http://www.mukeshkapila.org/download/Item%2021.pdf [accessed 4 December 2013]. Authors' interview with Adriaan Kooijmans, 16 September 2013.

145 Authors' interview with Adriaan Kooijmans, 16 September 2013.

146 MacKinnon (2010), p. 84.

initiative, but Kapila was always directed to the US and the UK for further international political involvement in Darfur.[147] But these two countries, consciously decided not to do so.

Quiet Diplomacy

Several countries pressured the Sudanese government on the deteriorating situation in Darfur, especially on the limited access for humanitarian workers and aid. Diplomatic pressure was primarily put on the Sudanese government to open up for humanitarian workers. The United Kingdom, US and the Netherlands brought up these issues directly with the government in the early stage of the conflict.[148] These concerns were mainly voiced behind closed doors. The most far-ranging forms of diplomacy were the mediation efforts by the government of Chad. In the course of 2003, President Déby of Chad tried several times to mediate in the conflict. In particular, there were attempts to negotiate ceasefires in September and November 2003 (see above).[149]

Kapila said that the US was "keen to press the [Sudanese government] to fulfil its responsibilities to protect its own people [and] many other countries were not in a mood to hear the concerns voiced by the [US]" in late 2003 and early 2004.[150] The US was, however, not so forthcoming in confronting the government in most of 2003, because it was initially not aware of what exactly was happening in Darfur, believing that the government was only undertaking a limited counter-insurgency operation (see previous section).[151] When the actual nature of the conflict became clearer and USAID more outspoken, the highest levels of the White House took up contact with the Sudanese government in October 2003. What is described as "quiet diplomacy," President Bush, Secretary of State Powell and National Security advisor Rice called their Sudanese counterparts in the fall of 2003.[152]

UK Secretary of State for International Development, Clare Short, already raised the issue of Darfur in conversations with the Sudanese government in

---

147   Kapila (2013), p. 106–107; Traub (2006), p. 215.

148   Slim (2004), p. 814; Mayroz (2008), p. 376; MacKinnon (2010), p. 96.

149   Toga, D. (2007) "The African Union mediation and the Abuja peace talks," in *War in Darfur and the search for peace*, by de Waal, A., (ed.), Global Equity Initiative, Harvard University, p. 215.

150   UK House of Commons, 2005, Volume I p. ev 51.

151   Supra n 135.

152   Igiri and Lyman (2004). There was another call by President Bush in December, asking on the development of the North-South talks, but not on Darfur (Prunier, 2007, p. 108).

April 2003.[153] Her successor Hilary Benn stated to have raised humanitarian access with the Sudanese government when visiting Sudan in December up to the Sudanese President al-Bashir.[154]

Dutch Minister for Development Cooperation Agnes van Ardenne visited Sudan in November 2003. She urged the Sudanese government to increase humanitarian access to Darfur.[155] There was another Dutch ministerial visit in January 2004. Van Ardenne, joined by Foreign Minister Bot, and Minister of Defence Kamp had meetings in Africa for three days and one of the countries they visited was Sudan.[156] Although the initial plan was to only discuss the North-South conflict, Darfur was also brought up. The Ministers met on January 28 in Sudan with Taha (Vice-President), Ismail (Minster of Foreign Affairs) and Hasan (Deputy Minister of Defense) and pressed each of them for a solution on Darfur. It was decided that the Netherlands – as the acting EU president in Sudan – would take the lead in initiating mediation or ceasefire talks between the Sudanese government and the rebels and would therefore contact the leaders of the SLM.[157] The following day this initiative was already discussed in the framework of the EU Common Foreign and Security Policy. It consisted of (1) the possibility of an unilateral cease fire at 2 February, (2) the provision of a safe passage of the SLM/A rebels to meet the local EU Presidency in order to persuade them to accept the ceasefire and (3) the extension of support for Chad in its efforts to mediate. It was made clear that Ismail rejected any EU fact-finding mission. The United Kingdom immediately "congratulates the Netherlands on the excellent efforts".[158] France also reacted positively and put forward that the initiative could be discussed in Paris when President Déby visited Paris in the first week of February. French Minister of Foreign Affairs, de Villepin, would press the Darfur agenda during his visit on 18 and 19 February to Chad and Khartoum. In the following chapter we will demonstrate that

---

153   Bieckmann (2012), p. 264. Williams, P. (2010) "The United Kingdom," *The International politics of mass atrocities. The case of Darfur*, by Williams, P. and Black, D. (eds.), London, New York: Routledge, p. 198.

154   UK House of Commons, 2005, Volume II, pp. ev 28, ev 86; BBC Panorama, 3 July 2005, Fergal Keane interview with Hilary Benn, available at http://news.bbc.co.uk/2/hi/programmes/panorama/4647195.stm [accessed 18 November 2013].

155   Dutch Parliamentary Doc.: Tweede Kamer, 2003–2004, 29 237 and 29 234, nr. 4, 9 December 2003.

156   Dutch Parliamentary Doc.: Tweede Kamer, 2003–2004, 29 237 en 29 278, nr. 7, 27 Februari 2004.

157   Authors' interview Adriaan Kooijmans, 16 September 2009.

158   Archive Ministry of Foreign Affairs in the Netherlands, DAF/2015/00646, Period December 2003-June 2004.

France tried in vain to put the Darfur situation on the Security Council agenda in February 2004.

The Government of Sudan attacked the border area near the town of Tine some days after the meeting with the three Dutch Ministers in January 2004. The local EU Presidency wanted to criticise this action contrary to the earlier promises in a demarche to Ismail on 8 February and to Taha on 10 February. The results were discussed by the EU Heads of Missions in Khartoum and they asked their capitals for a common EU statement in particular now President al-Bashir claimed that he had achieved a decisive military victory over the rebels. In February the local EU presidency in Khartoum prepared a draft statement. This statement communicated to all EU member states was followed by a EU Troika mission on 12 and 13 February to West and North Darfur (Section 5.2.2). The EU declaration by the Presidency on behalf of the European Union on the situation in Darfur was made public on 25 February 2004.[159] The EU Presidency expressed its "serious concern" and urged the Government of Sudan to stop *Janjaweed* militias from "systematically target[ing] villages."[160]

Further Political Involvement: No Security Council Involvement
Powerful actors such as the UK and the US, as well as the UN Secretariat had decided during the last months of 2003 that Darfur should not put the North-South talks in jeopardy and should therefore not be put on the agenda of the UNSC. An illustration of this approach is that the UNSC released a Presidential Statement concerning Sudan in October 2003 under the US Presidency that did not mention Darfur at all.[161] In it the Security Council welcomed the progress that was made in the North-South talks and looked forward to a successful conclusion. There was no reference or hint in the statement that the Security Council was concerned about the raging conflict in Darfur. An early opportunity to bring the situation to the world's attention was missed. The next presidential statement on Darfur would only come 7½ months later on 25 May 2004.

That this did not happen was largely the result of the conscious decision by the UK and US not to bring the situation of Darfur to the Security Council. The conclusion of a peace agreement between the Sudanese government and the SPLM/A was deliberately prioritised over Darfur and it was decided to follow a sequential strategy instead of conducting negotiations in parallel or integrate

---

159   Authors interview with Adriaan Kooijmans, 16 September 2013; personal communication
       29 December 2013.
160   EU Doc.: 6750/04 (Presse 66) P 26/04, 25 February 2004.
161   UN Doc.: S/PRST/2003/16, 10 October 2003.

Darfur into the North-South negotiations.[162] This decision might not have been "malign," but – as it later turned out – was certainly "misguided."[163] When Kapila pressed UK officials in October 2003 for political involvement, the UK policy was laid out to him: "Naivasha is key." When Kapila told that SPLM leader Garang would consequently stall the talks unless Darfur was dealt with first, the position of the UK was unchanged. Kapila was simply told: "Don't rock the boat."[164] when he made another appeal to the UK Foreign Office to make Darfur an agenda item for the Security Council in early 2004. Kapila believed that his own government would be supportive of his recommendation, even more so since he was formally still a member of the Foreign Office and therefore was believed to have some credibility. Kapila was again informed about the decision not to prioritise the conflict for fear of disturbing the Naivasha negotiations: "We sympathise with the problems of Darfur but do not make too much noise and trouble now, let us sort this Naivasha thing out and then everything will be alright."[165] When he urged to bring Darfur to the Security Council's attention, he was told "not yet."[166] There was a fear that confronting the Sudanese government too much would "paint Khartoum into a corner."[167] Kapila argued that the negotiations were already disturbed since neither the North (Governement of Sudan) nor the South (SPLM) wanted to deal with the issue of Darfur in a 'Government of National Unity'. Unimpressed, the UK refused to bring it to UNSC. Kapila was allegedly said to be "a nuisance."[168]

There was also a strong push by Egeland to have the UNSC adopt Sudan/Darfur on its agenda. He "pestered everyone" in the beginning of 2004 with this request. He had, just like Kapila, trouble convincing policy-makers that further involvement at the political level was necessary.[169] Egeland observed: "The notion was in some circles that you shouldn't bring in Darfur as an alien element that would cause problems for the effort to get parties to make peace, finally, [N]orth-[S]outh."[170] Oliver Ulich, Egeland's Chief of staff added: "Neither the UK nor the US wanted Darfur on the agenda until March [of 2004] (...) we were pressing them from

162   Flint and De Waal (2008), pp. 179–183; Mayroz (2008), p. 364; MacKinnon (2010), p. 88.
163   UK House of Commons report, Volume II, p. ev 58, stated by MEP Berkov in the hearing with Dr. Mukesh Kapila.
164   Kapila (2013). pp. 108–109.
165   UK House of Commons, 2005, Volume I, p. 36; Kapila (2013), pp. 108–109.
166   UK House of Commons, 2005, Volume I, p. 36.
167   Kapila (2013), p. 184.
168   Kapila as quoted in Cockett (2010), pp. 205–206.
169   Traub (2006), p. 215. Cockett (2010), p. 198.
170   BBC Panorama, 3 July 2005, "Never again programme transcript," available at http://news .bbc.co.uk/2/hi/programmes/panorama/4654093.stm [accessed 18 November 2013].

December/January."[171] Like the UK, US Special Envoy for Sudan John Danford, urged Egeland: "Don't rock the boat, we're trying to finish this [North-South peace agreement]."[172] Dutch ambassador Kooijmans also noted that the US and the UK "were so concerned about the Comprehensive Peace Agreement (CPA) that they blocked any Security Council discussion on Darfur."[173] The US government even put pressure on Western aid workers in Darfur to "keep quiet about Darfur, not to make it a big issue," according to Reuters journalist McDoorn.[174]

It seems that the US – and also the third member of the Troika, Norway – primarily deferred to the UK and did not want to make an independent call themselves.[175] At the US State Department Kapila was told that the US was in favour of addressing Darfur but would not do so if the UK does not want it.[176] For the US two reasons appeared to play a role and were used as an argument not to press for more action. Firstly, the support they received from the UK in Iraq made them grant the UK "autonomy" or the lead role on Sudan; also because it is a former British colony.[177] Secondly, some officials in the State Department did agree with the analysis that pressuring the Sudanese government on Darfur might hurt the Naivasha negotiations. For instance, Egeland stated that US ambassador to the UN Negroponte, knowing little about Darfur, agreed with his analysis of addressing Darfur in the Security Council, but his staff pushed back.[178]

By late 2003, the US and the UK representatives in Khartoum had received their orders that there would be no Security Council involvement for fear that the Naivasha talks might unravel. US Chargé d'Affaires Gerard Galluci indeed acknowledged that he was instructed by Washington that he could only focus on the negotiations and on the counterterrorism cooperation.[179] This policy decision was not necessarily in line with the thinking and preferences of the ambassadors in Khartoum. UK Ambassador Patey is known to be unhappy with this decision given his more "progressive" background as an official from the Department for International Development (DFID), but he followed

---

171   Ulich as quoted in Cockett (2010), p. 198; Authors' interviews with Jan Egeland, 28 November 2012; Olivier Ulich, 1 June 2005.
172   Danforth as quoted in Hamilton (2011a), pp. 23–24.
173   Kooijmans as quoted in Hamilton (2011a), p. 20; Authors' interview with Adriaan Kooijmans, 16 September 2013.
174   McDoorn as quoted in Cockett (2010), p. 195.
175   Kapila (2013), pp. 106, 118; UK House of Commons, 2005, Volume II, p. ev. 57.
176   Kapila (2013), p. 118.
177   Idem.; Cockett (2010), p. 196.
178   Egeland (2010), p. 90; Authors' interview with Jan Egeland, 28 November 2012.
179   Galluci as paraphrased in Hamilton (2011a), p. 20.

the orders.[180] US Chargé d'Affaires Galluci also had difficulties with the instructions from Washington.[181] He attempted to persuade his superiors in the State Department to move beyond the mere provision of food supplies[182] Other (Western) embassies were also in favour of a greater political involvement of their respective governments. As stated above, Kapila, for example, sent a memo to New York in December 2003 stating that western embassy missions were in favour of international monitoring of a ceasefire.[183] In Kapila's own account, the western embassies appeared largely supportive of his efforts and tried to help him in pressuring their own ministries. Especially, UK Ambassador William Patey takes initiatives to address the issue. Another illustration of the more 'activist' line of the embassies in comparison with their capitals is the joint statement which was issued by key diplomats from the UK, US, France and the Netherlands in support of Kapila's statement in March 2004 (see next chapter).[184]

In addition to the UK and US, the UN SG and Secretariat were also unwilling to put the issue of Darfur on the agenda of the UNSC. Kapila tried to get the UN Secretariat involved through reports and with explicit calls on his visits to New York, first in the fall of 2003, and a second time in early 2004.[185] UNHCR Lubbers also noted how Kapila and his own early warnings since November 2003 fell on deaf ears within the UN.[186] When Kapila asked Egeland how he could make the UN politically involved in the crisis, he was told to meet with UN Department of Political Affairs head Kieran Prendergast. Prendergast however, saw no use for the UN to get involved in Darfur.[187] Kapila was allegedly told that the Sudanese should fight it out among themselves.[188] The analysis in the UN Secretariat was also that the North-South negotiations should be prioritised, in

---

180   Authors' interview with Adriaan Kooijmans, 16 September 2013; Bieckmann (2012), p. 257–258. Patey's occasional different view relative to London can also be observed from the account of Kapila (2013).

181   Authors' interview with Adriaan Kooijmans, 16 September 2013.

182   Galluci as quoted in Hamilton (2011a), p. 29.

183   Kapila, M. (2013), p. 164; Internal UN Memo from Mukesh Kapila to Kieran Prendergast and Jan Egeland, 18 December 2013.

184   "We of the British, French, Dutch and American diplomatic community in Khartoum wholly commend the stand taken by UN resident coordinator Dr Mukesh Kapila, and endorse what he has said about the serious events now unfolding in Darfur" (Kapila, 2013, p. 238).

185   Kapila (2013), pp. 114, 187; Traub (2006), p. 215.

186   Lubbers as referred to in Bieckmann (2012), p. 176.

187   Kapila (2013), p. 112–114.

188   Kapila as quoted in Cockett (2010), p. 194.

line with the Troika countries.[189] So the UN Secretariat, and in particular Secretary-General Annan and UN DPA head Kieran Prendergast chose not to speak out on Darfur as a strategy to obtain results for the Naivasha talks, and because they were aware that this was not supported by member states (for a further discussion of the role of the UN, see Section 5.5.4).[190] According to Kapila, the attention within the UN headquarters "focused laser-like on [North-South] peace talks, with everything else being ignored."[191] Likewise, an evaluation of MSF's humanitarian efforts concluded:

> When the crisis emerged, agencies in Sudan were like rabbits caught in the headlights, with their attention focused almost exclusively on the Naivasha process and preparations for post-peace rehabilitation and development. (...) Attention was firmly on the Naivasha peace process and the UN therefore took a cautious line on Darfur.[192]

5.5   Explaining the Warning – Response Gap

As was mentioned in Chapter 1, many previous analyses of the response of the international community to the situation in Darfur relied on realist explanations as to the absence of national and geopolitical interests of the powerful states and the absence of the limited political will. Some within the US government, for example, prioritised the good anti-terrorism cooperation over confronting the government of Sudan over Darfur, since the former is intimately connected to its own security interests.[193] This prioritisation is understandable from a realist and rational decision-making point of view. This section will complement such explanations by focusing on the theoretical elements discussed in Chapters 2 and 3.

---

189   PBS Frontline interview with Kieran Prendergast, 29 June 2007.

190   Annan later acknowledged that this approach was made irrelevant as "evidence of gross human rights violations in Darfur [emerged]" a few months later (Traub, 2006, p. 125).

191   Kapila (2013), p. 95.

192   MSF the Netherlands, January 2005, "Darfur 2004: a review of MSF-Holland's responsiveness and strategic choices", available at www.alnap.org/pool/files/erd-3291-full.pdf [accessed 18 November 2013], pp. 7, 11.

193   US State Department official Charles Snyder qualified in the following way: "I would say now the level of cooperation we have with them is among the best in the world in terms of practical terms." (BBC Panorama, 3 July 2005, "Never again programme transcript," available at http://news.bbc.co.uk/2/hi/programmes/panorama/4654093.stm [accessed 18 November 2013]).

5.5.1   *Wishful Thinking and Cognitive Dissonance with Respect to the North-South Negotiations*

The first factor that prevented an early response from the international community were the – at that time ongoing – North-South negotiations. This factor has often been approached implicitly from the perspective of the rational actor model whereby it is emphasised that several states, most notably the "Troika countries" of the US, UK and Norway, had invested a good deal of time, energy and resources to settle this conflict. The Troika countries feared that too much pressure on the Sudanese government over Darfur would put these negotiations at risk, which would be a costly affair in terms of resources spent and unrealised benefits in the form of ending a conflict which had raged for more than twenty years and had cost the lives of two million people.[194] Hilary Benn, Secretary of State for International Development – although he claimed that there were attempts to address both South-Sudan and Darfur together – emphasised the urgency of addressing North-South by referring to "longest running civil war in Africa that killed over...about 2½ million people. (...) It also provides the opportunity for southern Sudan in particular – this is one of the poorest places on earth – now at least to have the chance of some development."[195] There was also an idea that the negotiations could lead to a transition from an authoritarian regime into a democracy with a Government of National Unity.[196] Vraalsen, for example, argued: "we wanted to screen that conflict from other conflicts like Darfur."[197]

Not achieving an agreement would thus be costly for Sudan, but also for the Troika countries. There was undeniably an element of prestige involved for the third parties involved in the negotiations. There were hopes of signing an agreement on the White House lanes, which could consequently be heralded as an example of diplomatic and foreign policy success that was badly needed after the controversial invasion of Iraq in the spring of 2003.[198] In addition, the US government also sought to satisfy the demands of domestic Christian

---

194   Slim (2004), p. 822; Traub (2006), p. 215; Prunier (2007), p. 141; Flint and De Waal (2008), p. 127–128.

195   BBC Panorama, 3 July 2005, Fergal Keane interview with Hilary Benn, available at http://news.bbc.co.uk/2/hi/programmes/panorama/4647195.stm [accessed 18 November 2013]. Although we stated that this civil war had cost the lives of 1½ million people, much higher figures are regularly used as well (see Section 4.4).

196   Hamilton (2011a), p. 20.

197   AlertNet's interview with Tom Vraalsen, 8 July 2004, "Sudan: interview. Darfur access improving but risks ahead," available at http://reliefweb.int/report/sudan/sudan -interview-darfur-access-improving-risks-ahead-un [accessed 29 November 2013].

198   Igiri and Lyman (2004), p. 12; Cockett (2010), p. 177.

evangelic groups who had been fervently lobbying for a peace deal. Such a peace deal was seen by President Bush as crucial for his re-election in November 2004.[199] Several diplomats also had associated or committed themselves wholeheartedly to solving the issue. Traub, for example, referred to US Special Envoy for Sudan Danforth's "long-sought goal of ending the civil war."[200]

Several cognitive and psychological mechanisms might further explain why third parties stuck so fervently to this prioritisation of the North-South negotiation while "allowing Darfur to fester."[201] Firstly, in 2003 there was a great deal of wishful thinking and optimism that the negotiations would soon be over and that successful finalisation of North-South would help solve the problem in Darfur as well. Over the course of 2003 there was an idea that a peace agreement was within reach, although these optimistic expectations needed to be adjusted constantly. There was, for instance, already a three-day donor conference in the Netherlands in April 2003 about possible reconstruction efforts after a peace agreement.[202] The idea at that time was that a peace agreement would be reached by the end of June 2003.[203] By December 2003, the negotiators were so convinced that a deal was forthcoming that two seats were reserved for al-Bashir and SPML leader Garang at the State of the Union to be given by US President Bush on 21 January 2004.[204] At the same time, the UN Secretariat started planning for a new peacekeeping force to support the implementation of a future peace agreement prior to a request from the parties.[205] As was mentioned in the previous section, it was at the end of 2003 when the optimism reigned, that there was a full awareness among most international actors as to the (ethnic and genocidal) dimensions of the Darfur conflict.

Secondly, there was also an element of cognitive dissonance among some actors. Hamilton noted: "Faced simultaneously with information that

---

199   Cockett (2010), pp. 177, 199.

200   Traub (2006), p. 242.

201   Idem.

202   1–3 April 2003, Donor meeting in Noordwijk, the Netherlands, see Grünfeld, F. and Vermeulen, W.N. (2014) "The role of the Netherlands in the international response to the Crisis in Darfur," Maastricht Faculty of Law Working Paper No. 2014-2 (available at http://ssrn.com/abstract=2418398 [accessed 2 April 2014]).

203   See http://www.sudan-forum.de/meeting.html.

204   Samantha Power, "Dying in Darfur. Can the ethnic cleansing in Sudan be stopped?," The New Yorker Magazine, 30 August 2004. A US Cable also referred to the end of 2003 (US State Department Cable, Brussel, 25 March 2004, No. 1174). According to Kapila, Norgewian Minister Johnson expected the peace to be signed within two to three months when asked about this in October 2003 (Kapila, 2013, p. 107).

205   MacKinnon (2010), pp. 73, 84.

Khartoum was both set to deliver a historic North-South agreement and responsible for mass murder in Darfur, officials in Washington found it initially easier to discount information about Darfur than to revisit the highly attractive idea that a once-in-a-generation diplomatic breakthrough was about to occur in Sudan."[206] The cognitive dissonance is well illustrated by a quote from a US politician who argued: "We so wanted to get peace in the South that it was like the Simon and Garfunkel song: 'A man hears what he wants to hear and disregards the rest.'"[207]

5.5.2   Disbelief

There was no outright denial of the warnings by government officials and diplomats. It is, however, not unthinkable that there was a certain amount of disbelief of the horrific facts. A US State Department official, for example, noted on a fact-finding trip to Darfur in February 2004: "We were astounded by what we saw. It was instantly clear that the situation was worse than we imagined, beyond our wildest dreams."[208] For Lorne Craner, Assistant Secretary for Democracy, Human Rights, and Labour at the US State Department "it was not clear (...) that Darfur presented a situation in which they would have to shift into the 'no Rwandas' mode of action" when he was listening to USAID head Natsios' predictions about the increasing death rate in Darfur.[209] Hamilton referred in this context to the information-processing heuristics human beings use when confronted with an enormous amount of information. She noted that Darfur did not fit the pre-existing Rwanda like genocide schema that officials had in mind. Darfur was consequently overlooked.[210] Danforth, added: "I don't think it was a Rwanda type situation."[211] Gerard Galluci, the top US diplomat in Khartoum also noted that "there was a tendency not to see Darfur initially for what it was."[212]

Another element that contributed to a denialist tendency among policymakers is to question the reliability of all incoming information. The scholar

---

206   Hamilton (2011a), p. 30.

207   Congressman Frank Wolf as quoted in Samantha Power, "Dying in Darfur. Can the ethnic cleansing in Sudan be stopped?," The New Yorker Magazine, 30 August 2004.

208   US official as quoted in Hamilton (2011a), p. 30.

209   Hamilton (2011a), p. 29.

210   Idem.

211   BBC Panorama, 3 July 2005, Fergal Keane interview with John Danforth, available at http://news.bbc.co.uk/1/hi/programmes/panorama/4647211.stm [accessed 5 October 2013].

212   Michael Abramowitz, "U.S. promises on Darfur don't match actions. Bush expresses passion for issue, but policies have been inconsistent," Washington Post, 29 October 2007.

Theriault noted more generally how the increasing call for "critical thinking" and "the other side of the story" could actually lead to a form of denial in cases of clear one-sided violence.[213] There is a tendency among scholars, journalists and decision-makers to always challenge the facts, whereby situations are always portrayed as complex and uncertain. This is, for example, visible in the reasoning of Prendergast: "I think when you're dealing with issues which are always complex, they're very easy to present in the media or for NGOs to present as extremely black-and-white, very clear-cut. They tend on the ground to be pretty complex."

5.5.3   Conflict Framed and Represented as a Humanitarian Crisis or Civil War

As was mentioned in the previous section, the underlying political dynamics of the conflict were initially not properly understood. There was an idea that the situation in Darfur could be addressed through the provision of humanitarian aid, without addressing the underlying (political) causes of crisis. This had two implications. Firstly, the humanitarian efforts, such as the funding for the Greater Darfur initiative, created the idea among third parties that they were seized of the matter and doing all they could. This was also observed by Egeland who noted rather critically that: "too often the world sends us, the band aid, and the world believes that we keep people alive and then they don't have to take a political and security action. This is wrong and that's why we are really tired of being that kind of a substitute for political and security action."[214] Secondly, the US State Department officials were rather content with viewing Darfur as a humanitarian crisis over the course of 2003 and the beginning of 2004, since this did not necessitate a confrontational response that would disturb the Naivasha negotiations.[215]

Another element that played a role was that the conflict in Darfur was at times treated more as an inevitable "civil war" or "recurrent tribal conflict"[216] which erupted as a result of centuries old (ethnic) hatred than top-down orchestrated atrocities by the Government of Sudan which would require

---

213   Theriault, H.C. (2013) "Denial of ongoing atrocities as a rationale for not attempting to prevent or intervene," *Impediments to the prevention and intervention of genocide*, by Totten, S. (ed.), New Brunswick, London: Transaction Publishers, pp. 58–59.

214   UK House of Commons, 2005, Volume I, p. 33.

215   Hamilton (2011a), p. 29.

216   Office of the RC/HC Sudan, Doc 5A, 15 September 2003, "Greater Darfur Special Initiative," available at http://www.mukeshkapila.org/book/sudan-archive.html [accessed 22 October 2013], p. 8.

immediate action.[217] Likewise, Snyder stated that many US officials of the State Department "were saying that this was just a standard African civil war," and not genocide or mass killing.[218] The latter was also visible in the statements of Prendergast as paraphrased by Kapila: "these people, have been fighting each other for a very long time, so what's new in all of this? It escalates, it de-escalates, and eventually they will fight each other to a standstill."[219]

By arguing in the abovementioned ways, the violence in Darfur is qualified as almost natural or unavoidable. For instance, Hilary Benn, UK Secretary of State for International Development, pointed to the "complex crisis with long history, difficult origins."[220] It is therefore not surprising that Prunier said: "For the world at large Darfur was and remained the quintessential 'African crisis': distant, esoteric, extremely violent, rooted in complex ethnic and historical factors which few understood."[221] The consequence of such views is that by describing the conflict in such terms, the urgency to act is diminished and third parties are relieved from any duty to act since there is little possibility of resolution.[222]

5.5.4   Why was the UN Secretariat so Cautious?

Even though high UN officials, including UN SG Annan, publicly acknowledged the tragedy in Darfur relatively early, there were hardly any initiatives taken by the SG to, for example, bring the issue of Darfur to the UNSC agenda. Annan himself chose to approach Darfur carefully and "subtly" also because he wanted to make sure the Naivasha negotiations would not fail.[223] Prunier likewise observed: "Annan tried to act without upsetting things, to scold without being threatening and to help without intruding too much. The result was that he appeared weak and irresolute."[224] Even though Annan – in his words – tried

---

217   Power, S. (2007 [2003]) *Problem from Hell: America and the Age of Genocide*. New York: Perennial, London: Flamingo, pp. 285, 373.

218   Snyder as quoted in Cockett (2010), p. 196.

219   Kapila (2013), p. 114.

220   BBC Panorama, 3 July 2005, Fergal Keane interview with Hilary Benn, available at http://news.bbc.co.uk/2/hi/programmes/panorama/4647195.stm [accessed 18 November 2013].

221   Prunier (2007), p. 124.

222   This was also noted by Piiparinen in relation to Rwanda (Piiparinen, T., 2010, *The transformation of UN conflict management. Producing images of genocide from Rwanda to Darfur and beyond*. London, New York: Routledge, p. 170).

223   Annan, K. (2012) *Interventions: A Life in War and Peace*. The Penguin Press HC, p. 124. This line is also put forward by DPA head Kieran Prendergast (PBS Frontline interview with Sir Kieran Prendergast, 29 June 2007). See also Cockett (2010), p. 198.

224   Prunier (2007), p. 142.

"to raise the level of the discussion and raise awareness to try and mobilise support and attention," he was, however, reluctant to come up with any proposals in the first year of the conflict.[225]

This section will examine why the UN SG (or the broader UN Secretariat) was so reluctant to come up with any concrete policy recommendations or to make use of its powers to introduce Sudan to the Security Council on the basis of Article 99 of the UN Charter.[226] In addition, why was there hardly any response to the early warnings from Kapila who felt a "growing sense of isolation" as a result of the "deafening silence," but also others like Egeland and Lubbers, within the UN system?[227]

Bureaucratic Culture and Inflexible Rules

A first explanation for the absence of any UN action or forward looking policy recommendations is the cautious bureaucratic culture within the UN Secretariat. The Secretariat was cautious and reluctant to come up with policy advice with respect to Darfur out of its own motion, because it also anticipated that UNSC members were not very willing to receive this.[228] Prendergast, for example, believed that the UN Secretariat was not able to push member states in the direction that Kapila proposed, and therefore should not even try.[229] The cautious approach of the Secretariat is also visible in its reluctance to draw up a strong and integrated mandate for Kapila's successor Pronk, as will be discussed further in Section 7.3.

The behaviour of the UN Secretariat and the UN SG can also be explained by reference to the fear that the SG's political capital would diminish when he is too "activistic" and strongly challenges the will of the members of the SC.

---

225 BBC Panorama, 3 July 2005, Fergal Keane's interview with Kofi Annan, available at http:// news.bbc.co.uk/2/hi/programmes/panorama/4647177.stm [accessed 18 November 2013]. See also MacKinnon (2010), p. 85. See also UK Ambassador Patey in Khartoum as paraphrased in Kapila (2013, p. 96).

226 CBC Radio, 16 May 2013, "As it happens," interview with Mukesh Kapila.

227 Note, however, that Kapila stated that the first clear expression by Annan only appeared at the end of March 2004, while Annan already voiced his concern in December 2003 (Kapila, 2013, pp. 119, 152).

228 MacKinnon (2010), p. 85. The idea that a Secretary-General does not use its power to introduce items to the Security Council agenda without Council member support is described in Karns, M.P. and Mingst, K.A. (2004) *International Organizations*, p. 118.

229 Kapila (2013), pp. 114, 187. In an interview Pronk stated that in general Secretary-Generals barely have had the political power to overrule UNSC member states on the agenda. This was valid even more so for Annan at that time (Authors' interview with Jan Pronk, 2 September 2013).

This bureaucratic calculation is, for example, visible in Prendergast's statement that the UN, after the affair with Iraq, cannot "waste [its] political capital on Darfur."[230] It is less risky or costly to ignore warnings or respond in a minimal way, because this diminishes the expectations of future action.[231] Such a cautious bureaucratic culture of minimising risks also seemed to exist with respect to the UN response to Darfur. It was feared that if the SG actively takes up the issue, this could lead to "more aggressive proposals for action from within the UN." This was not seen as desirable, especially at a time during which the UN was already overstretched.[232] The latter might explain why Kapila referred to the UN bureaucracy as a "massive, immovable steel and concrete wall."[233] He also referred to the "concerted conspiracy of silence," which means that the issue is downplayed all the time.[234] UN officials also tended to safeguard themselves against any personal "failure" by constantly ensuring that they have the approval from New York. When UN Special Envoy Tom Vraalsen briefed the diplomatic community of the situation in Darfur in July 2003, Kapila noted that he watered down the briefing. When asked about this, Vraalsen replied that he did not want to be more explicit "without first discussing it with New York."[235] Therefore, according to Kapila, Vraalsen's presentation was less blunt than it could have been. This discrepancy was also noted by UK ambassador William Patey.[236]

Another element from the organisational behaviour model is the inflexibility of rules and procedures. One issue which played a role with respect to Darfur was the strict interpretation of the mandate of the UN Resident Coordinator Kapila, which was only humanitarian. Kapila was being told by the UN headquarters that "this was a political issue, and that [his] mandate

---

230   Kapila (2013), p. 114.
231   This was also noted by Piiparinen in relation to the UN response to Rwanda (Piiparinen, 2010, p. 112).
232   MacKinnon (2010), p. 85. This might explain why any (early) military intervention was ruled out from the start. Kapila suggestion as to the deployment of peacekeepers was laughed away ("a pipe dream"), since Khartoum would never consent to it and UN is "massively overstretched." (Kapila, 2013, p. 187–188). For a further discussion of this issue, see Section 8.7.
233   Kapila (2013), p. 164.
234   Ibid., pp. 165, 217.
235   Ibid., p. 95. Kapila earlier noted that "Tom Vraalsen was far from the proving the great ally that I had hoped for," because Vraalsen preferred to be patient and have trust in the Sudanese government (Ibid., p. 77).
236   Ibid., p. 89–90.

was purely humanitarian."[237] He was urged to simply focus on getting aid into Sudan. UN DPA head Prendergast turned Kapila's warnings down and appeared annoyed that Kapila did not stick with his humanitarian tasks. Kapila paraphrased Prendergast: "You're straying way outside of your remit, which is what concerns me most. You're the resident and humanitarian coordinator for Sudan – that's your remit, and you need to stick to it."[238] The distinction is crucial since framing Darfur as a humanitarian problem actually downplayed the urgency for the UN Secretariat to inform the UNSC about Darfur.[239] The distinction also (partly) explains why Kapila's early memos lack urgency.

Kapila's Memos and His Authority

Another explanation for the timid UN response is that Kapila's initial "warnings" (until December 2003) contained a rather bureaucratic or diplomatic language and miss the sense of urgency demanded by the situation on the ground. The memos are mainly about the humanitarian issues and the problem of limited (humanitarian) access on the ground, and not so much about the violence instigated by government/*Janjaweed* as the main problem. This was also noted in an evaluation of DFID and UNICEF. The evaluation concluded that Darfur was only discussed at the end of August 2003 during the meetings of the UN country team headed by Kapila, but that it was still not seen as a priority. It further held that the minutes of these meetings "reflect a general lack of urgency until December 2003."[240] Prendergast also claimed that when he met Kapila in November 2003, he was not so explicit about the situation in Darfur and did not use the terms "ethnic cleansing."[241] As was discussed in Section 5.2.2, it was only at the end of November 2003 that a political solution and a political role for the UN was suggested by Kapila. The lack of urgency might have been affected by the difficulty of and the limited resources for collecting accurate information about the situation in Darfur (Section 5.3).

A textual analysis of the memos actually confirms the reading that Kapila did not communicate the severity of the conflict in an urgent way. One example of the lack of urgency is the Darfur update of 14 September 2003. This update only mentioned that "low intensity conflict is a likely scenario for the

---

237   Ibid., p. 70.

238   Kapila (2013), p. 187.

239   Cockett (2010), p. 194.

240   Joint UNICEF-DFID Evaluation of UNICEF preparedness and early response to the Darfur emergency, UNICEF, New York, March 2005, p. 37.

241   PBS Frontline interview with Kieran Prendergast, 29 June 2007.

future of Darfur."[242] Likewise, the introductory paragraph of the Greater Darfur Special Initiative of 15 September spoke about "this is a timely chance to consolidate a fragile peace."[243] Another example of the euphemistic framing of the situation in Darfur is the following paragraph of the latter document, which only mentioned the conflict related IDPs at the end, after discussing more common patterns of displacement:

> North Darfur: Successive drought, recurrent tribal conflict and deteriorating economic conditions are the major causes of human displacement in the state. The seasonal migration of men in search of farm and off-farm labour in farming schemes in North Darfur and large towns is common. In bad crop production years, the migration starts early and can include the women or whole family. There are approximately 110.000 IDPs in North Darfur, mainly as a result of recent conflict.[244]

This paragraph also emphasises the root causes of the conflict, which are more difficult to address, instead of the proximate causes.

As said, the initial memos were mainly about addressing the delivery of humanitarian aid, development aid and the "urgent human survival and welfare needs."[245] A "Darfur Humanitarian Needs Profile" from 29 November 2003 only referred to the "humanitarian emergency in Darfur" with policy recommendations focused on humanitarian efforts and food and health supplies. Only on pages 4–6 were there passing references to the atrocities committed: "In certain areas almost all villages have been completely looted and burnt causing displacement (...) Entire villages have been wiped out and hundreds of lives have been lost (...) A large proportion of the villages were burnt to the ground. As a result, 89 villages were destroyed."[246] By mentioning these atrocities only on pages 4-6, the memo downplayed the role of preventable manmade violence while emphasising the humanitarian aspects that can only be alleviated reactively.

---

242   Office of the RC/HC Sudan, Doc 4, 14 September 2003, "Darfur Update," available at http:// www.mukeshkapila.org/book/sudan-archive.html [accessed 22 October 2013].

243   Office of the RC/HC Sudan Doc 5A, "Greater Darfur Special Initiative," 15 September 2003, available at http://www.mukeshkapila.org/book/sudan-archive.html [accessed 22 October 2013], para. 1.

244   Ibid., p. 8.

245   Ibid., para. 1.

246   Office of the RC/HC Sudan, Doc 7, 29 November 2003, "Darfur Humanitarian Needs Profile," available at http://www.mukeshkapila.org/book/sudan-archive.html [accessed 22 October 2013], paras. 11, 16, 18.

The lack of urgency may explain why the highest levels within the UN did not accord the priority to Darfur that it deserved, with all the other issues, such as Afghanistan and Iraq, warranting attention. Prendergast, for example, wondered why "the humanitarians" in Sudan did not raise the issue in the Cabinet or in the Executive Committee on Peace and Security or in the Executive Committee on Humanitarian Affairs when they regarded Darfur as a "political crisis requiring political action."[247]

Another possible explanation as to why Kapila's warnings were not taken as seriously as they should have been by the UN system and also by officials from other countries, had the do with the status and authority of Kapila himself. Kapila was seen by officials from the UK Foreign Office as hysterical and a person who over-dramatises.[248] Kapila had incurred the hostility of UN staff and organisation inside and outside Sudan because of his anti-corruption agenda.[249] He was also regarded as "an irritant" by those who favoured a strategy of quiet diplomacy.[250] Cockett aptly observed: "Impatient, passionate, unorthodox, belligerent and clever, Kapila was no respecter of the byzantine, turf-obsessed bureaucracy of the UN (...) He was regarded by many knowledgeable and honourable people who worked with him in Khartoum as arrogant and hard to work with."[251] It was allegedly also because of his "imperious temperament" that Prendergast actually warned him that he would probably be fired.[252] Kapila described himself as an outsider to the UN system.[253] It is not unthinkable that because Kapila was not always taken seriously, his warnings suffered the same fate.[254] Kapila himself reported how Hawkesley-Smith, the key advisor on the UK Darfur policy of the Foreign Office responded to Kapila's warnings in January: "Look, Mukesh, old chap, don't you think you're over-dramatising things a little? You do have something of a reputation for exaggeration, and you're behaving close to hysterical at the moment, which is far from convenient."[255]

---

247 PBS Frontline interview with Kieran Prendergast, 29 June 2007.
248 Kapila (2013), p. 182.
249 Lubbers as referred to Bieckmann (2012), p. 176; Authors' interview with Adriaan Kooijmans, 16 September 2013.
250 UK House of Commons, 2005, Volume I, p. 28.
251 Cockett (2010), pp. 203–204.
252 Ibid., p. 204.
253 Kapila (2013), p. 19.
254 See also Cockett (2010), p. 204.
255 Kapila (2013), p. 183.

CHAPTER 6

First Actions and Increased Public Outcry
March 2004–May 2004

We will focus in this and the following chapters primarily on the actions of bystanders, and in particular on the way they attempted to respond to the crisis in Darfur, while taking into account their wider interest in Sudan and relations with other states and organisations. It should be noted that most of the fighting was quickly diminishing over 2004 although clashes and bombings still took place regularly. As was presented in Chapter 1, there is a certain mismatch between the developments in Darfur and how the situation is presented by policymakers, part of which can be explained by limited information on the extent of the fighting and real number of casualties in this period.

6.1   Situation in Darfur

In spite of the growing concern for Darfur and the recurrent articles seemingly regurgitating the same information (especially at the IRIN[1]), *Janjaweed* attacks again intensified at the beginning of March 2004. The terrifying image of hordes of "devils on horseback" was witnessed across Darfur with haunting frequency, and attacks over the course of 5 to 7 March reportedly involved the execution of 170 civilians, with gangs of up to 400 attacking single villages. In the subsequent days, more reports came of government bombings, with the *Janjaweed* lying in wait ready to burn what the bombs had missed, rape whoever remained alive and loot whatever was left over. The Guardian newspaper also brought attention to the growing ambitions of the *Janjaweed* in launching raids on refugee camps in Chad,[2] and though taking the lead on reporting the story in the UK, the newspaper was perhaps guilty of a degree of credulity. Indeed, its article suggested that Khartoum was no longer in control of the *Janjaweed* – a claim strongly contradicted by an earlier Amnesty International press release unequivocally stating that, "[t]his is not a situation where the

---

1   In the space of a week the IRIN ran stories with the headlines, "Sudan: One million at 'imminent risk' in Darfur, says US government" (3 March 2004), "Sudan: More violence reported in Darfur" (5 March 2004) and "Sudan: Militias ravage Darfur in gangs of Hundreds" (10 March 2004).
2   The Guardian, 18 March 2004, "Sudanese refugees flee killer militias."

central government has lost control. Men, women and children are being killed and villages are burnt and looted because the central government is allowing militia aligned to it to pursue what amounts to a strategy of forced displacement through the destruction of homes and livelihood..."[3] A report from the European Parliament delegation's visit to Darfur also recognized "that the militias have received financial, logistical and other support from Government authorities."[4]

The conflict had escalated over 12 months and what was left was crisis management and attempts to bring the parties to ceasefires. It was in these chaotic circumstances that international actors became politically active in Sudan and had to leave quiet diplomacy quickly for discussions on coercive methods.

By the end of March 2004, the humanitarian aid had been greatly expanded. The UN now had US$61 million in pledges for both Darfur and eastern Chad – a ten-fold increase from 4 months earlier, 49% of that from the US and 50% from European countries. No other countries except Japan, for 0.6%, had pledged or donated anything.[5] This situation would not change much over the year. Twelve months later another 15-fold increase in pledged funds (US$936.6 million), of which 90% came from the US, Canada and European countries.[6]

6.2 The 8 April N'Djamena Ceasefire

As was mentioned in the previous chapter, President Déby of Chad tried several times to mediate in the conflict during the course of 2003. In particular, there were attempts to negotiate ceasefires in September and November 2003. Further international involvement in Darfur especially increased in February 2004 when actors started to realise that "something had to be done."[7] There was

---

3   AI doc.: AFR 54/028/2004, 16 March 2004, "Sudan: Darfur – attacks against civilians ongoing."
4   EU Parliament doc.: Internal document 300769, 29 January 2004, see further discussion below.
5   Office of the RC/HC Sudan, 22 June 2003, "Conflict in Darfur region of Sudan – a briefing note," available at http://www.mukeshkapila.org/book/sudan-archive.html [accessed 22 October 2013].
6   UK House of Commons, International Development Committee, "Darfur, Sudan: The responsibility to protect" Fifth Report of Session 2004–05, Volume II Oral and Written Statements, p. ev. 92–93 (hereafter UK House of Commons, 2005, Volume II). This excludes the private funds (5.8%), which likely also originate from the main donor countries.
7   Slim, H. (2004) "Dithering over Darfur? A preliminary review of the international response," *International Affairs*, Vol.: 80(5), p. 816. Prunier also referred to the spring of 2004 that the international community started to take the situation in Darfur seriously (Prunier, G., 2007, *Darfur: An ambiguous genocide. Revised and updated edition 2007*. London: C. Hurst & Co., publishers, ltd., p. 90).

an unsuccessful attempt to restart mediation talks in Geneva in February 2004. By March 2004, the international community had become increasingly engaged with the situation in Darfur and a resumption of talks was eventually decided to take place in N'Djamena under the auspices of Déby and assisted by the Chair of the AU, Baba Gana Kingibe.[8] Lacking success, and since Déby's impartiality was questioned, the AU obtained a more central position in the negotiations with the rebels and the Sudanese government, even though the mediation rounds were still to taking place in Chad.[9]

Western governments were supportive of the rounds, firstly by being present as "international facilitators," and quickly by offering financial support and pressuring the government and rebel groups to accept compromises. France was especially eager to have the talks take place in Chad.[10] Once the UK and US had decided to forgo the option of bringing the situation to the UN Security Council, their ambassadors in Khartoum and Chad became active in trying to set up a ceasefire conference, which was the first time that the western countries became more involved at the political front. The US, particularly through USAID, was active in working towards such talks, as was Tom Vraalsen in liaison with UN DPA in New York.[11] Initially each of these parties was working on its own channels without much coordination between them. Moreover, the preparations were hampered by Sudanese military and secret service obstructions.[12] As discussed in the previous chapter, during January, February and the preparation for the ceasefire talks, the government and *Janjaweed* undertook large offensive operations with the aim quashing the rebellion.

Once the talks were certain to take place by the end of March, the different international parties started to coordinate as well. Specifically, US diplomats discussed the upcoming mediation rounds with EU counterparts in Brussels. Their strategy was to focus the first talks squarely on a humanitarian ceasefire, without including political demands in these talks. The European Commission was involved offering financial means to the Geneva based NGO Centre for Humanitarian Dialogue (CHD), which had its own connections with the Darfuri

8   Slim (2004), p. 816.

9   Badescu, C. and Bergholm, L. (2010) "The African Union," in *The International politics of mass atrocities. The case of Darfur*, by Black, D.R. and Williams, P.D. (eds.), London, New York: Routledge.

10   The Dutch were reluctant towards a mediating role of Déby (Jean-Christophe Belliard who coordinated the French Darfur policy as quoted in Bieckmann, F., 2012, *Soedan. Het sinistere spel om macht, rijkdom en olie*. Amsterdam: Balans, p. 267–268).

11   US State Department Cable, Brussels, 25 March 2004, No. 1174; Authors' interview with Jan Egeland, 28 November 2012.

12   Authors' interview with Adriaan Kooijmans, 16 September 2013.

rebels and the Sudanese government. Official EU representation on the ground came from French diplomats in Chad and Dutch diplomats from Sudan.[13] The US delegation consisted of officials from State Department and USAID.[14]

Despite the preparations, negotiations were problematic. The different tracks that were followed to pressure the government and rebels into the talks did not lead to full information sharing and a common strategy among the international parties. For instance, the EU appointed two chairpersons: the Dutch, who were the local EU presidency in Khartoum, and the French, as the presidency *sur place* in N'djamena.[15] The US delegation internally had no common position or strategy as delegates of USAID had a much less compromising view towards Khartoum than their State Department colleagues.[16] The NGO Centre for Humanitarian Dialogue was in close discussions with the US in the talks, while it had given the impression that the talks were an EU initiative.[17] The Sudanese government was initially against the participation of international observers in the talks, and did not want to speak directly to the rebel groups, but gave in after some further pressure.[18] In Brussels, a US proposal for a joint EU-US public statement was dismissed by an Irish Foreign Affairs official representing the EU Presidency.[19] This American proposal for a public statement was made a few days after Kapila's radio interview, discussed below. It would appear therefore that the US wanted to use the sudden surge of media attention to the benefit of constructing a common public position of western governments.

As the talks in N'Djamena were going on during the last week of March and the first week of April, there was a large increase in diplomatic activity

---

13   Authors' interview with Christian Manahl, 26 August 2013. Manahl stated that the mediation was a EU Commission initiative after which other international parties jumped on the bandwagon. Although the EU Commission financed the talks, State parties and the UN were already planning the meeting for some time.

14   US State Department Cable, Brussels, 19 March 2004, No. 1151; Authors' interview with Adriaan Kooijmans, 16 September 2013.

15   Archive Ministry of Foreign Affairs in the Netherlands: DAF/2015/00646, Period December 2003–June 2004.

16   Authors' interviews with Adriaan Kooijmans, 16 September 2004; The hard line view of USAID was also observed by Kieran Prendergast, who links it to the suspicion in Khartoum of US' ulterior motives for their role in Darfur (PBS Frontline interview with Sir Kieran Prendergast, 29 June 2007).

17   Authors' interviews with Adriaan Kooijmans, 16 September 2004; Christian Manahl, 26 August 2013.

18   Toga, D. (2007) "The African Union mediation and the Abuja peace talks," in *War in Darfur and the search for peace*, by de Waal, A., (ed.), Global Equity Initiative, Harvard University, p. 216.

19   US State Department Cable, Brussel, 25 March 2004, No. 1174.

regarding Darfur as well as an increasing public outcry. On 2 April, the UNSC issued a statement expressing "deep concern" on the situation in Darfur after a briefing by the OCHA head Jan Egeland.[20] A day later the UN issued a statement on behalf of UNSG Annan and the heads of all UN agencies, bodies and funds expressing their concern over Darfur.[21] Annan had pressured President al-Bashir on the ceasefire and humanitarian access just days before in a private telephone call.[22] A UN fact-finding mission, set up by acting High Commissioner for Human Rights Ramcharan, started its mission in Chad.[23] US President Bush issued a statement expressing concern on Darfur.[24] At the same time, "leading members of the US administration" expressed their concern to the Sudanese leadership over telephone calls and applied firm political pressure.[25] It is likely that at least some of these actions were an attempt by those international parties to put pressure on Sudan and convince the rebels that they now had international support and could start talks. Vice-President Taha reportedly ordered his delegation to sign the agreement in order to release some of the pressure that was building on the government.[26]

The increase in public outcry, on top of the statements from the US government and the UNSG, helped to further highlight the seriousness of the situation.[27] For instance, eight UN Human Rights experts expressed their concerns for the situation on 26 March, recommending accountability for perpetrators "in conformity with international standards."[28] On 31 March, the European

---

20 UN Doc.: SC/8050 AFR/883, 2 April 2004, further discussed below.

21 UN News, 3 April 2004, "Sudan: UN officials urge end to human rights abuses in Darfur."

22 Annan, K. (2012) *Interventions: A Life in War and Peace*. The Penguin Press HC, p. 122–123.

23 UN News, 6 April 2004, "Sudan: UN human rights fact-finding team begins work as conditions worsen."

24 US White House press office, 7 April 2004, "President Condemns Atrocities in Sudan," available at archived website http://georgewbush-whitehouse.archives.gov/news/releases/2004/04/20040407-2.html [accessed 13 June 2013]. At the same time, "leading members of the US administration" might have sought direct contact with Sudanese leadership conveying their concern (Slim, 2004, p. 825).

25 Slim (2004), p. 825; Authors' interview with Adriaan Kooijmans, 16 September 2013; US State Department cable, Washington D.C., 3 July 2004, No. 145183, available at: http://www2.gwu.edu/~nsarchiv/NSAEBB/NSAEBB335/Document3.PDF [accessed 2 December 2014].

26 Hamilton, R. (2011a) *Fighting for Darfur: public action and the struggle to stop genocide*. New York: Palgrave Macmillan, p. 33.

27 See further below.

28 UN Press Release, AFR/873 HR/CN/1065, 29 March 2004. The eight experts are Theo van Boven, Yakin Ertürk, Doudou Diène, Paul Hunt, Asma Hahngir, Juan Miguel Petit, Jean Ziegler, Francis Deng.

Parliament issued a resolution regarding Sudan, with particular concern for Darfur.[29] Official European actors, apart from the Parliament, demonstrated remarkably less public activity at this moment.

An agreement was signed on 8 April.[30] The ceasefire agreement foresaw a joint monitoring "ceasefire commission" and future talks on political issues. The agreement appeared possible because the Government of Sudan thought it had gained the upper hand in Darfur, while the rebels found recognition of their cause with international actors. However, a strong commitment from the warring parties was lacking. Meant to last for repeated 45-day periods, the ceasefire was allegedly broken within hours.[31] A formal break of the agreement came when the Sudanese government announced that delegations went beyond their mandate even though President al-Bashir had had contact with AU Chairperson Konaré on 6 April endorsing the ceasefire.[32] There were also two versions of the agreement. The Sudanese government had allegedly written some additional terms on their own copy, presenting it as the only true one.[33]

6.2.1 Start of the AU Observer Mission AMIS

From early on UN, EU and US officials were aware of the necessity of some form of observer mission in case a ceasefire was agreed. Such a mission had already been, proposed by Kapila and also was advised by the diplomatic missions in Khartoum by the end of 2003 (e.g. see Section 5.2.2). In March 2004, during the preparation for the ceasefire mediation there were discussions on implementation and monitoring between EU officials and US diplomats. These discussions included the option of using international military and civilian staff, which were already available in Sudan monitoring a ceasefire with the SPLM, who would have been able to start up such a mission. However, none of these early discussions led to actual preparations that could have sped up deployment once the ceasefire was signed.

The N'Djamena ceasefire agreement of 8 April established a ceasefire monitoring commission, consisting of representatives of all parties of the agreements. The UN was not willing to be responsible for or get involved in the monitoring of the ceasefire.[34] It was the AU Peace and Security Council which

---

29   EU Parliament Doc.: P5_TA(2004)0225, 31 March 2004, "Resolution on Darfur/Sudan."

30   The text of the ceasefire of 8 April 2004 is available at http://www.sudanembassy.ca/Docs/darfur_humanitarian_ceasefire_agreement.pdf [accessed 13 June 2013].

31   Prunier (2007), p. 114.

32   Totten and Markussen (2006), p. 15; Toga (2007) in de Waal, p. 216.

33   Toga (2007) in de Waal, p. 217.

34   Authors' interview with Adriaan Kooijmans, 16 September 2013.

quickly endorsed both the ceasefire and the monitoring commission.[35] The mission was called the African Union Mission in Sudan (AMIS). The EU was directly involved in the ceasefire commission by becoming vice-chair under the AU, and would contribute observers and planners from its member states.[36] However, a month after the ceasefire was signed, the EU was still in discussions with the AU on how to deploy monitors and which resources would be necessary, including the organisation of protection for the observers,[37] while an AU reconnaissance mission was still looking into these aspects at the end of May.[38]

6.3   Increased Public Outcry

As the talks in N'Djamena were ongoing the Darfur unrest became more widely covered in public media. The talks were not covered directly in the media, but coincidently the new public outcry probably added to the pressure that was already put on the Sudanese government to stop its military operations and rein in the *Janjaweed*.

6.3.1   *Kapila's "Whistleblowing" and SG Annan's Response*
Kapila, dissatisfied with the continuing lack of outcry over Darfur, and in his eyes a wrong analysis of the peace negotiations in the south, decided – in his own words – to "blow the whistle."[39] Convinced that he had tried all possible channels to request the attention that Darfur deserved, he arranged an interview with the BBC.[40] He had heard that Prime Minister Tony Blair listened to the morning broadcast.[41] In this interview he drew a picture of a full-blown crisis situation with mass human rights violations.[42] Following the broadcast

---

35   AU Doc.: PSC/PR/Comm. V, 13 April 2004.

36   US State Department Cable, Brussels, 4 June 2013, No. 2410.

37   US State Department Cable, Brussels, 3 May 2013, No. 1897.

38   AU Doc.: PSC/AHG/Comm. X, 25 May 2004.

39   Another reason was that he was already dismissed by UNDP, and therefore had nothing more to loose from going public. See his book for his considerations (Kapila, M., 2013, *Against a tide of evil*. Edinburg: Mainstream Publishing).

40   Kapila (2013), p. 217.

41   Traub states the interview too place for the 8.00am live broadcast on 21 March 2004, according to the BBC the interview is at 6h47 on 19 March 2004, see below (Traub, J., 2006, *The Best Intentions: Kofi Annan and the UN in the Era of American World Power*. New York: Farrar, Straus and Giroux, p. 219).

42   BBC Radio 4 Today Program, 19 March 2004 – (6h47) in the 2½ minute interview he managed to put in the following: "*Janjaweed* allied with the government," "worst crises of the

he received immediate response from other media outlets, but there was none directly from the UN. After the interview, he sent another memo to Iqbal Riza (staff chef of Annan), with a copy to Mark Malloch Brown (UNDP) and Kieran Prendergast (DPA), and others, in which he stated that he considered the situation in Darfur "ethnic cleansing." In this note he asked the UN Secretariat to become involved. Concretely he recommended (again) an internationally monitored ceasefire, a humanitarian briefing to the Security Council, to "develop a position as and when there are calls made by other in the international community for the perpetrators of the ethnic cleansing policy to be brought to justice – in line with similar recent accountability efforts in other situations." Furthermore, he repeated his assertion of the radio interview, writing: "[There is concern] that the situation in Darfur is reminiscent of the earlier period of the crisis in Rwanda, which ultimately progressed to genocide because of lack of timely recognition of the problem and action by the international community."[43]

Although not heard on the radio, the BBC website also stated that Kapila compared the situation in Darfur with the Rwandan genocide, which happened to be commemorated only a few weeks later at a ten year memorial.[44] There was an indirect response from the UN; the speechwriter for Kofi Annan, Edward Mortimer, "rewrote the address" for the Rwanda anniversary.[45] In his speech at the Rwanda commemoration in Geneva, Annan addressed the situation of Darfur expressing his "deep sense of foreboding."[46] He even held: "If that [humanitarian assistance] is denied, the international community must be prepared to take swift and appropriate action. By 'action' in such situations I mean a continuum of steps, which may include military action. But the latter should always be seen as an extreme measure, to be used only in extreme cases."[47]

---

world today," "systematic scorched-earth," "systemized rape," "loot," "torture," "close to ethnic cleansing," "this is ethnic cleansing, this is the world's worst humanitarian crisis, and I don't understand why the world isn't doing more about it."

43   Office of the RC/HC Sudan, RCHC/SUD/Note 39, 22 March 2003, "Note to Mr. Riza – Sudan: Ethnic Cleansing in Darfur," available at http://www.mukeshkapila.org/book/sudan-archive.html [accessed 22 October 2013].

44   BBC news, 19 March 2004, "Mass rape atrocity in west Sudan."

45   Traub (2006), p. 219–220.

46   UN Press Release, SG/SM/9245 AFR/893 HR/CN/1077, 7 April 2004, "Secretary-General Kofi Annan speech to the Commission on Human Rights in Geneva," available at http://www.un.org/News/Press/docs/2004/sgsm9245.doc.htm [accessed 21 August 2013].

47   Idem.

By doing this Kofi Annan probably went against his political advisor Prendergast, who was not happy with the methods and strong words used by Kapila in his radio interview, as well as statements by Annan and Egeland (see also the previous chapter). On Kapila's methods Kieran Prendergast says: "I was very surprised when Mukesh rent his garments. What's he been doing the rest of the time?"[48] Some days later Egeland was allowed to brief the Security Council on Darfur. On this briefing Prendergast says: "By the absence of diplomacy and by the use of very emotive terms, we almost guaranteed failure," and a "great disservice" was done by those that convinced Annan to "make reference to the possibility of military action.[49]

Although Kapila might have felt that nothing was being done for Darfur, we have seen that Western embassies in Khartoum and Chad as well as the capitals tried to become more involved, albeit not too publicly. From different sides, including the UN Secretariat, there were contacts with the government and rebels to set up a ceasefire conference. But since Kapila did not have a political mandate, and his position was under pressure, he was not involved in these developments. This isolation in turn contributed to his sense of helplessness that made him choose to go to the international media. Once the story is out, western countries generally but slowly become more outspoken on the issue and also change policy.

6.3.2   *Increased Media Attention*
Some have noted that New York Times columnist Nicholas Kristof had been crucial to further drive the topic among diplomats and the wider media.[50] Kristof's first opinion article was published on 24 March.[51] Jack Christofides, a UN DPA official, held: "When we were in Khartoum, after reading a Nicholas Kristof article in the New York Times we could set our stopwatches to see how long it would take New York to do something."[52] Other media followed suit, especially in the beginning of April when the tenth anniversary of the Rwandan genocide was commemorated.

---

48   Traub (2006), p. 219.
49   PBS Frontline interview with Sir Kieran Prendergast, 29 June 2007.
50   Authors interview with Olivier Ulich, 1 June 2005.
51   Nicholas Kristof, "Ethnic cleansing, again," *New York Times*, 24 March 2004, p. 21. "Will we say never again, again?," *New York Times*, 27 March 2004, p. 15.
52   Christofides as quoted in Cockett, R. (2010) *Sudan: Darfur and the Failure of an African State*. New Haven: Yale University Press, p. 216.

6.3.3 *European Parliament Resolution of 31 March 2004*

A delegation from the European Parliament Committee on Development and Cooperation, led by the British PPE[53] member John Corry had visited Sudan and Darfur from 19 to 24 February. The delegation had met with government representatives, including President al-Bashir, as well as representative NGOs and representatives of opposition parties in of the parliament.[54] Among the members of the delegation the British were most concerned about Darfur and addressed the issue during their meetings with Sudanese officials.[55]

The committee wrote a report and drafted a resolution for the European Parliament. The resolution stated that the Sudanese government was complicit in the attacks of the *Janjaweed* and "systematically [delayed] and obstructs" humanitarian aid. It explicitly called for a UN monitored no-fly zone over Darfur.[56] Interestingly, the delegation's report does not mention a no-fly zone as a recommendation or otherwise,[57] but Mukesh Kapila notes that he was consulted over the resolution during his last days in Khartoum.[58] The resolution explicitly referred to his recent radio statement.

The European Parliament had no real power to establish a no-fly zone. However, it is remarkable that they made this public proposal based on real knowledge from their own visit and concern for the situation in Darfur. A real no-fly zone would never be established but would become a recurring policy option that was discussed among western governments.

6.4 UN Commission on Human Rights

The US and European countries planned to adopt a resolution on Sudan during the 60th session of the UN Commission of Human Rights (CHR) in April, with a special reference to Darfur. The plan was already discussed with EU officials in March, where the US had indicated that it wanted a stronger resolution than what the EU officials deemed possible to adopt in the CHR.[59] Indeed, an EU

---

53   European Peoples Party.

54   EU Parliament Doc.: Internal document 300769, 29 January 2004.

55   Authors' interview with Cees Bremmer, 28 August 2013.

56   EU Parliament Doc.: P5_TA(2004)0225, 31 March 2004, "Resolution on Darfur/Sudan."

57   European Parliament, Committee on Development and Cooperation, 15 March 2004, "Report of the ad hoc delegation of the Committee on Development and Cooperation on its mission to Sudan from 19 to 24 February 2004."

58   Kapila (2013), p. 243.

59   US State Department Cable, Brussels, 25 March 2004, No. 1151.

draft resolution was weakened in the negotiations with African countries. During the sessions the US tried to add extra paragraphs, sourced from the earlier EU draft. These paragraphs would condemn directly the *Janjaweed* militia's attacks on the African tribes in Darfur, and call upon the Sudanese government to protect its citizens. The US pushed for a vote to include each of these paragraphs in the resolution. They had European support, but the proposals were subsequently rejected due to overwhelming African and other non-western opposition.[60] The resolution that was adopted referred neither to the *Janjaweed* nor to the scale and severity of the conflict and its ethnic dimensions.[61] The US was the only country voting against the final resolution, while Sudan voted in favour. The resolution also installed an independent expert to report on the situation of human rights in Sudan to the UN general Assembly and the next years' Commission of Human rights session.

The divergence between the EU and US was later discussed among diplomats. The US wanted a more outspoken approach to exert more pressure on Sudan even if the cost would be to have no resolution at all. Whereas the EU aimed at having broader support, in particular from African states, in order to move Sudan.[62] That is why for instance in the Netherlands, which was at the time acting as EU Presidency in Sudan, the resolution was still seen as a success. In the words of the Dutch Foreign Minister Bot, African countries are usually rather hesitant to adopt any resolution that is critical towards one of their own. The watering down of the resolution was a necessary part of the bargaining to get it adopted.[63] Human Rights Watch called it a failure of the CHR to not condemn the actions of Sudanese government in Sudan. It concluded that Sudan had African and Arab states sufficiently on its side to make the EU back down from its initially stronger draft resolution.[64] However, not only African

60   UN Doc. E/CN.4/2004/SR.61, 9 December 2005, "Commission of Human Rights, 60th session, summary record of the 61st meeting on 23 April 2004."

61   UN Doc. E/CN.4/2004/128, 23 April 2004, "Situation of human rights in the Sudan." One criticism on the N'Djamena 8 April humanitarian cease-fire is that the Sudanese Government managed to keep the *Janjaweed* out of the agreement, referring only to "neutralizing the armed militias [under their control]." The same formulation is used in CHR resolution.

62   US State Department Cable, Brussels, 3 May 2004, No. 1897. The outspoken US position is also note in the literature, e.g. Totten and Markussen (2006, pp. 116–117) and Hamilton (2011a, p. 35).

63   Dutch Parliamentary Doc.: Tweede Kamer, 2003–2004, Aanhangsel 1613, question 26 April 2004, reply 26 may 2004; Aanhangsel 1620, question 29 April 2004, reply 26 May 2004.

64   Human Rights Watch, No. 16, 5a, "Darfur in flames: atrocities in western Sudan," 15 April 2004.

and Arab states were against the condemning draft resolution. Also Russia, China and the Southeast Asian countries Pakistan, India, and Indonesia voted in line with Sudan.[65]

One of the defences that were put forward by the African group against a stronger resolution was that an investigative team sent by Acting High Commissioner for Human Rights Ramcharan was still in Darfur and hence had not yet issued a report.[66] However, there was already a report, one based on a previous visit to refugees from Darfur in Chad. The Sudanese government had only allowed a UNHCR team to enter Darfur after it had seen this earlier report on 20 April, making sure that Ramcharan would not issue this report officially and hence it could not discussed in the Commission.[67]

6.5 Route to the Security Council

The pressure to discuss the situation in Darfur in the Security Council increased as well. At a UN Donors Principal Meeting on 4 March it was put forward that the UNSC should now discuss the issue and that the SG of the UN should at least give the same message as High Commissioner Lubbers who spoke about "atrocities." Anyhow, the representatives concluded that the Government of Sudan was not responsive to the international pressure to allow access for humanitarian assistance. Moreover, because the government of Sudan did not stop the ethnic cleansing activities of the *Janjaweed* the international pressure should be enhanced.[68]

As discussed in the previous chapter, Mukesh Kapila and Jan Egeland tried several times to have Darfur adopted on the agenda of the Security Council. Some countries supported them, but others were fiercely against. Egeland

---

65 A further moralistic narrative in the UN from the side of the US was hampered when images of US torture and prisoners' mistreatment at the Iraqi prison Abu Graib were published. The event caused the US to lose international credibility on human rights issues and allowed Sudan to counter US criticism on Darfur (Hamilton, 2011a, p. 35).

66 UN Doc. E/CN.4/2004/SR.61, 9 December 2005, "Commission of Human Rights, 60th session, summary record of the 61st meeting on 23 April 2004," p. 2, statement by Mr. Menga (Congo).

67 Ramcharan, B., (2005) *A un High Commission in defence of human rights*. Leiden, Boston: Martinus Nijhuff Publishers, p.14–16.

68 Archive Ministry of Foreign Affairs in the Netherlands, DAF/2010/00185, Period 2003–2004.

asserts that it is the Pakistani delegation that withheld its support and therefore he had to wait for the German Presidency before the conflict would be discussed in the Security Council.[69] However, this cannot be correct since Pakistan would have the UNSC presidency after Germany.[70] According to the German UN ambassador Pleuger, most resistance to start discussions in the Council actually came from the US, aided by the UK, and China. He attributes their opposition to the interests they have in collaboration with the Sudanese government (in particular US' interest in intelligence on Islamic terrorists) and oil interests (China). The UK instead served mainly to hide the US' interests in blocking the Council's involvement in Darfur. According to the German UNSC Representative, the US let the UK voice its (public) concerns so that it could remain silent itself. Thus, the UK simply followed the US' line.[71] Germany and France allegedly worked closely together on the Council in this period, where the German UN Ambassador even speaks of an *Alliance Franco-Allemande*.[72] Hence, before Germany, France had the Security Council presidency, but it was unable to overcome their opposition. Therefore, the following month Germany took a different approach. It invited Jan Egeland to brief the Council on humanitarian situations in Africa, knowing that Egeland would take the opportunity to address Darfur.[73] Egeland noted the lateness of his address: "I regret that we couldn't get it on the Council's agenda at least two months earlier. If we

---

69   Egeland, J. (2010) *A Billion Lives: An Eyewitness Report from the Frontlines of Humanity.* New York: Simon & Schuster, p. 90; Authors' interview with Jan Egeland, 28 November 2012; Traub (2006, p. 215) mentions the same, without citing Egeland, and repeats it in an interview for PBS Frontline (conducted 13 September 2007). Kofi Annan makes the same claim (Annan, 2012, p. 125) as does Hamilton (2011a, p. 34) citing Jan Egeland.

70   The sequence of UNSC Presidency is the following, starting in October 2003 to November 2004, USA (October), Angola (November), Bulgaria (December), Chile (January), China (February), France (March), Germany (April), Pakistan (May), Philipines (June), Romania (July), Russia (August), Spain (September), UK (October), USA (November), according to the website of the UN Security Council, http://www.un.org/en/sc/.

71   Authors' interview with Pleuger, 5 November 2013. By contrast, according to Cockett, the UK was more inflexible and less nuanced than the US, who *appeared* at least more willing to consider action (Cockett, 2010, pp. 195–196).

72   Authors' interview with Gunter Pleuger, 19 October 2010; telephone call to authors, 5 November 2013. This ambassador's account of a close relationship with France and in opposition to the US and UK could probably be explained partly by the issue of Iraq.

73   Authors' interview with Gunter Pleuger, 19 October 2010; telephone call to authors, 5 November 2013.

had gotten it earlier on the agenda we might have gotten access earlier, we might, and if we had gotten access earlier we would have saved a lot of lives."[74]

And so Egeland was able to give a dramatic depiction of the situation in Darfur on 2 April 2004. After the meeting towards the press, he accused the Sudanese government of aiding the *Janjaweed* in their "scorched earth" tactics and "ethnic cleansing".[75] However, still facing the same opposition from China, the US and the UK, Germany could not have the Council adopt a Presidential Statement let alone a Resolution. It indicated after the briefing to the other Council members that it would make a statement to the press as Council President, and only broadly indicated the points it would address in the statement. Even though other members could overrule the president, this is extremely rare. Therefore, Germany was free to issue its own statement, in which it expressed a "deep concern" of the situation.[76] Nevertheless, this press statement is considered "extremely weak."[77] Although the weakest instrument, it was the strongest measure available at that point. The most important thing was that Egeland's briefing had as a consequence that Darfur could become its own agenda item.[78]

The pressure to discuss Darfur in the SC not only as a humanitarian crisis but as a massive violation of human rights was put forward by Human Rights Watch on May 3.[79] In May, during the Pakistani Presidency, the Security Council discussed Darfur informally. Firstly, on 7 May, under consultations for "other matters," the Council was briefed by Ramcharan, who by this time had a new report finished based on an investigation in Darfur.[80] On 24 May, Germany took the initiative to arrange a so-called 'arria-meeting' for Darfur, where the Security Council met with NGOs.[81] This detour from 'other matters' towards becoming an agenda item by itself was a "trick" necessary to overcome the resistance of

74   BBC Panorama, 3 July 2005, "Never again programme transcript," available at http://news
        .bbc.co.uk/2/hi/programmes/panorama/4654093.stm [accessed 18 November 2013].

75   UN IRIN interview with Jan Egeland, 2 April 2004, available at http://www.irinnews.org/
        report.aspx?reportid=49400 [accessed 21 August 2013].

76   UN Doc.: SC/8050 AFR/883, 2 April 2004.

77   Authors' interview with Olivier Ulich, 1 June 2005; Jan Egeland, 28 November 2012.

78   Authors' interview with Gunter Pleuger, 19 October 2010; telephone call to authors, 5
        November 2013.

79   Archive Ministry of Foreign Affairs in the Netherlands, DAF/2010/00185, Period
        2003–2004.

80   Ramcharan (2005), p.16; UN Doc.: S/2004/614, 10 August 2004.

81   UN Doc.: S/2004/614, 10 August 2004.

those Security Council members that wanted to keep Darfur out of it.[82] This combination of briefings then led to a Presidential Statement on 25 May.

6.6   First Security Council Action

6.6.1   *Security Council Statement of 25 May*
Under the Pakistani Presidency, the Security Council Presidential Statement of 25 May was clear.[83] The Council

> expresses its grave concern over the deteriorating humanitarian and human rights situation in the Darfur region of Sudan. Noting that thousands have been killed and that hundreds of thousands of people are at risk of dying in the coming months

It abstained from explicitly mentioning the perpetrators of the violence in Darfur by saying it

> [strongly condemns] indiscriminate attacks on civilians, sexual violence, forced displacement and acts of violence, especially those with an ethnic dimension (…), stresses that all parties to the N'djamena humanitarian ceasefire agreement committed themselves to refraining from any act of violence (…) against civilian populations, in particular women and children, and that the Government of Sudan also committed itself to neutralizing the armed *janjaweed* militias urges all parties to take necessary steps to put an end to violations of human rights and international humanitarian law.

The Presidential Statement continued by insisting on access for humanitarian workers, observing the ceasefire and disarmament of the *Janjaweed*. This is interesting since the government of Sudan managed to keep *"Janjaweed"* out of the 8 April ceasefire agreement and the CHR resolution. Furthermore, the Presidential Statement also referred to the recommendations of the High Commissioner for Human Rights in his report. One of these recommendations included the establishment of an international Commission of Inquiry.[84]

---

82   Authors' interview with Chris Coleman, 24 May 2005.

83   UN Doc.: S/PRST/2005/18, 26 May 2004.

84   UN Doc.: E/CN.4/2005/3, 7 May 2004. The international commission of inquiry is recommend in paragraph 104.

The Council further acknowledged the role played by the African Union in the ceasefire agreement and encouraged member states' support for the observer mission. As a measure to start addressing the crisis the Security Council itself demanded an

> immediate appointment and appropriate accreditation of a permanent Resident Coordinator/Humanitarian Coordinator to ensure daily coordination in order to address impediments to humanitarian access brought to the UN's attention by the international aid community.

The statement closed with an acknowledgement of the severity of the crisis as it

> requests that the Secretary-General keep it informed on the humanitarian and human rights crisis as it unfolds, and, as necessary, to make recommendations.

There were mixed reactions to this statement. On the one hand the statement was detailed and strong. On the other hand, besides the timing – which was rather late – the Security Council endorsed the leading role of the African Union while there were doubts that it may not be able to fulfil this role adequately.[85]

The invitation for the Secretary-General to make recommendations stood in contrast with the lack of UN Secretariat initiatives described in the previous chapter. However, Annan was slowly becoming more involved. Starting with the Rwandan commemoration discussed above, in a personal communication he urged the Sudanese government to find a political solution and offered to mediate himself.[86]

Taken together with preceding events, one may deduce that the US and UK were still against strong Security Council involvement by April. Their decision in the fall of 2003 to treat Darfur under the radar was still maintained, but slowly policy was changing. As more information on the situation in Darfur became public and as the story was being framed in the context of Rwanda, some western countries, in particular the US and the UK, changed policy to be more in line with their domestic audiences. A stronger US position in the

---

85 Authors' interview with Olivier Ulich, 1 June 2005.

86 UN News, 13 May 2004, "Annan writes Sudanese President Urging disarmament of militias"; UN Darfur time line, available at http://www.un.org/News/dh/dev/scripts/darfur_formatted.htm [accessed 19 June 2013].

Commission of Human Rights might have been one indication, except that the US was pushing for a resolution everyone knew was unable to be adopted. The US also took the lead in drafting the Presidential Statement.[87] Once the situation was on the agenda of the Security Council, discussions quickly resolved around sanctions, with the US and UK as two of the most vocal proponents. This change of attitude may not have been completely sincere on their part, since they had been well aware of the situation for many months; really it was an opportunistic sway for domestic political purposes.[88]

6.6.2   UN *without Leadership in Sudan*
The request for the appointment of a UN Resident Coordinator hinted at an intriguing affair between the UN Secretariat and the Sudanese government. Kapila was implicitly forced out of his function because the UN no longer supported him for his anti-corruption measures applied to UN programmes in Khartoum, and for being too vocal on Darfur. During his visit to New York in January, his boss at UNDP Mark Malloch Brown, had made clear that he was to be replaced.[89] Since he had spoken out on Darfur on BBC radio he expected that the Sudanese government would quickly declare him *persona non grata*, and made his own decision to leave on 31 March.

One year later, when asked by a UK House of Commons subcommittee, Secretary of State for International Development Hilary Benn acted like he did not know why Kapila had to leave.[90] He reported back to the subcommittee, writing that the UN had explained him that Kapila was replaced according to normal proceedings as the signing of the North–South peace agreement foresaw a new UN team coming in.[91]

During three months that were critical for the development of an international response towards Darfur – until the appointment of Jan Pronk as UN Secretary-General Special Representative for Sudan in July – the UN office in Khartoum was without leadership. Temporarily, another Dutchman, Eric de Mul (from UNDP), was put in charge of operations.[92] As the departure of Kapila was

---

87   Igiri, C.O. and Lyman, P.N. (2004) "Giving meaning to 'Never again'. Seeking an Effective Response to the Crisis in Darfur and Beyond." Council on Foreign Relations No. 5, 5 September 2004, p. 12.

88   Seymour, L.J.M. (2013) "Let's Bulshit! Arguing bargaining and dissembling over Darfur." *European Journal of International Relations*, forthcoming.

89   Kapila (2013), p. 188.

90   UK House of Commons, 2005, Volume II, p. ev 34.

91   Idem. p. ev 96.

92   Idem. p. ev 34; Dutch Parliamentary Doc.: Tweede Kamer, 2003–2004, 29 237, nr. 13, 10 June 2004; Authors' interview with Adriaan Kooijmans, 16 September 2013.

foreseen in New York, his successor was being sought. Before Kapila had left by the end of March, the UN proposed to Sudan to replace him with the Brit Allan Doss as Humanitarian Coordinator. The Sudanese rejected Doss based on his nationality. An interim replacement, the American Kevin Kennedy, had his credentials similarly not accepted due to his nationality and because he was not intended as a permanent replacement. A UK House of Commons subcommittee thought it "not wise" of the UN to propose these British and American candidates, without clarifying what would have been a more suitable alternative.[93]

Egeland believes that the Sudanese only aimed to postpone a replacement as long as possible, and did not want to have someone strong in that function.[94] This is also what Kapila was told by Sudanese officials when he was leaving. They "did not want a strong head to create the sort of trouble that [he] had created for them and (...) they were going to delay accepting any replacement for as long as they possibly could."[95] Even after the Security Council referred to the replacement issue in the Presidential Statement of 25 May, Sudan was able to keep the UN office in Sudan without senior leadership for another month. Furthermore, the top of the UN, which could act politically, including SG Annan and UN DPA head Prendergast, chose not to do so. It appears that those countries that were deeply involved in Sudan (the UK, the US and Norway) did not desire the UN to have a greater role before the crisis. This did not refrain Dutch Development Minister van Ardenne from criticizing the UN for lacking capacity and leadership in Sudan to deal with the situation.[96]

A 'lame-duck' Kapila and subsequent leaderless UN office, combined with the fact that the Resident Coordinator (including temporary replacements) had no political mandate, probably explains largely the absence of the UN (Secretariat and other offices) during this early stage of international involvement.[97]

6.7   Start of the Deployment of AMIS

As discussed before, although the EU and other international parties supported the African Union in establishing its observer mission in Darfur, the planning

---

93   UK House of Commons, International Development Committee, "Darfur, Sudan: The responsibility to protect" Fifth Report of Session 2004–05, Volume I Report, para. 40 (hereafter UK House of Commons, 2005, Volume I).

94   UK House of Commons, 2005, Volume II, p. ev 43.

95   Idem., p. ev 49.

96   Dutch Parliamentary Doc.: Tweede Kamer, 2003–2004, 29 237, nr. 13, 10 June 2004.

97   See also the discussion in the previous chapter.

had not started until after the signing of the N'Djamena ceasefire agreement. And only after several months were the first observers and their protection forces active in Darfur.

The JEM, SLM/A and the Government signed an agreement for the actual deployment of AMIS observers on 28 May 2004.[98] Deployment was planned to start in early June, with 80 observers and a protection force of 300 military soldiers, supplied mainly by Rwanda and Nigeria.[99] This military force was primarily for the protection of the observers, not for the people of Darfur. The first observers arrived in June, and by 19 June the Ceasefire commission was called "operational."[100]

However, the deployment of the protection force did not develop without problems. Nigeria said in July that it still needed material and airlift support, initially understood to be provided by the US, but in the end it was executed by the UK.[101] Even when such help and cooperation was agreed at the Nigerian presidential and highest military levels, lower military commanders appeared initially unaware of the British involvement.[102] 150 Rwandese soldiers arrived on 15 August, airlifted with Dutch support[103] but at that time it was still unclear how Nigeria would deploy their 170 soldiers in Darfur.[104] At the same time, France deployed 200 troops already present in Chad to the Chadian border with Sudan to aid humanitarian efforts, but they appeared not to be involved in facilitating the AU mission.[105] The EU Commission was concerned with transferring funds to the AU for the financing of the observer mission but also countered problems due to lack of AU capacity to handle the transfers and the refusal by some AU officials to allow non-Africans, i.e. Europeans, to help out managing the tasks.[106]

---

98   AU Press release 51/2004, 28 May 2004.

99   Badescu and Bergholm (2010) in Black and Williams, p. 103.

100   Toga (2007) in de Waal, p. 219.

101   US State Department Cable, Abuja, 19 July 2004, No. 1260. The US embassy in Nigeria received information that the 170 Nigerian soldiers needed material support and airlift facilities from international donors in order to be able to deploy in Darfur. Many questions remained on the specifics, such as what material was needed, where they would initially be flown to, whether other international partners would take up some of the support, and to what extent the US was willing to donate and support the requested help.

102   US State Department Cable, Abuja, 12 August 2004, No. 1382.

103   Totten and Markussen (2006), Ch. Chronology.

104   US State Department Cable, Abuja, 12 August 2004, No. 1382; US State Department Cable, Abuja, 16 August 2004, No. 1396.

105   Igiri and Lyman, p. 14.

106   US State Department Cable, Brussels, 23 July 2004, No. 3140.

6.8   Theoretical Reflections: Bureaucratic Politics within the UN

A relevant question is whether there were significant disagreements between the different departments of the UN, as Section 6.3.1 already hinted at in relation to the speech of UN SG Annan during the Rwanda commemoration in Geneva. Annan probably went against his political advisor Prendergast (DPA) who was not in favour of using emotive terms. Underlying these in the words of Prendergast himself were "genuine differences of view," between the "humanitarians" and the "political officers."[107] As will be argued in Chapter 8, similar divisions existed within the US and UK governments and these divisions might partly account for the inconsistencies within the policy of both.

As for the UN, there were on the one hand people like Egeland (OCHA) and Kapila who were vocal, outspoken and preferred a more confrontational approach towards the governing regime.[108] On the other hand, the political officers of DPA, like Prendergast favoured a more diplomatic course. Prendergast and his chief political assistant Menkarios preferred to strengthen the moderate voices within the Sudanese government and therefore did not want to "bash the supposed moderates over the head with allegations of ethnic cleansing or genocide."[109] Prendergast was therefore sceptical when Egeland was pushing Darfur to the agenda of the UNSC and also because he was of the view that the situation in Darfur was more complicated.[110] Prendergast himself stated in this context: "I also happen to think that Jan Egeland was mistaken in insisting in his first briefing of the Security Council to which you refer, in referring to "ethnic cleansing." I advised him not to use that term. And why? Not because I and the political department were afraid to call a spade, but because once you use very emotive terms of that kind, you change the nature of the debate." Prendergast also tried to avoid that the UN would waste its political capital on Darfur, as was argued in Section 5.5.4

The fact that the "political officers" at DPA generally have the ultimate say over political matters of peace and security[111] within the UN hierarchy explains the cautious approach of the UN SG Annan, who was reluctant to come up with

---

107   Cockett (2010), p. 200; PBS Frontline interview with Kieran Prendergast, 29 June 2007.

108   Authors' interview with Jan Egeland, 28 November 2012.

109   Cockett (2010), p. 200.

110   Authors' interview with Jan Egeland, 28 November 2012.

111   This is illustrated by the Egeland's referral of Kapila to Prendergast, when Kapila asked Egeland how he could make the UN politically involved in the crisis in Darfur (Kapila, 2013, p. 112–114).

concrete policy recommendations or to put Darfur on the UNSC agenda (Section 5.5.4). DPKO was barely involved with respect to the situation in Darfur at this period in time. As will be discussed in the next chapter, it actually tried to minimise its involvement, because it did not foresee a role for itself since there was no peace to keep (Section 7.8.4).

CHAPTER 7

Increased International Activity and Decision-Making
June 2004–September 2004

Now that the Darfur ceasefire was signed, Darfur had entered the agenda of the Security Council and humanitarian aid was quickly expanding. The next months were dedicated to maximising the pressure on the Sudanese government to reign in the *Janjaweed* and start political talks with the rebel groups. This chapter will look into the international attempts to achieve these goals.

7.1   Situation in Darfur

The disparity between the dire situation on the ground – 2 million affected by the conflict,[1] 120,000 refugees in Chad,[2] "mass starvation"[3] looming ominously in the background and WFP Executive Director James Morris admitting he had "never seen people who are as frightened as those displaced in Darfur"[4] – and the policies adopted at the UN emphasising gentle persuasion, solidarity and the outright avoidance of strong action against Khartoum, was palpable.

Despite the surge in media attention directed towards Darfur both regionally, nationally and internationally,[5] with damning judgments of Sudan and

---

1   UN News, 17 May 2004, "UN estimates 2 million Sudanese in Darfur area now affected by conflict."

2   UN News, 14 May 2004, "Sudan: UN in 'desperate need' of funds for Darfur refugees as rains approach."

3   Médecins Sans Frontières Press Release, 20 May 2004, "On the brink of mass starvation in Darfur."

4   UN News, 7 May 2004, "Sudan humanitarian crisis characterized by violence and fear, UN official says."

5   See for example: The Daily Telegraph, 3 May 2004, "In this ravaged land, the old insanity of racism is breeding imminent catastrophe. Ethnic violence is ripping apart Darfur in western Sudan. Author Irvine Welsh, the first person to report from the region, sees the tragedy"; CNN, 12 May 2004, Christiane Amanpour. "Sudan's hellish humanitarian crisis"; de Volkskrant, 12 May 2004, "Sudan sluit vrede terwijl de volgende oorlog woedt; Oplaaiende strijd rond Darfur draait niet alleen om grotere autonomie, het gaat uiteindelijk om de macht in Khartoem" [Sudan secures peace while the next war rages; Conflict blazing in Darfur is not only about autonomy, it concerns power in Khartoum]; The Economist, 15 May 2004, "Fleeing the horsemen who kill for Khartoum-Sudan"; The International Herald Tribune, 15 May 2004, "A complex ethnic reality with a long history; Darfur"; The Boston Globe, 20 May 2004, "Stopping

the international response employing the term 'genocide' with increasing frequency, evidence suggests that such attention did not correlate to the intensity of violence on the ground. Of course attacks such as the *Janjaweed* incursion into a border-town in Chad[6] continued, but in the weeks following the 8 April ceasefire the brutalities significantly decreased. Indeed, the preceding months of February and March witnessed some of the most devastating and bloodthirsty attacks in the entire Darfur conflict, whilst in April and May there were few reports of the mass rapes and other atrocities that had characterised those earlier months.[7] It has been argued that this situation demonstrates the greater scrutiny of Khartoum as a result of the by-now wide international and public awareness of Darfur. In contrast, others such as UN emergency relief officer, Daniel Augstburger, on returning from Darfur, offered the opinion that the situation had calmed only "because there are no more villages to burn."[8] Whatever the truth, and the decrease in violence notwithstanding, disease, malnutrition and the other horrors that quickly follow the mass displacement of entire populations ensured that the death toll in Darfur continued to rise towards catastrophic proportions.

In Darfur itself, refugees and IDPs, terrified of the *Janjaweed* and fearing becoming the targets of attacks, and who had earlier refused aid for the same reasons now began to refuse to return home,[9] preferring the relative sanctity provided by their squalid camps. Yet even this was being increasingly threatened as Chadian forces began to clash with the *Janjaweed*.[10] The contradictions continued as reports of government bombings at the end of the month, and accusations by either side over the killing of civilians marked something of an official breaking of the 8 April ceasefire,[11] while the African Union released a

---

Sudan's slow-motion genocide"; The Times, 18 May 2004, "Cleansing in Sudan may soon become genocide"; The Observer, 30 May 2004, "Empty villages mark trail of Sudan's hidden war: Carter Dougherty reports from west Darfur, where Khartoum's genocidal killers have made a million homeless"; The Washington Post, 30 May 2004, "The Darfur Catastrophe."

6   Agence France Presse, 29 April 2004, "Sudan pro-government militia attacks Chad border town: official."
7   See also Figure 1 in Chapter 1.
8   Agence France Presse, 12 May 2004, "Sudan's Darfur calm because 'no more villages to burn,' UN official says."
9   The New York Times, 8 May 2004, "Uprooted Sudanese balk at invitation to return home."
10   Associated Press, 9 May 2004, "Dozens killed as Chadian army battles Sudanese militia inside Chad."
11   Agence France Presse, 24 May 2004, "Khartoum accuses Darfur rebels of truce violation"; The New York Times, 24 May 2004, "Raid in Sudan claims 56, villagers say."

communiqué proclaiming an agreement between the government and rebels paving the way for international observers in Darfur.[12]

By June 2004 the UN was estimating that the horrendous daily reality had produced over 2 million war-affected civilians,[13] with every fifth child in Darfur reportedly suffering severe malnutrition.[14] Amnesty International predicted[15] that the situation described as "catastrophic"[16] by the Secretary-General would only get worse with the onset of the imminent rainy reason, with efforts by the UNHCR to relocate 90,000 refugees to safer camps in Chad also offset by renewed flows of refugees across the border. A regular flow of reports from Darfur described sustained civilian assaults,[17] government air strikes,[18] clashes between Chadian soldiers and the *Janjaweed*,[19] the murder and rape of black Africans,[20] and *Janjaweed* militias now burning, looting and killing their way through south Darfur.[21]

7.2   UNSC Resolution 1547

The first resolution in which Darfur was mentioned in 2004 was on 11 June, two weeks after the Presidential Statement.[22] Despite the focus on Darfur that the Presidential Statement expressed, this resolution was focused for the main part on the North–South Peace Agreement and was adopted unanimously. It established the South Advanced Mission in Sudan (UNAMIS), which was mandated to prepare for the various UN missions that would start with the signing of the Comprehensive Peace Agreement (CPA). UNAMIS was provisioned

---

12 African Union Press Release: 51/2004, 28 May 2004.

13 Prunier, G. (2007) *Darfur: An ambiguous genocide. Revised and updated edition 2007* London: C.Hurst & Co. (publishers) ltd., p. 150.

14 Totten, S. and Markussen, E. (eds.) (2006) *Genocide in Darfur, investigating the Atrocities in the Sudan.* New York/London: Routledge, p. xxiii.

15 AI Doc.: AFR 54/066/2004, 1 June 2004, "Sudan: 130,000 refugees on the Chad border."

16 UN Doc.: S/2004/453, 3 June 2004, Report of the Secretary-General on the Sudan.

17 Agence France Presse, 1 June 2004, "Twenty-four dead in government strike on Darfur village: rebels."

18 Agence France Presse, 4 June 2004, "Sudan air force bombs Darfur market: Chadian mediators."

19 Associated Press, 17 June 2004, "Chadian soldiers kill 69 Sudanese Arab militiamen."

20 Totten and Markusen (2006), p. xxiv.

21 UN News, 23 June 2004, "Sudan: UN filed workers report fresh attacks by Janjaweed militias in Darfur."

22 UN Doc.: S/Res/1547, 11 June 2004.

to be under the control of a Special Representative of the Secretary-General.

Even though the resolution was focused on South Sudan, it recalled the specific Presidential Statement of 25 May 2004, repeated many of its provisions, and called on all parties to stop all "acts of violence and violations on human rights and humanitarian law." Nevertheless, whereas the Presidential Statement was specifically concerned with those acts "with an ethnic dimension," this resolution refrained from mentioning this.

In the sixth operative paragraph of the resolution Darfur is mentioned, in which the SC

> Calls upon the parties to use their influence to bring an immediate halt to the fighting in the Darfur region, (...) urges the parties to the N'Djamena Ceasefire Agreement of 8 April 2004 to conclude a political agreement without delay.

It is said that the inclusion of Darfur in this resolution was the result of the considerable lobby of the French Ambassador to the UN, Levite.[23] After the vote the UK, Germany and the US made a statement, mentioning Darfur.[24] The UK wished that all

> Pay particular attention to the situation in Darfur and ensure that all of us and the humanitarian agencies play our part to avert any humanitarian catastrophe in that area.

Germany referred to the report of the Acting High Commissioner for Human Rights, mentioned above, and stated:

> We believed that it was indispensable that this overall context of the conflict should also be appropriately reflected in the resolution.

Finally, the US made a statement, saying it is concerned with the

> Continuing reports of gross violations of human rights, many with an ethnic dimension.

---

23   Mayroz, E. (2008) "Ever again? The United States, genocide suppression, and the crisis in Darfur," *Journal of Genocide Research*, Vol.: 10(3), p. 369. As discussed in the previous chapter, France and Germany were very much in favour in addressing Darfur in the Security Council (Authors' interview with Gunter Pleuger, 5 November 2013).

24   UN Doc.: S/pv.4988, 11 June 2004.

It addresses a paragraph on Darfur, and demanded that Sudan

> Respect the ceasefire, allow unimpeded humanitarian access (...) displaced to return safely (...) disarm immediately the Janjaweed and other armed groups which are responsible for massive human rights violations in Darfur.

All these aspects would become important in the following resolutions, as they were measures on which the cooperation of the government was tested. The statement of the US was a partial repetition of a declaration made a day earlier by the Group of 8 (G8).[25] Certain states were not in favour of a motivation of the vote because they did not want to condemn the government of Sudan in public. They therefore agreed to repeat the statement which the G8 had already issued.[26] Interestingly, the G8 referred to the "*Janjaweed* and other armed groups responsible for massive human rights violations." In contrast the resolution and previous Presidential Statement referred to "all violations of human rights and humanitarian law by all parties," which would also include the Sudanese government. However, the resolution failed to explicitly mention the *Janjaweed*, and did not mention the "ethnic dimension" as was done in the Presidential Statement.

7.3 Annan Moves UN Back into Action

All over the world the pressure increased to act. With the humanitarian aid scaling up and the first Security Council Resolution on Sudan adopted, UN SG Annan made several decisions to give the UN Secretariat a bigger political role in Sudan, and Darfur in particular. An important decision by the UN was that Annan appointed his Special Representative Jan Pronk and visited the region in order to pressure the Sudanese government on Darfur.

As discussed above, a major issue for the UN was its lack of strong presence in Sudan. Until then it had a Resident Coordinator for Humanitarian Affairs, which had no political mandate. The official explanation by the UN for Kapila's departure was the preparation for a new country team that would come in for

---

25 US White House press office, "G-8 Statement on Sudan," 10 June 2004, available at http://georgewbush-whitehouse.archives.gov/news/releases/2004/06/20040610-7.html [accessed 22 August 2013].

26 Archive Ministry of Foreign Affairs in the Netherlands: DAF/2015/00646, Period December 2003–June 2004.

the period of CPA implementation, which was to be combined with a major peacekeeping force.[27] This was partly true. People had already been approached in December 2003 for this new UN position. Both Tom Vraalsen and Jan Pronk were on this shortlist. Pronk was sounded out on 2 December.[28] Tom Vraalsen had been active in OCHA and DPA until then, and appears in Kapila's account as a timid diplomat. Sudan rejected his candidacy based on his nationality, since Norway was too much on the side of South Sudan according to Khartoum,[29] and perhaps his proximity to Jan Egeland, who had been much too vocal on Darfur according to the Sudanese government.

In contrast, Jan Pronk is a politician, having served as Minister for Development in the Netherlands. From that capacity he had obtained a great knowledge of Sudan, and was known in Khartoum. Additionally, he had worked within the UN at UNCTAD and therefore had experience with the particular UN bureaucracy. Even though the Netherlands were pressuring the Sudanese government privately on Darfur, their new commitment to donor funding for Sudan, as exemplified in a donor meeting for Sudan organised in the Netherlands in Noordwijk, made the Dutchman acceptable to Sudan.[30] However, Pronk himself had some demands for the UN.

The proposal for the new UN team in Sudan was focused on the North–South situation. UN SG Annan had initially proposed to the Security Council to appoint a Special Representative and two deputies, including one who would serve as Resident/Humanitarian Coordinator. The tasks spelled out for this team completely focused on the final stages of the Naivasha talks and implementation of the CPA, including heading the UN peacekeeping mission for South Sudan (UNAMIS).[31] The Security Council in UN Resolution 1547 endorsed this proposal of Annan, thus creating a direct mandate for the Special Representative. When Pronk was approached for the position of Special Representative in early June, he further demanded that he would have full authority to act in the situation in Darfur as well.[32] He saw Darfur as the much

---

27   UK House of Commons report, Volume II, p. ev 96.

28   Archive Ministry of Foreign Affairs in the Netherlands: DAF/2015/00646, Period December 2003–June 2004.

29   Authors' interview with Jan Pronk, 2 September 2013.

30   Grünfeld, F. and Vermeulen, W.N. (2014) "The role of the Netherlands in the international response to the Crisis in Darfur," Maastricht Faculty of Law Working Paper No. 2014–2 (available at http://ssrn.com/abstract=2418398 [accessed 2 April 2014]).

31   UN Doc.: S/2004/453, 3 June 2004, "Report of the Secretary-General on the Sudan," paras. 11–17.

32   Bieckmann, F. (2012) Soedan. Het sinistere spel om macht, rijkdom en olie. Amsterdam: Balans, p. 176; Authors' interview with Jan Pronk, 2 September 2013; email to authors, 13 October 2013.

more urgent situation that needed to be addressed since the Naivasha talks were well underway (about to be finalised), while the ceasefire between North and South was maintained. Therefore, it was on Pronk's own initiative that his mandate was changed to encompass Darfur as well and this forced Annan to focus on Darfur.[33] Furthermore, he demanded to have the authority over all UN bodies and missions, which included the future UNAMIS and UNMIS missions for the South, as well as all the other humanitarian bodies in the UN structure. Pronk called this the "unified approach."[34]

Annan agreed with Pronk's vision for the coordination and responsibility of UN organisations in Sudan and his mandate over Darfur, so Pronk became the UN Secretary-General Special Representative (SGSR) on Sudan. Pronk would report to Annan via DPKO whereby copies of his reports were sent to OCHA, DPA as well as the Human Rights offices in Geneva. At the meeting of his appointment were – as well as Annan – the heads of DPA (Prendergast) and DPKO (Guéhenno).[35] Although he managed to have a more unified system of responsibilities in Sudan, decision-making among the different UN agencies remained largely uncoordinated.[36] Pronk was not given additional means to deal with Darfur. UNAMIS had not yet started so there were no military personnel. Furthermore, he had no additional finance apart from what was available for the UNAMIS mission. Pronk had to do with the means of "good offices"; diplomacy and coordinating with other stakeholders such as the western embassies.[37]

After his appointment on 18 June, Annan and Pronk travelled to Sudan on 30 June.[38] Annan visited IDP camps in Sudan and refugee camps in eastern Chad. These visits gave plenty of opportunities for media coverage.[39] Their visit fell together with one of US Secretary of State Colin Powell, which helped to increase the pressure on the regime even further. After the visits, Annan and Pronk had meetings with President al-Bashir and Minister of Foreign Affairs Ismail. In this meeting of four, they negotiated an agreement for Darfur,

---

33 Authors' interview with Jan Pronk, 2 September 2013; email to authors, 13 October 2013.

34 Authors' interview with Jan Pronk, 21 Augustus 2006.

35 Archive Ministry of Foreign Affairs in the Netherlands: DAF/2015/00646, Period December 2003–June 2004.

36 Idem.

37 Authors' interview with Jan Pronk, 2 September 2013.

38 UN Doc.: Press release SG/A/877 AFR/974 BIO/3577, 21 June 2004.

39 UN News, 25 June 2004, "Annan vows to press Sudan to protect Darfur's civilians from catastrophe"; UN News, 1 July 2004, "Annan vows that Darfur's displaced will not have to go home unless safe"; UN News, 2 July 2004, "Annan hears reports of 'gross and systematic' abuses of human rights against Sudanese."

presented as a Joint Communiqué on 3 July, in which the government committed to retreat the military in Darfur to their camps, and disarmament of the
Janjaweed.[40] Pronk saw it as an important step in the negotiations with the
government, despite the fact that the time frame to implement these agreements would not be respected. The importance of the Communiqué came
from the fact that the UN Secretary General and the President of Sudan had
agreed to the terms in direct talks and had signed this document. As such it
functioned as an authoritative basis for future negotiations.[41]

7.4   Discussing Sanctions

The EU and the UN could have applied sanctions in the first six months of 2004.
The US already had an extensive set of sanctions applied. From the moment
Darfur was first discussed in the Security Council the sanctions under discussion were mainly "targeted sanctions" at individuals and "economic sanctions,"
in particular an oil-boycott. Additionally, the conditionality of future donor
funding was strengthened from signing the CPA to signing the CPA and a peace
settlement in Darfur. Other economic sanctions were barely proposed or
discussed.

There were several constraints in applying sanctions on Sudan or individual
members of the regime. Firstly, the US and the EU already had a wide range of
sanctions in place at the start of the Darfur conflict, resulting from the conflict
in the south and Sudan's role in supporting terrorism. The US had more measures in place than the EU. With respect to the possibility of economic sanctions, the US maintained a wide range of financial and trade restrictions and
kept access to donor funding conditional on the successful conclusion of the
CPA.[42] The EU had an arms embargo in place, but some European countries

---

40   The communiqué is to our knowledge not archived as an official UN document. The text
       can be found online, e.g. http://www.issafrica.org/AF/profiles/sudan/darfur/uncommjul04
       .pdf [accessed 15 November 2013].

41   Authors' interview with Jan Pronk, 2 September 2013.

42   12 unilateral sanctions in September 2004 according to Igiri, C.O. and Lyman, P.N. (2004)
       "Giving meaning to 'Never again.' Seeking an Effective Response to the Crisis in Darfur
       and Beyond." Council on Foreign Relations No. 5, 5 September 2004, note 51. For instance,
       President Clinton enacted trade sanctions in 1997, see Executive Order 13067 (5 November
       1997). BBC Panorama, Fergal Keane interview with John Danforth, 3 July 2005, available
       at http://news.bbc.co.uk/1/hi/programmes/panorama/4647211.stm [accessed 5 October
       2013].

were still trading significantly with Sudan, such as Germany and the UK.[43] One of the consequences of these existing restrictions was the limited scope for a Western unilateral oil-boycott, since companies from the US and Europe were already not allowed to deal with Sudan, directly or indirectly. Hence, none of the big western oil companies (e.g. BP, Royal Dutch Shell, Total, ExxonMobil, Chevron, Statoil) had producing facilities in Sudan in 2004.[44] However, Sudan produced at that time a surplus (i.e. production in excess of domestic consumption) of 150,000 barrels per day, which were mainly exported to China and to a lesser extent Japan.[45] India and Malaysia also had oil stakes in the country. Therefore, any further economic sanctions for Sudan had to be negotiated at the UN level.

Secondly, in particular with respect to targeted sanctions, their effectiveness was in doubt, and as such sanctions were reduced to symbolic signals rather than real coercive instruments.[46] If one considered the *Janjaweed* as bands of nomads, then asset-freezes or travel restrictions would arguably not be very threatening to those subjected to it. However, if one considered the Sudanese government as the ultimate perpetrator, then the situation would become more complicated. As shown before, any measures were not to threaten a successful finalisation of the Naivasha talks. This aspect also reduced the leverage

---

43   Germany and the UK account jointly for more than 10% of Sudan's imports. See The World Factbook 2004, Sudan, available at http://www.umsl.edu/services/govdocs/wofact2004/geos/su.html [accessed 11 June 2013].

44   According to each of their 2004 Annual Reports. Some of them had producing facilities in the past but had withdrawn due to the sanctions regime. They might still have concessions in the country but were at the time not involved in production. One of the last to leave was Canadian based Talisman Energy, which sold its last concession in 2003 according to its annual report. Sweden based Lundin Petroleum still owned a minority share in one field, and noted in its 2004 Annual Report that it hoped that the signing of the CPA would allow "operations to resume in the near future." For a discussion on Western oil companies' involvement and the subsequent Asian, including Chinese, take over. See Johnson, D.H., (2003 [2011]) *The root causes of Sudan's civil wars. Peace or truce?* Revised edition. Kampala: Fountain Publishers, pp. 162–165; Leach, J.D. (2011) *War and Politics in Sudan. Cultural identities and the challenges of the peace process.* London, New York: I.B. Taurus, pp. 144–146.

45   The World Factbook 2004, Sudan.

46   "Effectiveness" here means the ability to change a target's conduct away from what is considered harmful by those that apply the sanction (Grünfeld, F., 1999, "The effectiveness of United Nations economic sanctions," in *United Nations sanctions: effectiveness and effects, especially in the field of human rights. A multi-disciplinary approach,* by van Genugten, W.J.M. and de Groot, G.A. [eds.], Antwerpen: Intersentia).

of threatening with sanctions, often a more effective method then the actual adopted sanctions.[47]

Finally, the Sudanese government had not shown to be very sensitive to sanctions (e.g. the existing sanctions had not made the government more open to attempt to settle the Darfur conflict early and peacefully). The regime was willing to pass negative consequences of sanctions to civilians, especially those outside its core powerbase, while harnessing a growing nationalistic support.[48] In short, Sudan appeared to be neither susceptible to external pressure nor internal pressure. Hence, theory would predict that sanctions would not be effective.[49] However, as will be discussed below, there were signals that Sudan feared international sanctions, which could indicate the regime was much more susceptible to outside pressure than they showed. Furthermore, some argue that the regime was strongly reliant on the support of an Arab economic elite based around the Khartoum/Nile area, making any targeted sanctions on this elite's economic interests effective channels for internal pressure.[50]

What remained was the option of an international sanctions regime at the global level in the UN based on Article 41 under Chapter VII of the UN Charter. Therefore, with the preparation of the next mandatory resolution, Resolution 1556, there was a first strong and concerted push by the US to have the UNSC apply sanctions to Sudan. On 7 July, after a closed briefing of the Secretary-General to the Council, some ambassadors acknowledged that sanctions were discussed but they did not elaborate on their specifics. The new US ambassador to the UN John Danforth, previously Presidential envoy to Sudan, was the most explicit, giving only days to Sudan to show that it was sincere in arresting the *Janjaweed*.[51] A US drafted resolution included sanctions on the *Janjaweed*, while another source stated that the UNSC also considered an arms-embargo

---

47   Idem.

48   Although not specifically related to sanctions, during the famine in the 1980s the regime had no problem redirecting food aid to their core base, neglecting the people in the South and Darfur, see Chapter 4; de Waal, A. (1989 [2005]), *Famine that kills. Revised and updated edition.* Oxford: Oxford University Press.

49   Rosenau, J.N. (1966) "The adaptation of national societies: a theory of political behavior and transformation," in *The scientific study of foreign policy*, by Rosenau, J.N. (1980), New York, London: Frances Pinter Ltd.; Grünfeld (1999).

50   Authors' interview with Christian Manahl, 26 August 2013; Verhoeven, H. (2013) "The rise and fall of Sudan's Al-Ingaz revolution: The transition from militarised Islamism to economic salvation and the Comprehensive Peace Agreement," *Civil Wars*, Vol. 15:2, pp. 118–140.

51   Video recording after the briefing of 7 July 2004, available at https://www.un.org/webcast/arc2004c.html [accessed 18 June 2013].

and a travel ban.[52] The US then went around the world to seek support for adopting sanctions.

7.5   Creating Wider International Support

A few days before the adoption of Resolution 1547, the US and EU countries started planning to activate third parties in order to obtain wider support for condemnation of Sudan.[53] The focus was on approaching "friendly" Arab and African states. These approaches continued after the resolution were adopted in order to achieve maximum effect of this resolution and to build support for the preparations of new resolutions and the inclusion of sanctions therein. One such friendly state is the United Arab Emirates, which shared information with the US on Sudan and addressed the security situation in Darfur with a visiting Sudanese delegation.[54]

The Organisation of the Islamic Conference (OIC) was another potential partner. In July a former Turkish diplomat was elected to become the next Secretary-General of the organisation, starting in 2005. Following that election, both the US and Sudan approached Turkey to make use of its influence in the OIC. Both Turkey and the new OIC Secretary-General wanted the OIC to take a position on Darfur.[55] Sudan hoped that it would oppose sanctions, while the US wanted it to use its influence on Sudan to abide with the resolutions and disarm the *Janjaweed*. It is interesting that the US was briefed by Turkish officials on what was discussed between the Sudanese and Turkish Ministers during their meeting on 26 July. In particular, it is an indication that Sudan feared sanctions at that point.

In the Security Council the US started to share information with the other members as a way to convince them of the severity of the situation. In particular the US showed satellite pictures of burned villages to the other permanent members.[56] The Pakistani representative of the Security Council hinted that Pakistan's President Musharraf was also approached shortly before adoption of Resolution 1556 to "assist in resolving [the] humanitarian situation."[57]

---

52   Totten and Markussen (2006), Ch. Chronology; BBC News, 8 July 2004, "France opposes UN Sudan sanctions."
53   US State Department Cable, Brussels, 4 June 2004, No. 2410.
54   US State Department Cable, Abu Dhabi, 7 June 2004, No. 1880.
55   US State Department Cables, Istanbul, 13 July 2004, No. 1090; Ankara, 29 July 2004, No. 4227; Ankara, 18 August 2004, No. 4628; Ankara, 8 September 2004, No. 5029.
56   Totten and Markussen (2006), p. 37.
57   UN Doc.: S/pv.5015, p. 10.

7.6   EU Decision-Making under the Incoming Dutch Presidency

The Dutch EU Council Presidency started on 1 July. As stated before, since it represented the EU already from Khartoum since 1 January 2004, the Netherlands had a running start on the issue and was potentially well-positioned to streamline EU decision-making. Additionally, the EU was already engaged on the topic. The previous EU Council President, Ireland, had already put Darfur on the EU Council agenda since April.[58] Under the Irish presidency the importance of Darfur for the EU Council had increased with every meeting, as evidenced by the ranking on the agenda and the length of the statements/conclusions. The Netherlands planned to be much more active on Darfur and were in favour of much stronger action.[59] The Dutch official from the Ministry of Foreign Affairs, Schuthof, for example, argued that the draft of Resolution 1556 "did not go far enough" as he was of the opinion that sanctions should be imposed on both the Sudanese government and the *Janjaweed*.[60] Although the Netherlands was in favour of sanctions, it preferred a common EU position on this before it could support such measures in public.[61]

Consequently, the first EU Council conclusions on Darfur under the Dutch Presidency were much stronger than the last ones, but not as strong as it had wanted. The EU Council conclusions of 14 July clearly set out a list of demands for the Sudanese government, which included implementation of the cease-fire, disarmament of the *Janjaweed*, access for human rights observers and humanitarian agencies etc., as conditions for further "normalization of relations." If demands are not met and civilians continue to being "exposed to death, atrocities and starvation, (...) the EU will consider taking further measures."[62]

---

58   Early press releases condemning the fighting were released on 22 December 2003 and 7 January 2004 (EU Doc.: Press releases 16357/03, 22 December and 5101/04, 7 January 2004). Under the Irish Presidency Darfur was first discussed at the EU Council meeting of 26–27 April (EU Doc.: Press Release 8567/04, 27 April 2004).

59   A US Cable also noted that the Dutch government is "fully seized [...] at all levels, and is actively engaging Europ[ean] colleagues to increase contributions." US State Department Cables, The Hague, 15 July 2004, No. 1777. Another cable had as its title "Dutch in driver's seat in Europe" and noted that the highest levels of the Dutch government, including the Prime Minister, are actively engaged. US State Department Cables, The Hague, 9 July 2004, No. 1721.

60   US State Department Cables, The Hague, 9 July 2004, No. 1721.

61   Grünfeld, F. and Vermeulen, W.N. (2014) "The role of the Netherlands in the international response to the Crisis in Darfur." Maastricht Faculty of Law Working Paper No. 2014–2 (available at http://ssrn.com/abstract=2418398 [accessed 2 April 2014]).

62   EU Doc.: Press Release 81416/04, 14 July 2004. This list ("a Dutch plan of action that sets specific benchmarks") was drawn up by the Dutch Foreign Ministry and included a

The EU had not used this kind of strong language before. The Dutch had drafted conclusions that referred to "sanctions" as opposed to "measures."[63] Only Germany was allegedly in favour of such a reference, while the rest of the EU members had pushed and succeeded to "weaken" the statement.[64] Nonetheless, the first benchmarks of EU actions were made explicit.

Besides a stronger EU position, the Netherlands wished for a more public position of the EU.[65] For instance, Minister Bot complained to a US diplomat that the EU had not received the credit that it deserved for its involvement.[66] This is interesting when recalling the US offer for a joint public statement in April, which was at that time not taken up by the EU. Furthermore, during the first days of July, the EU was not involved with the acts of Colin Powell, UN SG Kofi Annan and Jan Pronk in Sudan who pressed the Sudanese government into an agreement. Therefore, compared to the intention of the Dutch government of a more active and public position of the EU, the start of the Dutch Presidency appeared partly successful. The change of direction was towards more action on the EU side, implicitly threatening unilateral sanctions, but it missed its first opportunity for a public image.

In general in Europe there was a realisation that targeted sanctions, especially on members of the *Janjaweed*, would be of little practical effect, but could serve as a symbolic measure.[67] France, in particular, was publicly against sanctions. French deputy Foreign Minister Renaud Muselier stated, when asked on French radio on his thoughts on a German proposal of sanctions on the *Janjaweed* as well as the Sudanese government, that sanctions would not be helpful while a peace process is ongoing in Naivasha.[68]

The EU Council met two weeks later on 26 July, and needed to deal with the fact that its benchmarks regarding security were not met. The EU Council did so in two ways: (1) it called upon the UNSC to pass a resolution with a view of

---

timeframe with specific EU sanctions, including economic sanctions, asset freezing and travel restrictions (US State Department Cables, The Hague, 9 July 2004, No. 1721).

63 On 14 July, the Dutch government also delivered a statement to the Sudanese government that they "will not hesitate to apply sanction, however limited their effect might be." US State Department Cables, The Hague, 15 July 2004, No. 1777.

64 US State Department Cable, The Hague, 15 July 2004, No. 1777.

65 Dutch Parliamentary Doc.: Tweede Kamer, 2003–2004, 21 501–502, nr. 562, 9 July 2004.

66 US State Department Cable, The Hague, 9 July 2004, No. 1717.

67 US State Department Cable, Madrid, 14 July 2004, No. 2660; The Hague, 15 July 2004, No. 1777.

68 BBC News, 8 July 2004, "France opposes UN Sudan sanctions"; Radio Français Internationale, 8 July 2004, "Invite Afrique," interview with Renaud Muselier, available at http://www.rfi .fr/actufr/pages/001/page_63.asp [accessed 10 July 2013].

passing sanctions on Sudan conditional on non-cooperation, and (2) requested its secretariat to prepare a list of *Janjaweed* leaders which the Sudanese government ought to investigate.[69] This list of *Janjaweed* leaders already existed, and it was checked with a list of the US.[70] Additionally, the EU Council backed the recommendation of Ramcharan for a Commission of Inquiry. Finally, the EU further expanded its support to the AU mission with additional finance and logistical support.

The explicit call for UN sanctions was a change relative to the previous statement. However, this policy line was also not completely aligned to the position of the Dutch Presidency. For instance, in a reply to questions from the Dutch Parliament, Ministers Bot and Van Ardenne stated that the UNSC was considering sanctions that would go less far than what the EU countries were foreseeing.[71] Given that the EU Council was now leaving the actual decision-making about sanctions to the UNSC, rather than leaving the option of unilateral EU actions open, this could not be seen as a success for the Netherlands. It indicates that there were some European countries opposed to sanctions. Minister Bot needed to defend the EU position as EU Council president and commented after the meeting that sanctions at that stage would have been "completely pointless."[72]

7.7   Resolution 1556 of 30 July 2004

UN Resolution 1556 was adopted on 30 July, and dealt with Darfur exclusively.[73] The US had proposed a strong draft resolution but needed to water it down significantly due to the opposition of non-Western countries on the Council who were against any resolution with sanctions or the threat thereof, including China, Algeria, and Pakistan. Outside the Council, Sudan still had the support of international organisations such as the Arab League, which "cautioned the

---

69   EU Doc.: press release 81554/04, 26 July 2004.

70   US State Department Cable, Brussels, 23 July 2004, No. 3140. A month earlier the US ambassador for war crimes Prosper, in a hearing before the US congress, had publicly named 7 Janjaweed leaders. (Pierre-Richard Prosper, Ambassador-at-Large for War Crimes Issues Testimony before the House International Relations Committee, Subcommittee on Africa Washington, DC, 24 June 2004.

71   Dutch Parliamentary Doc.: Tweede Kamer, 2003–2004, Aanhangsel 1979, send 12 July, replied 21 July.

72   NRC Handelsblad, 26 July 2004, "Bot: nu nog geen sancties tegen Soedan; 'Stevige waarschuwing'" [Bot: no sanctions against Sudan yet; "strong warning"].

73   UN Doc.: S/Res/1556, 30 July 2004.

Council to 'avoid precipitate action.'"[74] This situation sounds rather similar to what had led to the resolution in the UN CHR in April 2004. Consequently, the US drafted a new resolution in which the word "sanctions" was changed into "further actions, including measures as provided for in Article 41" (see below).[75] The new draft is relatively weaker compared to the previous one, and more focused on threats to the *Janjaweed* only, perceived to ease concerns of China, Algeria and Pakistan specifically.

The Security Council acknowledged the practical action of the African Union, in particular the observer missions and now condemned,

> Indiscriminate attacks on civilians, rapes, forced displacements, and acts of violence especially those with an ethnic dimension, [by all parties].

This differs from the previous resolution, which only mentioned "indiscriminate attacks" not the "ethnic dimension."

Additionally the refugee flows, both internal as those towards Chad are explicitly mentioned. The humanitarian crisis, the ongoing violence, and the refugee flows to Chad, made the Security Council determine

> That the situation in Sudan constitutes a threat to international peace and security and to stability in the region, Acting under Chapter VII of the Charter of the United Nations.

This was the first time that the situation in Darfur caused the Security Council to make this determination. This determination of a "threat to international peace and security" was based both on a traditional and a modern concept. The international refugee flows to Chad is a traditional reason, addressing the international dimension, whereas the violations of human rights and humanitarian law constitute a more modern interpretation for a threat to peace.[76] The determination that the situation was a threat to peace opened the way to potentially enact enforcement measures.

A number of obligations towards the government are then noted. These are based on the Joint Communiqué between the Secretary-General of the UN and the Government of Sudan of 3 July. These demands include the facilitation of

---

74   Traub, J. (2006) The Best Intentions: Kofi Annan and the UN in the Era of American World
      Power. New York: Farrar, Straus and Giroux, pp. 225–226.
75   US State Department Cable, Rome, 26 July 2004, No. 2874; Madrid, 26 July 2004, No. 2844;
      Mayroz (2008), p. 368.
76   Bothe (2007), p. 9.

humanitarian relief, a credible investigation into the crimes committed in Darfur, the establishment of security for the civilian population, the disarmament of the *Janjaweed* and the resumption of talks with the rebel groups. Further paragraphs are dedicated to the deployment of the international monitors as facilitated and mandated by the AU, the support donated and pledged by international donors such as the EU, the monitors sent by the UN High Commissioner on Human Rights and the need for respecting the ceasefire as negotiated on 8 April 2004 in N'Djamena. After mentioning the actions already underway and facilitated mainly by the AU, the Security Council repeated the demand to the Sudanese government to

> Fulfil its commitments to disarm the Janjaweed militias and apprehend and bring to justice Janjaweed leaders, (...) and further requests the Secretary-General to report in 30 days, and monthly thereafter, to the Council on the progress or lack thereof by the Government of Sudan on this matter and expresses its intention to consider further actions, including measures as provided for in Article 41 of the Charter of the United Nations on the Government of Sudan, in the event of non-compliance.

The threat of sanctions (Article 41 of the UN Charter states "measures not involving the use of armed force") only applied to the disarmament of the *Janjaweed*, and not to actively pursue peace negotiation, nor to facilitating freedom of access of the humanitarian workers and the monitors. In order to help the government to disarm the *Janjaweed*, and protect the civilians under threat, the Security Council notably applied one real measure, an arms embargo. However, this embargo was limited to non-governmental entities in Darfur only. Therefore, it included the *Janjaweed* (mentioned explicitly) as well as the rebel militias SLA and JEM (not mentioned) but not the government forces. In addition, the Government of Sudan was required to disarm the *Janjaweed* under threat of further sanctions.

Looking at the statements made by several Security Council members gives some understanding as to why this compromise arose.[77] Only China and Pakistan abstained from voting, while all other members voted in favour. China stated that it was opposed to the "mandatory measures against the Sudanese government" in the resolution. The only "mandatory measure" in the resolution was the demand of the disarmament of the *Janjaweed* as stated above. China put the primary responsibility for *resolving* the Darfur situation to the

---

77   UN Doc.: S/PV.5015, 30 July 2004.

government of Sudan. The reason it did not vote against the resolution was to support the leadership of the African Union. This may explain partly why most paragraphs enacted under the Chapter VII are referring to activities and plans already underway, not to new measures. Even the "mandatory measures" of *Janjaweed* disarmament were already agreed, for instance in the Joint Communiqué with the UN SG Annan from 3 July. The Security Council merely put a timeline on the measure. In addition, China, but also Pakistan's reason for abstaining, was that the resolution only mentions the *possibility* of future sanctions. Since the Chinese representative did not refer to the arms embargo this measure is seemingly of a lesser concern to China.

After the vote all the other members made their statements. The US contrasted the Chinese interpretation of the situation by stating that "the responsibility for this disaster lies squarely with the [Sudanese] government." The US further noted a list of promises made by the Sudanese government which were not fulfilled, notably the establishment of general security, the rebuilding of confidence with the civilian population, the immediate disarmament of the *Janjaweed* and the security of IDP camps. These commitments are regarded by the US as measure of compliance with the international community. However, except for the *Janjaweed* disarmament, none of these commitments were adopted in the resolution. Furthermore, the US underlined the current arms embargo and the prospect of sanctions. To all who might find this resolution too weak, because it does not refer to the atrocities as genocide, the US answers that it had succeeded to name and condemn the violence with an "ethnic dimension."

The UK emphasised that the "obligation to protect" lies with the government, while the rebels also share responsibility of the crisis. Furthermore, it gave a wide interpretation of the sanctions to be considered the following month as it put two further conditions not mentioned in the resolution, notably the start of constructive peace talks and an end of intimidation and atrocities by both the government and the rebels.

Russia on the opposite side, found it "of fundamental importance (...) that the resolution does not foresee possible further Security Council action with regard to Darfur." The Russian position was explained at the time in its economic ties with Sudan, delivering fighter planes at the same moment this resolution was adopted.[78]

---

78 Peterson, Scott, "Sudan's Ties at the UN," Christian Science Monitor, 31 August 2004, available at http://www.csmonitor.com/2004/0831/p01s02-wogi.htm [accessed 15 October 2013] cited in Williams, P.D. and Bellamy, A.J. (2005) "The responsibility to protect and the crisis in Darfur," *Security Dialogue*, Vol.: 36(1), p. 33.

Germany repeated its support for the recommendations made in the report of the UN High Commissioner for Human Rights mentioned in Resolution 1547. It explicitly called, for "the establishment of an independent international commission of inquiry into the abuses committed in Darfur." This was a repetition of the EU Council declaration a few days earlier, discussed above, and consequently was backed by Spain and France as well. France mainly emphasised the solution to the humanitarian disaster by granting access of aid, and bringing the *Janjaweed*, "whose behaviour has been atrocious," to justice. One sole sentence was dedicated to the commitment of the ceasefire and peace talks.

Sudan gave a closing, but lengthy and angry, response to the current debate, suggesting US conspiracies. Sudan initially refused to accept the resolution. Egypt's Foreign Minister at the time, Abu'l Gheith, urgently called members of the Sudanese government in order to convince them that under the circumstances this resolution was the best deal they could get and that they thus should accept it.[79]

7.8   International Actors Dealing with the Sudanese Government

Sudan was now condemned for its actions in Darfur in the Security Council. However, there were no automatic mandatory measures adopted (apart from a limited arms embargo), and international actors had to do their utmost to have the Sudanese government change its actions. Intense diplomatic activity can be observed during this period from many sides.

7.8.1   *Incoherent Demands*

The US and European countries aimed to maximise pressure, but they failed to form a common line on perhaps the most important aspect, the timeline for disarmament of the *Janjaweed*. The Sudanese government was given multiple contrasting deadlines to comply with the demands given. There is the Joint Communiqué of 3 July with UN SG Annan, which included the "immediate" start of *Janjaweed* disarmament, but the communiqué does not mention a timeframe.[80] After a closed UNSC briefing on 7 July, the US ambassador to the UN, while referring to the Joint Communiqué, said that the government needed

---

79   According to Egypt's ambassador in Khartoum at the time in a conversation with Adriaan Kooijmans. Authors' interview with Adriaan Kooijmans, 16 September 2013; personal communication 29 December 2013.

80   UN News, 3 July 2004, "At end of Annan's trip, Sudan pledges to end conflict in Darfur."

to act "in days."[81] Resolution 1556 demanded from the UN SG a report on the progress of *Janjaweed* disarmament in 30 days after adoption on 30 July and monthly thereafter. The EU Council decided to follow a 90-day period that was given by the UN.[82] Even, the Sudanese UN ambassador complained that a 90-day period, which according to him had started with the signing of the Joint Communiqué, had not yet passed at the time that Resolution 1556 stipulates the 30-day reporting obligation.[83] On 5 August, UN SGSR Pronk signed and another agreement with Sudan Foreign Minister Ismail, intended as a follow up to Resolution 1556, which committed the government to take "detailed steps" to disarm *Janjaweed* in the following 30 days.[84]

7.8.2   UN SGSR *Pronk and Visits of* UN *Experts*

In Khartoum UN SG Special Representative Pronk tried to execute Resolution 1556 by agreeing with the government to a 'Joint Implementation Mechanism,' which spelt out in more detail which actions of the government were needed in order for Pronk to report back to the Security Council that Sudan was cooperating. In particular it included a 'plan of action' or 'Pronk plan', described in his August report to the UNSC.[85] This plan proposed designating 'safe areas' from where the government troops and its militias would withdraw.

Pronk later tried to introduce the plan in the negotiation talks in Abuja, but this was not supported by the US and EU observers. The US and the EU did not support the concept of safe areas and objected to its introduction in the Abuja negotiations, because they believed the strategy of 'safe areas' was wrong. The government tended to abuse the notion of safe areas to attack those areas that fell outside it.[86] Additionally, the plan was a commitment between the UN and the Sudanese government, and hence excluded the rebels. The US complained that it was not consulted on the plan, and would not commit to the actions and demands set forth in the plan, but instead would keep with its own list of requirements for the Sudanese government.[87] For Pronk it was rather a way to get involved into the negotiations rather than trying to hijack it.[88]

---

81   UN webcast of 7 July 2004, available at https://www.un.org/webcast/arc2004c.html [accessed at 19 July 2013].

82   US State Department Cable, Brussels, 27 July 2004, No. 3195.

83   UN Doc.: S/pv.5015, 30 July 2004, p. 12.

84   UN News, 5 August 2004, "UN envoy and Sudanese Foreign Minister pen deal to disarm militias in Darfur."

85   UN Doc.: S/2004/703, 30 August 2004.

86   US State Department Cable, Brussels, 20 September 2004, No. 3989.

87   US State Department Cable, Brussels, 20 September 2004, No. 3989.

88   Authors' interview with Adriaan Kooijmans, 16 September 2013.

Nevertheless, Pronk's contacts and negotiations with the government were in close cooperation with diplomatic missions, in particular the Netherlands, US, UK, and Norway.[89] Pronk, as a UN Special Representative with responsibility for the UN day-to-day operations, faced more constraints in criticising the government openly than diplomats in Khartoum did. In a game of 'good cop, bad cop', Pronk would invite diplomats from western, African and Arab countries to participate in monthly coordination meetings that he co-chaired with Foreign Minister Ismail who coordinated the interaction, from the Sudanese side, between the UN and the various ministers and government agencies. In these meetings, Western ambassadors felt free to speak their mind and complain about perceived Sudanese violations of the various UNSC resolutions whereas Pronk had to tread more carefully and avoid antagonising his Sudanese counterparts (at least not in the presence of ambassadors). In this manner these coordination meetings proved to be reasonably productive despite the obstruction from the Sudanese side that the UN was facing in its daily operations.[90]

Actions from other UN departments since April 2004 were characterised by the build-up of a large humanitarian effort and the visits of a number of special rapporteurs. Firstly two "fact-finding missions" were sent in April. The first, on the request of Acting High Commissioner Bertrand Ramcharan, visited the refugee camps in Chad to document human rights violations in Sudan and later to Darfur.[91] Ramcharan briefed the Security Council on the report of this mission in a closed meeting on 7 May.[92] The second was sent on 28 April as a high-level mission lead by James Morris, the Executive Director of the UN WFP, and focused on assessing the needs for humanitarian action.[93]

Around and following Annan's visit in early July and while the Security Council was following the situation in Darfur, there were seven UN special representatives and rapporteurs visiting Sudan in a short time span. In June Special Rapporteur for extrajudicial, summary or arbitrary executions Asma

---

89   Authors' interview with Jan Pronk, 2 September 2013.

90   Authors' interview with Adriaan Kooijmans, 16 September 2013.

91   UN News, 6 April 2004, "UN human rights fact-finding team begins work as conditions worsen"; See previous chapter.

92   UN Doc.: E/CN.4/2005/3, 3 May 2004; UN News, 7 May 2004, "UN finds Sudan has carried out massive human rights violations in Darfur."

93   UN Doc.: AFR/908 IHA/895, 23 April 2004. The mission was officially on the invitation of the Sudanese Government. According to Egeland the mission was led by Morris since the Government was angry with him for having given a dramatic account to the Security Council and in the media (Authors' interview with Jan Egeland, 28 November 2012).

Jahangir visited Darfur, and reported to the UNCHR.[94] In the last week of July Francis Deng, Secretary-General's Representative on IDPs, visited Darfur.[95] On 30 August the Director of the UN's Internal Displacement Division Dennis McNamara visited the region for one day.[96] Emmanuel Akwei Addo visited the country in August as independent expert pursuant to a resolution adopted by the CHR.[97] Later in September, after the Security Council decided to authorise a Commission on Inquiry to establish whether genocide had occurred in Darfur, UN SG Annan sent two more envoys High Commissioner for Human Rights Louise Arbour and Special Advisor on the Prevention of Genocide Juan Méndez. However, their assignment was "not to describe or characterize what is happening, but to see what more can be done to stop it, and to prevent further abuses."[98] They reported to the Security Council on their return, but actually described the current situation and advised further international action rather than keeping strictly with the assignment.[99] Finally, the UNCHR Special Rapporteur on violence against women, its causes and consequences Yakin Ertürk also visited Sudan and Darfur and also writes a report for the CHR.[100]

There are several observations to make. Firstly, Each of these representatives and rapporteurs told a similar story on the appalling situation in Darfur, the lack of action from the side of the Sudanese government to make the situation better, or even the government's direct responsibility for the continuing violence. Secondly, these envoys and rapporteurs came both from the UN in New York and from the humanitarian side in Geneva and they reported on their missions to both places.

However, the visits did not seem very well coordinated as each of them visited Sudan on their own schedule, which did occasionally overlap. Pronk stated

---

94   UN News, 29 June 2004, "UN human rights expert expects large number of deaths in Darfur"; UN Doc.: E/CN.4/2005/7/Add.2, 6 August 2004.

95   UN Doc.: AFR/1005 HR/4785, 2 August 2004. The statement acknowledges that his visit follows that of many high profile actors in recent months, but that nonetheless his mission has value, since Mr. Deng is Sudanese as well as a Special Representative for the UNSG.

96   UN News, 30 August 2004, "Darfur's displaced remain traumatized and at risk of rape, harassment – UN official."

97   UN Doc.: E/CN.4/2005/11, 28 February 2005.

98   UN SG press statement, 16 September 2004, available at http://www.un.org/sg/offthecuff/?nid=629 [accessed 8 July 2013].

99   UN News, 30 September 2004, "UN rights officials tell Security Council international police are required in Sudan."

100   UN Doc.: AFR/1035 HR/4795, 27 September 2004; UN Doc. E/CN.4/2005/75/add.5 (23 December 2004).

that this unorganised situation is characteristic for how the UN functions, as each rapporteur feels the need to come for his/her own mandate.[101] His 'unified approach' was starting to work in Sudan, but the offices in New York and Geneva had not changed their practices. One could see these visits also in a different light. For instance, eight UN human rights experts had issued a joint statement of concern over Darfur already back in March.[102] By visiting Sudan regularly over the following months they kept up the pressure on the Sudanese government to heed their concerns.

7.8.3   *First Mediation Rounds*

Another way for international actors to try to address the conflict was through intensive support of political talks. The ceasefire agreement of 8 April in N'Djamena foresaw the organisation of talks for a political settlement. Hence, the first attempts to set up proper negotiations for a lasting settlement are by the end of April 2004.[103] However, the initial attention went primarily to the humanitarian situation and access for relief workers. As discussed before, Annan tried to push for the start of such talks in May. There was a first negotiation attempt in July in Addis Ababa, on the sidelines of an AU meeting, but not much came out of this.[104] The rebel groups and government mainly exchanged accusations and demands.[105]

In July the Vatican based group Sant'Egidio proposed to the US to mediate between the rebels and the Sudanese government.[106] It indicated that it had good relationships with both sides, but asked permission from the US to proceed. Also the Geneva based NGO Centre for Humanitarian Dialogue was already involved and closely cooperating with the US. These mediators were present during negotiations but appeared not to be in a leading position in the negotiations.[107] This involvement of mediation experts contrasts with the

---

101   Authors' interview with Jan Pronk, 21 August 2006.

102   UN High Commission for Human Rights, 26 March 2004, "Eight UN Human Rights experts gravely concerned about reported widespread abuses in Darfur, Sudan," see Chapter 4. Some of the signatories later also visited Sudan, notably Yakin Ertürk, Asma Jahangir and Francis Deng.

103   Totten and Markussen (2006), p. 15.

104   AU press release, Addis Ababa, 7 August 2004.

105   Toga, D. (2007) "The African Union Mediation and the Abuja Peace Talks," in *War in Darfur and the search for peace*, by de Waal, A. (ed.), Global Equity Initiative, Harvard University, p. 220.

106   US State Department Cable, Vatican, 26 July 2004, No. 2892.

107   Sant'Egidio is present as observer at the negation rounds in August/September (US State Department Cable, 3 September 2004, Abuja, No. 1515). Centre for Humanitarian Dialogue

assertion of some authors that the EU left the negotiations to local diplomats who lacked that experience.[108] This is therefore only partly true. Mediation experts were involved, but the AU was in the lead.

On 23 August, political negotiations started under the auspices of the AU led by President Obasanjo of Nigeria in Abuja.[109] The real negotiation sessions were initially closed to the international observers of the UN, the US and the EU. Obasanjo had purposely organised it this way, whereas the rebel group preferred that the international observers would be present at all sessions. This was later granted. The western delegations in turn were instrumental in moving the rebels towards serious negotiations. In general, the representatives of the rebel groups were inexperienced in negotiations tactics and had no clear strategy or well-defined aims for the talks. The US and EU observers urged the rebels to keep a constructive position in the negotiations. For instance, the observers argued to the rebels that they could risk losing influence on future solutions, such as was the case under the Pronk plan, if they would not be sufficiently constructive.[110] In addition, also the AU mediators are described as inexperienced, albeit sincerely dedicated.[111]

As the AU-led negotiations were continuing in September, US Secretary of State Powell made a declaration that the US government had concluded that genocide had occurred in Darfur (see below). US diplomats noted that after this statement the Sudanese government representatives became more accommodative in negotiations, agreeing to a larger AU force and committed to disarming the *Janjaweed*.[112] This round of negotiations, which did not yield much apart from having the parties agreed to talk seriously, were ended by 14 September to be continued in late October.

In short, although a real negotiation process was now underway, it did not proceed smoothly. Compounding the lack of trust between the warring parties were the amateurish negotiation skills of the rebels. The Sudanese government

---

is present during the talks of the N'Djamena 8 April ceasefire, and training the JEM for the second round of talks (US State Department Cable, Brussels; 19 March 2004, 1151; Abuja, 26 October 2004, No. 1811).

108 Keane, R. and Wee, A. (2010) "The European Union," in *The International politics of mass atrocities. The case of Darfur*, by Black, D.R. and Williams, P.D. (eds.), London, New York: Routledge, p. 124.

109 UN News, 24 august 2004, "UN observes latests round of peace talks between Sudan and Darfur rebel groups"; UN Doc. press release SC/8173 AFR/1014, 24 August 2004.

110 US State Department Cable, Abuja, 13 September 2004, No. 1573.

111 US State Department Cables, Abuja, 24 August 2004, No. 1456; Abuja, 25 August 2004, No. 1461; Abuja, 3 September 2004, No. 1514; Abuja, 3 September 2004, No. 1515.

112 US State Department Cables, Abuja, 13 September 2004, No. 1573.

in contrast was an experienced machine, having had years of experience in negotiations with the SPLM, always trying to take advantage of divisions. Although the western countries and the UN sometimes appeared to lack coordination, their aim was to not allow the Sudanese government to take advantage of that.[113]

7.8.4   Decision on No other Military Involvement but the Expansion of AMIS

The decision on a non-African intervention by either western nations or through the UN is related to the decision to expand AMIS to a peacekeeping force. Within the US, EU and UN there were discussions on the need for an international intervention. But these discussions remained in a very preliminary state because of the limitations on both the side of the potential "sending countries" and on the characteristics of the conflict and the location, as will be explained in this section.

There were, firstly, limitations on the side of sending countries. Since the US and the UK were heavily involved in Iraq, the practical limits of their militaries may have been reached, if not operationally then politically.[114] Without being to formal about this position, smaller contributions were still a possibility. The UK did suggest it was preparing for a deployment during 2004, putting 5000 troops on standby.[115] However, this may have been more for diplomatic pressure and to satisfy domestic audiences than actual planning.[116] Within the EU there was some speculation of US intervention after their strong position against Sudan in the Commission on Human Rights in April.[117] In fact, in the summer of 2004 some "lower-ranking government officials" and US diplomats in Khartoum had allegedly advised to use a limited US military contribution to bolster AMIS, but the idea was never taken up in Washington.[118] Some authors

---

113   Idem.

114   Having attacked Iraq and Afghanistan in recent years, the "US could not be seen 'as invading another Muslim country'" (The Washington Post, 29 October 2007, "U.S. promises on Darfur don't match actions").

115   BBC News, 25 July 2004, "UK troops 'ready to go to Sudan'"; Bieckmann (2012), pp. 260–261.

116   EC Commission official Manahl qualified these rumours as "a trial balloon that enjoys no support elsewhere in the EU," also because the UK had not mentioned the idea during official EU meetings. US State Department Cable, Brussels, 29 July 2004. See also Cockett, R. (2010) Sudan: Darfur and the Failure of an African State. New Haven: Yale University Press, pp. 227–228.

117   US State Department Cable, Brussels, 3 May 2004, No. 1987.

118   The Washington Post, 29 October 2007, "U.S. promises on Darfur don't match actions."

have noted that President Bush did look into the possibility of intervention, but this was only in late 2005.[119] France, which was not involved in Iraq, had military stationed in the region, close to the Chad-Sudan border in Abaché, Chad, as well as in Djibouti. 200 of those troops were deployed to protect refugee camps in Chad in the summer of 2004.[120] One author highlights that France certainly had the capacity to intervene in the region, but generally tends to do so only on its own terms for its own interests.[121] The EU discussed internally within the European Commission the possibility of setting up a EU mission to Darfur. However, the option was quickly discarded. The conclusion was that contributions of EU forces are "highly unlikely."[122] Another anonymous EU official stated that, however frustrated European leaders are with the situation in Darfur, the EU is "simply not up to something like [military intervention] yet."[123]

Another option that was considered was linking the planning of UNMIS, the UN mission for peacekeeping once the CPA would be signed, and the need for troops in Darfur.[124] The idea was that the future UN mission could potentially incorporate Darfur as well. However, this idea never got very far either, mainly due to lack of support from both the UN DPKO as well as Sudan.[125] DPKO was primarily against because there was no peace to keep.[126] Pronk remembered

119   Hamilton, R. (2011a) *Fighting for Darfur: public action and the struggle to stop genocide.* New York: Palgrave Macmillan, p. 77–79; Seymour, L.J.M. (2013) "Let's Bulshit! Arguing bargaining and dissembling over Darfur." *European Journal of International Relations,* forthcoming, p. 11.

120   Igiri and Lyman (2004) p. 10. Agence France Presse, 27 August 2004, "Chirac: la France continuera à participer activement à l'aide au Darfour" [Chirac: France continues to participate actively in the aid to Darfur]. France supplied air transport for humanitarian aid to the camps in Chad, and security along the border. The operation was called *Opération Dorca,* and received support from French troops that were stationed since long time in Chad under *Opération Epervier.*

121   Charbonneau, B. "France," in *The International politics of mass atrocities. The case of Darfur,* by Black, D.R. and Williams, P.D. (eds.), 2010, London, New York: Routledge.

122   US State Department cable, Brussels, 16 July 2004, No. 3055.

123   The Economist, 29 July 2004, "The world notices Darfur."

124   E.g. Dutch Minister for Development Cooperation van Ardenne suggests this in the Dutch Parliament (Dutch Parliamentary Doc.: Tweede Kamer, 2003–2004, meeting 89, p. 5691, 29 June 2004.

125   A more thorough discussion on this option is presented below.

126   Cockett (2010), p. 229; Hamilton (2011a), p. 86; Natsios, A. (2012) *Sudan, South Sudan and Darfur: what everyone needs to know.* Oxford: Oxford University Press, p. 159. According to Pronk, DPKO changed its position in January 2006 (Authors' interview with Jan Pronk, 2 September 2013).

that DPKO instructed him not to pressure for greater UN involvement alongside or instead of AMIS.[127]

Secondly, there were limitations related to the particularities of Darfur. All western countries that would consider getting involved faced a conflict that was taking place across a vast territory; Darfur is often compared to the size of France or the state of Texas. Additionally, Darfur was far away from supply lines such as major seaports and airports, while the main perpetrator, the government in Khartoum, was not located in the same area. There was no peace agreement, a ceasefire only on paper, and many warring parties. Any involvement would potentially risk many casualties and an indeterminate exit. These considerations were instrumental in the avoidance of any specific proposals from the West on military interventions.[128] For instance, even Mukesh Kapila, one of the more vocal actors with respect to the use of multiple instruments, notes that a robust presence would have had problems achieving its goals due to these aspects.[129]

Thirdly, there were multiple political constraints on foreign intervention. Even though the African Union was quick in agreeing to a mission in Darfur, African countries that were in favour of strong AU action were simultaneously against western intervention. Nigerian President Obasanjo was credited with being very active in moving the parties during negotiations and in committing troops to the AU mission, but he was similarly a firm believer in the doctrine, "African solutions to African problems."[130] The AU limited the US and European help to facilitation, planning, administration and financing. This does not mean that the West wanted things organised differently. One observer stated that the emphasised "African character" of AMIS (and the later hybrid AU-UN missions for Darfur) is ultimately a western invention,

127   Pronk as referred to in Mackinnon, M.G. (2010) "The United Nations Security Council," in *The International politics of mass atrocities. The case of Darfur*, by Black, D.R. and Williams, P.D. (eds.), London, New York: Routledge, p. 86.

128   Authors' interviews with Christian Manahl, 26 August 2013; Eckhard Straus, 1 June 2005; see also discussion in Chapter 8.7.

129   UK House of Commons, International Development Committee. "Darfur, Sudan: The responsibility to protect" Fifth Report of Session 2004–05, Volume II Oral and Written Statements, p. ev54. However, at the time he did tell to the UN Secretariat that troops should be considered (Kapila, M., 2013, *Against a tide of evil*. Edinburg: Mainstream Publishing, p. 188).

130   Badescu, C. and Bergholm, L. (2010) "The African Union," in *The International politics of mass atrocities. The case of Darfur*, by Black, D.R. and Williams, P.D. (eds.), London, New York: Routledge, p. 100.

since the US and EU countries had no wish to put their own military on the ground.[131]

Another political constraint lay with the Sudanese government. Sudan was naturally firmly against foreign intervention. It had no reason to accept any forceful international force on its territory. If Sudan was careful enough to keep the situation in Darfur a domestic issue, then it would be feasible to maintain the support within the UNSC of those permanent members that classically defend national sovereignty. AMIS was and would remain a force that was in Darfur with the permission of the Sudanese government. In this way Sudan maintained a strong control on AMIS' operational capacity.

As stated, the deployment of the AU observer mission did not proceed without problems. Despite, or perhaps because of, these problems, the AU with western support decided in August 2004 that the observer mission needed to be changed to a peacekeeping mission, both in terms of the mandate and number of troops. A vital change was that the mission would now be authorised to protect civilians, whereas the original AMIS mission was officially only authorised to protect the ceasefire monitors.[132] UN DPKO, in helping the AU to plan for the new mission, made an informal plan for a 3000 strong military and police mission, which was subsequently taken over by the AU.[133] However, the new AMIS was not tasked to actively disarm militias, which instead remained the responsibility of the government.

The Nigerian government approved such an expansion of AMIS on 19 August with the pledge to send an additional 1500 troops.[134] During negotiations that were going on at that time in Abuja, the Sudanese government agreed to an expanded AU mission. Subsequently, the first weeks of September were used to arrange all the formal support for such a mission. On 2 September UN SGSR Pronk recommended formally to the UNSC to expand the AU mission.[135] Nigeria started to push other African countries for more observers, and intended to demand the support from the UN via UN SG Annan and the UNSC president.[136] The EU Council, the AU PSC and finally the UNSC all endorsed the plan.[137]

---

131   Authors' interviews with Christian Manahl, 26 August 2013.

132   Authors' interview with Eckhart Straus, 1 June 2005.

133   Authors' interview with Chris Coleman, 24 May 2005.

134   Totten and Markussen (2006), Ch. Chronology.

135   UN Doc. S/2004/703, 30 August 2004. Pronk briefs the Council on his report on 2 September.

136   US State Department Cable, Abuja, 6 September 2004, No. 1528.

137   AU Doc.: PSC/PR/Comm. XVI, 17 September 2004; UN Doc. S/Res/1564 (2004), 18 September 2004.

In addition, the EU, in its endorsement, proposed a EU police support mission to the AU in Darfur.[138]

7.9   Towards Resolution 1564

As UN Resolution 1556 stipulated a reassessment of the situation in Darfur within 30 days after its adoption, a new resolution was on the table in early September. The report by SGSR Pronk indicated that there was no improvement on the disarmament of the *Janjaweed*, but there was improvement on the access of humanitarian workers to the region.[139]

7.9.1   *The US Calls the Situation in Darfur "Genocide"*

The US is often cited as the only country to have called to situation in Darfur 'genocide'. US Secretary of State Powell did this on 9 September 2004. At the same time Powell underscored that "no new action is dictated by this determination."[140] The decision of the White House to call the situation in Darfur genocide was primarily due to domestic politics, rather than strategic foreign policy, or conclusive evidence. The process leading up to the genocide statement started with pressure in the US Congress. In late June Congressman Donald Payne started the legislative procedures to have the US Congress declare the situation in Darfur a genocide with the introduction of a bill to the House of Representatives, followed with a call on the State Department to determine whether genocide was occurring in Darfur.[141] Already at that moment legal counsellors of the State Department argued that a determination of genocide would not obligate a US military intervention, opening the way for a research.[142] The State Department set up an investigation team that would interview refugees from Darfur in eastern Chad.[143] While this process was

---

138   EU Doc.: Press release 12068/04, 13 September 2004. The discussions surrounding the EU police mission is presented below.

139   UN Doc.: S/2004/703, 30 August 2004.

140   He consequently argued: "We have been doing everything we can to get the Sudanese government to act responsibly. So let us not be preoccupied with this designation of genocide." Secretary Colin L. Powell, "The Crisis In Darfur," Written Remarks Before the Senate Foreign Relations Committee Washington DC, 9 September 2004, available at http://2001-2009.state.gov/secretary/former/powell/remarks/36032.htm [accessed 16 December 2013].

141   US Congress, H.Amdt. 651 to H.R. 4754, 7 July 2004.

142   State Department internal memo, authored by William H. Taft, IV, 25 June 2004, "Genocide and Darfur." See also Hamilton (2011a), p. 36.

143   Markussen & Totten, 2006.

underway the US Congress declared formally that genocide occurred in Darfur on 22 July.[144] It is generally understood that the proactive position of the US Congress was due to pressure from the conservative Christian groups as well as African American communities (for a further discussion, see Section 7.10.2).

Internationally, the US Congress resolution meant that the UN, especially Annan, was confronted with questions on his opinion as to the (legal) qualification of the conflict. He generally kept with the view that the label mattered neither for the people of Darfur nor for those who can offer solutions.[145] The assembly of the African Union rejected the label of genocide.[146]

The American investigation team returned to the US by mid-August and issued a report some weeks later.[147] The evidence of this investigation turned out to be of secondary importance. The US Government Accountability Office later added reservations to the report, but already at the time of issue Powell was aware that it lacked indisputable evidence for the determination of genocide.[148] One of the main problems was to prove 'intent', and the evidence from the investigation was not able to provide the evidence for this directly. The question of intent had to be seen from the circumstances of the attacks and the failure of the government to act against the *Janjaweed*.[149] Given the actions from the US Congress, the pressure was high on the White House to make a decision on the situation in Darfur. Several sources agree that the domestic pressure was so high for Secretary of State Powell that he had no choice other than to declare that genocide had occurred in Darfur.[150] It was a judgement call, made by Powell and not prevented by President Bush or National Security Advisor Condoleezza Rice.[151] Powell made the statement on 9 September 2004

---

144 H. CON. RES. 467, 108th congress, 2nd session, 22 July 2004. "Concurrent resolution, declaring genocide in Darfur, Sudan."

145 UN, Off the Cuff, Secretary-General's press conference, 25 June 2004, available at http://www.un.org/sg/offthecuff/?nid=600 [accessed 14 October 2013].

146 AU Doc.: Assembly of the African Union, Third Ordinary Session, 6–8 July 2004, Decision on Darfur.

147 US Bureau of Democracy, Human Rights, and Labor and the Bureau of Intelligence and Research, "Documenting Atrocities in Darfur," State Publication 11182, September 2004.

148 Seymour (2013).

149 Kostas, S.A. (2006) "Making the determination of genocide in Darfur," in *Genocide in Darfur: Investigating the atrocities in the Sudan*, by Totten, S. and Markussen, E. (eds.), London, New York: Routledge, pp. 120–122.

150 Prunier (2007), p. 140, based on an anonymous US official; Authors' interview with Jan Pronk, 21 August 2006; Seymour (2013), p. 10.

151 Hamilton (2011a), p. 38; Hamilton, R. (2011b) "Inside Colin Powell's decision to declare genocide in Darfur," *The Atlantic*, 17 August 2011.

in front of the Senate Foreign Relations Committee.[152] He barely needed to consult with other members of the administration; instead they were just notified. There is no indication that any of its international partners, either the UN Secretariat or EU leaders, were given early notice, which further indicates that the issue was driven more by domestic factors than by the necessity to organise an common international approach against Sudan.[153]

The statement caused some response from the EU and from negotiating parties at the ongoing Darfur talks in Abuja. As discussed above, US diplomats in Abuja noticed that the Sudanese government shifted towards a greater accommodation to western demands. On the other hand, Pronk noted that for the rebels it might have worked in the opposite direction. Their hard line position was rewarded with strong US language and, despite Powell's claims otherwise, suggestions of US intervention.[154] They understood that there was no need for them to compromise.

US ambassador to the UN Danforth stated that in his eyes, this event had no real effect for the situation in Sudan: "it was something that would appeal to the constituency (...) this was something that was said for internal consumption within the United States, I did not think it would have very much effect within Sudan."[155] Seymour quoted one senior UN official who stated that Powell had also as much as admitted in a closed meeting that "it was made in response to domestic pressure, that he was personally sceptical and that the issue was proving to be a distraction."[156] Several authors also argued that the genocide rhetoric was primarily adopted as a substitute for stronger action.[157]

7.9.2   *European Response to US Genocide Declaration and New Initiatives*

Pieter Feith, the Deputy Director General for Politico-Military Affairs of the Council of the EU and adviser to High-Representative Solana, visited Sudan

---

152   Secretary Colin L. Powell, Testimony before the Senate Foreign Relations Committee, United States of America, 9 September 2004. The report on which the statement is based does not use the term genocide. See also Seymour (2013), p. 11.

153   However, Hamilton (2011a, p. 38) notes that Powell may have considered that his statement could help push the UNSC to adopt stronger actions.

154   Authors' interview with Jan Pronk, 2 September 2013; Seymour (2013), p. 17.

155   BBC Panorama, Fergal Keane interview with John Danforth, 3 July 2005, available at http://news.bbc.co.uk/1/hi/programmes/panorama/4647211.stm [accessed 5 October 2013].

156   Seymour (2013), p. 10.

157   Heinze, E.A. (2007) "The rhetoric of genocide in U.S. foreign policy: Rwanda and Darfur compared," *Political Science Quarterly*, Vol.: 122(3), p. 362; Mayroz (2008), p. 381; Flint, J. (2010) "Rhetoric and reality: The failure to resolve the Darfur Conflict," Small Arms Survey, Geneva; Seymour (2013).

and the AU Head Quarters in a fact-finding mission looking into the possibility for EU cooperation to further support the African Union mission in Sudan.[158] This emphasis on AU support made sure that the mission was conducted with the authorisation of the Sudanese government.[159] Once returned, in a radio interview, he "refrains from making any statement on whether the situation constitutes a genocide," when asked to do so.[160] This is because Feith felt that he did not have the competences. This does not mean, however, that he was of the opinion that the situation in Darfur did *not* constitute genocide, nor was he downplaying the situation.[161] The media nonetheless misinterpreted his statement as if he considered that the situation did not constitute genocide.[162] During a meeting between American diplomats and officials from the EU Commission and the Netherlands, Feith's statement was briefly discussed. A Dutch Foreign Affairs official regretted his statement if it "allowed the [Sudanese government] to get the misimpression that the EU was less concerned than the US about the situation."[163] The confusion over Feith's statement was also discussed in the Dutch Parliament. Foreign Minister Bot stated that Feith did not have the mandate to make a "political judgment" on the situation but should have kept with his mission. Bot stated that it is up to the UN to investigate it, by the special advisor on the prevention of genocide Juan Méndez for example.[164]

More importantly, Feith had identified a potential role for the EU in a police mission in Darfur. This proposal would not necessarily mean European forces, but at least very strong European support, including police training.[165] This proposal fitted in the general willingness among EU countries to do more than humanitarian aid and was henceforth discussed in the EU Council. The EU indicated from an early stage that it had wanted to go beyond humanitarian

---

158   Pieter Feith is a career diplomat from the Netherlands, having been active in Dutch for-
        eign service and NATO. He had served in Khartoum as *Chargé d'Affaires* during the 1980s,
        effectively the most senior Dutch diplomat in Sudan since the Netherlands had no ambas-
        sador in Sudan at that time.

159   Authors' interview with Pieter Feith, 28 August 2013.

160   Idem.

161   Idem. Email of Pieter Feith to the authors, 21 December 2013.

162   De Volkskrant, 10 August 2004, "EU: Sudan beschermt burgers niet" [EU: Sudan does
        not protects its citizens]; Guardian, 10 August 2004, "Sudan massacres are not genocide,
        says EU."

163   US State Department Cable, Brussels, 20 September 2004, No. 3989.

164   Dutch Parliamentary Doc.: Tweede Kamer, 2003–2004, 29 501–502, nr. 577, 1 September
        2004.

165   Idem.

assistance, and considered the contribution of own personnel already in late April.[166] Following the fact-finding mission of Pieter Feith in August, the EU indicated on multiple occasions that it wanted to organise a police mission in Darfur.[167]

In September the EU Council met again, once informally in the Netherlands ('Gymnich-meeting'), and two weeks later for new decisions. A few days before the Gymnich meeting UN SGSR Pronk delivered his report on the progress the Sudanese had made with respect to their agreements with the UN.[168] As expected by the ministers, the government failed in providing security and disarming of *Janjaweed*. During the Gymnich meeting the European ministers agreed to further support an expanded AU mission, while the EU police mission was discussed. In principle this EU police mission was supported but "some countries" demanded that support is only provided if the AU would take full responsibility.[169] Additionally, High-Representative Solana and Commissioner Patten were asked, again, to quickly create a list of options for sanctions. An oil-boycott was not discussed as one of the options, but when asked about it Minister Bot was sceptic to its use and effects.[170]

At the second September meeting, the Dutch presidency aimed to change the focus from sanctions to AU support.[171] According to the Netherlands, the UNSC would discuss the previously mentioned report of Pronk, and it was up to the Security Council to make a decision on sanctions, not the EU any longer. In the EU Council conclusion the ministers maintained a threat of sanctions, supported a proposed Commission of Inquiry on the question of genocide and offered help for an AU police unit.[172] The request to Solana for a list of options on sanctions is repeated as a way to prepare for possible future decisions.[173]

---

166   US State Department Cable, Brussels, 3 May, 2004, No. 1897; This information is at this stage still debated internally. The cable refers to an European Council meeting of 27 April. The press release after this statement does not indicate that the EU intends to offer more help (EC Press release 8567/04, 27 April 2004).

167   US State Department Cable, Brussels, 8 September 2004, No. 3772; EC Press release 12068/04, 13 September 2004.

168   UN Doc.: S/2004/704, 30 August 2004.

169   Dutch Parliamentary Doc.: Tweede Kamer, 2003–2004, 21 501–502, nr. 569, 7 September 2004.

170   US State Department Cable, Brussels, 8 September 2004, No. 3772; Dutch Parliamentary Doc.: Tweede Kamer, 2003–2004, 21 501–502, 21 501–520, nr. 577, 1 September 2004.

171   Dutch Parliamentary Doc.: Tweede Kamer, 2003–2004, 21 501–502, nr. 570, 13 September 2004.

172   EU Doc.: press release 81897/04, 13 September 2004.

173   Idem; US State Department Cable, The Hague, 10 September 2004, No. 2289.

However, the conclusions also stated that decisions of sanctions must be in accordance to UNSC Resolution 1556.

The ministers were taken aback by US Secretary of State Powell 'genocide-statement'. France dismissed the term genocide and stuck to the label of civil war. The Belgian Minister of Cooperation also argued that the genocide finding was "inappropriate and simplistic."[174] Even UK officials refrained from using the label.[175] Within the Dutch Foreign Ministry Department of International Law the label was discussed at the end of July and in August.[176] The government was not in favour to take a position at that moment and it argued that it was up to the UNSC to decide on the issue.[177] Therefore the EU Council did not want to make a similar statement as the Americans, but felt that it needed to acknowledge Powell's declaration in some way.[178] The general opinion among EU foreign ministers was that it would be up to the UN to make such calls, not individual governments. In order to be in line with UNSC and Special Representative Pronk, the EU Council supported a Commission of Inquiry to investigate the situation, including with the task to determine whether genocide had occurred.[179] Finally, the EU conclusions had been changed during the meeting from "moratorium on all military air operations" to "moratorium on military operations."[180]

There are three observations to make. Firstly, the EU was unwilling to make any concrete decisions as to unilateral EU sanctions and the determination of genocide. The EU deferred instead to the UN, in particular the Security Council. During the meeting of 26 July, the EU Council merely left it to the UNSC to consider or implement sanctions, rather than making their own decision. European leaders preferred a common international line on Darfur at the UN level. Henceforward, the mention of sanctions was always in relationship with the Security Council rather than on the EU's own demands. The interaction between the UNSC and EU Council appeared one way, with the UNSC leading, and the EU Council following. Since the non-permanent European members of

---

174   Smith (2010), p. 224 as quoted in Seymour (2013), p. 12.

175   Idem.; Williams, P. (2010) "The United Kingdom," *The International politics of mass atrocities. The case of Darfur*, by Black, D. and Williams, P. (eds.), London, New York: Routledge.

176   Archive Ministry of Foreign Affairs in the Netherlands: djz/ir/na/00210, 2004–2004.

177   Dutch Parliamentary Doc.: Tweede Kamer, 2003–2004, Aanhangsel 1979, question 12 July 2004, answer 21 July 2004; 2004–2005, Aanhangsel 200, question 16 September 2004, answer 20 October 2004.

178   US State Department Cables, The Hague, 16 September 2004, No. 2346.

179   US State Department Cable, Brussels, 10 September 2004, No. 3840; 14 September 2004, No. 3897.

180   Idem; EC press release 12068/04, 13 September 2004.

the UN Security Council lacked strong influence on the politics within the UN, they were left with conforming to the position set out there. For instance, in the meeting of 13 September, the EU Council went to some length to "be in line with UN process."[181] Additionally, the EU Council let their decisions depend on (future) reporting by the UN SG Special Representative Pronk. Likewise, the Special Rapporteur on the prevention of genocide Juan Méndez was sometimes referred to as the person to make a call on the situation in Darfur (while he did not have such a mandate). When an EU Commission official, Pieter Feith, allegedly made a qualifying statement on the situation he was quickly reprimanded. After the Commission of Inquiry was established, no more decision-making took place as European leaders awaited the report of this commission.

Secondly, even when trying to be in line with the UN, the EU went notably less far in their statements than the Security Council. In the conclusions of 26 July, where a formulation of "sanctions" was replaced by "measures," the more general "military operation" put less pressure on Sudan compared to the narrower but more explicit "military air operations," that was proposed in the draft conclusions. In contrast, the next UNSC resolution (1564), which was adopted five days later, told Sudan explicitly under a Chapter VII headline, to "refrain from conducting military flights in and over the Darfur Region."[182] Furthermore, this resolution explicitly mentioned targeting Sudan's petroleum sector. Each of these aspects was consciously left out of the EU conclusions. In addition to the EU's softer language, the EU was also rather slow in its response. There was no discussion or meeting at the EU level scheduled during the summer recess, between the 26 July meeting and the Gymnich meeting of 3 and 4 September, despite that fact that the summer of 2004 was a crucial period in terms of international decision-making over Darfur. The slowness of the response of the EU was also noted by the Dutch Foreign Affairs official Schuthof who complained in July 2004 that the EU "has lagged behind" and that specific EU actions would only be discussed in September.[183]

Thirdly, from an early stage, the EU had indicated that it wanted to go beyond humanitarian assistance, and already considered the contribution of its own personnel in late April.[184] Following the fact-finding mission by Pieter Feith in

181   US State Department Cable, Brussels, 14 September 2004, No. 3897.

182   UN Doc.: S/Res/1564, 18 September 2004, operating paragraphs 1 and 11, see discussion below.

183   US State Department Cables, The Hague, 9 July 2004, No. 1721.

184   US State Department Cable, Brussels, 3 May, 2004, No. 1897; This information is at this stage still debated internally. The cable refers to a EU Council meeting of 27 April.

August, it indicated at multiple occasions that it wanted to organise a police support mission in Darfur.[185] It is doubtful whether the Sudanese government would ever have allowed such a mission, but there was no wider support from either the US or the AU. If the AU had backed the proposal, Sudan would have had much less possibility to refuse it. However, Nigerian President Obasanjo, as President of the AU, was not keen either. When briefing the UNSC on 24 September, he was asked directly: "Why is the EU not invited to organise a police mission?"[186] Although not answering this question specifically, he indicated a preference for an AU-led mission only, with support from the international community outside of actual personnel, meaning financial, material and logistical support only.[187]

In general, we can identify the actions of the EU as a difference in strategy (or objectives) compared to those of the US. Whereas the US called the situation genocide adding that it would not do anything against it, the EU was more careful in its words but actually hinted towards contributing police to AMIS. In discussions on labelling the situation genocide, or condemning the Sudanese government with other equally strong terms, some actors considered the counterproductive effects such an action might have on the ground.[188] For instance, the Sudanese government could deny access again to humanitarian workers and diplomacy might fail.

Following the resolution in the US Congress, the European Parliament adopted its own 'genocide-resolution'. On 16 September it adopted a resolution that described the situation as "tantamount to genocide."[189] Based on a recent mission to Sudan in early September, the EP resolution was in general much more outspoken on the atrocities and violations committed by the parties in the conflict than the EU Council. It spoke of the attacks of military aircraft, the support of the government for targeting civilians including sexual violence against women, general bad governance and politics of marginalisation.

The press release after this statement does not indicate that the EU intends to offer more help (EU Doc.: 8567/04, 27 April 2004).

185   US State Department Cable, Brussels, 8 September 2004, No. 3772; EC Press release 12068/04, 13 September 2004.

186   UN Doc. S/pv.5043, 24 September 2004.

187   Ibid., p. 17. Obasanjo states: "[W]e in the AU now have a Constitutive Act that does not regard an African troop anywhere in Africa as a foreign troop."

188   Piiparinen, T. (2007) "Reconsidering the silence of the Ultimate Crime: A functional shift in the crisis management from the Rwanda Genocide to Darfur," *Journal of Genocide Research*, Vol.: 9(1) pp. 71–91.

189   EU Doc.: P6_TA(2004)0012, 16 September 2004.

It called on the UN and AU to coordinate and work more closely together and for Eritrea to stay out of the conflict. It asked the UNSC to consider a global arms embargo, targeted sanctions against the worst perpetrators as well as international prosecution through the ICC. A US diplomat reporting back to State Department called it a "strong resolution," and quoted a European Commission official who had told him that "the value-added of the [Members of the European Parliament] is that they can say what many others are thinking, but cannot express publicly."[190]

7.9.3   Designing a Commission of Inquiry

The next UNSC Resolution on Sudan, to be adopted in September, would establish a Commission of Inquiry (COI) that would eventually lead to the SC referral of the situation in Darfur to the International Criminal Court. Already several times, in various circumstances, a Commission of Inquiry was proposed as a policy measure for Darfur. However, the kind of commission that was proposed by Amnesty International (AI) and supported by Special Representative to the UN Commission on Human Rights Gerhart Baum in 2003 was not the same as what was finally established.[191] The AI proposal was rather general, welcoming any advice such a commission would give, and was not aimed at justice and accountability *per se*.[192] Kapila did have in mind a COI that would function as a starting point for an international prosecution.[193] Acting United Nations High Commissioner for Human Rights Ramcharan submitted a report on Sudan to the Commission of Human Rights with a detailed recommendation for a Commission of Inquiry, which includes among other things the task to identify perpetrators and to recommend options for accountability.[194] The EU Council endorsed the idea of a COI as proposed by Ramcharan in their July statement. The rebels made such an international commission of inquiry one the demands during negotiations in the first Abuja negotiations in July and September.[195] However, western observers pushed back such demands, telling the rebels that they could not introduce demands to the international community in their

---

190   US State Department Cable, Brussels, 21 September 2004, No. 4016.
191   A UNSC mandated Commission of Inquiry is not a fixed established measure. For instance it is not set out as measure in the UN Charter. Neither does this measure have a large historic precedent that would imply certain customs.
192   AI Doc.: AFR 54/004/2003, 21 February 2003.
193   UK House of Commons, International Development Committee. "Darfur, Sudan: The responsibility to protect" Fifth Report of Session 2004–05, Volume II Oral and Written Statements, p. ev53.
194   UN Doc. E/CN.4/2005/3 (7 May 2004), in particular para. 103–104.
195   Toga (2007) in de Waal, pp. 220, 223.

negotiations with the Sudanese government.[196] Therefore, the Commission of Inquiry that was considered appeared to be one originating from the UN Commission on Human Rights, tasked to look at the responsibility of individuals in the violence.

The statement on genocide by Secretary of State Powell probably changed this proposal. Firstly, Powell's statement put both the UN and EU in an uncomfortable situation, as they were confronted with the question over whether they agreed with the US' conclusion. However, the same day that Powell made his statement before Congress, the US also introduced a new draft resolution that included a clause to establish a COI.[197] Therefore this suggests that the US proposed 'a way out' for countries that were confronted with their stark conclusion, namely they could support a special commission, which would report back to the Security Council. This commission is then tasked to not only identify perpetrators and look at accountability, but additionally to look explicitly into the question of whether genocide had occurred. This solution fitted well with the aforementioned European opinion that it was up to the UN classify the situation.

7.9.4   *Resolution 1564*

From the above discussion, the ingredients on the table for a new resolution were clear: sanctions and a Commission of Inquiry, which could also look into the determination of genocide. However, the exact types of sanctions were still undetermined. Targeted sanctions were under discussion, but the lack of progress in the EU Council signalled a lack of support for it. Economic sanctions, such as an oil-boycott, were also considered. The Chinese representative stated after Council discussion on the draft resolution that China had "some difficulties" with the draft resolution but the possibility of an oil-boycott was not one of these.[198] The initial US draft referred to a ban on Sudanese military flights over Darfur, but this was watered down to an appeal to the government to stop these flights.[199] Likewise, suggestions in the US draft of international

---

196 US State Department cable, Abuja, 13 September 2004, No. 1573. Besides a COI, the rebels had asked for peacekeepers and a no-fly zone.

197 This can be deduced from a US cable in which the US Ambassador to Brussels Schnabel reports that the prospected European Council conclusions conform to the US draft resolution, including the establishment of a Commission of Inquiry (US State Department cable, Brussels, 10 September 2004, No. 3840).

198 UN webcast of 16 September 2004, available at https://www.un.org/webcast/arc2004c .html [accessed at 19 July 2013].

199 Mayroz (2008), p. 369.

over-flights to monitor the situation in Darfur and targeted sanctions in the form of travel bans were not included in the adopted resolution.[200]

The new resolution was adopted on 18 September.[201] It acknowledged the conclusions of UN SG Annan's report by stating:

> Expressing concern that paragraphs 59–67 indicate that the Government of Sudan has not fulfilled the entirety of its commitments under resolution 1556 (2004).

The particular aspects of this lack of fulfilment primarily came down to the only conditions that would release further sanctions according to the previous resolution, namely

> the lack of progress with regard to security and the protection of civilians, disarmament of the Janjaweed militias and identification and bringing to justice of the Janjaweed leaders responsible for human rights and international humanitarian law violations in Darfur.

The other aspects which made the SC decide to consider the situation in Darfur a threat to international peace and security in Resolution 1556 – such as the humanitarian crisis, the continuing violence, and the refugee flows to Chad – were either not mentioned or were welcomed due to progress. Nevertheless, the determination that the situation was a threat to international peace and security was maintained and therefore decisions were made under chapter VII of the UN Charter. Welcoming the monitoring and negotiating efforts by the AU, the SC:

> Reiterates its call for the Government of Sudan to end the climate of impunity in Darfur by identifying and bringing to justice all those responsible, including members of popular defense forces and Janjaweed militias, for the widespread human rights abuses and violations of international humanitarian law, and insists that the Government of Sudan take all appropriate steps to stop all violence and atrocities;

An international Commission of Inquiry is to be established by the Secretary-General to,

---

200   Williams, P.D. and Bellamy, A.J. (2006) "The UN Security Council and the question of humanitarian intervention in Darfur", *Journal of Military Ethics*, Vol.: 5(2), p. 152.

201   UN Doc.: S/Res/1564, 18 September 2004.

investigate reports of violations of international humanitarian law and human rights law in Darfur by all parties, to determine also whether or not acts of genocide have occurred, and to identify the perpetrators of such violations with a view to ensuring that those responsible are held accountable.

The resolution demanded from the Sudanese government that it complied with Resolution 1556, and cooperated fully with the African Union monitoring mission in order to avoid sanctions. These demands then covered more obligations for the government than before.[202] The threat of sanctions was slightly more explicit in this resolution, in that the Security Council,

> shall consider taking additional measures as contemplated in Article 41 of the Charter of the United Nations, such as actions to affect Sudan's petroleum sector and the Government of Sudan or individual members of the Government of Sudan,

as opposed to the formulation "expresses its intentions to consider" that was used in Resolution 1556. It was also more specific on the sanctions it would use, namely targeted sanctions and an oil-boycott.There was no certainty expressed in the resolution that sanctions will be enforced in case of noncompliance, but the conditions for compliance were widened. This was considered more forceful, and consequently China and Russia both abstained from voting.[203] Russia brings forth:

> that threatening sanctions is far from the best method of inducing Khartoum to fully implement its obligations to the United Nations [and] counterproductive.

It says so because according to the Russian representative there were many aspects on which the government had made progress. Additionally, the mediation efforts of the African Union as part of Chapter VIII of the UN Charter, concerning the cooperation with regional organisations, should not be linked with

---

202 Bothe, M. (2007) "International Legal Aspects of the Darfur Conflict" in *The law of international relations: liber amicorum Hanspeter Neuhold*, by Reinisch, A. and Kriebaum, U. (eds.), Eleven International Publishing, p. 11.

203 Vote: Algeria, China, Pakistan and Russia abstaining, rest in favor (UN Doc.: S/pv.5040, 18 September 2004).

sanctions. A similar statement came from China, which emphasised that the international community should work on cooperation, whereas this resolution did the opposite. However, despite the "serious reservations," it refrained from blocking because,

> a key element of the Council's work at present is support for the African Union in extending its deployment in Darfur.

The United States expressed a more fatalistic view of the situation. According to President Bush himself the resolution,

> throws the full weight of the Council behind the African Union in undertaking an increased mission in Darfur.(...) calls for the completion, on an urgent basis, of the Naivasha and Abuja negotiations and calls on the international community to fulfil urgently its pledges of humanitarian assistance to the people of Darfur.

The United States seemed to be in favour of more sanctions by emphasising this possibility in case of non-compliance and it felt the need to defend itself for not being able to impose them already by saying:

> The resolution (...) reflects the wishes of some delegations to recognize that the Government of the Sudan has met some of its commitments with regard to access for humanitarian assistance. But no one should be under the slightest illusion as to why the Government of the Sudan met even that commitment.

It went on by strongly accusing Sudan by stating that:

> [m]ore than 2.2 million people have been victimized in one way or another by the actions of the Sudanese Government. (...) [T]he disaster in Darfur is entirely manmade, (...) entirely avoidable.

The European countries are less focused on the blaming of Sudan. Germany acknowledged the necessity of pressure because,

> there was no verifiable progress in key areas of resolution 1556 (2004), such as the disarmament of the Janjaweed (...) but we also want to pursue a dialogue with the Sudan.

It supported the

> commission of inquiry to end the culture of impunity in the Sudan and help restore some measure of trust that justice will be done.

France was similarly reluctant to strongly accuse Sudan but stated that they,

> are still waiting for the Janjaweed militia to be disarmed as soon as possible and for the perpetrators of violations of human rights and international humanitarian law to be identified and punished.

The UK took a stance somewhere between the US and the other European countries. It did not directly accuse Sudan but acknowledged that,

> it is the pressure of the international community that has been chiefly responsible for (...) progress.

Although the US and the UK were vocal in criticising the Sudanese government, they did not go as far as Romania and the Philippines in advocating for a more active approach of the UNSC. Rather, they and the European countries primarily supported the expanded AMIS mission of the African Union. Romania and the Philippines argued that the UNSC itself should take up a responsibility to protect the civilians in Darfur as well.[204] Romania, for example, stated:

> In our twenty-first-century world, it should not be possible for the international community – for the Security Council in particular – to confine themselves to only taking a political look at events that involve tens of thousands of victims of targeted violence, especially when we hear no denial of such tragic reported facts. There should be no moral hesitation in the Council in taking up its responsibilities.

The Philippines likewise stated:

> A state has the responsibility to protect its citizens, and, if it is unable or unwilling to do so, the international community – the Security Council – has the moral and legal authority to enable that State to assume that responsibility.

---

204 Williams and Bellamy (2006), p. 153.

Sudan was again displeased with the resolution. Interestingly, it declared that,

> The roots of the problem lie in the country's economic and social back-
> wardness. Hence, we wonder whether the sanctions measures will help
> to resolve the problem or whether, on the contrary, they will in fact com-
> plicate it by hindering measures aimed at solving it.

This is a direct reaction to the claim of the US, which stated it was "entirely
manmade."

7.10   Reflections

7.10.1   *The Results of the Increased International Activity*

This chapter has shown that there was a peak in international activity and
decision-making in the period between June and September 2004. This is also
illustrated by Figure 2 in Chapter 1 which shows that the number of actions
taken were highest in this period. But what were the results achieved?

Simply said, the policies adopted at the UN level can be described as the
outright avoidance of strong action against the Sudanese government. No
sanctions were adopted, but the possibility was left open in future. However,
this was an empty threat because many states had already expressed their
reluctance, or opposition to them. Another aggravating factor in this context
was that the various demands and timelines for Khartoum were unclear and
inconsistent. At the same time, stronger (military) measures, such as a no-fly
zone or a military mission were not even seriously discussed. The deployment
of the small AMIS force with a limited mandate was slow and there was a reluctance of several countries (US and France) in helping the facilitation and logis-
tics. In addition, the response of the EU was not only slow, but it also failed to
come up with a strong policy on Darfur. The US used bold words and rhetoric
by labelling the situation in Darfur as 'genocide', while it explicitly ruled out
any implication of such a determination on the US policy. Other Islamic and
African countries remained generally silent. The only real 'actions' taken by
international actors, include the appointment of Jan Pronk as Special
Representative who immediately employed several initiatives after an absence
of a head of the UN country team in Sudan for almost three months. In addition, a Commission of Inquiry was established, but such a commission could
and should obviously have been established much earlier.

How can it be explained that the response of the international community
was so weak? Firstly, there was China and Russia who as permanent members at

the Security Council could block any – in their view – undesirable action. Given their national *realpolitik* interests in continuing the flow of oil (China), the trade in arms (Russia) and their general preference for avoiding international interference in the domestic affairs of other states, made them unwilling to consider more forceful action. Secondly, the international dynamics at that time also prevented many states from joining more activist states as the US and the UK in their efforts of exerting more international pressure on Khartoum. In particular, the "isolation" of the US and UK can be explained as the result of discontent among many states over the invasion of Iraq, the policies of Guantanamo Bay and the torture at Abu Ghraib. Mortimer, a top assistant of SG Annan, held that many countries did not want to cooperate with the US as a result of their irritation over Iraq.[205] This was also noted by Samantha Power, who pointed to as examples the absence of European support for the US resolution in the Human Rights Commission and the limited humanitarian assistance of Germany and France (US$1 million and nothing respectively compared to the US' contribution of US$28 million).[206] Thirdly, by giving the AU the primary responsibility over Darfur, the UNSC deliberately limited its future possibilities for taking stronger action. The latter explanation will be further explored in the next chapter.

7.10.2   *Theoretical Reflections: Explaining the U-turn of the US*

This chapter highlighted the rather vocal public approach of the US with respect to Darfur in the summer of 2004. This 'activist' position of the US stands in sharp contrast with its role in the previous year, which was marked by a conscious decision to keep (publicly) quiet about Darfur and outright resistance to have Darfur put on the agenda of the UNSC. As was discussed in Chapter 5, this decision was based on the fear that confronting the government of Sudan over Darfur might jeopardise the North–South negotiations. It is remarkable that the position of the US changed even though there was no North–South peace agreement yet. As was discussed in Section 6.2, the US government also exerted leadership and strong political pressure to secure a ceasefire agreement in March and April 2004. A strong linkage between the Naivasha process and Darfur was consequently made under US leadership from May 2004 as well.[207] What explains this U-turn in the position of the US?

---

205   Michael Abramowitz, "U.S. promises on Darfur don't match actions. Bush expresses passion for issue, but policies have been inconsistent," Washington Post, 29 October 2007.

206   Samantha Power, "Dying in Darfur. Can the ethnic cleansing in Sudan be stopped?," The New Yorker Magazine, 30 August 2004.

207   Slim, H. (2004) "Dithering over Darfur? A preliminary review of the international response," *International Affairs*, Vol.: 80(5), p. 822.

It would be tempting to answer this question by referring to the domestic sources of foreign policy-making, as many authors and policy-makers have done.[208] In this context one can especially point to the media coverage which started at the end of March 2004 (Section 6.3.2) and especially the attention to Darfur in the US Congress since the beginning of May.[209] There had also been increased political pressure from Christian groups and African American communities on the US government and Congress since June 2004. This culminated in a letter by 52 Senators of both the Democrats and Republicans urging Powell to strengthen the US response on 25 June and the genocide determination of the Congress of 22 July.[210] As was mentioned already in Section 7.9.1, the genocide statement of Powell was largely made in order to satisfy a domestic audience.

But does this sketch fully capture the political dynamics of US foreign policymaking? Several sources claim that the US policy and the attitude of the top level within the US government had already changed before the involvement of Congress and the media coverage by March 2004. Secretary of State Powell, Under Secretary of State Grossman and Deputy Secretary of State Armitage allegedly said to lower ranking US officials: "Don't filter the information – write what you think is true – just tell it like it is."[211] It was also in March 2004 that USAID head Natsios was sent to Naivasha by President Bush to deliver the message that the US would not normalise its relations with the Sudanese government while atrocities were ongoing in Darfur.[212]

Therefore, it seems that there have been some sincere attempts, albeit maybe not sufficient, of part of the US government since March 2004 to address the situation in Darfur. This stands in sharp contrast with the previous policy of deliberately keeping Darfur silent and away from the UNSC agenda. This

---

208   See, for example, Hamilton (2011a). Stedjan and Thomas-Jensen (2010) "The United States," in *The International politics of mass atrocities. The case of Darfur*, by Black, D.R. and Williams, P.D. (eds.), London, New York: Routledge, p. 158–160. BBC Panorama, 3 July 2005, Fergal Keane interview with John Danforth, available at http://news.bbc.co.uk/1/hi/programmes/panorama/4647211.stm [accessed 5 October 2013].

209   US Senate, "Condemning the Government of the Republic of Sudan," Proceedings and debates of the 108th Congress, second session Vol. 150 No. 62, 6 May 2004, available at: http://beta.congress.gov/crec/2004/05/06/CREC-2004-05-06-pt1-PgS4931-7.pdf [accessed 11 December 2013].

210   Heinze (2007), p. 386.

211   Craner as quoted in Hamilton (2011a), p. 31.

212   PBS Newshour, 24 June 2004, Fred de Sam Lazaro interview with Andrew Natsios, available at http://www.pbs.org/newshour/bb/africa/jan-june04/sudan_6-24.html [accessed 29 November 2013].

'change' came at a time when there was no domestic pressure and therefore no domestic political costs for not acting. This actually contrasts with Samantha Power's conclusions that US officials tend not to be interested and willing to respond to warnings when there is no media attention and public shame for inaction.[213] There are two possible explanations, which might account for this discrepancy in the case of Darfur. Firstly, the US government might have anticipated future domestic pressure (Section 2.2). Secondly, the US government was not solely based on a calculation of *domestic* political costs and benefits, but also a belief based on "a larger sense of morality" as US Special Envoy Danforth claimed.[214] President Bush was allegedly moved and angered by the situation in Darfur. Some of his staff even called him the "Sudan desk officer" because of his involvement in the issue.[215]

---

213 See Chapter 2. Power (2007), p. 270, 281 and 508.
214 See also Cockett (2010), p. 226–227. He also stated about Darfur/ Sudan: "This isn't a country that has much strategic interest for the US." Michael Abramowitz, "U.S. promises on Darfur don't match actions. Bush expresses passion for issue, but policies have been inconsistent," Washington Post, 29 October 2007.
215 Stedjan and Thomas-Jensen (2010) in Black and Williams (eds.), p. 161.

CHAPTER 8

No Further Decisions
October 2004–January 2005

The months following Resolution 1564 were characterised by the execution of the limited decisions that the international actors had taken, rather than discussing new measures. Since the Commission of Inquiry started its investigation in October, new decision-making was hampered for four months. Only once the commission reported back to the Security Council in January 2005 could new measures be discussed.

In the mean time, the African Union mission was becoming a fully-fledged peacekeeping mission, which needed strong western support in order to realise the deployment. The parties in the Naivasha talks were fully pressured to finish their talks into an agreement, in order for a new government to be installed and subsequently deal with Darfur. Simultaneously, the peace talks for Darfur in Abuja would resume again. This time with even stronger international supervision in order to help broker a peace. It brought the situation in Sudan to the awkward situation where one peace deal was closed while another, barely started, was already unravelling, and a UN peacekeeping mission was to be deployed in the South while the AU mission in Darfur was failing.

8.1   Situation in Darfur

Faced with more evidence of the plight of Darfur and attacks on civilians, Khartoum maintained its stance of denial and understatement of compelling evidence. In spite of the World Food Programme announcing that it had fed its highest number of people in September since the crisis erupted,[1] the World Health Organization stating that 70,000 people had died since March 2004 from causes excluding the violence,[2] and the Red Cross reporting on the collapse of agriculture in the region,[3] the Sudanese Foreign Minister insisted,

---

[1] UN News, 6 October 2004, "UN food relief agency helps 1.3 million people in Sudan's Darfur region".

[2] Totten, S. and Markussen, E. (eds.) (2006) *Genocide in Darfur, investigating the Atrocities in the Sudan.* London, New York: Routledge, p. xxxii.

[3] Prunier, G. (2007) *Darfur: An ambiguous genocide. Revised and updated edition 2007* London: C. Hurst & Co. (publishers) ltd, p. 120.

© KONINKLIJKE BRILL NV, LEIDEN, 2014 | DOI 10.1163/9789004260405_009

"...there is no famine...[and] no epidemic."[4] Yet the evidence from the three international bodies was symptomatic of the situation that had once again deteriorated in October following the passing of Resolution 1564, exemplified by increased violence and ceasefire violations across Darfur.[5] Once again attacks involving the looting, rape and burning of villages intensified, as did the violence against IDPs forced to return to their villages with the *Janjaweed* lying in wait. OCHA now believed that as many as one in three Darfurians were affected by the violence,[6] which took on similar patterns wherever it was perpetrated in Darfur.[7] Médecins Sans Frontières lambasted the failure of the government and the "international community," describing the persecution of civilians in Darfur as "...pervert[ing] the very idea of refuge..." since "[p]eople escape the attackers once, yet they cannot feel real safety."[8] The information was also brought before the Security Council as Jan Pronk reported on the continued sponsoring of violence by Khartoum and its utter failure to disarm the *Janjaweed*.[9] In a telling interview, Arab militiamen (*Janjaweed*) revealed to the Associated Press that they were armed and paid by the central government, with titles such as "Border Intelligence Division." "If I'm given to the court," one militiaman asserted, "I'll be given with all the government...[b]ecause we are all doing this together."[10]

---

4   Associated Press, 1 October, "Sudanese foreign minister: Darfur crisis 'tribal conflict,' not genocide".

5   See UN Doc.: S/2004/881, 2 November 2004, Report of the Secretary-General on the Sudan pursuant to paragraph 15 of Security Council resolution 1564 (2004) and paragraphs 6, 13 and 16 of Security Council resolution 1556 (2004), November 2 2004. In this report Kofi Annan stated that, "The situation became ever more intense in October, and there was less security and more violence than in the preceding month."

6   OCHA, "One in three people in Darfur now affected by crisis", 22 October 2004.

7   See for example, IRIN. "Sudan: Continuing violence breeding tension in North Darfur – sources", 1 October 2004; Amnesty International. "Sudan: Civilians still under threat in Darfur. An agenda for human rights protection", 12 October 2004 (AFR 54/131/2004); Associated Press, 15 October 2004, "U.N. says it is continuing to receive reports of attacks in Sudan's Darfur region". In his monthly report for November, UN Secretary-General Kofi Annan also detailed various attack from October directed against civilians, including an attack on 19 October over several days that caused "a considerable number of fatalities", a massacre at a marketplace, and fighting involving around 100 *Janjaweed* militias between 14 and 20 October (UN Doc.: S/2004/881, 2 November 2004, para. 5).

8   Médecins Sans Frontières, 29 October 2004, "Persecution, intimidation and failure of assistance in Darfur".

9   UN News, 2 October 2004, "Sudan has failed to disarm militias or prevent more attacks in Darfur – UN envoy".

10   Associated Press, 2 October 2004, "Arab militiamen say they collect paychecks from Sudan's government".

At the beginning of the November, the UNHCR reported at least six raids on refugees near the Chadian border in Darfur, perpetrated by *Janjaweed* militias.[11] An attack by Sudanese forces on the El-Jeer refugee camp,[12] bombing and then bulldozing the temporary homes of those already displaced, as well as the raping of women under the noses of aid workers and AU officers, typified the increased violence in November, as did the growing number of attacks characterised by Jan Pronk as "flagrant violation[s] of international humanitarian law."[13] During many similar attacks, refugee camps and villages would be surrounded, and then emptied, to force the involuntary return of refugees back into Darfur. Despite numerous accounts, also detailed in the Secretary-General's monthly reports to the Security Council, now indicted war crimes suspect, Ahmed Haroun denied the attacks, concocting a belief that the returns were voluntary and followed the stabilisation of the situation after the deployment of police.[14] These obvious fabrications ran in total contradiction to the situation described by a Human Rights Watch report as the "consolidation of ethnic cleansing" where Sudanese forces and militias had "systematically targeted civilian communities that share the same ethnicity as the rebel groups."[15]

The report from the international human rights NGO also illustrated the newly-emboldened rebels, whose forces had multiplied the number of their attacks against government troops, also targeting strategic posts with greater frequency. More significantly, over the course of October and November 2004, rebel forces were more often themselves accused of violating international law through targeting civilians, looting villages and using child soldiers, as well as provoking attacks on refugees through the abduction of 'Arab' civilians. In fact, while Kofi Annan warned the Security Council that security conditions had rapidly deteriorated, with a host of government-sponsored assaults on Darfur's civilians, he reported that the rebels were responsible for the greater number of ceasefire violations over the preceding month.[16] The Darfur conflict was once again changing. And with this change came the emergence of a new rebel movement – the National Movement for Reformation and Development

---

11   Totten and Markusen (2006), p. xxxiii.

12   Prunier (2007), p. 121.

13   Agence France Presse. 2 November 2004, "UN official says Sudanese forces pressuring Darfur refugees to return home against their will".

14   Agence France Presse 3 November 2004, "Sudan denies forced relocation of Darfur refugees".

15   Human Rights Watch, 15 November 2004, "'If we return we will be killed': Consolidation of Ethnic Cleansing in Darfur, Sudan".

16   UN Doc.: S/2004/881, 2 November 2004.

(NMRD) – from within the ranks of JEM. Once unified by their common cause of historical marginalisation, in-fighting and manifest splits surfaced within rebel movements, whilst details of the beginnings of clashes between rebel groups were also reported. With banditry also on the rise, Jan Pronk was left with little choice than to describe the evolving situation as descending into "total anarchy."[17]

8.2   Further Deployment of AMIS

Although everyone was in favour of the new expanded AU mission, later called AMIS II, implementation was again problematic. First of all, Sudan was not eager and tried to refuse the larger AU force permission to access to the country. Only after intervention of Egypt did it give in.[18] Operationally, the deployment was again less than fluent. In one episode, US diplomats caused problems over the selection of a Nigerian battalion that was implicated in Nigerian human rights violations three years earlier.[19] The US refused to airlift this unit. A new unit was subsequently selected, but needed to be prepared, while the previous battalion had spent several weeks in preparations, while the individuals that were involved with this past event were no longer in the battalion.[20] The issue caused some bad relations between US officials and Nigerian military, which came on top of what US diplomats perceived as problematic Nigerian military administration and rule of command.[21]

Analysis of an EU military committee on the AU plans for AMIS II addressed the dangers for the mission. The committee noted that it was mainly organised as an observer mission that assumed both sides wanted to implement the ceasefire. If this would turn out not to be true – for which there were plenty of indications – then the mission would not be able to enforce it, and there was no planning on how the mission might want to respond to such a situation. This was not a new observation. Officials of UN DPKO who had helped draft the plan had explicitly taken this as a working assumption.[22] Other risks were related to a lack of AU capacity to plan such a mission well, and not accepting sufficient help from international partners for advice and personnel for

---

17   Prunier (2007), p. 123.
18   Authors' interview with Christian Manahl, 26 August 2013.
19   US State Department Cable, Abuja, 22 October 2004, No. 1793.
20   US State Department Cable, Abuja, 23 October 2004, No. 1801.
21   US State Department Cable, Abuja, 10 December 2004, No. 2039.
22   Authors' interview with Chris Coleman, 24 May 2004. See also Section 7.8.4.

the planning.[23] One account also pointed to the lack of professionalism, human and material capacity of the AU and AMIS as the main explanation for the lack of effectiveness of the mission.[24] By the end of 2004, AMIS' deployment reached 800 of a planned 3000. In the mean time, the security situation in Darfur worsened.

8.3   Humanitarian Missions

In contrast, humanitarian agencies were much better prepared to deploy their staff and material when the ceasefire in April was agreed and access for humanitarian agencies was granted. The Sudanese government tried to stop, prohibit or obstruct humanitarian agencies and their staff and material from reaching Darfur, but with the political pressures that built up over the summer the situation remarkably improved. By the end of 2004 a "massive" operation was underway in Darfur.[25]

The history of their deployment is rather different from the one by the AU observer mission. Kapila recounted that by September 2003 he was already discussing plans with OCHA head Jan Egeland on how to respond to the upcoming humanitarian crisis in Darfur.[26] The UN lost access in December 2003 and January 2004 due to Kapila's evacuation order. By February some access was granted again and humanitarian and emergency relief agencies were deploying as much and fast as possible.[27]

In the following months, the UN, by means of the UN Secretary-General, other high-level UN officials, diplomats and visiting ministers from western countries kept pressing the Sudanese government for further access and for

---

23   US State Department Cable, Brussels, 26 November 2004, No. 5014; This attitude on the side of the AU is also confirmed by Dutch minister for Development Cooperation van Ardenne (Dutch Parliamentary Doc.: Tweede Kamer, 2004–2005, 21 501 02, nr 594, 28 October 2004).

24   Flint, J. and de Waal, A. (2008) *Darfur: a new history of a long war*. London, New York: Zed Books, p. 177.

25   Interview Grünfeld with Jan Egeland, 28 November 2012.

26   Kapila, M. (2013) *Against a tide of evil*. Edinburg: Mainstream Publishing, p. 112. Egeland states that when he started as head he wanted to focus on crises that received less attention. His staff pointed out Darfur (Interview Grünfeld with Jan Egeland, 28 November 2012, see also Egeland, J., 2010, *A Billion Lives: An Eyewitness Report from the Frontlines of Humanity*. New York: Simon & Schuster).

27   Markussen and Totten (2006), Ch. Chronology; Prunier (2007), p. 112; UN News, 10 February 2004, "UN hails Sudan's agreement to let aid workers in troubled Darfur region".

the abolishment of bureaucratic restrictions. By the end of April a high-level UN team visited the area to assess humanitarian needs.[28] A new way of supplying the IDP camps was negotiated with Libya, allowing shipments to Libyan ports and subsequent transportation by road through the Sahara desert to camps in eastern Chad and Darfur.

The push for greater humanitarian access was concerted from all sides, including the UN, AU, EU, individual European countries, and the US. In the last report from the Secretary-General in 2004 on Sudan, 6500 humanitarian workers, including 800 international staff were active in Darfur.[29] The bad and deteriorating security situation also had its repercussions on the aid workers, who became subject to kidnappings and violence themselves.[30] While the *Janjaweed* and other government militias occasionally attacked IDP camps, neither government troops nor AMIS were able to guarantee protection for the people and aid workers.

8.4   Further Mediation

A new round of talks started by the end of October in Abuja. US diplomats noted a messy start due to apparently bad preparation on the part of the AU and internal leadership issues among one of the rebel movements, the SLM/A. From western countries, apart from the US, The Netherlands as EU representative, a Swedish advisor for the European Council and a French representative were present. External non-governmental organisations, namely International Crisis Group and Centre for Humanitarian Dialogue, allegedly advised and trained the rebel groups in negotiation strategy.[31] In general, diplomatic communications indicate that the US and the EU blame the warring parties, rather than the AU, themselves or outside mediators, for the failure of concrete progress during these rounds of talks.

The talks in October showed the first signs of splintering among the rebel groups, which negatively affected the outcome of the negotiation rounds. During the meeting in December, the SLM/A failed to show up altogether due

---

28   UN News, 28 April 2004, "UN missions examine conditions in strife-torn Darfur region of western Sudan."

29   UN Doc. S/2004/947, 3 December 2004, para. 28.

30   Prunier (2007), p. 121; Totten and Markussen (2006), Ch. Chronology; UN News, 7 January 2004, "UN envoy for Sudan expresses concern at increasing harassment of aid workers in Darfur".

31   US State Department Cable, Abuja, 26 October 2004, No. 1811.

to leadership infighting.[32] At the same time the Sudanese government conducted further military attacks.[33] The combination of the two led to a collapse of the talks by the end of 2004.

8.5   Security Council Meets in Africa

At the initiative of the US presidency of the UNSC, in particular Ambassador John Danforth himself, the Security Council met in Nairobi in November to discuss Sudan. However, the main topic of the day was meant to be the finalisation of the Naivasha talks, resulting in the CPA. Statements on this occasion mainly underlined the vision of prioritising the resolution of North–South over Darfur, so that the CPA could function as a benchmark for a settlement in Darfur. In consequence there was strong resistance to mentioning Darfur at all.

Nevertheless, the decision to let 'Nairobi' be only about North–South and not about Darfur did not have wide support within the UN Secretariat. For instance, UN Secretariat officials had strongly advised Annan to address Darfur with the argument that one "cannot separate different conflicts with the same government."[34] Annan, for example, already encouraged the UNSC "to consider creative and prompt action to ensure effective implementation of the demands set out in it earlier resolutions."[35] Similarly, SGSR Pronk tried to arrange (informal) talks between delegates and Darfur rebels, in order to leverage the presence of all external actors, but no delegations were willing to do so.[36] The US was especially reluctant to have the UNSC address Darfur (formally).[37]

Two days are used for Security Council meetings on Sudan. Both days were highly focused on the peace agreement between the Sudanese government and the SPLM, while the crisis in Darfur was shifted into the background despite

---

32   Toga, D. (2007) "The African Union mediation and the Abuja peace talks", in *War in Darfur and the search for peace*, by de Waal, A. (ed.), Global Equity Initiative, Harvard University, p. 229.

33   US State Department Cables, Abuja, 14 December 2004, No. 2060; Abuja, 15 December 2004, No. 2068.

34   Authors' interview with Eckhart Strauss, 1 June 2005.

35   BBC News World Edition, 4 November 2004, "'Prompt action' needed in Darfur".

36   Bieckmann, F. (2012) *Soedan. Het sinistere spel om macht, rijkdom en olie.* Amsterdam: Balans, p. 172.

37   Ibid., p. 153.

the acknowledged "deteriorating situation."[38] The first day, 18 November was reserved for speakers of regional organisations and representatives of Sudan to make a statement.[39] Also the Secretary-General of the UN Kofi Annan made a statement. In accordance with the different views within the Secretariat he stated:

> I cannot help feeling that the formation of a north–south Government in the Sudan would add weight and impetus to the search for a settlement in Darfur.

Acknowledging that most of the day would be about the North–South peace agreement he asked for attention for Darfur and the troubles "both natural and man-made."

The Sudan government representative, SPLM leader John Garang and IGAD Chairman, President Museveni of Uganda made statements that underlined the vision that 'their' peace agreement would help solve Darfur as well. But remarks on the crisis in Darfur are only noted as an aside of what was otherwise a festive event.[40]

The following day Resolution 1574 was adopted.[41] As the day before, most attention was drawn to the North–south peace agreement. Despite references to the conflict in Darfur, the resolution, was about the North–South peace agreement, so the Security Council did not impose mandatory measures under Chapter VII, and hence it was merely:

> [d]eeply concerned by the situation in Sudan and its implications for international peace and security and stability in the region.

In reference to Darfur, the threat of sanctions was reduced to:

> In accordance with its previous resolutions on Sudan, decides to monitor compliance by the parties with their obligations in that regard and,

---

38   UN Docs.: S/pv.5080, 18 November 2004, statement by the Secretary-General; S/PV.5082, 19 November 2004, statement by the German representative; S/2004/881, 2 November 2004, "Report of the Secretary-General on the Sudan"; Jan Pronk, 2 November 2004: "whole region descending in anarchy and warlordism" (Prunier (2007), p. 123).

39   UN Doc.: S/pv.5080, 18 November 2004.

40   E.g. President Museveni talks for 40 minutes, but only mentions Darfur in two sentences: "dealing with southern Sudan is part of dealing with the question of Darfur. If you deal with southern Sudan correctly, then you will be able to deal with Darfur more easily."

41   UN Doc.: S/Res/1574, 19 November 2004.

subject to a further decision of the Council, to take appropriate action against any party failing to fulfil its commitments.

The resolution further supported explicitly the new expanded AMIS mission. The result of this text was that it was unanimously adopted in contrast to the previous two resolutions on Sudan.

Everyone wanted to say something on such a special occasion. Many delegates, including China, Russia as well as the Sudanese government and SPLM leader Garang underlined that the CPA would need to function as a roadmap for Darfur. On the other side, western countries tried to interpret the resolution as strongly as possible and emphasised the previous demands on the Sudanese government. For instance, the UK representative stated that:

> The provisions of previous resolutions remained valid today. (...) No one should interpret this resolution as reducing their commitments and obligations, as set out in Security Council resolutions 1556 (2004) and 1564 (2004). (...) We remind them of the prospect of measures under Article 41 of the Charter for those who do not comply.

Of all the members, the United States had the strongest urge to defend itself for voting for this resolution. Anticipating the critical reactions of people who might disdainfully call this session a "photo opportunity" or "two beautiful days in Nairobi, filled with grand words but the event was an illusion," Danforth stressed that the message of having this session in Nairobi should be understood as very strong.

> ...Darfur, where chaos and cruelty remain the order of the day. As political institutions are established nationwide and as security is established across the country, the process of bringing justice to the oppressed people of Darfur must continue. I want to be very clear: the violence and the atrocities being perpetrated in Darfur must end now. You have heard this message clearly from the Security Council; heed it. I cannot emphasize this point more strongly.

But at the same time, the US was reluctant to propose or even discuss further measures that the UNSC could take, out of fear for undermining the progress over the North–South. Danforth had stated two weeks before the Nairobi meeting that "It's not so much the stick; it's the carrot."[42]

---

42   BBC News, 4 November 2004, "'Prompt action' needed in Darfur".

The EU statement, given by the Dutch ambassador for Sudan, was last and appears to be the strongest of the day.[43]

> ...progress made at the negotiating table has not been reflected yet in tangible progress on the ground. (...) the situation in Darfur has further deteriorated in recent weeks due to ceasefire violations and continued attacks on civilians. (...) the Government has not fulfilled many of its obligations (...), in particular disarming the Janjaweed and other militia groups, as well as bringing perpetrators of human rights violations to justice. (...) The EU will continue to exert pressure (...) and will take appropriate measures, as contemplated in Article 41 of the United Nations Charter, if no tangible progress is achieved in this respect.

SGSR Pronk had reported that the Sudanese government had fallen short of their obligations in Resolutions 1556 and 1564, with particular respect to security and disarmament of the *Janjaweed*.[44] Despite these facts Darfur was not allowed into the deliberations and Sudan was not confronted with its lack of compliance. Recalling the different time limits put upon and agreed with Sudan, all of them had now long expired. Yet nothing was done in Nairobi to make the government refrain from continuing its war in Darfur.

8.6   Discussions on How to Stop the Air Attacks

Since the start of the conflict it was clear that the Sudanese military was involved in the conflict in Darfur, especially through the use of aircraft and helicopter gunships. This aspect triggered some recommendations for measures against these attacks, ranging from a no-fly zone to installing observers at airports in Darfur to monitor their use.

A no-fly zone implies deploying fighter jets in the region with the power to attack illegal uses of aircrafts by the subjected government. It was a strong measure and implied direct military involvement by western nations, since only these countries have such capabilities. The European Parliament had proposed this in their March resolution and the rebels also had indicated at the

---

43   Statement made by the Dutch Ambassador to Khartoum Adriaan Kooijmans. With the help of the Dutch government he had to make a strong effort to be allowed in the meeting and make a statement (Authors' interview with Adriaan Kooijmans, 16 September 2013). Bieckmann (2012), pp. 154, 167.

44   UN Doc.: S/2004/881, 2 November 2004.

talks during the summer that a no-fly zone ought to be considered.[45] During the fall and winter of 2004 and 2005, on request of his national parliament, Dutch EU Council President Bot also proposed a no-fly zone several times in the EU Council. He himself was sceptic of the measure's feasibility and he found no further support for the idea among the EU countries, NATO or the US. The main constraints that were mentioned were the region's size, remoteness and lack of an airbase.[46] Even when AMIS suffered casualties due to Sudanese air bombings in January, there was no support to even discuss a no-fly zone in the EU Council or elsewhere.[47]

There were also other measures that were considered after repeated requests from the rebels to Western observers in the negotiations to act against the government's continuing use of planes and helicopters in attacks.[48] The measure of air surveillance was considered in the summer.[49] In September, the US ambassador to Nigeria discussed with Nigeria's President Obasanjo, the possibility of deploying monitors at air bases.[50] Since any measure was unacceptable on the side of the Sudanese government, the mediators tried to reconcile both sides with interpreting the ceasefires to include air attacks.[51] This led to an agreement in the fall in which the Sudanese government agreed to end the hostile flights. Since there was no enforcement mechanism it only took days before it was violated.[52]

Explicit condemnations of the military air operations were all that remained. UN Resolution 1564 made an explicit reference under a Chapter VII paragraph to "recent (...) helicopter assaults." In contrast, the EU Council statement had been

---

45   US State Department cable, Abuja, 13 September 2004, No. 1573.
46   This is a remarkable coincidence of historical aspects regarding Darfur. As was recounted in Chapter 4, Darfur's remoteness from other power centres worked for long time in its favour as a natural defence, while the Darfur airbases had been upgraded during the First World War on orders of the Britain's Royal Air Force.
47   Grünfeld, F. and Vermeulen, W.N. (2014) "The role of the Netherlands in the international response to the Crisis in Darfur", Maastricht Faculty of Law Working Paper No. 2014–2 (available at http://ssrn.com/abstract=2418398 [accessed 2 April 2014]).
48   Toga, D. (2007) "The African Union mediation and the Abuja peace talks", in *War in Darfur and the search for peace*, by de Waal, A. (ed.), Global Equity Initiative, Harvard University, pp. 220, 223, 227.
49   US State Department Cable, Brussels, 23 July 2004, No. 3140.
50   US State Department Cable, Abuja, 6 September 2004, No. 1528.
51   Toga (2007) in de Waal (ed.), p. 228.
52   Mackinnon, M.G. (2010) "The United Nations Security Council", in *The International politics of mass atrocities. The case of Darfur*, by Black, D.R. and Williams, P.D. (eds.), London, New York: Routledge, p. 76.

changed from "moratorium on all military air operations" to "moratorium on military operations."[53] Even an explicit condemnation was not possible for the EU.

8.7 Theoretical Reflections: Why was There Not More Forceful Action by the UNSC?

This chapter showed that the Security Council and other actors like the EU were unable and unwilling to adopt more stringent measures in the fall of 2004, such as (targeted) sanctions or a no-fly zone. A military option was ruled out from the start and not seriously considered at all.[54] Rather, these actors endorsed the primary responsibility of the AU and supported the extension of AMIS. The UNSC – but also the EU – preferred the AU to take the lead role with respect to the political and security issues, with the UN focusing on humanitarian issues and merely supporting the AU in its endeavours.[55] The EU's support for the AU also served another (side) objective which was strengthening the profile and position of the AU with respect to peace and security in the African continent. As a result, the AU would not constantly need to call on other (Western) states to contribute to conflict resolution in Africa. Darfur was seen as a first step to acquire the necessary experience.[56]

Placing the responsibility for Darfur on the AU is rather remarkable since Darfur was the first occasion during which the AU could act in accordance with its mandate in the field of peace and security, which it had only assumed at the end of 2003. In addition, since mid-2004 it had become increasingly clear that the AU was unable to protect civilians and deter attacks by the warring parties. The US embassy in Sudan, for example, had already informed Washington in the summer of 2004 that the AU was incapable of dealing with the security situation in Darfur.[57] The US had no trust in the AU and ignored it until September 2004.[58] It is maybe because of this that the US did not offer to equip or transport the AU force.[59] Both the EU and US already anticipated in October 2004

---

53   See Section 7.4.2.

54   Slim, H. (2004) "Dithering over Darfur? A preliminary review of the international response", *International Affairs,* Vol.: 80(5), p. 818.

55   MacKinnon (2010) in Black and Williams (eds.), p. 84.

56   Authors' interview with Pieter Feith, 28 August 2013.

57   Michael Abramowitz, "U.S. promises on Darfur don't match actions. Bush expresses passion for issue, but policies have been inconsistent", Washington Post, 29 October 2007.

58   Bieckmann (2012), p. 295.

59   Samantha Power, "Dying in Darfur. Can the ethnic cleansing in Sudan be stopped?", The New Yorker Magazine, 30 August 2004.

that AMIS might be "a bridge to a fully-fledged UN peacekeeping operation."[60] In November 2004, Danforth held: "it's going to be failure to support the African Union."[61] Senior White House advisor Michael Gerson also concluded at the end of 2004 that the 7000 strong AU force was completely insufficient: "A bigger UN force would be the only thing to change the dynamic on the ground."[62]

These statements and observations raise the question: why did the EU and the US continue with their public support of the AU? This question can best be answered with reference to the organisational process model. This model points to the inflexibility of bureaucracies which hardly allows for change when a policy decision is made. This is the result of 'path dependence' which explains how the policy options actors have are limited by the decisions made in the past. Once actors start with a certain process, it takes a momentum of its own. This is exactly what happened over Darfur. The decision in early 2004 to give the AU the primary responsibility "virtually locked the Security Council into a cautious and reactive position."[63] Prendergast honestly admitted in 2007: "We knew that they wouldn't be able to do it, but they wouldn't step aside. So in a way, a very laudable attempt to accept their responsibility to bring African solutions to African problems actually made it more difficult for US to deal with. And that's a great pity, but it was a persistent factor."[64] This statement also mirrors an observation of US Special Envoy Danforth about the AU: "They were anxious to do the job, but they really weren't able to do it. But once they had volunteered, then it was difficult to kind of muscle them aside and say well you are not doing a very good job."[65]

The previous account seems to imply that the leading role of the AU restricted the policy options for other international actors to deal with Darfur *unintentionally*. Some scholars have noted that the dominance of the AU actually provided a fig leaf or 'convenient façade' for other actors to hide behind and reduce their own responsibility.[66]

---

60   US State Department Cable, Brussels, 14 October 2004, No. 4410.

61   Warren Hoge, "Diplomats at UN surprised by Danforth's resignation", New York Times, 3 December 2004.

62   Gerson as quoted in Cockett, R. (2010) *Sudan: Darfur and the Failure of an African State.* New Haven: Yale University Press, p. 226.

63   MacKinnon (2010) in Black and Williams (eds.), p. 85.

64   PBS Frontline interview with Kieran Prendergast, 29 June 2007.

65   BBC Panorama, Fergal Keane interview with John Danforth, 3 July 2005, available at http://news.bbc.co.uk/1/hi/programmes/panorama/4647211.stm [accessed 5 October 2013].

66   Williams, P.D. and Bellamy, A.J. (2005) "The responsibility to protect and the crisis in Darfur", *Security Dialogue*, Vol.: 36(1), p. 35.

The start of this section also mentioned that any military option was not seriously considered and practically ruled out from the start. One way in which actors tried to escape their responsibility was by framing the demands of a further (military) involvement in rather extreme terms. The best example of this was given by assistant Secretary for African Affairs Frazer, who recollected: "[Officials at the US Department of] Defense weren't keen, so they would come up with these ridiculous estimates like 'you need 120,000 troops to succeed.' Then of course they would say, 'Well, we don't have that because of Iraq'."[67] By framing the issue in such extreme terms, other less far-ranging alternatives were not seriously considered, such as further military assistance to AU in the form of stand-by tactical support unions or EU troops under AU command.[68] In addition, the US was not willing to militarily support the delivery of humanitarian relief in July 2004.[69] For example, Powell stated, "there would never be enough troops to impose order on this place." He consequently argued that the only solution for Darfur would be a "political settlement between the government and the rebels."[70] Likewise, Special US Envoy for Sudan and later US Ambassador at the UNSC, Danforth, held: "So [a military intervention] was not going to happen, wasn't going to happen, shouldn't have happened and wasn't going to happen."[71] UK Special Envoy for Sudan Alan Goulty also stated in May 2004: "Humanitarian intervention in Darfur would be very expensive, fraught with difficulties and hard to set up in a hurry."[72] UK Foreign Office Minister for African Affairs Mullin later elaborated upon the many complexities, including the size of Sudan, the danger of drawing in Jihadists from all over the world, the possibility of destabilising the entire country

---

67   Stephen Hadley, National Security Adviser, also noted that the Pentagon was not eager (Frazer and Hadley as quoted in Hamilton, R., 2011a, *Fighting for Darfur: public action and the struggle to stop genocide.* New York: Palgrave Macmillan, p. 75).

68   UK House of Commons, International Development Committee. "Darfur, Sudan: The responsibility to protect" Fifth Report of Session 2004–2005, Volume I, p. 48.

69   Fessenden as referred to in Heinze, E.A. (2007) "The rhetoric of genocide in U.S. foreign policy: Rwanda and Darfur compared", *Political Science Quarterly*, Vol.: 122(3), p. 368.

70   Michael Abramowitz, "U.S. promises on Darfur don't match actions. Bush expresses passion for issue, but policies have been inconsistent", Washington Post, 29 October 2007.

71   BBC Panorama, Fergal Keane interview with John Danforth, 3 July 2005, available at http://news.bbc.co.uk/1/hi/programmes/panorama/4647211.stm [accessed 5 October 2013].

72   Goulty as quoted in Prunier (2007), p. 141. The Telegraph [UK], May 31, 2004. See also Hilary Benn in The Guardian [UK], June 9, 2004.

resulting in a failed state and the risk of getting attacked by all sides in the conflict.[73] It is therefore not surprising that Kapila was told at the UK Foreign office that peacekeeping forces were "a pipe dream."[74] Likewise, Prendergast (UNDPA) held: "I was opposed to the reference to the possible use of armed force because it seemed to me that less than a year after the war in Iraq, there was zero possibility of effective military intervention in Darfur, zero possibility."[75]

8.8   Theoretical Reflections: Changes and Inconsistencies in the Policies of the US and UK

This chapter also showed the inconsistencies in the policy of the US. That is to say, the US shifted its attention back to the stalled North–South negotiations in November 2004 during the Nairobi meeting of the UNSC. The US was reluctant to propose or even discuss further measures that the UNSC could take out of fear for undermining the progress over North–South.[76] In addition, it preferred to focus on (economic) 'carrots' instead of confrontational 'sticks' (Section 8.6). This change is remarkable in light of the outspoken position of the US and its preference for sanctions during the summer of 2004. The inconsistencies in the policy of the US have been noted by several authors as well.[77] These inconsistencies can be explained by the bureaucratic or governmental politics model with its focus on inter-departmental policy differences. As will be shown below, this model highlights the different competing factions and departments within the US and UK administrations. Note that the model was earlier applied to the UN bureaucracy and the differences between the 'humanitarians' and the 'political officers' (Section 6.8).

The different factions within the US Administration can be reduced to those who favoured a confrontational 'stick' approach and those who preferred a

---

73   BBC Panorma, "The new killing fields", 14 November 2004.
74   Kapila (2013), p. 184.
75   PBS Frontline interview with Kieran Prendergast, 29 June 2007. See also section 6.3.1.
76   *Supra* n 42. Heinze (2007), p. 379.
77   Stedjan and Thomas-Jensen (2010) "The United States", in *The International politics of mass atrocities. The case of Darfur*, by Black, D.R. and Williams, P.D. (eds.), London, New York: Routledge, p. 157–158. Michael Abramowitz, "U.S. promises on Darfur don't match actions. Bush expresses passion for issue, but policies have been inconsistent", Washington Post, 29 October 2007.

softer approached based on 'carrots' and persuasion.[78] A rather similar distinction was made by Prunier when he referred to the "realists," which can primarily be found at the US State Department, the CIA and the Defense Intelligence Agency.[79] These realists, who are generally more interested in the security interests of the US, tend to favour an approach which does not harshly confront Khartoum in order to safeguard cooperation in the field of anti-terrorism. At the other end of the spectrum are those in favour of a more confrontational 'stick' approach by the US government, termed by Prunier as the "Garang lobby," including USAID.

These differences were also visible at a later stage in 2005 and 2006 when a UN peacekeeping force and possible NATO involvement were discussed. For example, Bush's National Security Adviser Hadley was in favour of maximum US pressure for a larger UN peacekeeping force. Likewise, senior White House official Gerson tried to persuade Bush into establishing a no-fly zone.[80] Several factions within the US Administration were against any further military involvement of the US. Deputy Secretary of State Zoellick held that the risks for failure for President Bush were too big and he preferred an approach based on engagement.[81] Likewise, Rumsfeld and the Department of Defence were hesitant to even spend time or start planning action because they were afraid that by doing so they would eventually be compelled to do something.[82]

The bureaucratic or governmental politics model is also visible within the UK government. The Minister of Foreign Affairs responsible for Africa, David Triesman, for example, asked for military assets to enforce a no-fly zone. The Ministry of Defence was against.[83] Likewise, as we have seen in Chapter 5, the UK Ambassador Patey was also more vocal given his "progressive" background as an official from the Department for International Development (Section 5.3).

---

78   Michael Abramowitz, "U.S. promises on Darfur don't match actions. Bush expresses passion for issue, but policies have been inconsistent", Washington Post, 29 October 2007.

79   Prunier (2007), p. 139–140.

80   Michael Abramowitz, "U.S. promises on Darfur don't match actions. Bush expresses passion for issue, but policies have been inconsistent", Washington Post, 29 October 2007.

81   Cockett (2010), p. 226.

82   Gerson as quoted in Cockett (2010), p. 227. Hamilton (2011a), p. 75–76.

83   Cockett (2010), p. 228.

CHAPTER 9

New Decisions of the Security Council
January 2005–March 2005

The Abuja peace talks had collapsed in December 2004 due to new attacks and offensive operations by the Sudanese military. The situation in Darfur escalated and even AMIS became involved, suffering casualties from aerial bombings. Nonetheless, the humanitarian situation had majorly improved over the months, as the camps could now be supplied by the huge logistical humanitarian aid that was rolled out. On diplomatic side, the first three months of 2005 were very intensive. Following the publication of the Commission of Inquiry's report, a further two months were needed to pave the way for the UNSC resolutions of March 2005.

9.1 Situation in Darfur

Although incomparable to the peak in violence and deaths at the start of the previous year, 2005 began with a latent omnipresence of impending anarchy throughout Darfur. The cracks in the rebel movements were becoming increasingly visible, while Khartoum looked set to change its tactics. As Flint and de Waal note, with the government achieving its immediate goals by 2005, its time for self-congratulation would be short given the certainty of the war in generating new rebel recruits and the problematic border areas, especially with Chad, allowing for the easy flow of weapons into Darfur. Khartoum's response was thus to redouble its mobilisation of the *Janjaweed*.[1]

On 9 January 2005, the CPA was signed by the Government of Sudan and John Garang's SPLA rebels, bringing an end to the North-South civil war. The historic agreement granted autonomy to the South and majority representation for the SPLA in a new Government of Southern Sudan, as well as a role in the government in Khartoum and the chance for the South to secede in a 2011 referendum. Hailed by the parties concerned, as well as outsiders, the agreement inspired the EU to end its 14-year freeze on development aid to

---

1 Flint, J. and de Waal, A. (2008) *Darfur: a new history of a long war.* London, New York: Zed Books, pp. 150–151.

Sudan by offering 400 million euro. Even the UN Secretary-General and President al-Bashir at least superficially seemed united, as each welcomed the agreement as a model and inspiration for resolving Darfur.[2] Al-Bashir exclaimed, "[f]rom now on we shall work for solving the conflict in Darfur and we shall bring about peace in Darfur as we did in the south."[3]

Following the CPA's conclusion, al-Bashir told a crowd of cheering supporters in Khartoum that, "[t]he joy is incomplete because there is suffering in Darfur, but our promise to you is that we will bring peace to Darfur."[4] The next day government air forces bombed Darfuri villages. In fact, despite various pledges and the commitments at the end of December 2004 to peace and a ceasefire, violence by militias and government forces directed against villages was sustained. One incident alone, condemned by UK Foreign Secretary Jack Straw, killed as many as 100 civilians and resulted in the declaration of a "no-go" area according to AU forces on the ground.[5] Satellite images, which showed around 370 villages destroyed in June 2004, revealed in January 2005 that the number had increased to 800.[6] The situation escalated and even AMIS became involved, suffering casualties from aerial bombings. Nonetheless, the humanitarian situation had majorly improved over the months, as the camps could now be supplied by the huge logistical humanitarian aid that was rolled out. During the Christmas days of 2004 the Asian Tsunami had struck Indonesia and its wider region, which subsequently called on OCHA and the rest of the aid community to respond urgently to this natural disaster. It has been argued that the already meagre media attention for Darfur suffered from this event. Although this is an intuitive argument there is not much evidence that the humanitarian aid was scaled back or otherwise suffered from this new emergency.

---

2 Kofi Annan expressed hope that the agreement would serve as a blueprint and source of inspiration for addressing Darfur, since, he concluded, "the situation remains horrific" (UN News, 9 January 2005, "Annan hails signing of Sudan peace accord but warns of 'daunting challenges' ahead").

3 Agence France Presse, 12 January 2005, "Sudan's Bashir vows to achieve peace in Darfur."

4 Associated Press, 12 January 2005 "Darfur conflict dampens joy over southern peace accord, says el-Bashir [sic]."

5 UN News, 27 January 2005, "UN official voices concern over reports of deadly bombing raid on Sudanese village."

6 Totten, S. and Markussen, E. (eds.) (2006) *Genocide in Darfur, investigating the Atrocities in the Sudan.* London, New York: Routledge, p. 36.

9.2   The Commission of Inquiry Report

On 7 October UN SG Annan presented the 5-member committee headed by
Antonio Cassese to the world.[7] Despite being mandated by the Security
Council, the COI remained well connected with the UN in Geneva. It was based
in Geneva and its support team consisted of staff coming from the office of the
UN High Commissioner on Human Rights.[8] They requested and received
reports from other UN bodies and NGOs but in the report do not quote such
material. They appeared to work very autonomously with neither intermediate
public statements nor internal contact with people working at the UN in
Geneva.[9] The COI started its research on 25 October. It visited Sudan twice, first
in November 2004, a second time in January 2005, while some of its support
staff remained active in Darfur even if the members were not in Sudan. It interpreted its mission using the UNSC resolution and jurisprudence concerning
international law. Specifically, the task of identifying the perpetrators of violence was addressed using examples set out by the International Criminal
Tribunal for the former Yugoslavia (ICTY), International Criminal Tribunal
for Rwanda (ICTR) and various other cases and courts. The COI decided to set
itself the benchmark of collecting evidence that would be necessary in court
but stopping short of passing judgement and keeping alleged perpetrators
confidential.

The COI reaches several conclusions based on evidence it collected
itself.[10]

(1)   Government forces and *Janjaweed* militias committed by far the most
       violations of human rights and humanitarian law, as opposed to rebel
       forces.
(2)   These violations are categorised as war crimes and crimes against human-
       ity and include mass killings, destruction of villages, forced displace-
       ments, rape and sexual violence, torture, plunder and abductions.

---

7   The other members are: former Foreign and Justice Minister of Peru Diego Garcia-Sayán,
     director of an Eqyptian human rights NGO Mohammed Fayek, UNSG Special Representative
     on Human Rights defenders Hina Jilani of Pakistan and former Ghanaian judge and dip-
     lomat Thérese Striggner Scott.
8   UN doc. S/2005/60, 25 January 2004, "Report of the International Commission of Inquiry
     on Darfur to the United Nations Secretary-General, Pursuant to Security Council
     Resolution 1564 of 18 September 2004" [Hereafter: COI report], para. 1.
9   Authors' interview with Eckhart Straus, 1 June 2005.
10   See COI report for details.

Individuals that the commission identified were in part connected to these crimes.

(3) What is popularly termed *Janjaweed* militias consists in reality of sections of the Sudanese military as well as militias that are supported by the government. This support consists in varying cases in the supply of arms, uniforms, money and commands or failure to offer protection to civilians against militia attacks on purpose. Therefore, the government, despite its denial, is responsible for the actions of the *Janjaweed*.

(4) There is no strong evidence that the government had 'genocidal intent' with its military actions in Darfur. However the commission also noted that it was not handed minutes of relevant government meetings and decisions. The COI was not able to deduce general government intent from the evidence it collected, but suggested that some identified perpetrators, including government officials, may have had the intent of committing genocidal acts individually.

(5) There was no suitable system in Sudan to counter the impunity for the crimes that were committed. Actions that were taken before and after international condemnations and pressure had been half-hearted and inadequate. Therefore the commission advised the UNSC to refer the cases for prosecution at the ICC, rather than any other framework such as an ad hoc international tribunal or local courts.

(6) The commission also advised to setup a compensation scheme so that not only the case of the perpetrators was addressed through prosecution, but also the case of victims through compensation.

The question remained why a COI was necessary at all instead of having the Prosecutor of the ICC decide whether the reports of the committed crimes merited prosecution.[11] In addition, since many reports had already been written, and the COI relied on this information, why was another investigation necessary?[12] In fact, the COI report has largely the same findings as the research commissioned by US State Department in the summer of 2004.[13] Multiple

---

11 Schabas, W.A. (2004) "United States hostility to the International Criminal Court: It's all about the Security Council", *European Journal of International Law*, Vol.: 15(4), p. 1707.

12 Alston, P. (2005) "The Darfur commission as a model for future response to crisis situations", *Journal of international Criminal Justice*, Vol.: 3(3), pp. 600–607.

13 Totten and Markussen (2006); Markusen, E. (2009) "Three empirical investigations", in *The world and Darfur. International responses to crimes against humanity in western Sudan*, by Grzyb, A. (ed.), Montreal: McGill-Queens University Press.

answers are available and have been proposed, some with the benefit of hind-sight, namely:

(a)   The COI was a delaying measure from implementing more forceful mea-sures such as sanctions or a military intervention;[14]

(b)   The CHR instruments (the various topical rapporteurs and envoys) are unable to provide reports of the same authority, scope and quality as a COI;[15]

(c)   The route via the COI was a deliberate manoeuvre by those that favoured ICC referral to make the conditions right for it to happen.[16]

a)   *The COI was a Delaying Measure for Implementing More Forceful Measures such as Sanctions or a Military Intervention*

The establishment of the COI can certainly be viewed as a delaying feature since it would not report fundamentally different facts from what was already established in previous UN reports of the experts that had visited Sudan in 2004. However, once the commission was established in September, other actors such as the EU, would refer to the awaited COI report before making new decisions.[17] Similarly, the CPA may have functioned in the same way as the COI. Only after the CPA was signed were new discussions on measures against Sudan possible.

It is much less clear whether the COI was used in the Security Council as an alternative for stronger actions, e.g. sanctions. The resistance to implementing sanctions was more widely shared than the often-cited permanent members Russia and China, and this decision should be analysed by itself. Additionally, looking forward to March 2005, the Security Council would initiate the process of applying targeted sanctions around the same time as it referred the situa-tion to the ICC.

---

14   Happold, M. (2006) "Darfur, the Security Council, and the International Criminal Court", *International and Comparative Law Quarterly*, Vol. 55, p. 226. Authors' interviews with Eckhart Straus, 1 June 2005; Olivier Ulich, 1 June 2005. Some have even suggested that it was an outright escape for further measures, rather than just a postponement.

15   Alston (2005), in particular pp. 603–604.

16   Authors' interview with Isabelle Balot, 2 June 2005; Shraga D. (2009) "Politics and Justice: The role of the Security Council", in *The Oxford Companion to International Criminal Justice*, by Cassese, A. (ed.) Oxford: Oxford University Press.

17   For instance, the Dutch EU Council president Bot expresses such a view after questions from the Dutch parliament on whether sanctions were still considered (Dutch Parliamentary Doc.: Tweede Kamer, 2004–2005, 21 501 20, nr 265, 3 November 2004).

b) *The* CHR *Rapporteurs are Unable to Provide Reports of the Same Authority, Scope and Quality as a* COI

This argument was forwarded after the publication of the COI and referral to the ICC. Rapporteurs and Secretary-General Annan or its SR Pronk had briefed the Security Council numerous times. However, since the report of COI was explicitly authorised through a Security Council resolution to report on specific questions it carried much more weight. Various reports of the CHR rapporteurs as well as international NGO's had not resulted in clear actions. One of the reasons that the CHR had been unable move decision-makers is suggested to be institutional. Alston (2005) recounts how reports of CHR rapporteurs are constrained to 22 pages, leaving limited scope to delve into legal discussions as the COI did. However, it appears that the rapporteurs themselves do not naturally cooperate well as is evidenced by their disconnected visits and focused topical reports. For these reasons the COI and its report were more authoritative than any of the earlier reports.

c) *The Route Via the* COI *was a Deliberate Manoeuvre by Those that Favoured* ICC *Referral to Make the Conditions Right for It to Happen*

It was known that any path towards an ICC referral would be difficult since the US, Russia and China, as permanent members of the Security Council, had not signed up or ratified the Rome Statute. The discussion on the decision-making after the COI report is discussed below, but the establishment of the COI may have been a deliberate first step towards such a referral, which would otherwise not have been possible. This hypothesis appears rather likely but first-order evidence is not available. There exists a large body of commentary concerning the ICC referral of Sudan, but most concern the US position and actions only, the role of third states and organisations is rather less analysed. UN officials were quite aware of the difficult political situation, where one former official recounts that the COI was a deliberate first step towards ICC involvement.[18] In that respect the appointment of (the late) Antonio Cassese as the head of the COI, former president and judge at the International Tribunal for the former Yugoslavia, and author/editor of multiple volumes concerning International Criminal Law and the ICC in particular, almost guaranteed a particularly favourable view from the independent commission towards ICC referral. There also exists a historical analogue. In 1992, with collapse of Yugoslavia, the US sponsored a UNSC resolution that established a commission of experts

---

18 Isabelle Balot calls the COI the first step to prepare the US for the ICC referral (Authors' interview with Isabelle Balot, 2 June 2005); Shraga (2009, p. 171), writing as Prinicipal legal officer at the UN, fully acknowledges the political dimensions of the situation.

to look into the reports of "ethnic cleansing," also with the aim to prepare for criminal prosecution.[19] This would later be executed by the specially established ICTY.

9.3   January to March 2005: New Decisions

The United States introduced a lengthy draft resolution in February, which included a proposal for a UN peacekeeping mission in the south and preparations for sanctions on the perpetrators in Darfur.[20] It also included a small reference to international prosecution but from the resolution it is clear that this was not yet a settled issue. The resolution would be split in three to allow discussions on the different topics, because the debate had been in a stalemate for weeks.[21] It is interesting however, that also the decision on UNMIS was delayed and the resolution only adopted together with two resolutions on Darfur by the end of March. Therefore the three topics, (1) peacekeeping in Sudan and Darfur, (2) sanctions on individual perpetrators in the Darfur conflict and (3) international criminal prosecution were discussed in parallel. We will discuss them sequentially.

9.3.1   *Peacekeeping, Resolution 1590*
Already back in the summer 2004, with the discussion on western intervention and the first expansion of AMIS, the link between the peacekeeping force in South Sudan, UNMIS and Darfur was made. For instance, when questioned by the Dutch Parliament on the possibility of UN peacekeepers for Darfur, the Dutch Minister for Development Cooperation referred to ideas of combining the two.[22]

During the second half of 2004 the North-South talks moved to their real final stages and with that the planning for UNMIS. Now the UN was in the

---

19   UN Docs.: S/Res/771, 13 August 2013; S/Res/780, 6 October 1992; Schabas (2004), pp. 707–708; Authors' interview with Oliver Ulich, 1 June 2005.

20   UN Doc. SC/556 (14 February 2005), Draft Security Council Resolution on Sudan.

21   Authors' interview with Isabelle Balot, 2 June 2005; Williams, P.D. and Bellamy, A.J. (2005) "The responsibility to protect and the crisis in Darfur", *Security Dialogue*, Vol.: 36(1), pp. 27–47, p. 155; Rebecca Hamilton mentions that this was the ingenuity of Robert Zoellick, a newly appointed US front man, to force the diplomatic negotiations in the Security Council on Darfur through (Hamilton, R., 2011a, *Fighting for Darfur: public action and the struggle to stop genocide*. New York: Palgrave Macmillan, p. 62).

22   Dutch Parliamentary Doc.: Tweede Kamer, 2003–2004, meeting 89, p. 5691, 29 June 2004.

awkward situation where it planned to deploy a 10,000 strong peacekeeping force in the south, which is already largely at peace, while a potential genocide is going on in the west of the country, without the possibility of intervention but for a small and inexperienced AU force. However, since the UN Secretariat was aware that there was no political backing for a UN mission in Darfur, there was also no initiative or proposal coming from the UN secretariat.[23] In October 2004, Annan was left with offering the AU some administrative support and helping to gather more funds.[24]

After the signing of the Comprehensive Peace Agreement in January 2005, the first Security Council sessions concerning Darfur were in January and February although the first resolutions would only be adopted by the end of March 2005. SGSR Jan Pronk urged repeatedly for a stronger military force in Darfur to provide security; the 2000 AU forces should rather be around 8000.[25] He briefed the Security Council on this subject.[26]

The UNSC and the UN Secretariat discussed the under-performing AU mission. When it was concluded that the AU did not have the means and resources for a full-blown peacekeeping mission, four proposals were put forward by the UN secretariat to the SC members, in order of likeliness: (1) strengthening the AMIS mission, (2) a combined AU-UN mission, (3) a full-blown UN mission and (4) a multinational force under Chapter VII.[27]

Another important factor was that the negotiations in Darfur had collapsed in December with no view on a quick political solution. The formal ceasefire from April 2004 had never existed in reality either. The classic way in which peacekeeping missions are planned is based on an existing political agreement. Peace-enforcement missions, against the will of the government, are rare in the history of the UN, since they require no opposition from the permanent members. A military invasion by a multinational force without a UN mandate is even less likely without strategic security interests, especially after the war in Iraq.

On the other hand, pressure from grass-roots organisations and NGOs in the United States became more organised and one of their prime goals was

23   Authors' interview with Eckhart Straus, 1 June 2005.

24   UN News, 4 October 2004, "Annan Proposes ways to help African Union expand its mission in Darfur, Sudan."

25   See Totten and Markussen (2006), Ch. Chronology, 4 February 2005 and 17 March 2005.

26   UNSC meeting 5109, 11 January 2005, on report S/2005/10, 7 January 2005.

27   Traub, J. (2006) *The Best Intentions: Kofi Annan and the un in the Era of American World Power.* New York: Farrar, Straus and Giroux, pp. 305–312; Authors' interview with Isabelle Balot, 2 June 2005.

peacekeepers/enforcers in Darfur with US backing.[28] President Bush was alleg-edly responsive to this argument and did propose a stronger NATO role for AMIS. Also from the EU there was an attempt to get NATO involved.[29] NATO itself was only marginally interested. Therefore, the weakest option, solely the AU, possibly strengthened and assisted by UN, EU and NATO, was chosen.[30] It helped that the AU itself was not eager to have its missions taken over by the UN or anyone else.[31] Finally, other measures against Sudan were also discussed again such as a no-fly zone or a stronger enforcement of the arms embargo already in place since Resolution 1556.[32]

Therefore, Resolution 1590 was adopted on 24 March 2005 and establishes a 10,000 strong UN mission for South Sudan (UNMIS) under Chapter VII author-ity.[33] Despite its focus on the CPA, the resolution does refer to the situation in Darfur, including through the acknowledgement of the COI's report, and makes an explicit request to the UN SG to come with further proposals on how UNMIS may help AMIS, but this should not be understood as a preparation for poten-tial UNMIS expansion into Darfur as it

> Emphasizes that there can be no military solution to the conflict in Darfur.

The resolution was adopted unanimously.[34] Except for a statement from the Secretary-General there was no further discussion after the vote.

9.3.2   Targeted Sanctions, Resolution 1591

This resolution adopted on 29 March 2005 and sponsored by the United States concerned individual-targeted sanctions and travel bans on members of the Sudanese government. For the first time the Security Council requested all par-ties of the CPA "to take immediate steps to achieve a peaceful settlement to the conflict in Darfur," implying that the SPLM would now also need to shoulder its responsibilities.

The Council repeated the condemnations of previous resolutions and, under a Chapter VII heading,

---

28   Hamilton (2011a).

29   Authors' interview with Pieter Feith, 28 August 2013.

30   Traub (2006) p. 308–311; Authors' interview with Isabelle Balot, 2 June 2005.

31   Authors' interview with Isabelle Balot, 2 June 2005.

32   Traub (2006) p. 305–306.

33   UN Doc.: S/Res/1590, 24 March 2005.

34   UN Doc.: S/pv.5151, 24 March 2005.

[d]eplores strongly that the Government of Sudan and rebel forces and all other armed groups in Darfur have failed to comply fully with their commitments

Specifically the Council referred to air strikes by the government in December 2004 and January 2005,[35] attacks on villages by rebels and the failure of the Sudanese government to disarm the *Janjaweed* and bring their leaders to justice. Despite the violence it,

Emphasizes that there can be no military solution to the conflict in Darfur (...) and urges the parties to the [CPA] to play an active and constructive role in support of the Abuja talks and take immediate steps to support a peaceful settlement to the conflict in Darfur.

The many claims of the previous year, that a peace agreement between North and South was the best way forward to peace in Darfur, were now strongly endorsed by the Security Council as it requested all the parties in the CPA to put maximum efforts in reaching a solution in Darfur. However, since the Sudanese government had failed to fulfil its commitments since Resolution 1556, it decided to set up a committee, consisting of delegates of all Security Council members, which would decide on a travel ban and economic sanctions. The sanctions will be applied to:

those individuals (...), who impede the peace process, constitute a threat to stability in Darfur and the region, commit violations of international humanitarian or human rights law or other atrocities, violate the measures implemented by Member States in accordance with [the arms embargo of resolution 1556 (2004)] or are responsible for offensive military overflights[36]

The last part suggests some form of enforcement against the government's aerial bombings. However, the first persons were only subjected to sanctions more than one year later, in Resolution 1672 (24 April 2006).

---

35 AU mission report on air strikes on 26 January 2005 (Totten and Markussen, 2006, Ch. Chronology).

36 The text in the square brackets are the authors' interpretation of the technical references in the resolution. The resolution actually extends the arms embargo to "all parties of the N'Djamena Ceasefire Agreement", thus the Sudanese government would now be included. However, the ceasefire commission could pre-approve movements of (government) military material.

This resolution was adopted with China, Russia and Algeria abstaining. The adoption of this resolution (and the abstention of these countries) was the result of considerable informal discussions following the initial US draft in which an oil embargo was proposed. Due to resistance, the US weakened this to travel bans and asset-freezing, but this was dismissed again by Russia and China.[37] The imposition of a travel ban was thus the watered down solution that would not result in a veto by China or Russia. They explained their position in statements after the vote, arguing that the CPA provided a positive momentum for Sudan that should not be spoiled with such measures.[38] However, Russia acknowledged that:

> [t]his, naturally, does not negate the justification for targeted pressure on those who in fact are creating obstacles to normalizing the situation in Darfur.

Similarly, China had "serious reservations" about the resolution. Given the situation it would not be right to impose "measures" as:

> the humanitarian crisis in the Darfur region has gradually eased [thanks to the efforts of the international community]

On which report China bases this statement is not very clear as even the AU speaks about a deteriorating security situation in the past four months.[39] Furthermore, it laid blame at the SC stating that:

> [t]here are many complex factors that could explain why it is so difficult to resume the Abuja political talks. One of these relates to the messages sent by the Security Council.

The Sudanese government was also allowed to speak and used the same words, saying that the adoption of sanctions made the situation more complicated. Moreover, Sudan accused the US Congress of having orchestrated this resolution, which the US ambassador rebuffed in a second statement.

---

37   Williams, P.D. and Bellamy, A.J. (2006) "The UN Security Council and the question of humanitarian intervention in Darfur", *Journal of Military Ethics,* Vol.: 5(2), p. 156.

38   UN Doc.: S/pv.5153, 29 March 2005.

39   See Totten and Markussen (2006, Ch. Chronology, 5 February 2005), for a more elaborate picture of the situation in Darfur, Pronk's briefing in the Security Council: "The security situation in Darfur is still bad. The humanitarian situation is poor" (UN Doc.: S/pv.5109, 11 January 2005).

9.3.3   *Pushing for the ICC*

The Report of the Commission of Inquiry was presented to the Security Council by Pronk.[40] One of the prime attention spots of the report by the COI was its argumentation on whether genocide occurred in Darfur. After the determination by the US government and the activist movement in the US that had already concluded that it was genocide, the COI conclusion felt like a betrayal, even though its reasoning was more in line with the analysis of NGOs.[41] The Sudanese government, which was given a copy before the public release, could make a public statement that the UN had found that there was no genocide in Darfur, while leaving out the other serious charges.[42] A sealed envelope with the names of 51 individuals, which the COI thought involved with the crimes, was given separately to the UN Secretary-General.

Since the Commission was so detailed in its legal argumentation, their findings initiate many responses from activists, who were mostly critical, and (legal) scholars.[43] Some authors have doubted the intentions of the Commission, suggesting its lead investigator Cassese was prejudiced.[44] Others noted, as was pointed out in the COI report, that the Sudanese government had obstructed the COI in finding all the evidence it needed to draw the conclusion.[45]

However, the determination of genocide was not the only, or even the main task of the COI. Its main task was to identify perpetrators and give some views on how to move forward with respect to accountability. It had identified 51 of those perpetrators.[46] Together with this list of names, it provided a detailed

---

40   UN Doc.: S/pv.5119, 8 February 2005.

41   Flint and de Waal (2008), p. 183.

42   BBC News, 31 January 2005, "UN 'rules out' genocide in Darfur."

43   One prominent activist, Eric Reeves, gives a two-part analysis on the alleged failure of the commission (available at http://www.sudanreeves.org [accessed 19 July 2013]). For scholarly articles see for instance Schabas, W.A. (2006) "Genocide, crimes against humanity, and Darfur: the Commission of Inquiry's findings on genocide", *Cardozo Law Review*, Vol.: 27(4), pp. 1703–1722; Kress, C. (2005) "The Darfur Report and Genocidal Intent", *Journal of International Criminal Justice*, Vol.: 3(3), pp. 562–578.

44   Totten, S. (2006), "The US investigation into the Darfur crisis and its determination of genocide", *Genocide Studies and Prevention*, Vol.: 1(1), pp. 57–78.

45   Fowler, J. (2006), "A new chapter of irony: the legal implications of the Darfur genocide determination", *Genocide Studies and Prevention*, Vol.: 1(1), pp. 29–40.

46   COI report, para. 645. Paragraph 531 breaks down the number; among the 51 individuals identified there are "10 high-ranking central Government officials, 17 Government officials operating at the local level in Darfur, 14 members of the Janjaweed, 7 members of various rebel groups and 3 officers of a foreign army (who participated in their individual capacity in the conflict) who are suspected of bearing individual criminal responsibility for the crimes committed in Darfur."

report of the crimes with which these 51 were associated. It is a readable report – but heavily based on legal arguments – and was written to prepare the way for a Security Council authorised prosecution of those suspected to be the most important perpetrators, including high-ranking Sudanese officials.

Once it was determined that Sudan would not prosecute their own citizens for events in Darfur, a fact that most countries agreed on, there were four options available to the Security Council:

(1)   Refer the case to the ICC;
(2)   Establish a new ad hoc court for Darfur;
(3)   Expand the jurisdiction of the court for the Rwanda genocide, the ICTR, to include the case of Darfur;
(4)   Decide to establish a mixed court where the Sudanese justice system cooperates with a UN counterpart.

These options were all discussed in the COI report where the Commission advanced the case for an ICC referral against the other three options. Interestingly, whereas the entire report relied heavily on legal argumentation concerning the crimes and the perpetrators, the argumentation for the ICC and against the alternatives was entirely based on practicalities such as finance, speed and efficiency.[47]

Since Sudan is not a party to the Rome Statute of the ICC (Sudan had signed but not ratified the Statute), the Court would have no jurisdiction unless the UNSC referred the situation to it.[48] After the publication of the COI "the majority" of the Security Council members were in favour of a referral to the ICC.[49] The challenge was finding a form that would not trigger a veto from any of the permanent members, and in particular not from the US. The US draft resolution of 14 February 2005 had barely touched upon the findings of the COI.[50] However, although this draft resolution does not indicate a concrete proposal for the prosecution of Sudanese perpetrators, there was already much diplomatic

---

47   COI report, paras. 573–582. One legal comment the commission could have made is that the Rome Statute defines a rigid jurisdiction; whereas an ad hoc court could have a jurisdiction specialised to the specific case of Darfur (Condorelli, L. and Villapando, S., 2002, "Can the Security Council Extend the ICC's jurisdiction?" in *The Rome Statute of the International Criminal Court: A Commentary.* Volume I, by Cassese, A., Gaeta, P. and Jones, R.W.D. [eds.], Oxford: Oxford University Press).

48   Art. 13(b) of the Rome Statute.

49   Shraga (2009), p. 171.

50   Neuner, M. (2005) "The Darfur referral of the Security Council and the scope of the jurisdiction of the International Criminal Court", *Yearbook of International Humanitarian Law,* Vol.: 8, pp. 320–343.

activity going on from the side of the US. In line with what appears the most fundamental objection of the US to the ICC, that it does not have full control over proceedings through the Security Council,[51] the US preferred a new ad hoc court based in Arusha, Tanzania, or an extension of the jurisdiction of the Rwanda court, already based in Arusha, shaped after their preferences. On the financial side, the US is willing to cover the cost for such a new ad hoc court, while it would refuse to shoulder anything for the ICC referral.[52]

In January and February the US diplomatic corps were put into action to convince the world of the superiority of its proposal, with a special role for Ambassador-at-Large for War Crimes Pierre-Richard Prosper who presented the US alternative proposal to members of the Security Council and to many African and European governments.[53] There is not much evidence that the US became active much earlier on the issue of which court to use. This is surprising by itself since it was expected from the start that the COI would advise for the ICC.[54]

Africa

There is at least one indication that the US was anticipating the ICC advice of the COI just before the public release of the COI report. In mid-January the US ambassador to Nigeria tried to convince the Nigerian president and the AU chairman to consider the alternative of an AU court.[55] Similarly, Tanzania, the host of the ICTR in Arusha, was approached early to make it warm for hosting a new court for Sudan. Tanzania was sympathetic to the idea, but its official line remained to support the ICC until there existed a wide support for another

---

51   Schabas (2004) provides an overview of the literature and the multitude of difficulties the
      US may have with the ICC. He concludes that the key objection lies in the control the
      Security Council has over the ICC.

52   Kaufman, Z.D. (2005) "Justice in jeopardy: accountability for the Darfur atrocities",
      Criminal Law Forum, Vol.: 16, p. 347. These costs are estimated to range between US$40
      million and US$150 million per year.

53   In an interview with a French newspaper, Prosper doubts whether a referral will have any
      added value to ameliorate the situation in Darfur. He further indicates that only after the
      publication of the COI report will there be a discussion on ICC referral if countries try to
      pursue that direction (Le Monde, 25 December 2004, "Trois questions à Pierre-Richard
      Prosper" [three questions for Prosper]). Prosper states the US objections for the ICC to
      members of the Security Council (Le Monde, 2 February 2005, "L'ONU ne conclut pas au
      génocide mais dénonce des 'crimes contre l'humanité' au Darfour" [The UN concludes no
      genocide but denounces crimes against humanity in Darfur]).

54   Authors' interview with Eckhart Straus, 1 June 2005.

55   US State Department Cable, Abuja, 14 January 2005, No. 59; 31 January 2005, No. 137. The
      formulation in the second cable suggest that the US was aware of the advice in the COI
      report but that the it did not know its contents exactly yet, as the meeting on which the
      cable reports took place on 29 January 2005.

direction.[56] The position of Chad was that the AU would not have the capacity to run its own court and it therefore supported the ICC.[57] Gabon and AU officials were, nonetheless, open to the US proposal presented by Ambassador Prosper. The AU was considering setting up its own court in the future, and the US tried to use this aspect to push for this AU court to take up the situation of Darfur.[58]

Europe

France is named as one of the more influential actors with respect to the discussion of Darfur and the ICC.[59] This role is highlighted in two mid/high-level meetings of American and French officials. During a meeting between a US embassy official and a French Foreign Affairs official on 10 February, the French official suggested that a new resolution could include special opt-outs for the US in a referral to the ICC.[60] Another high-level meeting between Ambassador Prosper and a French deputy director at the Ministry of Foreign Affairs set out the reasoning of both positions much more clearly.[61] The US could cooperate with the ICC, for instance through provision of evidence or financial means, the ICC was dealing exclusively with African issues (Uganda, Democratic Republic of Congo, contemplating Central African Republic and now Darfur) that it would not look very good for Africa. Expanding the ICTR to Darfur, with a vision of creating a new permanent AU/UN court for Africa would appear nicer. The French official cut apart all of the US' arguments and came back offering to support a resolution that would include exceptions for the US. The account also confirms that the US was the only member in the Security Council that was opposing the referral, indicating that the other permanent members, China and Russia, were not obstructing this process to the same extent. The bigger issue was that the US wanted to find a long-term workable solution for the ICC, but since this was proving harder than envisioned it needed to accept that Darfur would have to be dealt with first. The newly appointed Secretary of State Condoleezza Rice was in direct discussions with French Foreign Minister Barnier on the issue.[62]

---

56   US State Department Cable, Dar Es Salaam, 26 January 2005, No. 155; 1 February 2005, No. 206; 18 February 2004, No. 374.

57   US State Department Cable, Ndjamena, 18 February 2005, No. 260.

58   US State Department Cable, Ndjamena, 22 February 2005, No. 277.

59   Authors' interviews with Isabelle Balot, 2 June 2005; Olivier Ulich, 1 June 2005; Hamilton (2011a), p. 62.

60   US State Department Cable, Paris, 11 February 2005, No. 879. The meeting was between the US deputy chief of mission and French Ministry of Foreign Affairs cabinet director.

61   US State Department Cable, Paris, 17 February 2005, No. 1039.

62   US State Department Cable, Paris, 30 March 2005, No. 2110; Le Monde, 26 March 2005, "A L'ONU, la discussion sur le jugement des crimes commis au Darfour

The UK, as the other European permanent member of the UN SC, also aimed to find a way in which US would not veto a referral to the ICC. For instance it also offered exceptions for the US, similar to the once France offered.[63] The UK was involved in the drafting and sponsored the resolution that the Security Council finally adopted.[64]

The Netherlands, as host of the ICC, was also committed to the ICC and was not in favour of the establishment of a separate tribunal or the extension of the Rwanda Tribunal. Already on 11 August 2004 the Ministry of Foreign Affairs rejected a proposal for the extension of the Rwanda Tribunal because it preferred to make use of the momentum of the Darfur crisis to underline the relevance of the ICC.[65] However, in February Foreign Minister Bot sent a message to US Secretary of State Rice offering to "brainstorm" on different options and to "tone down the rhetoric and activities" of Dutch representatives in the world against alternatives to the ICC in this case.[66] In preparation for a EU Council meeting the Dutch government stated that in anticipation of the COI report it would argue for the ICC.[67] Besides the Netherlands, the UK, and France, Ireland,[68] Spain,[69] Austria,[70] and Finland[71] are documented to be in favour of an ICC referral. There is no indication that any European country was in favour of the alternative proposal. A declaration by the European Council supported the recommendation of the COI for the ICC, but the formulation is sufficiently ambiguous to allow some space for negotiation.[72]

The US

There is not much support from within the US for objecting to an ICC referral either. Some American commentators loathe the US stance that its opinion of

---

continue." [At the UN, the discussion continues on the trial of crimes committed in Darfur].

63 Le Monde, 18 Februari 2005, "Washington bataille contre la justice internationale" [Washington fights against international justice].

64 UN Docs.: S/2005/199; S/2005/218; S/pv.5158, 31 March 2005.

65 Archive Ministry of Foreign Affairs in the Netherlands: djz/ir/na/00210, 2004–2004.

66 US State Department Cable, The Hague, 16 February 2005, No. 451.

67 Dutch Parliamentary Doc. Tweede Kamer, 2004–2005, 21 501-02, nr. 603, 25 January 2005.

68 US State Department Cable, Dublin, 17 February 2005, No. 207.

69 US State Department Cable, Madrid, 15 February 2005, No. 617.

70 US State Department Cable, Vienna, 17 February 2005, No. 473.

71 US State Department Cable, Helsinki, 17 February 2005, No. 207.

72 EU Doc.: press release 6420/05, 21 February 2005: "...the [European] Council reaffirms the EU's constant support for the International Criminal Court and reiterates its common position on the International Criminal Court, while noting that it is for the United Nations Security Council to take a rapid decision on this matter."

the ICC has precedence over accountability for the perpetrators in Darfur.[73] Similarly, international NGOs such as Amnesty International, Human Rights Watch as well as American-based activist groups for Darfur all favoured the US government's cooperation with the Security Council on this issue.[74] Retiring UN ambassador Danforth wrote a note to Secretary of State Condoleezza Rice warning of the "train wreck" coming to the US.[75] Finally, there exists a large body of scholarly articles (from American authors) in the field of international and criminal law that analyses the US position on the ICC, which are often critical of the US policy and reasons of not acknowledging the ICC's jurisdiction.[76] An apparent refusal by US Congress to speak out against an ICC referral was another motivation for European countries to push even harder. Interestingly, the grass-roots movement, known as the "Save Darfur" campaign, was not involved much on this issue. Hamilton notes that a US abstention in the UNSC on this issue seemed so unlikely that some NGOs thought it not worth a big fight, while the "Save Darfur" campaign was partly supported by Jewish groups which were not too eager in looking to support the ICC either. Instead they focused on other measures such as trying to commit the US to act militarily.[77]

9.3.4   ICC, Resolution 1593

This resolution on 31 March 2005, sponsored by the UK, referred the situation of Darfur since 1 July 2002 to the International Criminal Court. In the resolution the Security Council:

> Decides that the Government of Sudan and all other parties to the conflict in Darfur, shall cooperate fully with and provide any necessary assistance to the Court and the Prosecutor pursuant to this resolution and, while recognizing that States not party to the Rome Statute have no obligation under the Statute, urges all States and concerned regional and other international organizations to cooperate fully.

---

73   Nicholas D. Kristof, 2 February 2005, New York Times, "Why should we shield the killers?"; Samantha Power, 10 February 2005, New York Times, "Court of first resort."

74   Amnesty International, AFR/024/2005, 21 February 2005, "Open letter to the members of the United Nations Security Council: The situation in the Sudan."; Human Rights Watch, 15 February 2005, "U.S. Proposal for a Darfur Tribunal: Not an Effective Option to Ensure Justice."

75   State Department Cable, US-UN mission New York, 7 January 2005, Nr. 34 (available at http://www2.gwu.edu/~nsarchiv/NSAEBB/NSAEBB335/index.htm [accessed 25 January 2013]; Hamilton (2011a), p. 58.

76   See Schabas (2004) for references.

77   Hamilton (2011a), p. 63.

Due to principle reservations by two permanent Security Council members, the US and China, special paragraphs were included for those countries which are not bound by the Rome Statute of the International Criminal Court:

> Decides that nationals, current or former officials or personnel from a contributing State outside Sudan which is not a party to the Rome Statute of the International Criminal Court shall be subject to the exclusive jurisdiction of that contributing State for all alleged acts or omissions arising out of or related to operations in Sudan established or authorized by the Council or the African Union, unless such exclusive jurisdiction has been expressly waived by that contributing State.[78]

In addition, the costs incurred by the court were not to be born by the US, neither directly nor indirectly, for instance through the UN. The resolution "[encouraged states] to contribute to the ICC Trust Fund for Victims."

The preamble of Resolution 1593 referred to an article in the Rome Statute, Article 98(2), which points to bilateral agreements of non-signatories. The US had been actively establishing such bilateral agreements in an effort to protect its citizens from the ICC prosecutor. It showed something of the US nervousness that this reference appears in this resolution where the threat to US (or Chinese/Russian) servicemen appears non-existent, and the mere indirect note in the resolution has no further value in international law.[79] This reference, together with the clauses that prevented prosecution of nationals of non-signatory countries and the exclusion of any direct or indirect bearing of the cost of prosecution combine to full protection of those countries uncomfortable with the ICC, except Sudan.

Because this was the first time the Security Council referred a situation to the ICC, there was a lengthy discussion on the specialties of the provisions that excluded non-signature countries of the Rome Statute of International Criminal Court. The US gave a clear reason why it would not object to the

---

78   For a more elaborate discussion on the legal obligations considered in this referral, see Bothe, M. (2007) "International Legal Aspects of the Darfur Conflict" in *The law of international relations: liber amicorum Hanspeter Neuhold*, by Reinisch, A. and Kriebaum, U. (eds.), Eleven International Publishing, in particular pp. 13–17.

79   Condorelli, L. and Ciampi, A. (2005) "Comments on the Security Council Referral of the Situation in Darfur to the ICC", *Journal of International Criminal Justice* Vol.: 3(3), pp. 590–599. The three "officers of a foreign army (who participated in their individual capacity in the conflict)" (COI report, para. 531) included in the list of identified perpetrators by the COI are likely to be Libyans or Chadians.

resolution while it continued to have fundamental objections to the Court saying:

> We decided not to oppose the resolution because of the need for the international community to work together in order to end the climate of impunity in the Sudan and because the resolution provides protection from investigation or prosecution for United States nationals and members of the armed forces of non-State parties.

The US and China would have preferred a regional court such as one proposed by Nigeria on behalf of the African Union.[80] The countries that endorsed the resolution, such as the United Kingdom, France and other European countries, refer to the recommendation as given by the international Commission of Inquiry and stated that they believed that the ICC would be the most effective institution to address the situation.

There is a remarkably large body of (mostly US based) scholarly commentary on this resolution on Darfur in which authors analyse the different clauses of the resolution and try to explain the US role in it in particular. These commentaries centre around the legal construct of the referral, the differentiating obligations of cooperation put on member states, the bilateral agreements of protection from the ICC and the (lack of a) compensation scheme for victims.

For instance, as discussed above, only the Security Council, per article 13 of the Rome Statute, could subject Sudan to the Court's jurisdiction. However, Resolution 1593 does not refer to this article explicitly in the preamble, which some authors think suspicious given the reference of some other articles in the resolution.[81] Additionally, only Sudan is obliged to cooperate with the ICC prosecutor, whereas the Security Council could have chosen to make the obligation much wider.[82] It decided not to do so, and the obligations imposed in the resolutions are according to established international law.[83] However, it is

---

80   UN DOC.: S/PV.5158, 31 March 2008. China refers to it by saying "the African panel for criminal justice and reconciliation, proposed by Nigeria on behalf of the African Union, could also serve as a way out" (p. 5). The USA declares that it "believes that the better mechanism would have been a hybrid tribunal in Africa" (p. 3).

81   Condorelli and Ciampi (2005).

82   Idem; Heyder, C. (2006) "The U.N. Security Council's Referral of the Crimes in Darfur to the International Criminal Court in Light of U.S. Opposition to the Court: Implications for the International Criminal Court's Functions and Status", *Berkeley Journal of International Law*, Vol.: 24(2), pp. 650–671.

83   Happold (2006).

still remarkable that the Security Council decision to refer the situation to the ICC does not imply that all members need to cooperate with the court. With respect to the ICTY and ICTR, the Security Council established this obligation for all countries and the courts had mechanisms to notify the Council in cases of non-compliance under which the Council could enforce it. It never decided to do so, instead measures outside the Council, unilateral positive incentives rather than sanctions, have proved rather effective in facilitating compliance.[84] Finally, the COI made a strong recommendation in their report for a compensation scheme for the victims in Darfur. Some authors find that the mere encouragement to donate to the ICC Trust fund for victims falls short.[85] However, the COI recommendation for individual compensations, independent of an identified perpetrator, is complicated without any arranged finance to allow for it.[86]

---

84   Shraga (2009).
85   Condorelli and Ciampi (2005).
86   Tomuschat, C. (2005) "Darfur–Compensation for the victims", *Journal of International Criminal Justice*, Vol.: 3(3), pp. 579–589.

CHAPTER 10

Epilogue

The International Response to Darfur after 2005

This research focused on the international response to the conflict in Darfur in the period between February 2003 and March 2005, while concentrating on the gap between (early) warnings and (early) actions. The conflict had not ended by March 2005 and the international community has remained involved, albeit to varying degrees. This chapter shortly sketches out the main measures taken by third parties to the conflict as well as the security situation in Darfur since 2005.

10.1   2005–2007: Getting UN Peacekeepers in Darfur

The international actions in the rest of 2005 and the beginning of 2006 were focused on securing a peace agreement, which was considered a prerequisite for the transition from an AU to a UN peacekeeping force. One of the major reasons behind the policy of making AMIS a UN mission was the donor fatigue of Western countries, who were the major financial sponsors of the AU force, coupled with concerns about AMIS' limited effectiveness (Section 7.8.4).[1] The US was especially determined to have a UN force as quickly as possible.[2] This hurriedness stemmed from the US government's aim to appease the vocal "Save Darfur" grassroots movement, which called for stronger US involvement.[3] Similar protests took place in other Western states, as Photo 1 on the next page illustrates as well.

The fifth round of negotiations resulted in the signing of the "Declaration of principles for the resolution of the Sudanese conflict in Darfur" on 5 July 2005 by the Sudanese government and the two original rebel groups, the SLM/A and JEM.

---

1   At the beginning of 2006, the AU Peace and Security Council finally supported the transfer from AMIS to UN command. See also Mackinnon, M.G. (2010) "The United Nations Security Council", in *The International politics of mass atrocities. The case of Darfur*, by Black, D.R. and Williams, P.D. (eds.), London, New York: Routledge, p. 91; Authors' interview with Jan Pronk, 2 September 2013.

2   de Waal (2006), A. "'I will not sign'. Alex de Waal writes about the Darfur peace negotiations", *London Review of Books,* Vol.: 28(23), pp. 17–20.

3   Flint, J. (2010) "Rhetoric and reality: The failure to resolve the Darfur Conflict", Small Arms Survey, Geneva, p. 14.

PHOTO 1   *Protest for UN peacekeepers to Darfur in The Hague: Photo made by Willem*
            Schalekamp on 18 September 2006, The Hague, the Netherlands.

According to Flint, this was the "high point" of international diplomatic endeavours to achieve a peace agreement, not least because it is still the only time that these two rebel movements committed themselves to the same agreement.[4] While in 2004 the first rounds of negotiations were led by the AU and the Chadian government together, since the seventh round, which started in November 2005, the AU had become the sole mediator. This was the result of the worsening relations between Chad and Sudan, who accused each other of backing rebel groups in each other's countries (the Chadian government started to actively support the JEM, while the Sudanese government backed Chadian rebels against Déby.).[5] The mediation was led by AU Special Envoy Salim. The UN only played an observer role, to the discontent of Pronk.[6] The seventh round lasted almost six months

---

4   Flint (2010), p. 9.

5   Marchal, R. (2006) "Chad/Darfur: How two crises merge", *Review of African Political Economy*, 33(109), pp. 467–482.

6   Another difficulty was that the Darfur Peace Agreement (DPA 2006) did not include any reference to a future transition from an AU to a UN force (Bieckmann, F., 2012, *Soedan. Het sinistere spel om macht, rijkdom en olie*. Amsterdam: Balans, p. 187; Authors' interview with Jan Pronk, 2 September 2013; Jan Pronk, "Weblog nr 23", 27 May 2006, available at: http://www.janpronk .nl/weblog/english/may-2006.html [accessed 17 December 2013]).

and resulted in the Darfur Peace Agreement (DPA 2006), signed in Abuja, Nigeria. The DPA 2006 was signed "with little of the fanfare that had accompanied the signing of the CPA."[7] Only the government and one faction of the SLM/A, led by Minni Minnawi, signed the agreement, while the JEM and the faction of the SLM/A led by Abdul Wahid al Nur refused to sign, despite the strong pressure of the mediators and international observer states. Civil society or tribal leaders were not involved in the process either. The incomplete peace process was largely the result of the haste with which several countries, most notably the US, were handling the peace negotiations.[8] One consequence of the imperfect peace process was that the Darfuri population saw the DPA 2006 as forced upon them.[9] As will be argued below, violence continued after the agreement, because the non-signing rebel movements were put aside as outlaws or spoilers. Those who had not signed were banished from the Ceasefire Commission on the request of the US and Sudan.[10]

The DPA 2006, nonetheless, paved the way for the transition from AMIS to a UN peacekeeping force, which was mandated by the UNSC under Chapter VII in Resolution 1706 on 31 August 2006. Resolution 1706 extended the mandate of UNMIS, which was already present in South Sudan, to also cover Darfur. UNMIS would have up to 17,300 additional troops and 3300 civilian police officers, and was initially planned to take over the AU-led AMIS force by 31 December 2006. The problem with the new resolution was, however, that it invited the consent of Khartoum. This invitation was the result of the insistence of China, who other-wise threatened to use its veto. Although such language is redundant from a legal point of view because the UNSC was acting under Chapter VII, states were reluctant to contribute troops without at least the passive acquiescence of Khartoum.[11] What is more, Khartoum used this provision as a pretext for rejecting a UN force.

As said before, violence continued despite the signing of the DPA 2006. Pronk already referred to the "significant risk" that the DPA would collapse at the end of June 2006.[12] IRIN likewise reported in August that the security in

---

7   Grünfeld, F. (2012) "Early Warning, Non-Intervention and Failed Responsibility to Protect in Rwanda and Darfur", in *Human Rights and Conflict, Essays in Honour of Bas de Gaay Fortman*, by Boerefijn, I., Henderson, L., Janse, R. and Weaver, R. (eds.), Antwerp: Intersentia, p. 146.

8   Bieckmann (2012), p. 189–190 and 351.

9   Jan Pronk, "Weblog nr 26", 28 June 2006, available at http://www.janpronk.nl/weblog/english/june-2006/weblog-nr-26june-28-2006.html [accessed 17 December 2013].

10   Flint (2010), p. 9. De Waal (2006).

11   Grünfeld (2012), p. 146.

12   Jan Pronk, "Weblog nr 26", 28 June 2006, available at http://www.janpronk.nl/weblog/english/june-2006/weblog-nr-26june-28-2006.html [accessed 17 December 2013].

Darfur was worse than in 2005, while Pronk noted that the DPA had "become a source of further disruption."[13] Pronk subsequently informed the UNSC on 18 September 2006: "The DPA is only four months old, but it is nearly dead. It is in coma. It ought to be under intensive care, but it isn't."[14] The DPA was in practice disregarded by the international community even though they paid it lip service.[15] The DPA fuelled the conflict between the non-signatories, on the one hand and Khartoum/ SLM/A Minnawi, on the other hand. Minnawi, who had signed and was awarded a position as senior assistant to President al-Bashir as chairman of the Transitional Darfur Regional Authority, started to attack his former allies to "punish" them.[16]

The conflict in this period started to become more complex, partly as a result of the DPA 2006. The earlier violence inflicted by Arab Khartoum-backed militias primarily against non-Arab groups in the period 2003–2005 was replaced by increased conflicts between Arab groups who started to fight the government and each other.[17] The fragmentation of rebel groups into dozens of factions grew as well, leading to internal rivalries. Rebel groups became ever more concerned with their own personal power, wealth and status. In addition, the conflict has become more complicated as a result of growing regional competition for influence, various internal conflicts and a war economy.[18] Increased attacks by *Janjaweed* militias across the border into Chad led to growing tensions between Sudan and Chad. In April 2006, Chadian rebels supported by Khartoum attacked N'Djamena from Darfur. Déby broke off diplomatic relations and increased his support for JEM, also with a view of

---

13   UN IRIN, 10 August 2006, "Sudan: Darfur insecurity much worse than last year", available at:
      http://www.irinnews.org/report/60073/sudan-darfur-insecurity-much-worse-than-last
      -year [accessed 18 December 2013]. Jan Pronk, "Weblog nr 32", 18 August 2006, available at
      http://www.janpronk.nl/weblog/english/august-2006.html [accessed 17 December 2013].

14   UN News, 18 September 2006, "UN envoy to Sudan says Darfur peace deal needs fresh dis-
      cussions to be effective". Earlier, he held that the DPA 2006 has led to more violence between
      the non-signatories (SLM/A Abdul Wahil al Nur) and the signatory faction SLA Minnawi and
      the government of Sudan (Jan Pronk, "Weblog nr 32", 18 August 2006, available at http://
      www.janpronk.nl/weblog/english/august-2006.html [accessed 17 December 2013]).

15   One symptom of this was when Slovenia, through its President Janez Drnovšek and activ-
      ist Tomo Križnar offered their own mediation services but were explicitly denied by the
      US to get involved in the Abuja talks (Križnar, T. and Weiss, M., 2008, "Darfur: War for
      Water", DVD: Bela Film, Tomo Križnar, RTV Slovenia).

16   Flint (2010), p. 18.

17   Gramizzi, C. and Tubiana, J. (2012) "Forgotten Darfur: Old tactics and new players", Small
      arms survey, Geneva, p. 13.

18   Flint (2010), p. 44.

diverting attention away from Chad's domestic problems. These developments thus injected an element of a proxy war between both countries.[19]

Other noteworthy developments in 2006 include the imposition of a travel ban and asset freeze on four individuals in April 2006.[20] In addition, Pronk was declared *persona non grata* on 24 October 2006, because he had criticised the Sudanese government for violations of international agreements and human rights on his weblog.[21] No protest was voiced by the UN Secretariat against his expulsion. Pronk later labelled this non-reaction as "a bureaucratic, a-political approach" and attributed this approach to the fear of the UN to risk friendly relations with a member state.[22] This non-reaction also stems from the dominant idea within the UN of the complete sovereignty of states over their internal affairs. It also illustrates the weak position in the UN system of persons who favour a more activist (human rights) approach, as we have also seen with Kapila (Section 6.6.2).

Much of the international involvement in 2007 consisted of seemingly interminable negotiations to actually get the UN force deployed in Darfur.[23] Khartoum only compromised on 31 July 2007 when the UN force was replaced by a hybrid UN-AU force, UNAMID (UN-AU Mission in Darfur), which was mandated in Resolution 1769. China played a crucial role in persuading the Sudanese government to agree with UNAMID. The latter also illustrates that the Chinese role has changed since the end of 2006 to the detriment of the Sudanese government, even before several human rights and civil society organisations started the Genocide Olympics campaign in mid-2007, which connected the Chinese role in Sudan with the Chinese organisation of the 2008 Olympics.[24]

---

19   Grünfeld (2012), p. 145–146; Marchal (2006).

20   UN Doc.: S/Res/1672, 25 April 2006.

21   Jan Pronk, "Weblog nr 40", 14 January 2007, available at http://www.janpronk.nl/weblog/ english/january-2007.html [accessed 17 December 2013]. De Waal also argued that Khartoum used Pronk's writing on the decreasing morale of the Sudanese army as a result of battlefield defeats against the National Redemption Front in North Kordofan as an excuse (de Waal, 2006). For the weblog, see Jan Pronk, "Weblog nr 35", 14 October 2006, available at http://www.janpronk.nl/weblog/englishoctober-2006/weblog-nr-35october -14-2006.html [accessed 17 December 2013].

22   Jan Pronk, "Weblog nr 40".

23   Grünfeld (2012), p. 147.

24   For example, Large noted how Guangya, the Chinese ambassador in the UNSC, played a crucial and constructive role during the negotiations in Addis Abada in November 2006 (Daniel Large, 2007, "Arms, oil and Darfur. The evolution of relations between China and Sudan", HSBA Issue Brief No. 7, Small Arms Survey, Geneva, p. 9; Holslag, J., 2007, "China's Diplomatic Victory in Darfur", *Asia Paper*, Vol.: 2[4], Brussels Institute of Contemporary China Studies, Vrije Universiteit Brussel, Brussels, p. 8).

Several authors have argued that the international community placed too much emphasis on peacekeeping instead of reaching a negotiated peace agreement. Senior UN and US officials argued that they spent five to ten times as much time on peacekeeping issues.[25] Pronk likewise stated that the UNSC was mistaken in considering only the instrument of peacekeeping and discussing the specific modalities. He argued for strengthened peacemaking efforts based on "vigorous multilateral diplomacy" that goes "beyond issuing resolutions or statements."[26] The latter however did not happen sufficiently. According to UN officials, the peace process has not been supported by robust and coordinated political *démarches* of Western governments and especially the US, UK and France.[27] A DPKO official contrasted this limited involvement with the response of these countries to the post-election violence in Kenya in 2007–2008: "There was 24/7 assistance from these countries (...). In Darfur, their attitude has been, 'Tap us on the shoulder when you have a deal, and we'll come and party with you'."[28] It has also been argued that the external involvement and the focus on peacekeeping had a counter-productive effect and actually contributed to conflict, because it had the effect of making the rebels less willing to compromise.[29] Alex de Waal, adviser to the AU during the Abuja negotiations, noted, for example, how "the prospect of being 'saved' by UN troops" made the rebels less eager to accommodate.[30]

The peace process was only restarted in February 2007, nine months after the DPA was concluded. The talks were led by Salim (AU) and Eliasson (UN). These talks quickly proved to be ineffective, also because the two mediators worked only part-time on Darfur and were not based in the region. Christofides, the director of political affairs of UNMIS, talking about the AU and UN led mediation, referred to "managerial incompetence of a very high order" and explained that "no one had a really good grasp of what was needed in the mediation

---

25   Flint (2010), p. 22.

26   Jan Pronk, "Weblog nr 40", 14 January 2007, available at http://www.janpronk.nl/weblog/
      english/january-2007.html [accessed 17 December 2013]. For a similar reasoning, see de
      Waal (2006).

27   Flint (2010), p. 12.

28   DPKO official as quoted in Flint (2010), p. 34–35.

29   Cockett, R. (2010) *Sudan: Darfur and the Failure of an African State*. New Haven: Yale
      University Press, p. 237.

30   de Waal, A. (2007a) "Darfur and the failure of the responsibility to protect", *International
      Affairs*, Vol.: 83(6), p. 1046. This tendency of the rebels to become less constructive in talks
      the larger the impression of foreign intervention was already noted during the first Abuja
      round in September 2004 (see Section 7.9.1).

effort."[31] Talks in Sirte, Libya, in October 2007 were, for example, boycotted by the three most important rebel groups, JEM and the two factions of the SLM/A.

10.2   2007: EU/UN Military Missions, the ICC and Sanctions

In 2007, the UN and EU authorised two complementary military missions to be deployed in Sudan's neighbouring countries Chad and the Central African Republic (RCA, French abbreviation for *République centrafricaine*). EUFOR-Tchad/RCA was authorised by the EU to "take all necessary measures" in both countries to protect refugees, facilitate humanitarian access and protect UN personnel. MINURCAT (*Mission des Nations Unies en République Centrafricaine et au Tchad*) was mandated by the UN to provide police support to the armed forces in both countries and to protect refugees as well. These two missions have been attributed to the growing pressure of 'Save Darfur' lobbies in various EU states and especially in France to do something for Darfur, largely in response to the failure of establishing a strong UN mission in Darfur.[32] Darfur figured prominently in the presidential elections in France in 2007 and all candidates promised to help protect refugees from Darfur. The new socialist Minister of Foreign Affairs Kouchner, who had a humanitarian background as a co-founder of Médecins Sans Frontières, was an important force behind the two missions. An additional reason for France to enhance its involvement was also related to its strategic interests in its former colonies, which are located in the centre of the Africa and are rich in natural resources. Besides humanitarian motives, France was also eager to support the regimes in both countries against domestic rebels, foreign rebel groups and militia, and prevent a spill-over of the conflict in Darfur so as to ensure stability. This active French role reflects its considerable involvement in '*la Francophonie*'.[33] In contrast, the UK is generally more reluctant to take up a proactive role in its former African colonies.

In April 2007, the ICC issued its first arrest warrants against the Minister of State for humanitarian affairs, Haroun, and militia leader, Kushayb, for war crimes and crimes against humanity in Darfur. In July 2008, the Prosecutor

---

31   Christofides as quoted in Flint (2010), p. 24.

32   Pohl, B. (2013) "To what ends? Governmental interests and European Union (non-) intervention in Chad and the Democratic Republic of Congo", *Cooperation and Conflict*, forthcoming.

33   For a discussion of the French role in Africa, see for example, Lanotte, O. (2007) *La France au Rwanda (1990–1993). Entre abstention impossible et engagement ambivalent*. Bruxelles: P.I.E. Peter Lang.

Ocampo filed an application for another warrant against President al-Bashir for the same crimes as well as genocide. This arrest warrant was issued by the ICC's Pre-Trial Chamber in March 2009, but it did not charge al-Bashir for genocide. Khartoum reacted immediately by expelling thirteen NGOs and closing three Sudanese human rights organisations. The African Union was also unhappy with the Prosecutor's decision and requested the UNSC put a halt to the Court's proceedings pursuant to article 16 of the Rome Statute.[34] The Security Council refused to use this power. From that moment onwards a fierce debate has been ongoing about the political role of the ICC in Sudan as well as elsewhere. The decision not to include genocide in the arrest warrant against President al-Bashir was appealed by the Prosecutor and consequently allowed by the Appeals Chamber. As a result of this, the Pre-Trial Chamber issued a second warrant which included genocide charges in July 2010.

The US imposed unilateral sanctions in May 2007 on two Sudanese government officials, Haroun and Ibn Auf, and JEM leader Ibrahim as well as 30 government-run companies. In addition, the US Congress also adopted the Sudan Accountability and Divestment Act at the end of 2007, which requires, amongst others, that companies who seek US government contracts show that they are not doing any business in Sudan.

10.3   2008–2011: Parallel Peace Initiatives

Hardly any progress was made in 2008 with the negotiations. Salim and Eliasson therefore resigned in June 2008. Eliasson described the situation at that time as "very, very sombre."[35] The two mediators were replaced by a single mediator leading an AU-UN mediation team, Bassolé. Bassolé led the so-called Doha negotiations under the auspices of the Qatari government between June 2008 and July 2011. The focus was shifted to negotiations with JEM. At the same time there were greater efforts to involve civil society actors from Darfur and Sudan in Doha in comparison with the earlier negotiations in Abuja, albeit with

---

34   UN Doc.: S/2008/481, 23 July 2008, annex, or AU Doc.: PSC/PR/Comm(CXLII) (142nd), 21 July 2008. This communiqué expresses the strong opposition of the African Union of the proposed indictment of the Sudanese for various reasons (including the belief that the indictment harms the peace process), and expresses concern with "the misuse of indictments against African leaders" and "perception of double standards." It requests the UNSC to apply Article 16 of the Rome Statue in order to defer the case of President al-Bashir.

35   Flint (2010), p. 32.

limited results.[36] Since 2009, the international interest for Darfur has started to decrease. This was also because the death toll dropped. In addition, the attention shifted to other matters which demanded the attention of the international community, such as the presidential elections in Sudan scheduled for April 2010 and the referendum on the future of South Sudan planned for 2011.

However, Bassolé was no longer alone, since there were several parallel and competing peace initiatives. These initiatives were partly influenced by international rivalries over control of the negotiation process.[37] In addition to Bassolé/Qatar, there were also initiatives by Libya, Eritrea, Egypt, the US and the AU. Egypt was "very, very angry" with Qatar's involvement and decided to start another process to "smash" the Qatari effort in July 2009.[38] In addition, US President Obama also appointed a new Special Envoy for Sudan, Gration, in March 2009 who also embarked on mediating efforts by trying to unite the different rebel groups and by pursuing a softer approach vis-à-vis Khartoum, based on dialogue. The priority of the US was, however, focused on saving the North–South Agreement and preventing a violent partition following a referendum on independence in South Sudan planned for 2011. The AU also appointed a High-Level Panel on Darfur chaired by former South African President Mbeki in March 2009 to draw up suggestions on how to achieve peace in Darfur. The AU Panel launched a separate process parallel (and for some a rival) to Doha which was to take place in Darfur, the Darfur Political Process.[39] The latter process proved to be subordinate to Doha, also because the US and the EU were not in favour of negotiations taking place in Darfur, given the security situations and concerns of freedom of speech.[40]

The 'Doha Document for Peace in Darfur' was signed five days after the independence of South Sudan on 14 July 2011 with only one rebel group, the Liberation and Justice Movement (LJM). The LJM was a merger of several factions of the SLM/A and JEM, and the result of the attempts of the international community between 2006–2010 to unite the rebels in order to facilitate the negotiations with the Sudanese government.[41] However, several of the

---

36   Civil society had a more instrumental role as supporting actors which could pressure the rebels in compromising, rather than an independent negotiating party. For a good description of the Doha process, see Tubiana, J. (2013) "Darfur after Doha", in Sudan divided, by Sørbø, G.M. and Ahmed, A.G.M. (eds.), Palgrave, p. 166–172.

37   Tubiana (2013), p. 178.

38   Egyption government official as quoted in Flint (2010), p. 38.

39   Tubiana (2013), p. 172–173.

40   Ibid., p. 173–174.

41   Ibid., p. 164–165.

strongest factions defected from the LJM already before the conclusion of the agreement.[42]

UNAMID's limited effectiveness became increasingly clear. This was also largely the result of its limited mandate. Resolution 1769 had not mandated UNAMID to disarm militias and it did not include a clause authorising military force (e.g. "to take all necessary measures").[43] In addition, the Rules of Engagement were very weak and were respectful of the sovereignty of the government of Sudan.[44] Another complicating factor was that the actual deployment of UNAMID was also delayed because of Khartoum's obstruction and the slowness of states in contributing troops. Senior officials planning the transition already acknowledged in 2007 that the UN-AU force would be unable to be effective and deliver protection in the absence of an effective peace agreement or ceasefire, especially in such an enormous and complex region as Darfur.[45] Another complicating factor was that there was hardly any practical support from the Western countries and permanent members of the UNSC, except for the US and Germany.[46] Gramizzi and Tubiana thus referred to the "failure of UNAMID" which has been largely unable to protect the Darfuri civilian population. They and others referred to several instances of abuses against civilians close to the UNAMID bases that were not prevented.[47]

10.4   Since the End of 2010: Growing Insecurity and Ethnically Targeted Violence

The security situation in Darfur has worsened again since the end of 2010. The SLM/A led by Minni Minnawi, the only rebel group which signed the DPA 2006, restarted its rebellion against the government in December 2010.[48] At the same time, the Sudanese government has increased its support of non-Arab militias from the Bergid, Berti, Mima and Tunjur tribes and set them up against Zaghawa. The growing violence in Darfur also coincided with increased

---

42   Ibid., p. 165; Gramizzi and Tubiana (2012), p. 15.

43   Grünfeld (2012), p. 156.

44   Ibid., p. 147–148.

45   Flint (2010), p. 21.

46   Ibid., p. 44.

47   Gramizzi and Tubiana (2012), p. 35–36. Elbasri as quoted in Klaas van Dijken, "'VN liegen over oorlog in Darfur'; De waarheid over Darfur is taboe" [UN lies about war in Darfur; The truth about Darfur is taboo], *Trouw,* 14 December 2013.

48   Gramizzi and Tubiana (2012), p. 14.

violence and conflicts in the oil rich region of Abyei on the border between North and South Sudan, South Kordofan and the Blue Nile since 2011. Darfuri rebel groups have also extended their fields of activity towards South Kordofan.

In the light of the growing violence, it is surprising that UNAMID has claimed that violence has decreased in Darfur.[49] According to Gramizzi and Tubiana, UNAMID has publicly downplayed the intensity of the recent increase of violence in eastern Darfur and does not refer to the ethnically directed nature of the violence against the Zaghawa.[50] At the same time UNAMID has allegedly misrepresented the Doha Document as a significant achievement in an attempt to sell the agreement to the population.[51] Tubiana argued that because UNAMID is one of the few international actors who regularly reports on the situation in Darfur, this leads to overly positive assessments of progress.[52] It is therefore not surprising that the UNSC Panel of Experts on Darfur held that the Doha Document provided "a clear and relatively positive change compared to the [security] situation in the previous years (...) has set in motion a peace process that has been garnering support from the Darfur population at large."[53]

Several observers and organisations recently challenged these claims and argued that the conflict has actually worsened since the end of 2010 with a considerable offensive of the proxy militias backed by the Sudan Armed Forces, indiscriminate attacks and aerial bombardments against rebels but also civilians from the Zaghawa tribes in eastern Darfur.[54] According to Gramizzi and Tubiana this generated "some of the most significant ethnically directed

---

49   Head of UNAMID Gambari pointed in November 2011 to the "humanitarian gains made recently" and only noted the growing belligerent rhetoric of groups opposed to the Sudanese government. In February 2011, Gambari referred to the "simmering war". (UNAMID Press release, 29 November 2011, "UNAMID Chief Urges Firm International Backing for Darfur Peace", available at: http://unamid.unmissions.org/Default.aspx?tabid=11027&ctl= Details&mid=14214&ItemID=17505&language=en-US [accessed 17 December 2013]; Ibrahim Gambari, "Time for renewed effort to end conflict in Darfur", The Guardian, 25 February 2011, available at http://www.theguardian.com/global-development/poverty -matters [accessed 17 December 2013]).

50   Gramizzi and Tubiana (2012), p. 37.

51   Tubiana (2013), p. 181.

52   Ibid, p. 162.

53   Unreleased UN Doc.: Final report of the UNSC Panel of experts on the Sudan, 24 January 2011, authored by Claudio Gramizzi, Michael Lewis and Jérome Tubiana, available at http://dl.dropbox.com/u/72848070/Report%20of%20former%20members%20of%20 the%20unsc%20Panel%20of%20Experts%20on%20the%20Sudan%20January%202012 .pdf [accessed 21 December 2013].

54   Gramizzi and Tubiana (2012), p. 7; AI doc.: AFR 54/007/2012, February 2012, "Sudan: No End to Violence in Darfur"; AI Doc.: AFR 54/007/2013, March 2013, "10 years on. Violations remain widespread in Darfur".

violence since the start of the conflict in 2003 [including] deliberately targeting civilian settlements believed to be supportive or identified with rebel forces."[55] Amnesty International said that 500 people were reportedly killed and 100,000 displaced in the first three months of 2013.[56] The UN arms embargo against non-governmental and governmental entities (Resolutions 1556 and 1591) have remained ineffective, since arms supplies to Khartoum and the militias in Darfur have not been stopped.[57] The UN Panel of Experts on the Sudan also reached this conclusion and stated that the embargo "remains without discernable impact and ammunition, especially, has continued to enter Darfur since 2005."[58] These sources also claim that the government has conducted other rounds of aerial bombardments since 2011 irrespective of the prohibition issued by the UNSC.[59]

The version of Tubiana and Gramizzi was later confirmed by the former spokeswoman of the UNAMID, Elbasri, who stated that the policy of UNAMID was actually to *publicly* claim that the situation in Darfur is constantly improving. This was allegedly also the reason that Elbasri announced her resignation in April 2013, eight months after her appointment.[60] She herself tried to convince the management of UNAMID to be more open and transparent, but she did not receive an answer or she was being told that she took a dangerous course. She also stated that the UN Headquarters in New York has remained silent as well, despite the daily (internal) reports sent by UNAMID about the worsening situation in Darfur.[61] The management of UNAMID and the UN Headquarters consequently blocked the release of information that could give

---

55   Gramizzi and Tubiana (2012), p. 7, 11.

56   AI Doc.: AFR 54/007/2013, March 2013, "10 years on. Violations remain widespread in Darfur".

57   AI doc.: AFR 54/007/2012, February 2012, "Sudan: No End to Violence in Darfur", p. 16–22; Gramizzi and Tubiana (2012), p. 9.

58   UN Doc.: S/2011/111, 8 March 2011, "Report of the Panel of Experts on the Sudan established pursuant to resolution 1591 (2005)", p. 4.

59   AI doc.: AFR 54/007/2012, February 2012, "Sudan: No End to Violence in Darfur", p. 9–15; Gramizzi and Tubiana (2012), p. 9; UN Doc.: S/2011/111, 8 March 2011, "Report of the Panel of Experts on the Sudan established pursuant to resolution 1591 (2005)", para. 91–94.

60   The official explanation she gave at that time was: "I wasn't receiving the support I needed in terms of access to information in a timely manner" (Sudan Tribune, 24 April 2013, "UNAMID spokesperson resigns after 8 months in the post", available at http://www.sudantribune.com/spip.php?article46334 [accessed 17 December 2013]).

61   Elbasri as quoted in Klaas van Dijken, "'VN liegen over oorlog in Darfur'; De waarheid over Darfur is taboe" [UN lies about war in Darfur; The truth about Darfur is taboo], *Trouw*, 14 December 2013.

rise to doubts on UNAMID's image of a strong and robust mission capable of protecting the population.[62] An example of information that cannot be released is the denial of access to UNAMID by Khartoum to places where attacks and bombardments had taken place. At other times, information has been distorted. Elbasri gave the example of an incident that took place on 5 September 2012 two meters from a UNAMID compound in Kutum, North Darfur. Militias opened the fire on civilians while UNAMID stood by and did nothing to prevent this attack. At the same time, UNAMID troops photographed the incident.[63] The report of the Secretary-General Ban Ki-moon later wrote about this incident in rather vague terms, not mentioning that UNAMID was present at the location.[64]

One might wonder why the UN and AU swept information under the carpet? A similar question was raised as to the silence of the UN in the first year of the conflict in Darfur. This silence and the cautious response of the UN was explained by the bureaucratic culture of minimising risks and the preoccupation with the interests of the organisation (Section 5.4.4). A comparable mechanism seems at play with UNAMID, which appears primarily interested in its own image. Tubiana's citation of Barnett seems therefore justified to explain the behaviour of the UN and AU: "those in and around the UN come to have a stake in and identify with the bureaucracy, begin to evaluate strategies and actions according to the needs of the bureaucracy, and, accordingly begin to frame discussions and justify policies in a different manner."[65]

10.5   An Unprecedented International Engagement with Darfur, but What for?

Previous chapters and this Epilogue showed that the response of the international community over the last decade has been tremendous. This has been noted by several authors as well. According to Flint, the UNSC has approved "an unprecedented number of instruments to the Darfur crisis," including

---

62   Idem.

63   Idem.

64   "An exchange of fire left four attackers and two Government policemen dead. The following day, one civilian was killed and eight others were injured in the crossfire of a firefight between armed Arab militia and Government regular forces on the outskirts of the town." (UN Doc.: S/2012/771, 16 October 2012, "Report of the Secretary-General on the African Union-United Nations Hybrid Operation in Darfur", para. 26).

65   Barnett, M. (1997) "The UN Security Council, indifference and genocide in Rwanda", Cultural Anthropology, Vol.: 12(4), p. 576.

mediation, peacekeeping, arms embargoes and prosecutions by the ICC. Darfur has led to one of the largest humanitarian operations in the world, involving more than 13,000 humanitarian workers between mid-2004 and mid-2008.[66] Likewise, Lanz asserted that the "international engagement in the Darfur conflict eclipses most other responses to contemporary civil wars in Africa and beyond."[67] A different matter is whether these international endeavours have been enough? According to Flint, none of the efforts succeeded.[68] Pronk also held at the end of December 2006: "Policy makers in the capitals of the countries represented in the Security Council (...) have not shown an awareness of the urgent need to take prompt and effective action."[69]

This epilogue also casts doubts upon the achievements so far. The AU-UN peacekeeping force UNAMID has remained largely toothless while the arms embargo and prohibition of aerial bombardments of the UNSC have been ineffective and violated. In addition, the two peace agreements of Abuja and Doha have largely proven dead letters in practice. The perpetrators of the crimes committed in Darfur have not been brought to justice yet and the arrest warrants issued by the ICC are still outstanding. President al-Bashir actually travelled to several members of the ICC's Rome Statute, including Chad and Kenya, without being arrested. Above all, the situation in Darfur has entered a new phase which mirrors the period 2003–2005 with Khartoum supporting non-Arab militias and setting them up against the Zaghawa. Again, the UN (and AU) is silent and is burying its head in the dusty sand of the Darfuri desert.

66　Fabrice Weissman, 'Humanitarian dilemmas in Darfur', MSF Foundation, July 2008, available at: http://www.msf-crash.org/drive/6bde-fw-2008.humanitarian-dilemmas-in-darfur.pdf [accessed 20 December 2013]. Flint (2010), p. 11, 44.

67　Lanz, D. (2011) "Why Darfur? The responsibility to protect as a rallying cry for transnational advocacy groups", *Global responsibility to protect*, Vol.: 3, p. 226.

68　Flint (2010), p. 44.

69　Jan Pronk, "Weblog nr. 39", 27 December 2006, available at: http://www.janpronk.nl [accessed 17 December 2013].

CHAPTER 11

Conclusions

The chronological overview provided in the previous chapters makes it possible to answer the research questions on the (early) warnings on Darfur, and especially, whether these were received and read by the international bystanders. When did they realise the seriousness of the atrocities? Were they advised of the instruments or policy options to deal with the situation in Darfur and were these instruments also available? How did they respond to warnings, and were their actions successful? These first research questions were the following:

(1) When were the policy-makers aware of the severity of the impending crisis in Darfur (the knowledge question)?
(2) Were the policy-makers advised on feasible instruments to prevent conflict escalation and deteriorating human rights situation (the early warning question)?
(3) Were instruments available for the policy-makers to deploy in order to effectively prevent or deescalate the situation (question on availability of means)?

We will answer these question for the different periods dealt with in this book, which were:

a. February 2003–February 2004 (Chapter 5);
b. March 2004–May 2004 (Chapter 6);
c. June 2004–September 2004 (Chapter 7);
d. October 2004–January 2005 (Chapter 8);
e. January 2005–March 2005 (Chapter 9).

The explanations of the gap between the warnings and the responses are more difficult to give. This is because we want to delve deeper than the obvious answers based on the motives as national interest, general global indifference or lack of political will to act.

The questions formulated to address the explanations were:

(4) Did the policy-makers deploy these available instruments timely and effectively taking into account the need to alleviate or stop the suffering (question on decision-making)?

© KONINKLIJKE BRILL NV, LEIDEN, 2014 | DOI 10.1163/9789004260405_012

(5)   What other circumstances affected the decision-making. This includes factors such as international and domestic support to act, or developments in other parts of the world that called for attention as well (question on the environment and political will)?

For these explanations we made use of the academic literature in international relations on foreign policy decision-making and especially the three models originally developed by Allison. The decision not to act can be researched as well as the decision to act. In scrutinising the decision-making we also looked to the psychological and cognitive filters used for the incoming information in order to make these congruent with existing beliefs, disbeliefs and policy and institutional preferences. These academic tools are not unique for Darfur but are useful for the analysis of the response of third parties, both national and international, to conflicts and atrocities.

In Chapter 1, we explained the 'early warning-early action' approach and how to operationalise these concepts for our data gathering. In our study on Darfur, we made use of a wide variety of different sources, such as news reports, diplomatic cables, national and international documents, archives and interviews with decision-makers, in particularly those involved in decision-making at the UN and EU levels.

In Chapter 2 we elaborated on the academic literature of International Relations, including realism, pluralism/liberalism and the three foreign policy decision-making models. The applications of these theories on Rwanda and Srebrenica were presented in Chapter 3. These theories were used in the Chapters 5–9 for the explanation of the behaviour of national and international bystanders in the case of Darfur. When making use of pluralism/liberalism, we focused in particular on the domestic influences in Western democracies on the foreign policy-making of these governments. In order to understand the failures of the UN to act, prevent and rescue in Rwanda and Srebrenica, we discussed the use of 'institutional routinisation' linked with indifference to the outcome (organisational process model) and the bureaucratic compartmentalisation (bureaucratic politics) with the focus on the (differences) in interests of departments within government bureaucracies or international organisations. 'Where you stand depends on where you sit' is the slogan for this approach. The organisational process and bureaucratic politics model explain the mistakes of Kofi Annan as the head of the Department of Peace Keeping Operations (DPKO) in the genocide in Rwanda and Srebrenica. He deliberately misinformed the members of the Security Council in order to protect the survival of his own 'turf' (the administrative unit of the DPKO). DPKO – and the UNSC – also decided to withdraw the UN peacekeepers, because there was no peace to keep anymore. With the withdrawal of the UN force, the last defence for the Tutsi in Rwanda was removed and subsequently a large part of them were annihilated. More or less the same happened one year later for the Muslim male population in Srebrenica.

In our study on Darfur, we demonstrated that the bureaucratic politics and culture in the UN again meant that the alarm bells – which were particularly rung by persons of the Office of Humanitarian Affairs (OCHA) – were not heard and responded to by the top of the UN, including by Kofi Annan who, in the meantime, had been promoted to become the UN Secretary-General. Rather, the upper-echelons of the UN, including Security Council members, preferred to continue with silence, with the exception of some limited public statements on Darfur in December 2003. This decision and the cautious approach largely stemmed from the policy of focusing only on the North–South negotiations. The UN maintained this policy until spring 2004. From April 2004 it was no longer possible to remain silent as we have shown in this study, but the UN Secretariat was slower than some states in changing to a vocal and publicly active policy. It was thanks to Jan Pronk that Annan accepted that the mandate of his new Special Representative for Sudan would not be limited to aspects related to the North–South conflict but included Darfur as well. This was one factor which meant that since June 2004, Darfur was a hotly debated topic in international fora, including the UN Security Council. Unfortunately, it was in the period before this international attention that most Darfuri had lost their lives due to violence. The next section will provide the main conclusion for the different time periods.

11.1   Conclusions on Darfur

For the first period, February 2003–February 2004 (Chapter 5), we demonstrated that the embassies and UN mission in Khartoum became aware of the atrocities and the magnitude of the atrocities as late as summer 2003. The embassies and UN mission also informed their capitals and the UN New York headquarters. The ethnic dimensions of the conflict came to the forefront in November/December 2003 and it was also at that time that international actors started to realise the severity of the crisis. By the end of 2003, there was no doubt anymore about the close relationship between the *Janjaweed* and the Government of Sudan. Khartoum's denials of this linkage were not believed.

The instruments that were applied in this period were humanitarian assistance and quiet diplomacy. All western countries addressed Darfur at the highest levels with the Sudanese government, but strictly out of the public eye. At the same time, several western countries, including the UK and US, decided not to bring the situation of Darfur to the UNSC. The most far-ranging form of diplomacy was the mediation effort of the government of Chad during the course of 2003, which resulted in an (ineffective) ceasefire agreement in September. The focus in this period was clearly on the humanitarian aspects of the crisis and ensuring humanitarian assistance. However, during the period December 2003–February 2004 humanitarian assistance could no longer enter the region since the Sudanese government had denied access. This also meant that the perpetrators could execute the worst crimes without any spectators. The UN in New York never prevented the withdrawal of these humanitarian workers. The NGOs continued to issue warnings about the deteriorating situation in Darfur. OCHA chief Egeland also became more involved and vocal, but he was not able to open the UN debate on this topic that was framed solely in terms of a humanitarian crisis until the end of May 2004. This also downplayed the urgency for the UN Secretariat to inform the UNSC about Darfur.

Together with the early warnings, policy recommendations were given to decision-makers. A Commission of Inquiry was, for example, already proposed by UN Special Rapporteur (SR) Gerhart Baum in March 2003 in Geneva. This proposal was in turn based on the earlier suggestion by Amnesty International. The UN Resident Coordinator in Sudan, Mukesh Kapila, also made a similar request to the UN in New York. Again in May 2004 the UN Acting High Commissioner for Human Rights Ramcharan, asked the same of the UNSC. The European Council supported this call in a statement issued in July and Germany recalled this in the UNSC. The decision to establish the COI was eventually made in September 2004. In December 2003 the UN Resident Coordinator and the diplomatic missions in Khartoum favoured the preparation of an internationally monitored ceasefire and discussions in the Security Council. This is the second instrument that was advised. Despite the warnings and recommendations, a public debate on the crisis was still not possible until the spring of 2004.

For the second period March 2004–May 2004 (Chapter 6) we demonstrated that the warnings were not only received by the decision-makers but they also started to respond, albeit rather reluctantly. The UN Resident in Sudan Kapila, who knew already that he would be replaced by the UN, performed in his last days the role of 'whistleblower' and announced in a BBC interview that the situation in Darfur was like Rwanda with the only difference being its slower pace.

We have elaborated on how difficult it was to put the Darfur issue on the Security Council agenda in this period. Both the Secretary-General and the Department of Policy Affairs (DPA) within the UN opposed the debate on this issue in the main UN form and preferred to limit the topic as only one of humanitarian assistance. The theory of bureaucratic politics decision-making is useful to explain this decision, because it highlights the interest of the SG and DPA in safeguarding the political capital of the SG by preventing any risky undertakings. In addition, the rational decision-making theory explains why the UN and the Troika countries (US, UK and Norway) preferred to prioritise the North–South negotiations. They feared that Darfur was an obstacle to any progress on the North–South agreement, which could annul their large investment in the process.

The European states in the Security Council, France and in particular Germany, eventually succeeded with their initiative of issuing a press statement under the German Presidency with a view of opening the agenda for Darfur in April. During the following month Pakistan continued along this path and under its Presidency the Security Council issued a Presidential Statement. Additional pressure and publicity in these months came from the analogy that was made with the genocide of Rwanda, which had occurred exactly ten years before. For example, UN SG Annan, linked Darfur to the Rwanda genocide during a commemoration ceremony. At the same time, domestic pressures on Western governments increased, particularly in the US.

In April 2004 the instrument of diplomacy was successfully employed in the direction of Khartoum and resulted in the N'Djamena ceasefire of 8 April. The ceasefire also included the start of an observer mission, which would later expand to the AMIS peacekeeping force. This instance shows that combined pressure from both the UN and states can be effective. It illustrated that Sudan can be a rational actor that takes external demands into account when it fears the increasing pressures. For Khartoum, it was of the utmost urgency to respond positively and at least to show that it was willing to accommodate. Nevertheless, the ceasefire was already broken by the government of Sudan before the ink had dried. This behaviour on the part of Khartoum would repeat itself in the months and years to come. The pattern is roughly as follows: when the pressure from the outside world on the government of Sudan increases, it reacts and acts as if it is accommodating to the demands of the UN. The measures to threaten or punish are consequently postponed. The response of the government of Sudan consists often merely of words and intentions rather than concrete deeds or the change of behaviour and policy. However, it is often enough to satisfy the international community and it is highly effective in the sense that sanctions are not applied, or only in a limited form. The decreased pressure consequently gives Khartoum the freedom of manoeuvre to deal in an atrocious manner with Darfur.

This period can be seen as the first active political phase of international and multilateral decision-making, primarily at the UN level and by western countries. After great difficulties, Darfur could finally be discussed in the Security Council, even though the first resolution was yet to be adopted.

In the third period of June 2004–September 2004 (Chapter 7) we demonstrated that the increased international activity resulted in decision-making by the Security Council. The pressure on Sudan increased to comply with the external demands and targeted sanctions became an option. The instrument of military involvement was hardly considered seriously and restricted to assisting the Africans in a limited peacekeeping operation in Darfur (AMIS II). The UNSC and Western countries primarily tried to support the African Union in their efforts to deal with question of Darfur, rather than confronting African – and also Islamic – countries over their often uncritical public treatment of Khartoum. Several Western governments committed themselves to providing material and political support to the AU, albeit with delays and operational problems.

The newly appointed UN SG Special Representative Jan Pronk managed to have Annan extend his mandate so that it would also cover Darfur. His unified mandate also enabled Pronk to address issues in a comprehensive way in Sudan. As a result of his position as Special Representative, Pronk was in direct contact with the UN SC and the Secretary-General. Annan had initially proposed a restricted mandate for Pronk, in line with the positive view of a concluded North–South peace agreement. This illustrates that he was cautious in proposing concrete new policy options to the UNSC. This behaviour can be explained with the organisational process and the bureaucratic politics models, which highlight the risk-minimising approach and indifference of bureaucracies and the focus on departmental and organisational interests rather than the prevention of gross human rights violations in Darfur. This attitude was also visible in the behaviour of DPKO, which tried to avoid getting involved, and DPA, which was primarily interested in the political capital of the UN SG Annan.

Domestic pressure from western public opinion and parliaments increased, particularly in the US. This important factor contributed to an active role of Western states, such as the UK and US, which had remained rather passive in the international fora until spring 2004. The Americans changed their Permanent Representative in New York and appointed the former Special Envoy to Sudan, Danforth. Danforth had a strong authority and a profound knowledge on the situation in Sudan. World leaders such as Powell and Annan, under the influence of increasing political pressure to act on Darfur, visited Sudan at the same time to apply maximum pressure. Annan and Pronk signed a Communiqué with the President al-Bashir and Foreign Minister Ismail, on the withdrawal of the military in Darfur and the disarmament of the *Janjaweed*.

Resolutions with limited mandatory measures were adopted, such as the arms embargo against the *Janjaweed* and a threat on further sanctions.

Sudan, being a clever political actor in world affairs, accommodated by formally agreeing with the external demands as, for example, formulated in the Communiqué. However, the implementation of the proposed measures was deliberately postponed or not effectuated by Khartoum at all. The pressure on President al-Bashir diminished after his initial accommodation and that pressure was not renewed when it became clear that he had not acted upon his promises. This was also facilitated by Sudan's 'protection' in the Security Council, especially by the permanent members of China and Russia, who would not condemn Sudan immediately and could prevent more forceful measures from being adopted.

A good number of instruments were applied in this period. This includes the start of peace talks under Chadian/AU auspices with the help of Western diplomats. Moreover, Western countries supported the extension of AMIS with a mandate to protect civilians. This was an improvement, at least on paper, since AMIS I was only authorised to protect the ceasefire monitors. Other available and proposed instruments were however, not adopted. Neither the UNSC nor the EU Council agreed on stringent sanctions against the *Janjaweed* and their government supporters. The EU proposed a police mission in the framework of a European Common Security and Defence Policy, but this was never accepted by the African Union. The EU left decisions on sanctions and a determination of genocide to the UN, and was unwilling to take its own position on these issues, even though they knew that the decision-making at the Security would be hampered. The reason that an oil boycott was not installed, besides Chinese interests in safeguarding its oil imports, is probably also related to the fact that oil would become one of the biggest sources of income for South-Sudan. A boycott could not be installed on the North without hurting the South. The alternative would be a complex 'oil-for-food'-like program, but there appeared not to have been any appetite for that.

In the fourth period from October 2004–January 2005 (Chapter 8) the attention shifted again to the North–South negotiations. The situation in Darfur was excluded from these talks. This also explains why Darfur was hardly discussed at the November Security Council meeting in Nairobi. The threat of sanctions continued, but was never seriously considered. Humanitarian assistance continued as well, which resulted in an improvement in the Darfur area, despite continued fighting. A no-fly zone was discussed in the EU Council but there was no support for it among EU countries, NATO or the US. Further international decision-making in New York was also halted as a result of the establishment of the Commission of Inquiry on 7 October 2004. The Commission reported on 25 January 2005.

In the meantime, international actors were reluctant to take any decisions awaiting the outcome of the inquiry. Decisions were consequently only taken by the end of March 2005. Another factor that contributed to this was that decision-makers were also awaiting the conclusion of a North–South Agreement. The CPA, which was concluded in January, was, however, not followed by increased pressure on Sudan to deal with Darfur. The CPA was supported by a huge UN peacekeeping force of 10,000 soldiers but no significant linkage was made with the AMIS II mission in Darfur. Neither the UN Secretariat, nor Western or African countries were willing to give the AMIS mission a stronger mandate, despite increasing public demands for stronger actions.

The referral of Darfur case to the International Criminal Court took place in the fifth period from January 2005–March 2005 (Chapter 9). All European countries were unified in urging the US to agree with an ICC referral and not another ad hoc tribunal. The perpetrators have, however, still not arrived in The Hague at the ICC for their trial.

Chapter 10 (2005–present) provided an overview of the numerous measures and instruments that have been applied since 2005, including: mediation, peacekeeping, an arms embargo, targeted sanctions, humanitarian aid operations and prosecution by the ICC. The chapter, nonetheless, casts doubt on the effectiveness and achievements of these measures. The AU-UN peacekeeping force (UNAMID), which was only agreed upon mid-2007, experienced initial logistical problems and it took a while before it was fully deployed. Its weak mandate also made that it has remained largely toothless and has been unable to prevent the renewed violence since the end of 2010. In addition, the arms embargo and the prohibition of aerial bombardments by the UNSC have also been essentially ineffective and violated by Russia and China, and the government of Sudan respectively. The two peace agreements of Abuja and Doha which were concluded in 2006 and 2011, with considerable international involvement, have largely proven dead letters in practice. Furthermore, the arrest warrants of the ICC are still outstanding and perpetrators of the crimes committed in Darfur have thus not been brought to justice yet.

Our fifth and final research question concerned other circumstances that could have influenced the international decision-making on Darfur. In world politics, there is always a myriad of other influences and developments that have an impact on any particular case. For instance, the effectiveness of the US response and its genocide determination was diminished as a result of the publication of the torture photographs from Al Ghraib prison. The war in Iraq has led to a division between the UK and the US versus France and Germany, also in the SC. The Tsunami and other natural disasters attracted more media attention than the man-made disaster in Darfur.

Some have explained the failure in preventing the atrocities in Darfur by arguing that there was a confrontation between Western countries and the rest of the world, in particular Arab and African countries. In our view this is an incorrect assertion. The African Union and African states such as Chad (N'Djamena), Egypt, Nigeria (Abuja) and Rwanda already employed mediation and monitoring initiatives at an early stage. These and later efforts, including those in Qatar (Doha), were supported by Western states. Several Arab and African countries were also helpful in persuading Khartoum to comply with SC Resolutions, as Egypt role in July 2004 illustrates. The intention to avoid a confrontation was also demonstrated in the Commission on Human Rights' meeting in April 2004. African countries agreed with the EU to a resolution expressing concern on the human rights situation in Sudan. The resolution was severely weakened and fell far short of what the EU and US intended. Nevertheless participants, such as the Netherlands, considered the adoption a success since only in rare cases do regional blocs accept critical resolutions. It was a way of acting to keep 'Africa' and Sudan on board in the decision-making in Geneva and in New York. As we have demonstrated, the 'military instrument' was also put in the hands of the African Union with its AMIS I and II missions. Western states provided technical and financial support. The AU wanted to take up the responsibility to solve African issues itself. The AU role made it possible that the Sudanese government accepted a – albeit small – mission on Sudanese territory. Nevertheless, one cannot deny that this was also an easy escape for the UNSC, the US and the EU, who were not willing to adopt more stringent measures. Such measures were also made more difficult, because once it was decided to transfer the issue to the AU and afford the AU the primary responsibility it locked the SC in the distant and reactive position. So, it can also be argued that Western states actually used the adagio of 'African solutions for African problems' as a fig leaf not to become more involved themselves.

At many points in our study we have demonstrated the importance of the North–South conflict, the Navaisha peace process, and its impact on the Darfur situation. One direct connection is the support that the Darfuri rebels received from the Southern SPLM movement. In addition, the Southern success raised expectations for the Darfuri in their struggle for their rights. Above all, Western countries and the UN feared that addressing Darfur at the same time would undermine the Naivasha peace process. Therefore, states and the UN gave priority to the North–South peace process. This was one of the main causes of the limited progress in mediation and activities with regard to Darfur. The Sudanese government also (ab)used the Navaisha process by using it to keep international attention out of Darfur. As long as little or no progress was made on Naivasha, Khartoum realised that western countries would be hesitant to pressure the Sudanese government on the conflict in Darfur. The tactic also worked the other way around. When attention shifted to Darfur in the summer of 2004, it used this to argue it could not go forward with the talks in Naivasha. Thus the smart manipulation of the Sudanese leader al-Bashir showed 'divide and reign tactics' on the Darfur issue.

The priority for the North–South negotiations was considered from the rational actor model. Many states had invested a lot in this process in terms of resources and prestige and they, and especially the US, were under increased pressure from domestic civil society actors to deliver. Therefore, it was strongly felt that this process could not be jeopardised by the disturbance in Darfur. Additionally, the US' reluctance to directly criticise al-Bashir's government over Darfur was increased by the intelligence assistance Sudan gave to the US for its 'War on Terror'. Thus – in line with realism and the rational actor model – the US prioritised its national security interests after '9/11' over Darfur.

We also offered an explanation why several states and the UN stuck so fervently to this prioritisation of the North–South negotiation over Darfur, at a time when they were fully aware of the severity of the situation. There was a great deal of wishful thinking and optimism that the negotiations would soon be over, especially towards the end of 2003, exactly when most of the atrocities were taking place. The US already reserved two seats for President al-Bashir and SPLM leader Garang for the State of the Union ceremony in Washington in January 2004. Actors believed that they could quickly deal with the North–South and then move to Darfur. There was also a belief that such an accord would make it easier to solve the Darfur conflict as well, although the agreement between the North and South held no guarantees for Darfur or other marginalised regions in Sudan. It was also believed that as a consequence of the North–South peace agreement, a unified and possibly more democratic government for the whole of Sudan would stop the gross human rights violations in Darfur. We also used cognitive dissonance to explain why several actors simply did not want to hear what was happening and rather chose to disregard the negative signals from Darfur, while stressing the positive signals for the Naivasha talks. The latter happened when the entire Security Council moved in autumn 2004 to Nairobi to support the Naivasha negotiations and Darfur was simply ignored.

In short: realism, the rational actor model and cognitive dissonance all point in the same direction of limiting the attention to Darfur and avoiding a confrontation with the government of Sudan over Darfur.

11.2   *Comparative Conclusions*

The *génocidaires* got one week for Srebrenica, hundred days for Rwanda and more than ten years for Darfur. This means that the time period for international bystander to respond and prevent was different. The UN failed miserably for its own responsibility to protect test. The key for an explanation will be sought in the decision-making processes.

In all three cases warnings were known to the policy-makers but not discussed in the first preventive period. No response in the UN Security Council and the UN Secretariat was formulated when the first clear signals from within the UN system were put forward. In Rwanda the special rapporteur on extrajudicial executions of the UN Commission on Human Rights, Bacré Waly Ndiaye visited Rwanda in 1993 and already reported to Geneva about genocide in Rwanda. He wrote about attacks on Tutsis prior to the genocide of April-June 1994 who were targeted solely because of their membership of a certain ethnic group and for no other objective reason. He made clear that the criteria in making a difference was only birth and not political motivations or power-politics, and that is why he used the word 'genocide' and not, for instance, 'politicide'. He was pressured to delete the references to genocide, because the word genocide was seen as 'inappropriate' and because using the word genocide would threaten the Arusha Accords (the peace process to a transitional government in Rwanda), which were considered essential. He refused, regardless. However, his report had no impact on the decision-making to prevent the genocide in 1994.

The similarity with Darfur is striking. Not only were the same arguments used – prioritising the North–South peace process – but in both cases the label was genocide. In addition, in both cases the early warnings were swept under the carpet. In 2003 Gerhart Baum, the Special Rapporteur on the situation in Sudan, informed the UN Commission on Human Rights on the situation in Sudan and reported on 28 March 2003. In 2003, the UN Resident Coordinator in Sudan Mukesh Kapila also reported on an imminent ethnic cleansing or genocide in Darfur to the UN Secretariat and the heads of its main divisions OCHA and DPA, and also raised the issue with many governments directly. All these warnings were not taken into account. Bacré Ndiaye and Mukesh Kapila were both young diplomats with limited knowledge on the functioning of the UN and their authority and status was not very high. They described themselves as outsiders of the UN system. Their messages and memos sometimes lacked urgency but their importance was at the same time watered down by the higher authorities in the UN system. For instance, DPA chief Prendergast restricted Kapila in his activities and argued that he should stick to his humanitarian mandate instead of peace and security affairs. The lack of political backing for Kapila cost him his job and Kapila had to leave Sudan by the end of March 2004.

In all three cases, the severity of the violence of the aggressors was downplayed. The situation was represented as a civil war and an inevitable tragedy and not as a deliberate – and preventable – attack to annihilate a targeted eth-nic group. This also resulted in toning down the urgency of the warnings and made non-intervention more comfortable for the bystanders.

Darfur differs from Rwanda and Srebrenica in the sense that at last Darfur was discussed in the Security Council (since March 2004) when the atrocities were still on-going, even though it took more than one year before the debate in the SC started – from February 2003 till April 2004. The criticism on the UN for Rwanda and Srebrenica was that the available warnings were not discussed. In the case of Darfur, the warnings have been discussed since April 2004 and since then there was no doubt about the seriousness of the Gross Human Rights Violations. The SC was regularly informed by many actors from within the UN, including the Human Rights Division in Geneva, Special Representatives in Khartoum, the New York based Departments as DPA, DPKO and OCHA plus many rapporteurs and Commissions. Possible instruments were known and available to tackle the atrocities. Some were taken, albeit with significant delays, but the end result was as disappointing as with the tragedies in Rwanda and Srebrenica.

Realism can explain why a narrow understanding of the national interests of the bystanders played a role and why they prioritised the saving of their own nationals in all three cases. The military interventions of the UK, US, France, Belgium and Italy in Rwanda rescued only their own expatriates and the UN peacekeepers were ordered to support the national armies in this activity. However, a few days earlier, Annan had forbidden these same peacekeepers to protect the Prime Minister and other moderate members of the government of Rwanda, who were subsequently murdered. The peacekeepers were with-drawn when the genocide started in order to prevent endangering UN peace-keepers and to minimise risks. Halting the bombing on Srebrenica was another decision made by UN Special Representative of the SG, Akashi, to protect French and Dutch peacekeepers on the ground with the result that the Bosnian Serbs could conquer the so-called safe-area without any resistance and the genocide on Muslim men took place. The withdrawal of all UN humanitarian workers in November 2003 resulted in the absence of any international wit-nesses and in the most cruel and violent period in Darfur during which most Darfuri were killed and their houses and towns demolished. This UN decision was presented as a rational one to protect its own UN personnel. Another example of a risk-minimising strategy was the decision to deploy only a small AU force in Darfur with a limited mandate.

For all three cases, the decision-making within the UN and the role of the Secretary-General and the Secretariat is also relevant for the explanation of the gap between warnings and response. The bureaucratic politics model was helpful in showing the dominant position of DPKO in both Rwanda and Srebrenica concerning the peacekeeping missions at the time of the genocides. The aims of these missions were pre-determined and fixed. All information about the situation on the ground warranting a re-evaluation of the mandate or mission was discarded. DPKO dominated the SC agenda concerning these missions and only forwarded the selected and twisted information that safeguarded the interests of their own unit in order to ensure its continuation as a unit within the Secretariat. All incoming information was therefore made to fit with DPKO's preferred policy of continuing as planned. This is a good example of cognitive dissonance. This resulted in deliberately misinforming the SC in both Rwanda and Srebrenica as has been established afterwards in the UN inquiry reports. The dominant position of DPKO in Rwanda and Srebrenica and of DPA in Darfur with their preoccupation with their own departmental interests can be explained with the bureaucratic politics model. The continuation of the same policy and the inability of organisations to adapt is typical for the organisational process model.

Darfur is in this respect not different. For Darfur the dominant department within the UN Secretariat was not with DPKO but with DPA, since there was no peacekeeping force yet. The focus of DPA was on the Naivasha peace process. In addition, DPA preferred a cautious diplomatic approach instead of a confrontational policy. In contrast, OCHA was very outspoken and tried to broaden the issue from merely humanitarian to peace and security affairs, including military options. OCHA head Egeland and Sudan Resident Coordinator Kapila failed in doing so, because their mandate was purely restricted to humanitarian issues. Within a bureaucracy as the UN, such mandates are closely respected, in line with the organisational process model. The Secretary-General followed the policy line of DPA – in line with the bureaucratic politics model – and supported the policy of not bringing Darfur to the Security Council. Moreover, Annan was very cautious and accommodative to the wishes of the permanent members of the SC. The UK, the US, China and Russia, were not willing to discuss Darfur in the SC. There was also disagreement between DPA and OCHA on putting Darfur on the SC agenda. Darfur was framed or seen by DPA and several states as solely a humanitarian issue. This downplayed the urgency for the UN Secretariat to inform the UNSC about Darfur. The head of DPA Prendergast argued that Egeland's (OCHA) attempts to set the Security Council agenda and his strong statements stimulated the rebels to continue fighting, because it gave these rebels the impressions that the UN might intervene.

There are also differences between the three cases with respect to the domestic influences on the foreign policy of bystander states. These domestic influences were more relevant in the case of Darfur than in previous cases of

Gross Human Rights Violations in Rwanda and Srebrenica, because the available information for the general public about the genocide in these two instances was very limited. Although it took more than a year before the general public became somehow aware of the atrocities, the relatively high public interest and outcry had an important impact on the foreign policy of several states, in particular the US. This makes Darfur different from Rwanda and Srebrenica. International involvement in the latter two cases was much less driven by internal pressures within those countries that intervened or could intervene. For Darfur, the domestic influences in the US and other Western countries resulted in a change from quiet diplomacy to discussing the issue in public and proposing measures such as sanctions and to refer the Darfur perpetrators to the ICC. In addition, it was largely with a view to satisfying the American domestic audience that Powell made the genocide determination. The domestic pressures on Western governments to act, however, vanished the longer the struggle in Darfur continued even though ethnically targeted violence increased again towards the end of 2010.

In sum, gross human rights violations were not prevented in all three cases. No *effective* measures were taken to stop the atrocities. Darfur is not that different from Srebrenica and Rwanda in that respect. In Chapter 1 we depicted the role of the bystander in situations of Gross Human Rights Violations as burying one's head in the sand. Likewise, international bystanders have buried their heads in the dusty sand of the Darfuri desert. This happened despite the leading motive that is reiterated after each genocide; that such atrocities should "never again" be allowed to happen. What is the value of such repeated pledges? The statement on Darfur by one of the principle UN decision-makers on Darfur, the former head of DPA Prendergast, is striking:[1]

> We don't mean it when we say that we're not going to accept other Rwandas, further Rwandas. But I never thought we did mean it. It's a very sad conclusion, but I don't think there's any evidence to sustain the view that we did mean it. We may have meant it at a level of generalized indignation, but when it comes to accepting the consequences of that, we don't.

---

1   PBS Frontline interview with Kieran Prendergast, 29 June 2007.

Appendix
Timeline

Below we present a timeline of the main events concerning Darfur that are relevant to the main text. In addition we have indicated in this timeline whether we consider events an early warning (ew) or early action (ea), as defined in Chapter 1, including the criteria that determine whether we count events or not based on the completeness of information. The sum of all ew's and ea's for each month are represented by Figure 2 in Chapter 1.

Our timeline is not meant to be exhaustive and naturally does not represent in any way all the information that we used for our research. Several books on the Darfur crisis give an overview of some of the facts, while the NGO Coalition for International Justice has been particularly detailed.[1] We believe that the count represents a useful way of visualising some aspects of the "early-warning-response gap." However, in order to understand how we collected and selected the information, we present some more detailed comments on our methods.

Sources and Method

The qualitative data collected in the spread sheet represents a sample of information. Firstly, this is a sample related to the conflict in Darfur only, which we collected in order to start analysing the response of third parties to the conflict. Secondly, we never aimed to be exhaustive, collecting all existing information. However, we can be exhaustive with regards to certain sources. For instance, it is not very hard to ensure the inclusion of all relevant Security Council resolutions in the time period on the topic. Even collecting all relevant reports by a small number of rapporteurs or NGOs is something that can be done without much trouble. However, collecting all the news reports from multiple countries and multiple newspapers is not very useful, even though with modern databases this becomes feasible as well (e.g. the Coalition for International Justice chronology). The problems with including news articles are: (1) the sheer number of sources and events would overwhelm the numbers of the other categories, (2) even with a limited number of news sources, say two major newspapers, one would capture editorial decisions which are likely also based on domestic influences, which is not what we would like to capture here.

In terms of warnings we need to make a selection of sources, and news articles will mostly fall out of the category. The exception would be news reports on acts of key

---

1 Coalition for International Justice, February 2006, "Chronology of reporting on events concerning the conflict in Darfur, Sudan."

decision-makers. We would include such events if we believe that we can claim close-to-exhaustive knowledge of all the relevant acts of such an actor. For instance, we are reasonably sure that we have included all the relevant statements of the UN Secretary-General, even though we will occasionally refer to such statements by means of news reports, as opposed to his personal press office.

In general, when analysing situations such as the crisis in Darfur, some influential documents are known only in hindsight. For instance in the case of Rwanda, a prime example is Dallaire's Genocide-fax. It was a relevant warning, and known to (a select group of) key decision-makers. In the case of Darfur, there are also some memos available, written by the then UN Resident Coordinator Mukesh Kapila. However, if one was to include such a memo in the dataset then this would be a clear bias of events. These memos were arguably released for the purpose of driving action, or for other unknown (political) reasons. More importantly, if one would want to have some indication of a representative sample of internal memos, then we would need to include much more of the information between UN offices, as well as between embassies and their home ministries. Clearly, this information is not fully available. It would bias results if we were to include some memos released for unknown, but clearly not random, reasons. Therefore, it is better not to include such information in the count. They are vital for in-depth analysis and were used extensively in the study.

A similar argument holds for the US State Department Cables. Although a large number of them are available, they also present a selection of which the rule is unknown. From the entire set of cables available and from the subset that concerns Darfur, the number of cables available increases over time, unrelated to the conflict. This is probably because the original collector was more interested in recent communication. Additionally, some embassies are rather consistently included while others are not (Khartoum is absent until 2006, London, Moscow and Beijing are completely absent for Darfur). Communication is also largely one way, from the embassies to State Department, not the other way around. If for normative analysis it is important to be aware of these features, for quantitative analysis it is better to leave them out entirely in order to avoid a biased representation.

Our original dataset allowed several entries for the same event. For instance we can include both a Security Council resolution and a news article reporting on it. Multiple sources are very relevant for research, but there is no need to count the same event twice.

A subtle thing about counting in our context is that every event, once included based on the above criteria, is equally important. A Chapter VII Security Council Resolution establishing a 10,000 strong peacekeeping force is as important as the first statement by a whistle blower on a 7am radio show. This is clearly a drawback of the visualisation process. Including a process of weighting is technically feasible. However, how to define a weight is something that probably causes more headaches than insights. (How many whistle blowers equal a Security Council agenda item?)

Each of these decisions was guided by the definitions of early warning and early action as given in Chapter 1 and the selection-rules, which aim to avoid an unnecessarily biased representation. Nevertheless, it is possible to dispute our decision to include, exclude and categorise any single event. However, we believe that the pattern that is visible in Figure 2 would withstand such criticism. We hope to have been transparent on our method, allowing others to repeat our exercise on other datasets of Darfur or other situations.

Timeline

For many of the events we noted shortly where we found the information. For others the date and text is sufficient to identify the original source. Occasionally, we clarify our choice of classification and inclusion in the footnotes.

2003

6 Jan	ew	Report of the Special Rapporteur on the situation of human rights in the Sudan[2]
26 Feb		Darfur rebels attack Sudanese military garrison at the town of Golu. Nearly 200 soldiers are killed. Rebels call themselves Darfur Liberation Army (DLF)[3]
11 Mar		DLF changes name to Sudan Liberation Movement/Army (SLM/A). A few days after they make demands with the Sudanese government under a fragile ceasefire[4]
28 Mar	ew	Statement by UN Special Rapporteur Baum on Sudan in the CHR[5]
1 Apr		3-day Sudan Coordination meeting in Noordwijk, The Netherlands
25 Apr		Darfur rebels launch attacks against Sudanese military and police forces in Nyala and Al-Fashir. The Al-Fashir attack results in the death of more than thirty government soldiers, the destruction of several military aircraft and the capture of the commander of the Sudanese air force base. The attack was a combined SLA/JEM action. In addition there was an simulteneous attack on Kutum by SLM/A[6]

---

2   UN Doc.: E/CN.4/2003/42.
3   Totten and Markussen (2006), Ch. Chronology; Prunier (2007), p. 92.
4   Totten and Markussen (2006), p. 9–10.
5   UN CHR.
6   Totten and Markussen (2006), Ch. Chronology, p. 10; Prunier (2007), p. 95–96.

28 Apr	ew	Amnesty International report: Crisis in Darfur[7]
25 Jun	ew	ICG Africa Briefing 14
1 Jul	ew	Amnesty International report: Looming crisis in Darfur[8]
7 Jul	ew	ICG African report 65
16 Jul	ew	Amnesty International report: Empty promises?[9]
16 Sep	ew	MSF Chad: Thousands of Sudanese refugees caught in humanitarian disaster
17 Sep	ea	Tom Vraalsen, Secretary-General Kofi Annan's Special Envoy for Humanitarian Affairs in Sudan, announces the Greater Darfur Initiative, appealing for US $23 million to help those most in need[10]
1 Oct	ew	MSF reports that it provides health care for Sudanese refugees in Chad
7 Oct	ew	OCHA: Humanitarian situation worsens in greater Darfur region[11]
7 Oct	ew	UNHCR launches appeal for US $16.6 million to help Sudanese refugees in Chad
31 Oct	ea	US President Bush, Secretary Colin Powell and National Security Adviser Condoleeza Rice began to call their counterparts in Khartoum[12]
31 Oct	ew	Andrew Natsios (USAID) after visiting Darfur stated: "We don't want to have an end to the war and a new war starting in the West"[13]
7 Nov	ew	OCHA reports that displacement rises, while access declines[14]
8 Nov		Dutch Minister for Development Cooperation van Ardenne visits Sudan and urges for greater humanitarian access to Darfur[15]

---

7   AI Doc.: AFR 54/026/2003.
8   AI Doc.: AFR 54/041/2003.
9   AI Doc.: AFR 54/036/2003.
10   UN News. We consider the Initiative an early action, because it is the first concerted decision at the international level to start and coordinate humanitarian action for Darfur. This initiative also encompasses a warning to policy makers (e.g. UN Head Quarters and national capitals) since it aimed to mobilise political involvement from such decision makers. Other appeals for aid from humanitarian organisations will subsequently be categorised solely as early warnings.
11   UN OCHA: AFR/721-IHA/805.
12   Igiri and Lyman (2004), p. 10.
13   Prunier (2007), p. 108.
14   UN OCHA: AFR/748-IHA/818.
15   Dutch Parliamentary Doc.: Tweede Kamer, 2003–2004, 29 237 and 29 234, nr. 4, 9 December 2004. Although ministerial visits such as this one may be seen as clear direct interventions by policy makers, in the form of quiet diplomacy, we do not believe that we have a full overview of all such visits. Therefore, in order to avoid a bias we choose not to count such events.

11 Nov		Kapila starts sending memoranda to UN headquarters[16]
13 Nov	ew	UNHCR Director Lubbers calls for more attention on the problem[17]
5 Dec	ew	OCHA, Egeland: Humanitarian situation in western Sudan among world's worst[18]
8 Dec	ew	Vraalsen says humanitarian efforts have come to a near stand-still because of authorities' denials of access. After touring the affected area, he says he is shocked about the conditions faced by IDPS[19]
9 Dec	ea	SG Annan expresses alarm over human rights violations and the lack of humanitarian access. More than a million people estimated to need aid, including about 600,000 displaced persons[20]
9 Dec		UK Minister for International Development Benn visits Khartoum and presses for greater humanitarian access to Darfur[21]
11 Dec	ew	ICG Africa Report 73
17 Dec	ew	MSF: Refugee crisis in eastern Chad worsens

2004

7 Jan	ew	The Holocaust Memorial Museum in Washington issues a Genocide Warning for Darfur, expressing concern that the organised violence underway could result in genocide[22]
7 Jan	ea	EU Council Presidency declaration on the situation in Darfur-Sudan[23]
13 Jan	ew	The World Food Programme (WFP) calls for $11 million to help 60,000 of the refugees living in Chad[24]

---

16 Traub (2006), p. 214; Kapila (2013), p. xx.

17 Prunier (2007), p. 90.

18 UN OCHA: AFR/784-IHA/837; Prunier (2007), p. 90.

19 Totten and Markussen (2006), p. 13.

20 UN News. SG Annan's statements are often formulated in terms of warnings, and his direct actions are not always visible. We chose to interpret the statements by Annan on Darfur as actions in themselves given Annan's position as Secretary-General. Annan's statements are often the result or output of decision-making within the UN, rather than the input in the decision-making. Besides his statements increase the pressure on decision-makers as well as the parties in the conflict.

21 UK House of Commons, 2005, Volume II, p. ev. 86.

22 Totten and Markussen (2006), Ch. Chronology.

23 EU Doc.: 5101/04 (Presse 7) P 5/04.

24 UN News.

15 Jan	ew	MSF concerned for displaced following forced closure of camps by Sudanese authorities
15 Jan	ew	OCHA: Special Envoy seeks aid for Darfur refugees[25]
16 Jan	ew	HRW Sudan: Child Soldier Use 2003. Children have also been recruited to fight in Darfur
26 Jan	ew	All the ingredients are in place for a rapid deterioration of the humanitarian situation, WFP spokesman Rafirasme warned[26]
27 Jan		Dutch Ministers Bot (Foreign Affairs), van Ardenne (Development Cooperation) and Kamp (Defense) meet in Khartoum with their counterparts and discuss European involvement for Darfur mediation[27]
29 Jan	ew	MSF: Chadian civilians killed and injured by aerial bombings
3 Feb	ew	Amnesty International: Too many killed for no reason[28]
9 Feb		Sudanese President al-Bashir calls offensive successful and promises peace and access for UN and NGO[29]
17 Feb	ew	MSF: Massive aid urgently needed in Darfur, Sudan
18 Feb	ew	Egeland states: we are still not reaching the majority of those in need[30]
19 Feb		French Foreign Minister de Villepin visits Khartoum and plans to press the government on Darfur[31]
19 Feb		EU Parliament delegation visit to Sudan, from 19 to 24 March
24 Feb	ew	Egeland: prevented from delivering adequate aid up to now[32]
25 Feb	ea	EU Presidency declaration on the situation in Darfur-Sudan[33]
19 Mar	ew	Mr. Vraalsen describes Darfur situation as "one of the worst in the world." In a media interview, UN Humanitarian Coordinator for Sudan Mukesh Kapila says the situation in Darfur is comparable to what happened in the Rwandan genocide of 1994[34]

---

25 UN News.
26 Totten and Markussen (2006), p. 13.
27 Dutch Parliamentary Doc.: Tweede Kamer, 2003–2004, 29 237 and 29 278, nr. 7, 27 January 2004.
28 AI Doc.: AFR 54/008/2004.
29 Totten and Markussen (2006), p. 13; Prunier (2007), p. 112.
30 UN News.
31 Archive Ministry of Foreign Affairs in the Netherlands, DAF/2015/00646, Period December 2003–June 2004.
32 Idem.
33 EU Doc.: 6750/04 (Presse 66) P 26/04.
34 UN News, BBC.

22 Mar	ew	Kapila states: "The only difference between Rwanda and Darfur are the numbers involved. (…) there are no secrets, the individuals who are doing this are known"[35]
25 Mar	ew	ICG Africa Report 76
26 Mar	ew	UN OCHA: Eight UN human rights experts gravely concerned about reported widespread abuses in Darfur[36]
31 Mar	ea	EU Parliament resolution on Darfur/Sudan proposing a no-fly zone[37]
31 Mar	ea	SG Annan issues a statement saying he is disturbed by the continuing conflict, its impact on civilians and the ongoing problems with humanitarian access. He welcomes the start of peace talks in N'Djamena[38]
31 Mar	ew	First column of NYT columnist Nicholas Kristof on Darfur, Sudan[39]
1 Apr	ew	Amnesty International: Darfur: extrajudicial execution of 168 men[40]
2 Apr	ea	The German SC President issues a press statement in which it expressed a "deep concern" for the situation in Darfur[41]
2 Apr	ea	Jan Egeland (OCHA) briefs the UNSC and later asserts that the *Janjaweed* is carrying out a coordinated "scorched earth" campaign of ethnic cleansing against the African people of Darfur[42]
2 Apr	ew	Human Rights Watch: Darfur in Flames: Atrocities in Western Sudan[43]
3 Apr	ea	In a joint statement, the SG and the heads of all UN agencies, funds and programmes express their deepest concern over the serious human rights and humanitarian crisis in Darfur[44]

---

35   Prunier (2007), p. 114; Totten and Markussen (2006), Ch. Chronology; Igiri and Lyman (2004), p. 6, Kapila (2013).

36   UN OCHA: AFR/873 HR/CN/1065.

37   EU Parliamentary Doc.: P5_TA(2004)0225.

38   UN News.

39   New York Times.

40   AI Doc.: AFR 54/039/2004.

41   UN Doc.: SC/8050 AFR/883.

42   Totten and Markussen (2006), Ch. Chronology; UN News. We see many of Egeland's or OCHA's statements as warnings. However, as recounted in the text, the first briefing on the humanitarian situation in the UNSC was preceded by strong diplomatic lobbying from Egeland's side, among others. The briefing itself is thus the result or output of this lobbying process which we therefore classify as action in itself. At the same time, Egeland's statements are input for the subsequent decision making process in the UNSC.

43   HRW April 2004, Vol. 16, No. 5 (A).

44   Totten and Markussen (2006), Ch. Chronology; UN News.

6 Apr	ea	Upon the request of UN acting High Commisoner Bertrand Ramcharan, a fact-finding team from the UNHCR undertakes an investigation into the refugee camps in Chad to asses the extent of human rights violations that have been perpetrated in Dafur[45]
7 Apr	ea	During the course of the 10th year commemoration of the beginning of the Rwandan genocide, SG Annan asserts that he feared the unfolding of a similar tragedy in Darfur and calls on the international community to act[46]
7 Apr	ea	US President Bush makes a statement on Darfur[47]
7 Apr	ew	Amnesty International report: Deliberate and indiscriminate attacks against civilians in Darfur[48]
8 Apr	ea	Signing of the N'Djamena ceasefire in Chad after intensive mediation by western countries and parties
23 Apr	ea	CHR 60th adopt resolution on the situation of Human Rights in Sudan[49]
27 Apr	ea	EU General Affairs and External Relations Council conclusions include a discussion of Darfur for the first time[50]
4 May	ew	Following visit, Mr. Morris and other senior UN officials describe the Darfur situation as one of the worst humanitarian crises in the world. The number of IDPs estimated to now be above one million[51]
7 May	ew	Acting High Commissioner for Human Rights Ramcharan provides the UNSC with a report of the findings of the two UN-sponsered human rights invesitgations. He reports that they both found that the Sudanese government and the *Janjaweed* have commited massive human rights violations, which is determined to "constitute war crimes and/or crimes against humanity"[52]

---

45 Idem. Ramcharan made a conscious decision to deploy a mission to Darfur in order to move policy makers. Therefore, we classify the establishment of the fact-finding mission as an action. The resulting report from this mission is a warning (7 May).
46 Totten and Markussen (2006), Ch. Chronology, p. 176.
47 White House archived website; Igiri and Lyman (2004), p. 5.
48 AI Doc.: AFR 54/034/2004.
49 UN Doc.: E/CN.4/DEC/2004/128.
50 EU Doc.: 80143/04. We will not classify every EU Council conclusion or statement that mentions Darfur. In this case it is the first time that the Council explicitly discussed the situation.
51 Totten and Markussen (2006), Ch. Chronology; UN News.
52 Idem.; UN Doc.: E/CN.4/2005/3.

7 May	ew	Human Rights Watch report: Darfur Destroyed. Ethnic Cleansing by Government and Militia Forces in Western Sudan[53]
11 May		UK Foreign Minister Jack Straw meets with Sudanese Foreign Minister
11 May	ew	MSF: Catastrophic conditions for Sudanese refugees in Chad
13 May	ea	SG Annan writes to President al-Bashir, urging him to disarm the *Janjaweed*, maintain the ceasefire, improve access for humanitarian workers and negotiate a settlement to the conflict in Darfur[54]
17 May	ea	The Secretary-General meets Sudan's Permanent Representative to the UN to raise concerns about obstacles to humanitarian access such as visa delays and slow customs clearances[55]
20 May	ew	OCHA says all funds have been exhausted and there are shortfalls of food, water and health care services. Sudanese government announces measures to improve humanitarian access[56]
21 May	ew	MSF: Current crisis – future catastrophe in Darfur, Sudan, unless immediate action is taken
21 May	ew	Amnesty International report: In our silence we are complicit[57]
23 May	ew	ICG: Sudan: Now or never in Darfur[58]
24 May	ew	MSF: Humanitarian situation in Darfur, Sudan – statement to the United Nations Security Council
25 May	ea	UNSC Presidential Statement S/PRST/2004/18
26 May	ew	Jan Egeland informs the UNSC that the government continues to prevent humanitarian aid from reaching the IDP's in Darfur and that the number of IDPs has increased to 2 million people. The Sudanese government and rebel groups reach an agreement that allows the first international observers into Darfur[59]
27 May	ea	UN SG Annan's office announces that the SG continues to be deeply concerned over the situation in Darfur and that he is willing to mediate a settlement[60]

---

53   HRW May 2004, Vol. 16, No. 6 (A).
54   Totten and Markussen (2006), Ch. Chronology; UN News.
55   Idem.
56   Totten and Markussen (2006), Ch. Chronology; UN News.
57   AI Doc.: AFR 54/051/2004.
58   ICG African Report No. 80; Totten and Markussen (2006), p. 13.
59   Totten and Markussen (2006), Ch. Chronology; UN News.
60   Idem.

27 May	ew	UN Secretary-General Special Representative of human rights defenders, Hina Jilani, voices concern about recent treatment of human rights defenders working in Darfur[61]
1 Jun		US satellite reveals at least 377 villages destroyed. Pictures are shared with donors at meeting in Geneva[62]
8 Jun	ew	Amnesty International report: Darfur: Incommunicado detention, torture and special courts[63]
11 Jun	ea	UNSC Resolution 1547
14 Jun	ew	Following a visit to Darfur, Asma Jahangir, the UN's Special Rapporteur on extrajudicial, summary, or arbitrary executions claims that Sudanese government forces and the *Janjaweed* have committed numerous human rights violations, including the slaughter of civilians in Darfur villages[64]
15 Jun	ew	UN officials report that every fifth child in Darfur suffers from severe malnutrition. Additionally, it is reported that many children suffer from dysentery, measles, high fever, and that every day children in refugee camps are dying from starvation and exhaustion[65]
18 Jun	ea	UN SG Annan names former Dutch Environment Minister Jan Pronk as the UN Secretary-General Special Representative to Sudan. The US threatens to impose sanctions on Sudan due to the deteriorating humanitarian situation in Darfur[66]
21 Jun	ea	UN SG Annan says any peace accord in southern Sudan will be fragile unless the conflict in Darfur is resolved[67]
21 Jun	ew	MSF: Emergency in Darfur, Sudan: No relief in sight
24 Jun	ew	US Ambassador-at-Large for War Crimes Pierre Prosper asserts: "I can tell you that we see indicators of genocide and there is evidence that points in that direction." Prosper further states that the US government "is actively reviewing" the possibility that genocide is taking place in Darfur region[68]
30 Jun	ea	Arriving in Khartoum for a three-day visit to Sudan and Chad, SG Annan holds talks with Sudanese government officials and

---

61   UN News.
62   Totten and Markussen (2006), p. 36.
63   AI Doc.: AFR 54/058/2004.
64   Totten and Markussen (2006), Ch. Chronology; UN News.
65   Totten and Markussen (2006), Ch. Chronology.
66   Idem.; Dutch Foreign Ministry Archive.
67   UN News.
68   Totten and Markussen (2006), Ch. Chronology; State Department.

United States Secretary of State Colin Powell about the situation in Darfur and the obstacles faced by humanitarian workers in distributing aid[69]

2 Jul   ew   Refugees at a camp in eastern Chad tell UN SG Annan that there have been "gross and systematic" abuses of human rights by the *Janjaweed*. Later he meets Sudanese President al-Bashir for talks in Khartoum[70]

2 Jul   ew   Amnesty International report: Sudan: At the Mercy of Killers – Destruction of Villages in Darfur[71]

3 Jul   ea   The UN and Sudan sign a joint communiqué in which they both make pledges to resolve the conflict in Darfur. Khartoum vows to lift all restrictions on humanitarian access, bring to justice those responsible for human rights abuses, disarm the *Janjaweed*, protect IDPs from further attacks and resume peace talks with the rebels. The UN promises to help the AU quickly deploy ceasefire monitors and to provide more humanitarian relief. The two sides also agree to set up a Joint Implementation Mechanism to monitor the agreement[72]

6 Jul   ea   UN SG Annan tells AU summit in Addis Ababa that the Darfur crisis "could be a prelude to even greater humanitarian catastrophe" across the region[73]

7 Jul   ea   Briefing the Security Council by satellite link from Kenya, UN SG Annan describes the situation facing IDPs in Darfur as grave. Later, the Council's President for July, Ambassador Mihnea Ioan Motoc of Romania, calls for sustained pressure on Khartoum to resolve the crisis. Mr. Egeland warns "hundreds of thousands of people may die" if fighting does not stop and the *Janjaweed* are not disarmed[74]

9 Jul   ew   UN Special Rapporteur on the right to food Jean Ziegler expresses concern about the *Janjaweed's* destruction of food and water sources in West Darfur. UNICEF and the World Health Organization (WHO) vaccinate two million children against measles[75]

---

69   Totten and Markussen (2006), Ch. Chronology; UN News.
70   Idem.
71   AI Doc.: AFR 54/072/2004.
72   Totten and Markussen (2006), Ch. Chronology; UN News.
73   UN News.
74   Totten and Markussen (2006), Ch. Chronology; UN News.
75   Idem.

12 Jul	ea	EU General Affairs and External Relations Council statement on Darfur, threathens "further measures"[76]
13 Jul	ea	The US Congress adopts a resolution declaring that genocide has occurred in Darfur[77]
14 Jul	ew	Oxfam warns of the "spectre of disease" and an outbreak of cholera and/or malaria in the refugee camps based in Chad. The USHMM and American Jewish World Service host an emergency nongovernmental summit on Darfur, leading to the creation of the Save Darfur Coalition[78]
18 Jul		The SLM/A and JEM break off peace talks in Addis Ababa, Ethiopia, asserting they will not take part until the Sudanese government agrees to leave Darfur and to disarm the *Janjaweed*[79]
19 Jul	ew	Amnesty International report: Darfur: Rape as a weapon of war[80]
19 Jul	ew	UN agencies say the Sudanese government is trying to pressure Darfur's massive population of IDPs to return to their home villages, even though they remain afraid of *Janjaweed* attacks. The number of IDPs has swelled by 100,000 in the past month[81]
21 Jul	ea	SG Annan says the UN has received just $145 million of the $349 million it has requested to help the people of Darfur. He tells press conference that Khartoum has not taken "adequate steps" to meet its pledge to disarm the *Janjaweed*[82]
22 Jul	ea	In joint press conference, UN SG Annan and US Secretary of State Powell call for greater international pressure to make sure Khartoum meets its commitments[83]
22 Jul	ea	UNSC Resolution 1556
22 Jul	ea	In an unanimous vote, the US House of Representatives passes HR res.467, declaring the conflict in Darfur to be a case of genocide and urges the US government to take more robust action to intervene. The US Senate without dissent unanimously concurs[84]
26 Jul	ew	MSF: Darfur Sudan disaster, "Aid effort nowhere near enough"

---

76   EU Doc.: 11105/04.
77   US Congress S.CON.RES.124.
78   Totten and Markussen (2006), Ch. Chronology.
79   Idem.
80   AI Doc.: AFR 54/076/2004.
81   Totten and Markussen (2006), Ch. Chronology; UN News.
82   Idem.
83   Idem.
84   Totten and Markussen (2006), Ch. Chronology; US Congress.

26 Jul	ea	EU General Affairs and External Relations Council conclusions include demand for Commission of Inquiry[85]
26 Jul	ew	The US Holocaust Memorial Museum Committee on Conscience declares a genocide emergency for Darfur[86]
29 Jul	ew	SG Annan issues statement sounding alarm about continuing reports of rapes, attacks, acts of intimidation and threats against IDPS, especially in north and west Darfur[87]
30 Jul	ew	Amnesty International report: Sudan: Security Council resolution on Darfur welcome, but human rights recommendations sidelined[88]
30 Jul	ea	UNSC Resolution 1556
2 Aug	ew	Following a trip to Darfur, Francis Deng, UN Secretary-General Special Representative on IDPS, reports that Darfur remains in a state of crisis bereft of security and rife with human rights violations[89]
5 Aug	ea	Mr. Pronk and Sudanese Foreign Minister Mustafa Osman Ismail sign agreement committing Khartoum to take detailed steps in the next 30 days to disarm the *Janjaweed* and improve security for the IDPS. UN SG Annan later welcomes the agreement[90]
6 Aug	ew	Publication of the report of Secretary-General Special Representative for extrajudicial killings, Ms. Jahangir on the situation in Darfur and in southern Sudan. She finds that the Sudanese military and government-allied militias have carried out most of the extrajudicial killings[91]
9 Aug	ew	Amnesty International report: Surviving Rape in Darfur[92]
15 Aug	ea	Approximately 150 Rwandan troops arrive in Darfur to protect AU ceasefire monitors. They are to be stationed in 6 regions where large IDP camps are located[93]
19 Aug	ew	AU ceasefire monitors confirm the Sudanese military harassed and brutally treated IDPS a week ago at the Kalma camp in South Darfur and then looted the camp[94]
23 Aug	ew	ICG: Africa Report 83

---

85   EU Doc.: 11593/04.
86   Totten and Markussen (2006), Ch. Chronology.
87   Idem.; UN News.
88   AI Doc.: AFR 54/092/2004.
89   Totten and Markussen (2006), Ch. Chronology; UN Doc.: AFR/1005 HR/4785.
90   Totten and Markussen (2006), Ch. Chronology; UN News.
91   Idem.; UN Doc.: E/CN.4/2005/7/Add.2.
92   AI Doc.: AFR 54/097/2004.
93   Totten and Markussen (2006), Ch. Chronology.
94   Idem.; UN News.

25 Aug   ew   Declaring its operations in Sudan are "grossly under-funded," UN
               humanitarian agencies say they have received only $288 million of
               the $722 million it needs[95]

30 Aug   ew   Darfur's inhabitants are traumatized and humiliated and remain
               at risk of being raped, assaulted or forced to return to their homes,
               the Director of the UN's Internal Displacement Division Dennis
               McNamara tells press conference in Nairobi[96]

2 Sep   ew   Mr. Pronk tells Security Council that Khartoum has not disarmed the
               Janjaweed nor stopped their attacks against civilians. He calls for the
               AU mission to be expanded in size and mandate so that IDPs are bet-
               ter protected. But he adds that Khartoum deserves some praise for
               removing obstacles to humanitarian access and for deploying extra
               police. In Abuja, Nigeria, where AU-mediated talks are taking place,
               Khartoum and the rebels agree to draft protocol on relieving human-
               itarian situation[97]

3 Sep   ea   In his latest report to the Council, SG Annan says the international
               presence in Darfur must be enlarged as soon as possible because the
               "vast majority of militias" have not yet been disarmed. The report
               concludes a "scorched-earth policy" by the *Janjaweed* is responsible
               for most of the violence[98]

9 Sep   ea   Powell announces that the US government has concluded that the
               ongoing violence in Darfur constitutes genocide. It is the first time
               one sovereign nation has accused another nation of genocide while
               the conflict is still ongoing. US President Bush states: "We urge the
               international community to work with us to prevent and suppress
               acts of genocide"[99]

13 Sep   EU General Affairs and External Relations Council Council conclu-
               sion, proposing EU police support mission for Darfur[100]

13 Sep   ew   WHO survey shows more than 200 IDPs are dying every day in north
               and nest Darfur because of *Janjaweed* attacks and unhygienic condi-
               tions in camps[101]

---

95   Idem.
96   Idem.
97   Idem.; UN Doc.: S/pv.5027.
98   Totten and Markussen (2006), Ch. Chronology; UN News.
99   Totten and Markussen (2006), Ch. Chronology, Appendix 3; US State Department, New
      York Times, 9 September 2004, "Powell Says Rapes and Killings in Sudan Are Genocide".
100   EU Doc.: presse release 12068/04.
101   Totten and Markussen (2006), Ch. Chronology; UN WHO News.

16 Sep	ea	European Parliament calls Darfur "tantamount to genocide"[102]
16 Sep	ea	UN SG Annan announces he is dispatching High Commissioner for Human Rights Louise Arbour and Special Adviser on the Prevention of Genocide Juan Méndez to Darfur to assess the situation and recommend what can be done now to protect civilians. He tells reporters he has also told the Security Council's members that he wants a proposed commission of inquiry into whether genocide has occurred to proceed. The peace talks in Abuja, Nigeria, reach a stalemate[103]
17 Sep	ew	Amnesty International report: High Level Mission Update[104]
18 Sep	ea	UNSC Resolution 1564
22 Sep	ew	UN agencies report that the number of IDPs has swelled to 1,45 million and is still rising. SGSR Pronk visits Sudan's neighbours Eritrea and Ethiopia to discuss the situation in Darfur[105]
24 Sep	ea	SG Annan tells SC meeting that the "terrible violence" in Darfur means the crisis there is a global issue, and "not simply an African problem." Nigerian President and AU Chairman Olusegun Obasanjo says the AU force needs greater international funding and logistical support if it is to expand to a size of about three thousand troops and take on new responsibilities[106]
27 Sep	ew	MSF: Aid to displaced people in South Darfur remains insufficient
27 Sep	ew	Report of Francis Deng, Special Representative of the Secretary-General on IDPs: "Mission to the Sudan – The Darfur crisis"[107]
30 Sep	ew	Briefing Security Council on the findings of their mission, Mrs. Arbour and Mr. Méndez say international police officers are essential if the IDPs are to have any confidence that they will be protected if or when they leave their camps[108]
4 Oct	ea	UN SG Annan proposes four ways in which the UN can assist the AU to expand its mission, including by setting up a Darfur regional office of the UN Advance Mission in Sudan (UNAMIS)[109]

---

102   EU Parliamentary Doc.: P6_TA(2004)0012; Prunier (2007), p. 120.
103   Totten and Markussen (2006), Ch. Chronology; UN SG press office, statement available at http://www.un.org/apps/sg/offthecuff.asp?nid=629 [accessed 16 December 2013].
104   AI Doc.: AFR 54/123/2004.
105   Totten and Markussen (2006), Ch. Chronology; UN News.
106   Totten and Markussen (2006), Ch. Chronology; UN News; UN Doc.: S/pv.5043.
107   UN Doc.: E/CN.4/2005/8.
108   Totten and Markussen (2006), Ch. Chronology; UN News.
109   Idem.; UN Doc.: S/2004/787.

5 Oct	ew	UN SGSR Pronk tells Security Council that Khartoum made no progress last month in disarming the *Janjaweed*, stopping their attacks or prosecuting those responsible for the worst atrocities. Banditry is on the rise and both sides have frequently breached the ceasefire. Pronk tells reporters he is pressing the AU to expand the mission's size as soon as it can. He also says a solution to the long-running civil war in southern Sudan could serve as a model for the Darfur conflict.[110] In his regular report to the Council, UN SG Annan says the AU mission should have the power to protect IDPs and refugees, monitor the local police and disarm the fighters, including the *Janjaweed*
5 Oct	ew	ICG: Africa Briefing 19
7 Oct		Following UNSC Resolution 1564, UN SG Annan names the members of the UN COI whose task it is to conduct an investigation into the atrocities in Darfur[111]
13 Oct	ew	Amnesty International report: Civilians still under threat in Darfur[112]
15 Oct	ew	The WHO reports that at least 70,000 people have perished since March 2004 as a result of poor conditions in refugee camps. It states that the reguees have died of diarrhoea, fever, and respiratory diseases, and that that toll does not include those killed in the ongoing violence[113]
19 Oct	ew	Red Cross reports on Darfur agricultural collapse and estimates 2 million people IDPs by the end of the year[114]
28 Oct	ea	The AU announces that it starts to deploy more troops in Darfur to strengthen AMIS[115]
29 Oct	ew	MSF: persecution intimidation and failure of assistance in Darfur
2 Nov	ew	Jan Pronk warns that the whole province is descending into total anarchy and warlordism[116]
4 Nov	ew	UN SG Annan reports to the UNSC that there are "strong indications" that war crimes and crimes against humanity have occurred on a "large and systematic scale" in Darfur[117]
15 Nov	ew	HRW report: Consolidation of Ethnic Cleansing in Darfur[118]

110   Totten and Markussen (2006), Ch. Chronology; UN News; UN Doc.: S/pv.5050.
111   Totten and Markussen (2006), Ch. Chronology; UN News.
112   AI Doc.: AFR 54/131/2004.
113   Totten and Markussen (2006), Ch. Chronology.
114   Prunier (2007), p. 120.
115   AU Doc.: press release 098/2004.
116   Prunier (2007), p. 123.
117   Totten and Markussen (2006), Ch. Chronology; UN Doc.: S/pv.5071.
118   HRW November 2011.

16 Nov	ew	Amnesty International report: Arming the perpetrators of grave abuses in Darfur[119]
19 Nov		UNSC Resolution 1574[120]
1 Dec	ew	MSF: Escalating attacks in North Darfur, Sudan, force civilians to flee repeatedly
6 Dec	ew	Amnesty International: Open letter to all members of the Security Council with respect to the expected report of the COI[121]
16 Dec	ew	Amnesty International report: Darfur: What hope for the future?[122]
23 Dec	ew	Report of Yakin Ertürk, the visit of Special Rapporteur on violence against women to Darfur[123]

2005

7 Jan	ew	UN SRSG for Sudan Pronk expresses concern at increasing harassment of aid workers in Darfur[124]
12 Jan	ew	Pronk asserts that the crisis in Darfur has resulted in killing over 100,000 people. He warns that: "we may move into a period of intense violence unless swift action is taken and new approaches are considered"[125]
24 Jan	ea	UN SG Annan in a unprecedented meeting of the UNGA to commemorate the Holocaust, issues a dire warning about the violence in Darfur[126]
25 Jan	ew	UNSC COI releases its report to the SG. It concludes that serious violations of international law have occurred in Darfur, including "crimes against humanity." It does not though conclude that genocide has been perpetrated. The COI recommends the UNSC to refer the situation to the ICC[127]

---

119   AI Doc.: AFR 54/139/2004.
120   This UNSC resolution, adopted during meetings in Nairobi, Kenya, concerns primarily the North–south settlement. As discussed in the text, new action on Darfur was precluded.
121   AI Doc.: AFR 54/162/2004.
122   AI Doc.: AFR 54/164/2004.
123   UN Doc.: E/CN.4/2005/75/add.5
124   UN News.
125   Totten and Markussen (2006), Ch. Chronology; UN News.
126   Idem.
127   Totten and Markussen (2006), Ch. Chronology; UN Doc.: S/2005/60. Although some have suggested that the COI may have acted politically (i.e. early action), we view its report

26 Jan	ew	AU observers accuse the Sudanese Air Force of bombing villages in southern Darfur[128]
29 Jan	ew	Jan Egeland warns that violence and insecurity in Darfur is seriously impeding the delivery of humanitarian aid to displaced persons[129]
31 Jan	ea	EU General Affairs and External Relations Council conclusions welcome COI and support the ICC[130]
4 Feb	ew	Jan Pronk calls for a larger international military force in Darfur. He tells the UNSC that it is the only way to stop the raging violence. The Council debates whether war crimes trials should be held at the ICC[131]
16 Feb	ew	Arbour recommends that the UNSC refer the situation in Darfur to the ICC[132]
21 Feb	ew	Amnesty International: Open letter to the members of the United Nations Security Council[133]
7 Mar	ew	MSF issues a report stating that it has treated approximately 500 women and girls who were raped between October 2004 and mid-February 2005. The report asserts that the five hundred treated rape victims represent only a fraction of those who have been sexually assaulted[134]
8 Mar	ew	ICG Africa Report 89
24 Mar		UNSC Resolution 1590, creating a peacekeeping force for the South
29 Mar	ea	UNSC Resolution 1591, preparing targeted sanctions for perpetrators in Darfur
31 Mar	ea	UNSC resolution 1593, Darfur referred to the ICC

---

primarily as an analysis of the situation with explicit recommendations as requested by the UNSC (i.e. early warning). Clear actions are also taken in response to this report.

128 Totten and Markussen (2006), Ch. Chronology; UN News.
129 Totten and Markussen (2006), Ch. Chronology.
130 EU Doc.: 5535/05 (presse 15).
131 Totten and Markussen (2006), Ch. Chronology.
132 Idem.; UN News.
133 AI Doc.: AFR 54/024/2005.
134 Totten and Markussen (2006), Ch. Chronology.

Bibliography

Literature

Adelman, H. (1998) "Defining humanitarian early warning", in *Early Warning and Early Response*, by Schmeidl, S. and Adelman, H. (eds.), Columbia International Affairs Online, www.ciaonet.org/book/schmeidl/schmeidl01.html.

Adelman, H. and Suhkre, A. (1997) "Early warning and response: why the international community failed to prevent the genocide", *Disasters,* Vol.: 20(4), pp. 295–304.

Allison, G.T. (1969) "Conceptual models and the Cuban missile crisis", *The American political science review*, Vol.: 63(3), pp. 689–718.

Allison, G.T. (1971) *Essence of Decision: Explaining the Cuban Missile Crisis.* Boston: Little Brown.

Allison, G.T. and Zelikov, P. (1999) *Essence of Decision: Explaining the Cuban Missile Crisis.* 2nd edition. Pearson Publishers.

Alston, P. (2005) "The Darfur commission as a model for future response to crisis situations", *Journal of international Criminal Justice*, Vol.: 3(3), pp. 600–607.

Amnesty International Nederland (1991) E*en vergeten wetenschap; van onderzoek naar actie: over schendingen van mensenrechten en hoe die voorkomen kunnen worden.* Amsterdam, Mets.

Annan, K. (2012) *Interventions: A Life in War and Peace.* The Penguin Press HC.

Austin, A. (2004) "Early warning and the field: a cargo cult science?", in *Transforming ethnopolitical conflict: the Berghof handbook*, by Austin, A., Fischer, M. and Ropers, N. (eds.), Berlin: VS Verlag für Sozialwissenschaften.

Austin, A., Fischer, M. and Ropers, N. (eds.), (2004) *Transforming ethnopolitical conflict: the Berghof handbook.* Berlin: VS Verlag für Sozialwissenschaften.

Badescu, C. and Bergholm, L. (2010) "The African Union", in *The International politics of mass atrocities. The case of Darfur*, by Black, D.R. and Williams, P.D. (eds.), London, New York: Routledge.

Barnett, M. (1997) "The UN Security Council, indifference and genocide in Rwanda", *Cultural Anthropology*, Vol.: 12(4), pp. 551–578.

Barnett, M. (2003) *Eyewitness to a genocide: The United Nations and Rwanda.* Ithaca, N.Y.: Cornell University Press.

Barnett, M. (2012) "Duties beyond borders", in *Foreign policy. Theories, actors, cases*, by Smith, S., Hadfield, A. and Dunne, T. (eds.), Oxford: Oxford University Press.

Bartrop, P.R. and Totten, S. (eds.), (2013) *The genocide studies reader.* London, New York: Routledge.

Bassil, N.R. (2013) *The post-colonial state and civil war in Sudan. The origins of conflict in Darfur.* London, New York: I.B. Taurus.

Bieckmann, F. (2012) *Soedan. Het sinistere spel om macht, rijkdom en olie*. Amsterdam: Balans.

Black, D.R. and Williams, P.D. (eds.), (2010) *The International politics of mass atrocities. The case of Darfur*. London, New York: Routledge.

Boerefijn, I., Henderson, L., Janse, R., and Weaver, R. (eds.), (2012) *Human Rights and Conflict, Essays in Honour of Bas de Gaay Fortman*. Antwerp: Intersentia.

Boom, B.E. van der (2012) *Wij weten niets van hun lot*. Amsterdam: Boom.

Bothe, M. (2007) "International Legal Aspects of the Darfur Conflict" in *The law of international relations: liber amicorum Hanspeter Neuhold*, by Reinisch, A. and Kriebaum, U. (eds.), Eleven International Publishing.

Brazeal, G. (2011) "Bureaucracy and the U.S. Response to Mass Atrocity" *National Security & Armed Conflict Law Review*.

Cassese, A. (ed.), (2009) *The Oxford Companion to International Criminal Justice*. Oxford: Oxford University Press.

Cassese, A., Gaeta, P. and Jones, R.W.D. (eds.), (2002) *The Rome Statute of the International Criminal Court: A Commentary*. Volume I. Oxford: Oxford University Press.

Charbonneau, B. (2010) "France", in *The International politics of mass atrocities. The case of Darfur*, by Black, D.R. and Williams, P.D. (eds.), London, New York: Routledge.

Clarke, J.N. (2005) "Early warning analysis for humanitarian preparedness and conflict prevention", *Civil Wars*, Vol.: 7(1), pp. 71–97.

Cockett, R. (2010) *Sudan: Darfur and the Failure of an African State*. New Haven: Yale University Press.

Cohen, S. (2001) *States of denial: knowing about atrocities and suffering*. Cambridge: Blackwell Publishers.

Condorelli, L. and Ciampi, A. (2005) "Comments on the Security Council Referral of the Situation in Darfur to the ICC", *Journal of International Criminal Justice* Vol.: 3(3), pp. 590–599.

Condorelli, L. and Villapando, S. (2002) "Can the Security Council Extend the ICC's jurisdiction?" in *The Rome Statute of the International Criminal Court: A Commentary*. Volume I, by Cassese, A., Gaeta, P. and Jones, R.W.D. (eds.), Oxford: Oxford University Press.

Coomans, H., Grünfeld, F. and Kamminga, M. (eds.), (2009) *Methods of Human Rights Research*. Antwerp: Intersentia.

Cushman, T. (2003) "Is Genocide Preventable? Some Theoretical Considerations", *Journal of Genocide Research*, Vol.: 5(4), pp. 523–542.

Daillaire, R. (2004) *Shake Hands with the Devil, The Failure of Humanity in Rwanda*. London: Arrow Books, 2004 (originally published in Canada by Random House Canada, 2003).

Daly, M.W. (2010) *Darfur's Sorrow. The forgotten history of a humanitarian crisis*. 2nd Edition. Cambridge: Cambridge University Press.

Degomme, O., and Guha-Sapir, D. (2005) "Darfur counting the deaths. Mortality esti-mates from multiple survey data." Centre for Research on Epidemiology of Disaster, University of Louvain.

Degomme, O. and Guha-Sapir, D. (2010) "Patterns of mortality rates in Darfur conflict", *The Lancet*, Vol.: 375(9711), pp. 294–300.

Dunne, T., Kurki, M. and Smith, S. (eds.), (2008) *International Relations Theories*. Oxford: Oxford University Press.

Egeland, J. (2010) *A Billion Lives: An Eyewitness Report from the Frontlines of Humanity*. New York: Simon & Schuster.

Flint, J. (2010) *Rhetoric and reality: The failure to resolve the Darfur Conflict*, Small Arms Survey, Geneva.

Flint, J. and de Waal, A. (2008) *Darfur: a new history of a long war*. London, New York: Zed Books.

Fowler, J. (2006), "A new chapter of irony: the legal implications of the Darfur genocide determination", *Genocide Studies and Prevention*, Vol.: 1(1), pp. 29–40.

Genugten, W.J.M. van and de Groot, G.A. (eds.), (1999) *United Nations sanctions: effec-tiveness and effects, especially in the field of human rights. A multi-disciplinary approach*. Antwerpen: Intersentia.

George, A.L. and Holl, J.E. (1997) *The warning-response problem and missed opportuni-ties in preventive diplomacy*. Carnegy Commission on Preventing Deadly Conflict, Carnegie Corporation of New York.

Goldhagen, J.D. (2009) *Worse than war*. New York: Perseus Publishers.

Goldstone, R.J. (2011) "The role of economic sanctions in deterring serious human rights violations: South Africa, Iraq and Darfur", in *Confronting Genocide*, Ius Genrium: Comparative perspectives on law and justice 7, by Provist, R. and Akhavan, R. (eds.), Springer.

Gramizzi, C. and Tubiana, J. (2012) *Forgotten Darfur: Old tactics and new players*, Small Arms Survey, Geneva.

Grünfeld, F. (1999) "The effectiveness of United Nations economic sanctions", in *United Nations sanctions: effectiveness and effects, especially in the field of human rights. A multi-disciplinary approach*, by van Genugten, W.J.M. and de Groot, G.A. (eds.), Antwerpen: Intersentia.

Grünfeld, F. (2003) *Vroegtijdig optreden van omstanders ter voorkoming van oorlogen en schendingen van de rechten van de mens*, Utrecht: Utrecht University.

Grünfeld, F. (2008) "The Role of Bystanders in Rwanda and Srebrenica: Lessons Learned", in *Supranational Criminology: Towards a Criminology of International Crimes*, by Smeulers, A. and Haveman, R. (eds.), Antwerp: Intersentia.

Grünfeld, F. (2012) "Early Warning, Non-Intervention and Failed Responsibility to Protect in Rwanda and Darfur", in *Human Rights and Conflict, Essays in Honour of Bas de Gaay Fortman*, by Boerefijn, I., Henderson, L., Janse, R. and Weaver, R. (eds.), Antwerp: Intersentia.

Grünfeld, F. (2014), "Do bystanders exist?", in *Facing the Past*, by Malcontent, P.A.M. (ed.), forthcoming.

Grünfeld, F. and Huijboom, A. (2007) *The Failure to Prevent Genocide in Rwanda: The Role of Bystanders*. Leiden, Boston: Martinus Nijhoff Publishers, Brill.

Grünfeld, F. and Verlinden, S. (2012) "Mensenrechtenschendingen als vroegtijdige waarschuwingen voor conflictpreventie", *Vrede en veiligheid: tijdschrift voor internationale vraagstukken*, Vol.: 40(2/3), pp. 167–185.

Grünfeld, F. and Vermeulen, W.N. (2009) "Failures to Prevent Genocide in Rwanda (1994), Srebrenica (1995) and Darfur (since 2003)", *Journal of Genocide Studies and Prevention*, Vol.: 4(2), pp. 221–238.

Grünfeld, F. and Vermeulen, W.N. (2014) "The role of the Netherlands in the international response to the Crisis in Darfur", Maastricht Faculty of Law Working Paper No. 2014-2 (available at http://ssrn.com/abstract=2418398 [accessed 2 April 2014]).

Gryzb, A.F. (ed.), (2010) *The World and Darfur. International response to crimes against humanity in Western Sudan*. Montreal: McGill-Queens University Press.

Grzyb, A.F. (2010) "Media coverage, activism, and crating public will for intervention in Rwanda and Darfur", in *The World and Darfur. International response to crimes against humanity in Western Sudan*, by Gryzb (ed.), A.F., Montreal: McGill-Queens University Press.

Hamilton, R. (2011a) *Fighting for Darfur: public action and the struggle to stop genocide*. New York: Palgrave Macmillan.

Hamilton, R. (2011b) "Inside Colin Powell's decision to declare genocide in Darfur", *The Atlantic*, 17 August 2011.

Happold, M. (2006) "Darfur, the Security Council, and the International Criminal Court", *International and Comparative Law Quarterly*, Vol.: 55, pp. 226–236.

Harff, B. (2003) "No lessons learned from the Holocaust? Assessing risks of genocide and political mass murder since 1955", *The American Political Science Review*, Vol.: 97(1), pp. 57–73.

Harff, B. and Gurr, T.R. (1998) "Systematic early warning of humanitarian emergencies", *Journal of peace research*, Vol.: 35(5), pp. 551–579.

Heinze, E.A. (2007) "The rhetoric of genocide in U.S. foreign policy: Rwanda and Darfur compared", *Political Science Quarterly*, Vol.: 122(3), pp. 359–383.

Heyder, C. (2006) "The U.N. Security Council's Referral of the Crimes in Darfur to the International Criminal Court in Light of U.S. Opposition to the Court: Implications for the International Criminal Court's Functions and Status", *Berkeley Journal of International Law*, Vol.: 24(2), pp. 650–671.

Holslag, J. (2007), "China's Diplomatic Victory in Darfur", *Asia Paper*, Vol.: 2(4), Brussels Institute of Contemporary China Studies, Vrije Universiteit Brussel, Brussels.

Igiri, C.O. and Lyman, P.N. (2004) "Giving meaning to 'Never again'. Seeking an Effective Response to the Crisis in Darfur and Beyond", Council on Foreign Relations No. 5, 5 September 2004.

Jentleson, B. (ed.), (2000) *Opportunities missed, opportunities seized: Preventive diplomacy in the post-Cold War world.* Lanham: Rowan & Littlefield Publishers.

Johnson, D.H. (2011[2003]) *The root causes of Sudan's civil wars. Peace or truce?* Revised edition. Kampala: Fountain Publishers.

Kapila, M. (2013) *Against a tide of evil.* Edinburg: Mainstream Publishing.

Karns, M.P. and Mingst, K.A. (2010) *International Organizations: the politics and processes of global governance.* Boulder: Lynne Rienner Publishers

Karremans, Th. (1998) *Srebrenica, Who cares? Een puzzel van de werkelijkheid.* Nieuwegein: Arko Uitgeverij.

Kaufman, Z.D., (2005) "Justice in jeopardy: accountability for the Darfur atrocities", *Criminal Law Forum,* Vol.: 16, pp. 343–346.

Keane, R. and Wee, A. (2010) "The European Union", in *The International politics of mass atrocities. The case of Darfur,* by Black, D.R. and Williams, P.D. (eds.), London, New York: Routledge.

Kostas, S.A. (2006) "Making the determination of genocide in Darfur", in *Genocide in Darfur: Investigating the atrocities in the Sudan,* by Totten, S. and Markussen, E. (eds.), London, New York: Routledge.

Kothari, A. (2010) "The framing of the Darfur conflict in the New York Times: 2003–2006", *Journalism Studies,* Vol.: 11(2), pp. 209–224.

Kress, C. (2005) "The Darfur Report and Genocidal Intent", *Journal of International Criminal Justice,* Vol.: 3(3), pp. 562–578.

Križnar, T. and Weiss, M. (2008) "Darfur: War for Water", DVD: Bela Film, Tomo Križnar, RTV Slovenia.

Landman (2009) "Social science methods and human rights", in *Methods of Human Rights Research,* by Coomans, H., Grünfeld, F. and Kammingo, M. (eds.), Antwerp: Intersentia.

Lanotte, O. (2007) *La France au Rwanda (1990–1993). Entre abstention impossible et engagement ambivalent.* Bruxelles: P.I.E. Peter Lang.

Lanz, D. (2011) "Why Darfur? The responsibility to protect as a rallying cry for transnational advocacy groups", *Global Responsibility to Protect,* Vol.: 3, pp. 223–247.

Leach, J.D. (2011) *War and Politics in Sudan. Cultural identities and the challenges of the peace process.* London, New York: I.B. Taurus.

Mackinnon, M.G. (2010) "The United Nations Security Council", in *The International politics of mass atrocities. The case of Darfur,* by Black, D.R. and Williams, P.D. (eds.), London, New York: Routledge.

Malcontent, P.A.M. (ed.), *Facing the Past: Finding Remedies for Grave Historical Injustices,* forthcoming.

March, J.G. and Olsen, J.P. (1998) "The institutional dynamics of international political orders", *International Organizations*, Vol.: 51, pp. 943–969.

Marchal, R. (2006) "Chad/Darfur: How two crises merge", *Review of African Political Economy*, Vol.: 33(109), pp. 467–482.

Markusen, E. (2009) "Three empirical investigations", in *The world and Darfur. International responses to crimes against humanity in western Sudan*, by Grzyb, A. (ed.), Montreal: McGill-Queens University Press.

Mayroz, E. (2008) "Ever again? The United States, genocide suppression, and the crisis in Darfur", *Journal of Genocide Research*, Vol.: 10(3), pp. 359–388.

Mearsheimer, J.J. (2008) "Structural Realism", in *International Relations Theories*, by Dunne, T., Kurki, M. and Smith, S. (eds.), Oxford: Oxford University Press.

Melvern, L. (2005) "The Security Council in the face of genocide", *Journal of International Criminal Justice*, Vol.: 3(4), pp. 847–860.

Meyer, C.O., Otto, F., Brante, J., and De Franco, C. (2010) "Re-casting the warning-response-problem: Persuasion and preventive policy", *International Studies Review*, Vol.: 12(4), pp. 556–578.

Mintz, A. and DeRouen Jr., K., (2010) *Understanding foreign policy decision making*. Cambridge: Cambridge University Press.

Moravcsik, A. (1993) "Preferences and power in the European Community: a liberal inter-governmentalist approach", *Journal of Common Market Studies*, Vol.: 31(4), pp. 473–524.

Mukimbiri, J. (2005) "The seven stages of the Rwandan Genocide", *Journal of International Criminal Justice*, Vol.: 3(4), pp. 823–836.

Natsios, A. (2012) *Sudan, South Sudan and Darfur: what everyone needs to know*. Oxford: Oxford University Press.

NCDO (1997) *From early warning to early action. A report on the European conference on conflict prevention*, Amsterdam: NCDO.

Nederlands Instituut voor Oorlogsdocumentatie (2002) *Srebrenica: een 'veilig' gebied. Reconstructie, achtergronden, gevolgen en analyses van de val van een Safe Area.* Amsterdam: Boom.

Neuner, M. (2005) "The Darfur referral of the Security Council and the scope of the jurisdiction of the International Criminal Court", *Yearbook of International Humanitarian Law*, Vol.: 8, pp. 320–343.

Peters, G.B. (2005) *Institutional theory in political science: The 'new institutionalism'.* Gosport: Ashford Colour Press Ltd.

Piiparinen, T. (2007) "Reconsidering the silence over the ultimate crime: A functional shift in crisis management from the Rwandan genocide to Darfur", *Journal of Genocide Research*, Vol.: 9(1), pp. 71–91.

Piiparinen, T. (2008) "The rise and fall of bureaucratic rationalization: Exploring the possibilities and limitations of the UN Secretariat in conflict prevention", *European Journal of International Relations*, Vol.: 14(4), pp. 697–724.

Piiparinen, T. (2010) *The transformation of UN conflict management. Producing images of genocide from Rwanda to Darfur and beyond.* London, New York: Routledge.

Pohl, B. (2013) "To what ends? Governmental interests and European Union (non-) intervention in Chad and the Democratic Republic of Congo", *Cooperation and Conflict*, forthcoming. (available at http://cac.sagepub.com/content/early/2013/07/15/0010836713482875.full.pdf+html [accessed 10 March 2014]).

Power, S. (1999) "To suffer by comparison", *Daedalus,* Vol.: 128(2), pp. 31–66.

Power, S. (2001) "Bystanders to genocide: Why the United States let the Rwandan tragedy happen", *Atlantic Monthly* Vol.: 288(2), pp. 84–108.

Power, S. (2007 [2003]) *Problem from hell: America and the age of genocide.* New York: Perennial, London: Flamingo.

Provist, R. and Akhavan, R. (eds.), (2007) *Confronting genocide,* Ius Genrium: Comparative perspectives on law and justice 7, Springer.

Prunier, G. (2007) *Darfur: An ambiguous genocide. Revised and updated edition 2007.* London: C. Hurst & Co. (publishers) ltd.

Putnam, R.D. (1988) "Diplomacy and domestic politics: the logic of two-level games", *International Organization* Vol.: 42(3), pp. 427–460.

Ramcharan, B., (2005), *A UN High Commission in defence of human rights.* Leiden, Boston: Martinus Nijhuff Publishers.

Reinisch, A. and Kriebaum, U. (eds.), (2007) *The law of international relations: liber amicorum Hanspeter Neuhold,* The Hague: Eleven International Publishing.

Reychler, L. (1999) *Democratic peace-building and conflict prevention: The devil is in the transition.* Leuven, Belgium: Leuven University Press.

Rosenau, J.N. (1966) "The adaptation of national societies: a theory of political behavior and transformation", in *The scientific study of foreign policy,* by Rosenau, J.N. (1980), New York, London: Frances Pinter Ltd.

Rosenau, J.N. (ed.), (1969) *International politics and foreign policy; a reader in research and theory,* revised edition. New York: The Free Press, London: Collier-Macmillan Limited, London.

Rosenau, J.N. (1980) *The scientific study of foreign policy,* New York, London: Frances Pinter Ltd.

Schabas, W.A. (2004) "United States hostility to the International Criminal Court: It's all about the Security Council", *European Journal of International Law,* Vol.: 15(4), pp. 701–720.

Schabas, W.A. (2006) "Genocide, crimes against humanity, and Darfur: the Commission of Inquiry's findings on genocide", *Cardozo Law Review,* Vol.: 27(4), pp. 1703–1722.

Schmeidl, S. and Adelman, H. (eds.), (1998) *Early Warning and Early Response,* Columbia International Affairs Online, www.ciaonet.org/book/schmeidl/schmeidl01.html.

Schmeidl, S. and Jenkins, J.C. (1998) "The early warning of humanitarian disasters: Problems in building an early warning system", *International Migration Review*, Vol.: 32(2), pp. 471–486.

Seymour, L.J.M. (2013) "Let's Bulshit! Arguing bargaining and dissembling over Darfur", *European Journal of International Relations*, forthcoming (available at http://ejt .sagepub.com/content/early/2013/05/28/1354066113476118.full.pdf+html [accessed 10 March 2014]).

Shraga D., (2009) "Politics and Justice: The role of the Security Council", in *The Oxford Companion to International Criminal Justice*, by Cassese, A. (ed.) Oxford: Oxford University Press.

Singer, J.D. (1961) "The level of analysis problem in international relations", in *International politics and foreign policy; a reader in research and theory*, revised edition, by Rosenau, J.N. (ed.), (1969) New York: The Free Press, London: Collier-Macmillan Limited, London.

Slim, H. (2004) "Dithering over Darfur? A preliminary review of the international response", *International Affairs*, Vol.: 80(5), pp. 811–828.

Smeulers, A. and Grünfeld, F. (2011) *International Crimes and other Gross Human Rights Violations. A Multi- and Interdisciplinary Textbook*. Leiden, Boston: Martinus Nijhoff Publishers, Brill.

Smeulers, A. and Haveman, R. (eds.), (2008) *Supranational Criminology: Towards a Criminology of International Crimes*, Antwerp: Intersentia.

Sørbø, G.M. and Ahmed, A.G.M. (eds.), (2013) *Sudan divided*. Palgrave.

Stanton, G.H. (1996) *The 8 stages of genocide*, Genocide Watch, Washington D.C.

Staub, E. (2000) "Genocide and Mass Killing: Origins, Prevention, Healing and Reconciliation", *Political Psychology*, Vol.: 21(2), pp. 367–382.

Stedjan and Thomas-Jensen (2010) "The United States", in *The International politics of mass atrocities. The case of Darfur*, by Black, D.R. and Williams, P.D. (eds.), London, New York: Routledge.

Stein, J. (2012), "Foreign policy decision making: rational, psychological, and neurological models" in *Foreign policy. Theories, actors, cases*, by Smith, S., Hadfield, A. and Dunne, T. (eds.), Oxford: Oxford University Press.

Stoel, M. van der (1999) "Early warning and early action: preventing inter-ethnic conflict", Speech given at the Royal Institute of International Affairs, 20 August 1999, OCSE Doc.: HCNM.GAL/5/99.

Suhrke, A. and Jones, B. (2000) "Preventive diplomacy in Rwanda: Failure to act or failure of actions?", in Opportunities missed, opportunities seized: Preventive diplomacy in the post-Cold War world, by Jentleson, B.W. (ed.), Lanham: Rowan & Littlefield Publishers.

Theriault, H.C. (2013) "Denial of ongoing atrocities as a rationale for not attempting to prevent or intervene", *Impediments to the prevention and intervention of genocide*, by Totten, S. (ed.), New Brunswick, London: Transaction Publishers.

Toga, D. (2007) "The African Union mediation and the Abuja peace talks", in War in Darfur and the search for peace, by de Waal, A., (ed.), Global Equity Initiative, Harvard University.

Tomuschat, C. (2005) "Darfur–Compensation for the victims", *Journal of International Criminal Justice*, Vol.: 3(3), pp. 579–589.

Totten, S. (2006), "The US investigation into the Darfur crisis and its determination of genocide", *Genocide Studies and Prevention*, Vol.: 1(1), pp. 57–78.

Totten, S. (ed.), (2013) *Impediments to the prevention and intervention of genocide*. New Brunswick, London: Transaction Publishers.

Totten, S. and Markussen, E. (eds.), (2006) *Genocide in Darfur, investigating the Atrocities in the Sudan*. London, New York: Routledge.

Traub, J. (2006) *The Best Intentions: Kofi Annan and the UN in the Era of American World Power*. New York: Farrar, Straus and Giroux.

Tubiana, J. (2013) "Darfur after Doha", in *Sudan divided*, by Sørbø, G.M. and Ahmed, A.G.M. (eds.), Palgrave.

Udombana, Nsongurua J. (2005) "When Neutrality is a Sin: The Darfur Crisis and the Crisis of Humanitarian Intervention in Sudan", *Human Rights Quarterly*, Vol.:27(4), pp. 1149–1199.

UK House of Commons, International Development Committee, "Darfur, Sudan: The responsibility to protect" Fifth Report of Session 2004–05, Volume I Report.

UK House of Commons, International Development Committee. "Darfur, Sudan: The responsibility to protect" Fifth Report of Session 2004–05, Volume II Oral and Written Statements.

Verhoeven, H. (2011) "The logic of war and peace in Sudan", *Journal of Modern African Studies*, Vol.: 49(4), pp. 671–684.

Verhoeven, H. (2013) "The rise and fall of Sudan's Al-Ingaz revolution: The transition from militarised Islamism to economic salvation and the Comprehensive Peace Agreement", *Civil Wars*, Vol.: 15:2, pp. 118–140.

Viotti, P.R. and Kauppi, M.V. (1999) *International Relations Theory*. 3rd edition. Longman Publishing Group.

Viotti, P.R. and Kauppi, M.V. (2012) *International Relations Theory*. 5th edition. Longman Publishing Group.

Vos, D. (2006) "Een onderzoek naar internationale nieuwsstromen en de Nederlandse nieuwsberichtgeving over de crisis in Darfur in de periode van Februari 2003-2006", PhD Dissertation, Utrecht University.

Waal, A. de (1989 [2005]) *Famine that kills. Revised and updated edition*. Oxford: Oxford University Press.

Waal, A. de (2006) "'I will not sign'. Alex de Waal writes about the Darfur peace negotiations", *London Review of Books*, Vol.: 28(23), pp. 17–20.

Waal, A. de (2007a) "Darfur and the failure of the responsibility to protect", *International Affairs*, Vol.: 83(6), pp. 1039–1054.

Waal, A. de (ed.), (2007b) *War in Darfur and the search for peace*. Global Equity Initiative, Harvard University.

West African Network for Peacebuilding (2000) *Preventive Peace Building in West Africa: West Africa Early Warning and Response*. Network training module, Accra, Ghana.

Williams, P. (2010) "The United Kingdom", *The International politics of mass atrocities. The case of Darfur*, by Black, D. and Williams, P. (eds.), London, New York: Routledge.

Williams, P.D. and Bellamy, A.J. (2005) "The responsibility to protect and the crisis in Darfur", *Security Dialogue*, Vol.: 36(1), pp. 27–47.

Williams, P.D. and Bellamy, A.J. (2006) "The UN Security Council and the question of humanitarian intervention in Darfur", *Journal of Military Ethics*, Vol.: 5(2), pp. 144–160.

Woocher, L. (2001) "Deconstructing 'political will': explaining the failure to prevent deadly conflict and mass atrocities", *Journal of Public and International Affairs* Vol.: 12, pp. 179–206.

Documents

UN Security Council resolution, reports and press releases are easily found and therefore not listed here. Similarly for EU and AU documents.

Archive Ministry of Foreign Affairs in the Netherlands

daf/2010/00185, Period 2003–2004.
daf/2015/00646, Period December 2003-June 2004.
djz/ir/na/00210, 2004–2004.

US State Department Cables
WikiLeaks
Abu Dhabi, 7 June 2004, No. 1880.
Abuja, 19 July 2004, No. 1260.
Abuja, 24 August 2004, No. 1456.
Abuja, 25 August 2004, No. 1461.
Abuja, 3 September 2004, No. 1514.
Abuja, 3 September 2004, No. 1515.
Abuja, 6 September 2004, No. 1528.
Abuja, 13 September 2004, No. 1573.
Abuja, 22 October 2004, No. 1793.

Abuja, 23 October 2004, No. 1801.
Abuja, 26 October 2004, No. 1811.
Abuja, 10 December 2004, No. 2039.
Abuja, 14 December 2004, No. 2060.
Abuja, 15 December 2004, No. 2068.
Abuja, 14 January 2005, No. 59.
Abuja, 31 January 2005, No. 137.
Ankara, 29 July 2004, No. 4227.
Ankara, 18 August 2004, No. 4628.
Ankara, 8 September 2004, No. 5029.
Brussels, 25 March 2004, No. 1174.
Brussels, 25 March 2004, No. 1151.
Brussels, 3 May 2013, No. 1897.
Brussels, 4 June 2013, No. 2410.
Brussels 16 July 2004, No. 3055.
Brussels, 23 July 2004, No. 3140.
Brussels, 27 July 2004, No. 3195.
Brussels, 29 July 2004, No. 3223.
Brussels, 8 September 2004, No. 3772.
Brussels, 10 September 2004, No. 3840.
Brussels, 14 September 2004, No. 3897.
Brussels, 20 September 2004, No. 3989.
Brussels, 21 September 2004, No. 4016.
Brussels, 14 October 2004, No. 4410.
Brussels, 26 November 2004, No. 5014.
Dar Es Salaam, 26 January 2005, No. 155.
Dar Es Salaam, 1 February 2005, No. 206.
Dar Es Salaam, 18 February 2004, No. 374.
Dublin, 17 February 2005, No. 207.
Helsinki, 17 February 2005, No. 207.
Istanbul, 13 July 2004, No. 1090.
Paris, 11 February 2005, No. 879.
Paris, 30 March 2005, No. 2110.
Madrid, 14 July 2004, No. 2660.
Madrid, 26 July 2004, No. 2844.
Madrid, 15 February 2005, No. 617.
Ndjamena, 18 February 2005, No. 260.
Ndjamena, 22 February 2005, No. 277.
Rome, 26 July 2004, No. 2874.
The Hague, 9 July 2004, No. 1717.

The Hague, 9 July 2004, No. 1721.
The Hague, 15 July 2004, No. 1777.
The Hague, 10 September 2004, No. 2289.
The Hague, 16 September 2004, No. 2346.
The Hague, 16 February 2005, No. 451.
Vatican, 26 July 2004, No.2892.
Vienna, 17 February 2005, No. 473.

Official Release

US-UN mission New York, 7 January 2005, Nr. 34 (available at http://www2.gwu
.edu/~nsarchiv/NSAEBB/NSAEBB335/index.htm [accessed 25 January 2013].

Washington D.C., 3 July 2004, No. 145183, available at: http://www2.gwu.edu/~nsarchiv/
NSAEBB/NSAEBB335/Document3.PDF [accessed 2 December 2014].

State Department internal memo, authored by William H. Taft, IV, 25 June 2004,
"Genocide and Darfur".

Interviews

Authors' Interviews

Isabelle Balot, UN DPA, Sudan desk, OCHA, 2 June 2005 (Fred Grünfeld).
Cees Bremmer, EU Parliament, 28 August 2013 (Fred Grünfeld and Jasper Krommendijk).
Prudence Bushnell, US State Department, Africa Desk, 27 May 2005 (Fred Grünfeld).
Chris Coleman, UN DPKO, 24 May 2005 (Fred Grünfeld).
Jan Egeland, UN OCHA, 28 November 2012 (Fred Grünfeld).
Pieter Feith, EU CFSP, 28 August 2013 (Fred Grünfeld and Jasper Krommendijk), email
to Fred Grünfeld, 21 December 2013.
David Harland, Author UN report on Srebrenica, 2 June 2005 (Fred Grünfeld).
Adriaan Kooijmans, Dutch Ambassador in Sudan, 16 September 2013 (Fred Grünfeld),
email to Fred Grünfeld, 29 December 2013.
Christian Manahl, EU CFSP and Commission, 26 August 2013 (Fred Grünfeld and
Wessel Vermeulen).
Luc Marchal, Belgian Commander of the sector Kigali of UNAMIR, 21 January 2005
(Fred Grünfeld and Anke Huijboom).
Anthony Lake, National Security Advisor to US President Clinton, 21 May 2005 (Fred
Grünfeld).
Gunter Pleuger, German UN Ambassador, 19 October 2010 (Fred Grünfeld) and tele-
phone call on 5 November 2013 (Fred Grünfeld).
Jan Pronk, Special Representative SG UN in Sudan, 21 August 2006 (Fred Grünfeld and
Anke Huijboom), 2 September 2013 (Fred Grünfeld and Jasper Krommendijk), email
to Fred Grünfeld, 13 October 2013.

Arjan Schuthof, Sudan Desk Dutch Ministry of Foreign Affairs, 2 September 2013 (Fred Grünfeld and Jasper Krommendijk).
Eckhart Strauss, UN office of Special Adviser on Prevention of Genocide, 1 June 2005 (Fred Grünfeld).
Oliver Ulich, UN OCHA, 1 June 2005 (Fred Grünfeld).

PBS Frontline Interviews
All interviews are available at the PBS Frontline website, http://www.pbs.org/wgbh/pages/frontline/darfur/interviews [accessed 31 August 2013].
Interview with Dr. Mukesh Kapila, 11 June 2007.
Interview with Sir Kieran Prendergast, 29 June 2007.
Interview with James Traub, 13 September 2007.

Other Interviews
BBC Panorama, 3 July 2005, Fergal Keane's interview with Kofi Annan, available at http://news.bbc.co.uk/2/hi/programmes/panorama/4647177.stm [accessed 18 November 2013].
BBC Panorama, 3 July 2005, Fergal Keane interview with Hilary Benn, available at http://news.bbc.co.uk/2/hi/programmes/panorama/4647195.stm [accessed 18 November 2013].
BBC Panorama, 3 July 2005, Fergal Keane interview with John Danforth, available at http://news.bbc.co.uk/1/hi/programmes/panorama/4647211.stm [accessed 5 October 2013].
BBC Radio 4 Today Program, 19 March 2004, interview with Mukesh Kapila, available at http://www.bbc.co.uk/radio4/today/listenagain/listenagain_20040319.shtml [accessed 21 August 2013].
CBC Radio, "As it happens", 16 May 2013, Interview with Mukesh Kapila, available at http://www.cbc.ca/player/Radio/ID/2385645213/ [accessed 12 June 2013].
UN IRIN interview with Jan Egeland, 2 April 2004, available at http://www.irinnews.org/report.aspx?reportid=49400 [accessed 21 August 2013].
Interviews by the UK House of Commons are transcribed in the second volume of UK House of Commons, International Development Committee. "Darfur, Sudan: The responsibility to protect" Fifth Report of Session 2004–05.
AlertNet's interview with Tom Vraalsen, 8 July 2004, "Sudan: interview. Darfur access improving but risks ahead", available at http://reliefweb.int/report/sudan/sudan-interview-darfur-access-improving-risks-ahead-un [accessed 29 November 2013].

Index

ve
the
tion
that
dona
assu
use ir
apro
organ
expre
all un
and re
On
ficatic

s fu
s